Euro-Asian Encounters on 21st-C
Competency-Based Curriculum F

Weili Zhao · Daniel Tröhler
Editors

Euro-Asian Encounters on 21st-Century Competency-Based Curriculum Reforms

Cultural Views on Globalization and Localization

Springer

Editors
Weili Zhao
Department of Curriculum and Instruction
The Chinese University of Hong Kong
Hong Kong SAR, China

Daniel Tröhler
Institute of Education
University of Vienna
Vienna, Austria

ISBN 978-981-16-3011-8   ISBN 978-981-16-3009-5 (eBook)
https://doi.org/10.1007/978-981-16-3009-5

© The Editor(s) (if applicable) and The Author(s), under exclusive license to Springer Nature Singapore Pte Ltd. 2021

This work is subject to copyright. All rights are solely and exclusively licensed by the Publisher, whether the whole or part of the material is concerned, specifically the rights of translation, reprinting, reuse of illustrations, recitation, broadcasting, reproduction on microfilms or in any other physical way, and transmission or information storage and retrieval, electronic adaptation, computer software, or by similar or dissimilar methodology now known or hereafter developed.

The use of general descriptive names, registered names, trademarks, service marks, etc. in this publication does not imply, even in the absence of a specific statement, that such names are exempt from the relevant protective laws and regulations and therefore free for general use.

The publisher, the authors and the editors are safe to assume that the advice and information in this book are believed to be true and accurate at the date of publication. Neither the publisher nor the authors or the editors give a warranty, expressed or implied, with respect to the material contained herein or for any errors or omissions that may have been made. The publisher remains neutral with regard to jurisdictional claims in published maps and institutional affiliations.

This Springer imprint is published by the registered company Springer Nature Singapore Pte Ltd.
The registered company address is: 152 Beach Road, #21-01/04 Gateway East, Singapore 189721, Singapore

Contents

Introduction

Euro-Asia Encounters on 21st-Century Competency-Based
Curriculum Reforms: A Historical and Cultural (Re)Turn 3
Weili Zhao and Daniel Tröhler

**The European Picture: Christian Protestant Ideals and
Curriculum Reforms**

The Transformation of Christian Missions to Educational
Colonization, or Motives of Speaking and Listening
in the One-Sided Euro-American-Asian Dialogue 21
Daniel Tröhler

From Knowledge and *Bildung* Toward Competences and Skills
in Finnish Curriculum Policy?: Some Theoretical, Historical,
and Current Observations Related to Finland 41
Tero Autio

Historical Trajectories of the Contract-School Model in Norway 57
Kirsten Sivesind

Globalization and Localization in the Shaping of the Danish
Public Education System: Recontextualization Processes in Four
Historical Educational Reforms 85
Christian Ydesen

Fixing the Future: Public Discourse on the Implementation
of Education Standards in Austria 111
Bernadette Hörmann

A Critical Review of the Competency-Based Curriculum in Spain 133
Ana Sánchez-Bello

Competence-Based Curriculum Reforms in the Context of University Engineering Education in the Post-Soviet Lithuania—Hope or Disappointment? 147
Rūta Petkutė

The East Asian Picture: Confucian Ideals and Curriculum Reforms

Nationalism and Globalism as Epistemic Entanglements: China's *Suyang* Curriculum Reform as a Case Study 163
Weili Zhao

Unpacking the Global-Local Entanglements in Hong Kong's Curriculum Reform 175
Min Lin and Yundan Zheng

Competency-Based Curriculum Reform and Its Making of Korean Global Citizens 195
Ji-Hye Kim

A Holistic Model of Competence: Curriculum Reforms for Pre-school Education in Singapore 211
Sandra Wu and Charlene Tan

The Global Inside the National and the National Inside the Global: 'Zest for Living,' the *Chi, Toku and Tai* Triad, and the 'Model' of Japanese Education 229
Keita Takayama

Editors and Contributors

About the Editors

Weili Zhao is an assistant professor in the Department of Curriculum and Instruction at the Chinese University of Hong Kong, China. With interdisciplinary training in linguistics and sociolinguistics, critical discourse studies, language philosophy, and curriculum studies, she has been doing research on China's education and curriculum reforms at the nexus of tradition and modernity, East and West. Her dissertation-turned book, *China's Education, Curriculum Knowledge and Cultural Inscriptions: Dancing with The Wind*, was out in June 2018 with Routledge, and she was the recipient of 2019 AERA Early Career Outstanding Research Award, SIG 171 (Confucianism, Taoism, Buddhism, and Education).

Daniel Tröhler is a professor of Foundations of Education at the University of Vienna since 2017 and a visiting professor at the University of Oslo since 2018. His research interests lie in the international and transnational developments of the last 250 years with a focus around 1800s and the Cold War. In doing so, he relates the history of modern ideas to the history of institutions in the context of a broader cultural history by focusing on (educational) political and educational ideas and their materialization in school laws, curricula, and textbooks, comparing different national and regional developments and investigating their possible mutual influences. He has published or edited over 50 books, 100 journal articles, and some 150 book chapters in seven languages. For the book *Languages of Education: Protestant Legacies, National Identities, and Global Aspirations* (Routledge 2011), he was awarded the Outstanding Book of the Year Award of the American Education Research Association AERA in 2012. He is currently working on the development of an ERC project proposal titled Nation state, curriculum, and the fabrication of national-minded citizens.

Contributors

Tero Autio Tampere University, Tampere, Finland

Bernadette Hörmann Department of Education, University of Oslo, Oslo, Norway

Ji-Hye Kim Korean Educational Development Institute, Jincheon-gun, South Korea

Min Lin Department of Curriculum and Instruction, The Chinese University of Hong Kong, Hong Kong SAR, China

Rūta Petkutė Tallinn University, Tallinn, Estonia

Ana Sánchez-Bello University of A Coruña, A Coruña, Spain

Kirsten Sivesind Department of Education, University of Oslo, Oslo, Norway

Keita Takayama Graduate School of Education, Kyoto University, Kyoto, Japan

Charlene Tan National Institute of Education, Nanyang Technological University, Singapore

Daniel Tröhler Department of Education, University of Vienna, Vienna, Austria

Sandra Wu National Institute of Education, Nanyang Technological University, Singapore

Christian Ydesen Department of Culture and Learning, Aalborg University, Aalborg, Denmark

Weili Zhao Department of Curriculum and Instruction, The Chinese University of Hong Kong, Hong Kong SAR, China

Yundan Zheng Department of Curriculum and Instruction, The Chinese University of Hong Kong, Hong Kong SAR, China

Introduction

Euro-Asia Encounters on 21st-Century Competency-Based Curriculum Reforms: A Historical and Cultural (Re)Turn

Weili Zhao and Daniel Tröhler

With the end of the Cold War in 1989, a view of current and future world affairs that assumed harmony, uniformity, and stability took hold. The magic word used to conceptualize this view was "globalization." "Globalization" was the epitome of the supposed analytical description of world development after 1989, which, in the meantime, called for an epistemological readjustment, namely an "intensification of consciousness of the world as a whole" (Robertson, 1992, p. 8). Epistemology is not harmless, however, but effective when it asserts itself because it predetermines one's view of the world in a certain way (and silences others) and suggests corresponding desiderata for action (and makes other courses of action seem inappropriate).

Perhaps the most famous course of action was to "free" the economy from the control mechanisms and regulations of the nation-states and release it into global competition. In a paradoxical way, however, this global competition presupposes the nation-state, because the competition is one between real entities, and not only of companies, but also of nation-states themselves. This has only been made abundantly clear in efforts to combat the Corona virus when for instance Russia made international propaganda that it was the first country in the world to vaccinate its people, when a little later the United Kingdom came along and boasted that it was the first *Western* country to vaccinate its population, and when Switzerland followed by emphasizing that it is the first country that has approved vaccination in an *orderly* (and not accelerated) way. Shortly after Israel proclaimed it wanted to be "world champion" in the vaccination of its national people, and the internationally operating pharmaceutical companies profited massively from the national race for the

---

W. Zhao
Department of Curriculum and Instruction, The Chinese University of Hong Kong, Hong Kong SAR, China

D. Tröhler (✉)
Department of Education, University of Vienna, Vienna, Austria
e-mail: daniel.troehler@univie.ac.at

© The Author(s), under exclusive license to Springer Nature Singapore Pte Ltd. 2021
W. Zhao and D. Tröhler (eds.), *Euro-Asian Encounters on 21st-Century Competency-Based Curriculum Reforms*,
https://doi.org/10.1007/978-981-16-3009-5_1

vaccines, when competition drove up prices, and alleged or actual supply shortages to at least some countries soon led to accusations of "vaccine nationalism."

The epistemology closely associated with "globalization" has underestimated the efficacy of the nation-state and its persistence, as evidenced by the rampant nationalism in the world today. While sociological theories—particularly of Anglosaxon provenience—propagated the historical process of the world becoming one, a certain form of policy-savvy test psychology helped educational policy to throw itself into the international competition for the best possible schools (Tröhler, 2021). In these tests, the paradox becomes particularly clear. An education policy that pretends to be global relies on competition in inter-national rankings. One can see here very nicely what this epistemology inherent in globalism as a discourse does: It appeals to the national pride of nation-states to be better than their neighbors, and preferably even better than the whole world. This is neither particularly harmonious, uniform, nor stable, but a bit childish. But politicians are also shrewd people. They have very often played the game of globalized education policy, but in order to pursue national goals that have hardly been made transparent (Piattoeva, 2019).

The price of this game was to make its own education system comparable and that meant the introduction of a certain kind of curriculum that supposedly focused less on knowledge and more on test-psychologically comparable "competencies." The extent to which this balancing act between globality and nationality corresponds to va banque gambling will be examined in this volume on the basis of individual case studies. Accordingly, this volume discusses globalized curriculum discourses as an epistemic site where varying historical-cultural-philosophical themes negotiate, collide, assemble, and suppress as an effect of modernity-coloniality of knowledge, power, and being. Such colonial effect is never disentangled from the negotiation of, as well as assemblage between, globalization and localization in the name of "modernization" and "glocalization."

Accordingly, the central concepts of competency, globalization, localization, glocalization, assemblage, history of present, and discourse are explored generally and in relation to the specific cases that are elaborated in this volume. These case studies were chosen quite deliberately. Based on the realization that this new education policy posing as global is largely an extrapolated national education policy (of the U.S.), i.e., an imperialism staged via transnational organizations such as the World Bank, UNESCO or, above all, the OECD, we have brought two regions of the world into the discussion that have quite obviously gotten involved in this game, but which are also culturally and historically very different. We were interested in how the cultural path dependencies of the individual nation-states in these supranational cultural circles in Asia and in Europe behaved and proved themselves in this game, and how they can tell each other about their experiences.

Of course, it is a gross oversimplification to simply speak of a Confucian Asia and a Christian Europe, which is why we had the religious-cultural configurations in each nation-state in mind when we invited colleagues to the conversation. This seemed legitimate to us insofar as this pretend global education policy itself emerged from an amalgam of American nationalism and Presbyterianism (Tröhler & Maricic, 2021). We have wondered how Asia and Europe, as potential colonies of this imperialism, have reacted, how their own wisdom of thought or religious-cultural understandings of the world have entered into this game, and how they can now, after many years of experience, report to each other. The selection of the two educational-cultural systems and wisdom of thought, the Christian and the Confucian, is to provide a unique springboard for conducting international curriculum studies beyond the usual confinement of geopolitical nation-state construct.

Globalization of OECD's "Competency" Curriculum Discourses as a Form of Epistemological Imperialism

We take it for granted that discourses and languages are never neutral and value-free. Instead, they can be treated as traces of epistemological reasoning, which is particularly visible in international comparisons in the field of education, too (Tröhler, 2011). Back in the 1960s, Huebner (1966/1999) vociferated that curriculum research is in search of a new language, i.e., a new style of reasoning, to counter the then predominant instrumental and managerial Tyler Rationale. Today, the predominant languages or discourses for curriculum reform worldwide are competencies, skills, and literacies as represented and re-iterated by, among others, the OECD's core competencies definitions in the 1990s and the US's twenty-first century skills configurations. These discourses are advocated in the name of empowering students with "indispensable" knowledge and skills that would enable them to *succeed* in the twenty-first century. Ever since, different nation-states have been re-contextualizing and re-assembling the OECD's and the US's discourses and frameworks with(in) their local-national contexts, striving to go global with the advanced West either for fear that, if not, their students would *fail* in the twenty-first century world, or, for fear that the domestic expectations would punish stakeholders in elections.

Of course, the discourses of competencies, skills, and literacies do not travel around by themselves but often along with an epistemic fluster of keywords like testing, assessment, evidence-based, efficiency, accountability, and datatification. All these discourses have woven into, or rather, been constructed upon what Tröhler and Maricic (2021) call a "sciento-social epistemology", ordering the way education and curriculum have been thought and reasoned in politically organizing social life in the US and the OECD member nation-states since the early twentieth century. Scientosocial epistemology, the authors argue, intrinsically inscribes faith in detected regularities and visions of salvation, and promises a secured or even blessed future through the (re-)organization of national society. Historically speaking, the scientific and objective methods of precise observation and experimentation in exploring the laws of nature was extended to the cultural, social, and educational world of mankind by means of questionnaires and tests. The statistically collected data ensured the design of efficient curricula that would prepare, administer, and empower schooling children as future bearers of social progress. In other words, the sciento-social epistemology has generated a system wherein science, education, and religion are intertwined to present curriculum knowledge as not only being apparently modern, scientific, rational and secular but also implicitly salvational and faith(ful) (Tröhler & Maricic, 2021, p. 2).

The implicit salvational and faith(ful) dimension of the sciento-social epistemology, the authors continue, belies an often-neglected religious root of educational thinking and practice, namely, "a long-standing religious, or more precisely Presbyterian, legacy of the social order and the way we think about education" (p. 13). The roots of this now-global educational doctrine lie in sixteenth-century Scotland, and they materialized in the United States around 1900, when the traditional congregationalist ideology—from which pragmatism emerged—no longer seemed able to solve the challenges posed by industrialization and immigration. The Presbyterian thought leaders and activists, with the help of the Rockefeller Foundations and especially domiciled at Teachers College with their anti-pragmatic scholars John McKeen Catell and Edward Thorndike, developed the efficiency-oriented and statistics-based expertocratic test psychology, which after Sputnik became the official educational policy doctrine of the USA and was disseminated globally via the USESCO and the OECD (Tröhler, 2014). In doing so, they globalized a very specific sciento-social epistemology that aimed to build a data-driven non-governmental centralized expertocracy that felt obligated to fabricate the "kinds of people" (Bürgi & Tröhler, 2018) that seemed so urgently needed for purposes of the Cold War. Missionization, nationalism and imperialism thus went hand in hand in the educational renewal, standardization and harmonization of the globe (Tröhler, 2010).

Within the framework of this sciento-social epistemology, the OECD in the 1990s proposed a number of key "competencies and skills" that would supposedly enable students to meet the challenges of the twenty-first century more successfully than they could have with traditional curricula. The self-confident view of the future and its challenges exposes the religious content of this proselytizing, because, after all, empiricists can be oriented only to the present, if only by their methodological preference; where their prognosis for the future comes from is—literally—written in the stars. Prophecy, is, in fact, strictly religious or astrological. It is this firm, ultimately religious belief that lies at the core of the education policy doctrine that presents itself globally and sets out to reform or standardize the world according to a model that is at the heart of this volume, or more specifically, how this mission is received and processed elsewhere.

How has this sciento-social epistemology been translated into different nation-states in different cultural eras of the globe? How are they assembled with or confronted by the other, local, cultural, and national forms of knowledge that have been sedimented and constructed along alternative epistemes than the Enlightenment logic of modernity? How are such local cultural forms of knowledge expressed in languages or discourses to counter against the predominant keywords of competency, skills, testing, accountability, and evidence-based measurement? This edited volume engages with experiences of the rise of powerful and globally dominant twenty-first century competency-based curriculum discourses and models and their recontextualizations across the transnational communities and how they can be reciprocally informed, shared, and understood. Toward that agenda, we call for a historical and cultural re-turn in understanding the entanglement of what presents itself as modernization, globalization, localization, and glocalization along the dynamic of cultural and policy imperialism and (de)colonialism as to be unpacked in the next section.

Modernization, Globalization, Localization and Glocalization: A Historical and Cultural (Re)Turn

Situating our discussions within the global dialogue on globalization and localization, this volume specifically addresses the new trends and issues, originating in a particular Cold War context and encountered in borrowing, resisting, and/or re-contextualizing transnational curriculum policies in different nation-states. For example, the age-old unilateral pattern for the Eastern nations to borrow West/Eurocentric educational policies and practices is partially giving its way to a bilateral borrowing, one example of which is China's recent export of the "Shanghai Model" to UK and other European nations. Yet, globalization and localization can never be simplistically expressed away through a one-way or two-way borrowing pattern, nor a power versus resistance dynamic. Instead, they are contested and entangled in a multilayered power relations wherein varying mechanisms, say, nationalism, globalism, culture, religion, ideology, epistemology, social control, and state governance, are interpellated in play with and against one another. Even within Europe where many nation-states share a certain set of cultural systems of thought, inter/trans-national curriculum policy borrowing is a complex cultural negotiation and confrontation of varied socio-politico-cultural-historical factors that are so far not enough reflected. Just as collective or collectivizing terms such as "Latin America", "Near East", "East Asia" are rarely helpful to understanding policies in the individual cultural territories of the modern nation-states, "Europe" is hardly helpful, given the rise of rabid nationalism from Turkey via the Balkans, Poland to the United Kingdom ("Brexit"), to name just the most radical ones. We have to drill deeper to understand the respective idiosyncratic experiences in dealing with imperial regimes, which, as it were, points to the cultural history of the countries, whose peculiarity can hardly be understood in any other way than comparison and encounter.

Indeed, things get more complicated when globalization and localization are intricated with (non-Western) nation-states' modernization process. As the Hong Kong sociologist and education scholar King (2018)—working in the a cultural blend between Western-British and Chinese culture—rightly argues, modernization in many non-Western nation-states is both a response to the intrusion of Western modernity (the "modern" Western civilization that has already undergone the modernization process) in the forms of imperialism and colonialism and the renewal and further development of traditional local civilization. Put differently, apart from the dynamic of power negotiation, globalization and localization are also intrinsically entangled within an epistemological confrontation and colonialism in the name of going modern and global. We base this also on Andreotti (2011) who argues, that "colonialism is constitutive of, rather than derivative from, modernity" (p. 383). Moreover, modernity is intricately entangled with a coloniality of knowledge, power, and being. Coloniality refers to the memory or legacy of the colonialism, which defines culture, labour, intersubjective relation, and knowledge production well beyond the limits of colonialism and long after the end of a colonial administration (Maldonado-Torres, 2007).

Nevertheless, a dominant, yet inadequate, sociological viewpoint prevails in the modernization and globalization literature, namely, "globalization is an inevitable result of modernization" (King, 2018, p. 121). Specifically, sociologists like Max Weber mainly conceptualized the Western "modern" in linkage with technological and bureaucratic organizations and ground the "modern" episteme on an economic, i.e., instrumental or means-ends, rationality. And such Western modernization process by economic rationality has—they conclude—universal applications, as all modernized societies will ultimately take on similar or identical forms of modernity, including but not confined to market economy, nation-state polity, and individualism. Many Western and non-Western societies have indeed transformed into a convergent form of modernity, featuring the growth of scientific consciousness, secularization of religions, development of instrumental rationality, changes in social movements, and industrialization. However, such a Weberian understanding of modernity, albeit dominant for perhaps two centuries, is critiqued as being "a-cultural" (Taylor, 1992) in that its focus on social change excludes culture as an indispensable factor of modernization and modernity. To Taylor, such an a-cultural theory of modernity wrongly interprets everything modern as derived from the "Enlightenment package" and fails, as King's (2018) paraphrases, "to see the full gamut of 'alternative modernities' that are in the making in different parts of the world" (p. 125).

Hence, this volume rightly foregrounds the possible roles that "culture" plays in experiencing and translating the rising dominant "competency" discourses and curriculum framework of the OECD to local contexts. Specifically, this volume focuses on the scope of our international dialogue between some selected European (say, Austria, Finland, Norway, Denmark, Lithuania, Spain) and Asian (Mainland China and Hong Kong SAR, South Korea, Japan, and Singapore) countries, the former with deep cultural-educational influence from Christian ideals which, especially in Protestantism, shape the soul either to ideals of public virtue (Swiss Reformation; Calvin, Zwingli) or to inner aesthetic harmony called *Bildung* (German Reformation; Luther) (see Tröhler, 2020) and the latter from the Confucian educational culture. In other words, we aim to explicate how these two in themselves hardly strictly coherent cultural-historical systems of thought and educational wisdom, the Christian-Catholic preoccupation with the organizational culture of hierarchic expertise, the Protestant preoccupation of transforming the soul in one of the two possible ways, and the Confucian teaching-learning, are re-conceptualized and mobilized, nationalistically or not, in different nation-states' localization efforts of the global curriculum policies and practices. The selection of the two educational-cultural systems and wisdom of thought, the Christian and the Confucian, is to provide a unique springboard for conducting international curriculum studies beyond the usual confinement of geopolitical nation-state construct. It not only sheds new light on each nation-state's curriculum policies and practices, but also creates new collaboration spaces within similar and across disparate cultural-educational regions.

Seen this way, this volume also calls for a "historical" return to better explicate the "cultural" nuances, "culture" understood as shared systems of making sense of the world. The "historical" mode of inquiry examines the conditions and positivity of curriculum knowledge (re)production on an international landscape. Doing so, it brings in multiple cultural forms of epistemic "reason" to challenge the doxa on comparative reason, transnational curriculum knowledge transfer, politics of knowledge and identity, and the making of twenty-first century educational subjects. In so doing, this volumn builds a new platform for conducing healthy and mutually informing dialogues among the Confucian educational cultural nation-states and the Christian European nations on transnational curriculum reforms and school practices, with a caution against both a relativist nationalism and a colonial globalism. The historical and cultural perspective also require us to look at comparative studies and approach differently, which we now turn to clarify more.

Euro-Asia Encounters: A Comparative "Inter-cultural" Approach

Inter-cultural comparisons and dialogues have always involved or engendered theoretical, methodological, and moral complexities. Comparative study, transdisciplinary from its very inception, appeared in the Western academia around the late eighteenth and early nineteenth century along with the emergence of a field-or-problem-focused horizontal scheme of ordering scientific activity, and a methodological emphasis on the radical re-evaluation of empirical evidence (see, Schriewer, 2006). Comparative study also philosophically engages with epistemological and ontological problems within a whole network of power interests and identity issue. For example, around the mid-nineteenth Century when European nations started to command their power on the land of Near Orient and later on Far Orient, comparative approach easily became an expedient tool for the West, through their viewpoints of Marxist historicism and linear progressive time, to construct "the Orient" as "inferior, exotic, backward," waiting to be ruled and transformed. As a case in point, China, an independent country from the West for thousands of years, entered into the scope of comparative study with the arrival of missionaries around the sixteenth century and has since been consciously and unconsciously embroiled within the catch-up-with-the-West mentality (Zhao, 2019).

Such a comparative mentality has caused an epistemological imperialism and colonialism on the international landscape, often depriving the non-West of its very agency in orginating and constructing its knowledge and practices. Edward Said's *Orientalism* (1978) is one incisive example to the extent that it represents the Orient from the European's vision and rationale and thus deprives the locals of their voice and power. In the beginning, however, there was fascination with the foreign, which served as a foil for criticism of one's own. The Western sympathy for the Orient had been triggered by sexually defused translations of the Middle Eastern folk tales *One Thousand and One Nights* between 1704 and 1717, which in turn triggered Montesquieu's *Persian Lettres* in 1721, in which he criticized French conditions in general and the French monarchy in particular against the background of fictitious Persians traveling to France and exchanging letters with friends back home. This was before the time of imperial nationalism, colonialism, which was, however, imminent. In this context, the terms changed, including that of the *Orientals*. What had not changed was the fact that people still knew or wanted to know little precise, but what had changed was the curiosity, the cultural appreciation which turned into colonialism. In other words, *Orientalism* had then little to do with the local people's cultural praxis, but came to terms with the Orient that is based on the Orient's special place in European Western experiences. Through this strategy, "European culture gained in strength and identity by setting itself off against the Orient as a sort of surrogate, an even underground itself" (Said, 1978, p. 3).

Then, what does it really mean to *compare*, and more important, how can we do a more robust comparative conversation, i.e., to compare without necessarily and unconsciously placing one, mostly the Western, epistemological framework on top of the other cultures and thus enclosing the others into its developmental reason within a binary-contrastive logic? To put differently, how is it possible to render intelligible and in modern English those non-Western contextual and historical sensibilities without using the English (Western) metaphysical frameworks and globalized (Westernized) language as a normative identity to frame the other cultures as mirrored contrastive differences? How can comparative thinking flatten out the binary tropes in our analysis, including but not confined to the similarity-difference, equality-difference, identity-difference, and self-others myths?

Our volumn calls for an inter-cultural encounter as an alternative approach to explicate cultural differences comparatively but not normatively. By that, we mean to accent the cultural preconditions and thesis that belie and have made possible the way we think about education and curriculum historically and culturally. However, these cultural preconditions are historically sedimented, culturally unique, and possibly cross-culturally intersected. Thus, understanding cultural influences as they are and in connection with other cultures is one of the fundamental challenges in cross-cultural encounters (Koerrenz et al., 2019). Specifically, this volume foregrounds a cultural epistemic negotiation, confrontation, and (dis)assemblage between the two cultural-historical systems of thought and educational wisdom (namely, the Christian-Protestant preoccupation of transforming the soul in one of the two possible ways and the Confucian teaching-learning) and the so-called "scientosocial" epistemology that is expressed by the OECD's competency-based discourses and practices.

The selection of the two educational-cultural systems and wisdom of thought, the Christian and the Confucian, is to provide a unique springboard for conducting international curriculum studies beyond the usual confinement of geopolitical nation-state construct. Upon closer examination of the historical and cultural negotiation and confrontation of globalization and localization in each individual nation-state, the purpose is to not only shed new light on each nation-state's curriculum policies and practices, but also create new collaboration spaces within similar and across disparate cultural-educational regions. In this way, commonalities and similarities are not discussed at a superficial level and from a normative perspective along an East-West framework, but along the historical conditions of possibility for each nation state, which in turn rendered visible the historicity of (inter-)cultural differences among these varied nation-states and alongside a Euro-Asia encounter.

This historical and inter-cultural approach of comparison resonates with Schriewer's (2006) argument on two methods of comparison, i.e., comparing essence versus comparing relations. The essence-comparison method consists in relating "observable facts" as such, regarding their actual concreteness with pre-existing resemblances, and thus differences would only remain at a "descriptive level" with no theoretical strength. The relation-comparison method "consists in relating relationships or even patterns of relationships to each other" through "systematically exploring and analyzing socio-cultural differences concerning establishing the credibility of general concepts, theoretical propositions or statements of equivalence" (p. 310). In other words, this social-historical-cultural comparison method bears a positivist bent and shows differences empirically not informatively. As Jullien (2004) rightly argues, "difference can't be made in kind, but have to be made intelligible" (p. 11).

Overview of the Chapters

This volume aims to unpack what roles the two educational-cultural systems and wisdom of thought, the Christian and the Confucian, play in nation-states' glocalizing the rising predominant competency discourses, and more importantly, the scietosocial epistemology, promoted by OECD and USA as an expression of epistemological colonialism. Structurally, the volum is divided into two parts that respectively depict the European and Asian pictures, the former with seven chapters about Christian ideals and curriculum reforms whereas the latter with five chapters about Confucian ideals and curriculum reforms. Below is a brief overview of the flow of the volume after this introduction chapter.

In overlooking the last 300 years, chapter Two by Daniel Tröhler (The Transformation of Christian Missions to Educational Colonization, or Motives of Speaking and Listening in the One-sided Euro-American-Asian Dialogue) puts the thesis forward, that the missionary attempts of Christianized Europe failed in Asia in general and China in particular, but eventually triumphed at least in matters of education, as can bee seen in the submission of Asian education policy to the regime of the international assessment culture in general and the OECD in particular. However, Tröhler argues, it is not so much their subordination to the PISA regime as such that bears witness to its triumph, but rather the adoption of a thoroughly educationalized culture in which large scale assessments currently appear to be the most efficient means of performing it. This is because it cooperates most closely and submissively with the normal political power structures which stem from the conviction of a very specific Protestant church order, Presbyterianism.

Next, in Chapter "From Knowledge and Bildung Toward Competences and Skills in Finnish Curriculum Policy? Some Theoretical, Historical, and Current Observations Related to Finland" (From Knowledge and *Bildung* toward Competences and Skills in Finnish Curriculum Policy? Some Theoretical, Historical, and Current Observations Related to Finland), Tero Autio vociferates that Finland's mystery of educational success lies not in following the policies recommended by the OECD, but in ignoring them. To Autio, the Finnish rendition of education, embodied in the blueprint of Peruskoulu, drew on the juxtaposition with inner development provided by German Bildung theories, and democratic pragmatic construction of society shaped by local, historical, and cultural factors, political struggles and international influences. Furthermore, many democratic ideas and practices in Finnish basic schooling, like trust, autonomy and cooperation between teachers, schools and municipalities supported by the state, strictly contrast with the OECD promotion of competition, competences and skills in the technicist, undemocratic policy recommendations "to influence variations of student performance". With the Finnish case, Autio warns us all that after the sixty years' experience of the OECD impact on education, it seems evident that education is definitely too important to be left for economists.

Chapter "Historical Trajectories of the Contract-School Model in Norway" by Kirsten Sivesind (Historical Trajectories of the Contract-School Model in Norway) argues that curriculum reforms in Norway were influenced by a pietistic reform trajectory in the eighteenth century, which were combined with both philanthropic and empirical rationales during the nineteenth and twentieth centuries. Furthermore, the contract-school model that governed education by law and simultaneously through the semantic of schooling is now contested by the prevailing empiricist view on the twenty-first century skills. However, Vivesind believes that one should consider curriculum-making in Norway a public project and an innovative practice that created space for both political and practical developments, rather than as beginning as a top-down effort in terms of universal reforms, or even serving as a form of centralized implementation of national reform during the nineteenth and twentieth century.

Chapter "Globalization and Localization in the Shaping of the Danish Public Education System: Recontextualization Processes in Four Historical Educational Reforms" by Christian Ydesen (Globalization and Localization in the Shaping of the Danish Public Education System: Recontextualization Processes in Four Historical Educational Reforms) moves to explore how globalization and localization processes impacted the Danish education system over 45 years. Through a discourse analysis method, Ydesen's chapter maps the main political discourses associated with the selected educational reforms and determines the extent to which OECD-driven and OECD-adopted discourses were recontextualized and reassembled in the reform processes. It also discusses which cultural-hegemonic values travelled to Denmark and to what extent they were implemented in the cultural ideals of the Danish public education system.

Chapter "Fixing the Future: Public Discourse on the Implementation of Education Standards in Austria" by Bernadette Hörmann (Fixing the Future: Public Discourse on the Implementation of Education Standards in Austria) unpacks the reconstextualization of the global model of education standards in Catholic Austria. Hörmann argues research on Austrian curriculum reforms has not hitherto revealed the actual reason for Austrian politicians, policymakers, and the public to treat standards as an appropriate reform measure. Using a discourse analysis approach, her analysis reveals how a Protestant-Presbyterian-shaped, globalised model of standards has been met, legitimated, and reshaped by a nation-state that is deeply rooted in Catholic and aristocratic structures.

Chapter "A Critical Review of the Competency-Based Curriculum in Spain" by Ana Sánchez-Bello (A Critical Review of the Competency-Based Curriculum in Spain) maintains that the official discourse of competency-based learning in Spain must be decoded in terms of the type of education offered to students: one based on participation in and reflection on the principles of critical, democratic, common-good citizenship; or one more focused on measurable, rankable indicators and outcomes. Compounding this tension, the attempt to curricularise competences such as citizenship has seen a resurgence of the tug of war between church and state in Spain, where the role of religion in schools is always the biggest stumbling block to agreement.

Chapter "Competence-Based Curriculum Reforms in the Context of University Engineering Education in the Post-Soviet Lithuania—Hope or Disappointment?" by Rūta Budrė (Competence-Based Curriculum Reforms in the Context of University Engineering Education in the Post-Soviet Lithuania - Hope or Disappointment?) explores, through the eyes of academics, how the globally pervasive competence framework is implemented and responded to in the specific cultural context of the post-soviet Lithuania and the disciplinary context of engineering. Through reading into academics' narratives collected from an empirical study, Budrė explicates a gap that possibly exists between the circulating cultural and disciplinary understandings of curriculum as expressed by university engineers and the new instrumental neoliberal logic as introduced through the standardized competence-based curriculum model. Academics demonstrate sceptical and cautious attitude towards the new curriculum trend, which Budrė argues can be explained by cultural and discipline-related reasons.

After that, the volumn shifts to portray the Asian picture of the ways in which Confucian ideals are still working in glocalizing the globalized competency discourses and the sciento-social epistemology. Chapter "Nationalism and Globalism as Epistemic Entanglements: China's Suyang Curriculum Reform as a Case Study" by Weili Zhao (Nationalism and Globalism as Epistemic Entanglements: China's *Suyang* Curriculum Reform as a Case Study) builds upon her previous research on globalizing discourses as epistemological colonialism (see, Zhao, 2019, 2020, 2021a, 2021b), and examines an epistemic negotiation, agglomeration, and confrontation in China's recontextualization of OECD's and USA's twenty-first century competency-based curriculum framework as the Chinese Students Core Suyang Frameworks. Striving to catch up with the West, China has been reinvigorating cultural and national discourses to counter against, or rather decolonize, the hegemonic colonialism or the coloniality of knowledge and being of the Western modernity. However, Zhao argues that China's policy makers and academia are still subjugated to a modernity-coloniality to the extent that their efforts of recalibrating China's suyang curriculum as a cultural matrix remains as nothing but a linguistic trap and trope. Instead, Zhao proposes an alternative episteme, namely, the Chinese body-thinking, as a new direction for China's suyang curriculum that both speaks to the Confucian tradition and constrains the grip of neoliberal education. In so doing, this chapter examines the entanglement of globalism and nationalism beyond a relativist nationalism and a colonial globalism.

Chapter "Unpacking the Global-Local Entanglements in Hong Kong's Curriculum Reform" by Min Lin & Yundan Zheng (Unpacking the Global-Local Entanglements in Hong Kong's Curriculum Reform) foregrounds the importance of cultural conditions in understanding the curriculum reform in Hong Kong SAR. As a post-colonial city and one of the world's financial centers, Hong Kong, in its policy making, is deemed as under greater influence by "globalization" than other Chinese cities. Drawing on Savage's conceptual notion of "assemblage," the authors examine multiple political-cultural-historical entanglements conditioning Hong Kong's current ccurriculum framework as being distinct from the OECD model.

Chapter "Competency-Based Curriculum Reform and its Making of Korean Global Citizens" by Ji-Hye Kim (Competency-Based Curriculum Reform and its Making of Korean Global Citizen) investigates unpacks how OECD's competency discourse has traveled to South Korea, and how it is re-territorialized as cultural principles in Korean national curriculum reform. Kim first of all examines Korean Confucianism and the idea of the traditional ideal educated person as a cultural context to help us better understand the traveling of global competency discourses into South Korea. Then, through South Korean curriculum reform documents, Kim discusses how the Korean curriculum reform embodied the effort to make the ideal Korean citizen by translating the global competency discourse together with Korean history and culture. In so doing, this study reveals the connectivity between the global and local education reform as well as contextual differences emerged from the nation-state's own process of re-territorialization.

Chapter "A Holistic Model of Competence: Curriculum Reforms for Preschool Education in Singapore" by Sandra Wu and Charlene Tan (A Holistic Model of Competmjnhence: Curriculum Reforms for Preschool Education in Singapore) discusses the curriculum reforms for preschool education in Singapore by drawing upon a holistic model of competence. They further extend this model by offering a Confucian interpretation where holism revolves around person-making. In so doing, they show how and the extent to which recent changes for preschool curriculum in Singapore transcend the definition of competencies as discrete skills to promote a set of complex and integrated attributes (knowledge, attitudes, values and skills) in young children so that they could thrive as confident individuals and active members of the community. The chapter also explores how the interaction of top-down and ground-up forces and social actors work together to improve preschool education in Singapore.

Keita Takayama ends the volumn with chapter Thirteen (The Global Inside the National and the National Inside the Global: 'Zest for Living,' the *Chi, Toku and Tai* Triad, and the 'Model' of Japanese Education). This chapter artfully historicizes a period when Japan's education policy is re-moulded by both transnational and national discourses and epistemes. With a focus on the shifting articulations of "competencies" from the mid-1980s to the present, it demonstrates the complex intersections between national and transnational and their increasingly blurred distinction. In so doing, it problematizes the uncomplicated demarcation between these spatial categories and proposes a view that the national constitution of "competencies" or education policy in general has always been both transnational and national simultaneously, aptly expressed by his chapter title, "the global inside the national and the national inside the global".

Conclusion

It can be argued that the volume, through approaching a Euro-Asian encounter on competency-based curriculum reforms, is to *make intelligible*, rather than *make*, cultural-national differences between the two historical-cultural systems of thought and educational wisdoms, as well as among the individually surveyed nation-states. Our intention is to render cultural-historical differences as they are, not in and through one particular norm(alized) lens, say, the Presbytarian/OECD's educational scientosocial epistemology. In this sense, this volume goes against the dominant power-resistance paradigm in international and intercultural (curriculum) studies to configurate the (dis)ordering between globalization and localization. As an alternative, it looks at traveling languages, discourses, and curriculum practices as the political site where the varied geo-cultural epistemes collide, clash, and combine through the mechanisms of translation, re-contextualization, and de-contextualization. Translation here is treated as historical-political occurrence embedded within contingent historical-cultural-political practices, legitimizing the meaning-making of traveling discursive practices in their fluidities, rather than reified as ahistorical ideas and concepts. Deconstructing the past-present and East-West tempo-spatial boundaries, this volumn pinpoints and interprets the historical moments and processes in which certain traveling themes, discourses, and practices become meaningful contextually and acquire legitimacy in a given language and educational context, no longer reducible to foreign impact nor the self-explanatory logic of the indigenous tradition.

References

Andreotti, V. (2011). (Towards) decoloniality and diversality in global citizenship education. *Globalisation, Societies and Education, 9*(3–4), 381–397.

Bürgi, R., & Tröhler, D. (2018). Producing the 'right kind of people': The OECD education indicators in the 1960's. In S. Lindblad, D. Pettersson & T. S. Popkewitz (Eds.), *Education by the numbers and the making of society. The expertise of international assessments* (pp. 75–91). Routledge.

Huebner, D. (1966/1999) Curricular language and classroom meanings. In V. Hills (Ed.), 1999, *The lure of the transcendent: Collected essays by Dwayne E. Huebner* (pp. 101–117). Lawrence Erlbaum Associates.

Jullien, F. (2004). *Detour and access: Strategies of meaning in China and Greece.* Zone Book.

King, A. (2018). *China's great transformation: Selected essays on Confucianism, modernization, and democracy.* Chinese University Press.

Koerrenz, R., Schmidt, A., Vieweg, K., & Watts, E. (Eds.). (2019). *West-eastern mirror: Virtue and morality in the Chinese-German dialogue.* Ferdinand Schöningh.

Maldonado-Torres, N. (2007). On the coloniality of being. *Cultural Studies, 21*(2–3), 240–270.

Piattoeva, N. et al. (2019). The nationalism-trap in education research: Shared pathos, practiced ideals, and spectra of banal nationalism. *Bildungsgeschichte. International Journal for the Historiography of Education, 9*(2), 244–278.

Robertson, R. (1992). *Globalization: Social theory and global culture.* Sage.

Schriewer, J. (2006). Comparative social science: Characteristic problems and changing problem solutions. *Comparative Education, 42*(3), 299–336.

Said, E. W. (1978). *Orientalism.* Vintage.

Taylor, C. (1992). *Sources of the self: The making of modern identity.* Harvard University Press.

Tröhler, D. (2010) Harmonizing the educational globe. World polity, cultural features, and the challenges to educational research. *Studies in Philosophy and Education, 29,* 7–29.

Tröhler, D. (2014). Change management in the governance of schooling: The rise of experts, planners, and statistics in the early OECD. *Teachers College Record, 116* (9), 13–26.

Tröhler, D. (2011). *Languages of education. protestant legacies, national identities, and global aspirations.* Routledge.

Tröhler, D. (2020). The lasting legacy of the European reformation of the 16th century: Protestant foundations of modern educational reasoning. *Journal of Beliefs & Values. Studies in Religion & Education* (41). https://doi.org/10.1080/13617672.2020.1818934

Tröhler, D. (2021). Magical enchantments and the nation's silencing: Educational research agendas under the spell of globalization. In D. Tröhler, N. Piattoeva, & W. F. Pinar (Eds.), *Education, schooling and the global universalization of nationalism* [World Yearbook of Education 2022]. Routledge.

Tröhler, D., & Maricic, V. (2021). Data, trust and faith: The unheeded religious roots of modern education policy. *Globalisation, Societies and Education, 19*(2). https://doi.org/10.1080/14767724.2021.1872371

Zhao, W. (2019). *China's education, curriculum knowledge and cultural inscriptions: Dancing with the wind.* Routledge.

Zhao, W. (2020). Problematizing "Epistemicide" in transnational curriculum knowledge production: China's *Suyang* curriculum reform as an example. *Curriculum Inquiry, 50*(2), 105–125.

Zhao, W. (2021a). Re-Turning to the "Cultural" foundations of China's curriculum reform: ICT and confucian "Wind" pedagogy. In J. Paraskeva (Ed.), *Itinerant curriculum theory a declaration of epistemological liberation.* Palgrave.

Zhao, W. (2021b). Toward a de-colonial language gesture in transnational curriculum studies. In B. Green, P. Roberts, & M. Brennan (Eds.), *Curriculum challenges and opportunities in a changing world: Transnational perspectives in curriculum inquiry.* Palgrave McMillan.

Weili Zhao is an assistant professor in the Department of Curriculum and Instruction at the Chinese University of Hong Kong, China. With interdisciplinary training in linguistics and sociolinguistics, critical discourse studies, language philosophy, and curriculum studies, she has been doing research on China's education and curriculum reforms at the nexus of tradition and modernity, East and West. Her dissertation-turned book, *China's Education, Curriculum Knowledge and Cultural Inscriptions: Dancing with The Wind*, was out in June 2018 with Routledge, and she was the recipient of 2019 AERA Early Career Outstanding Research Award, SIG 171 (Confucianism, Taoism, Buddhism and Education).

Daniel Tröhler is Professor of Foundations of Education at the University of Vienna since 2017 and Visiting Professor at the University of Oslo since 2018. His research interests lie in the international and transnational developments of the last 250 years with a focus around 1800s and the Cold War. In doing so, he relates the history of modern ideas to the history of institutions in the context of a broader cultural history by focusing on (educational) political and educational ideas and their materialization in school laws, curricula and textbooks, comparing different national and regional developments and investigating their possible mutual influences. He has published or edited over 50 books, 100 journal articles and some 150 book chapters in seven languages. For the book *Languages of Education: Protestant Legacies, National Identities, and Global Aspirations* (Routledge 2011) he was awarded the Outstanding Book of the Year Award of the American Education Research Association AERA in 2012. He is currently working on the development of an ERC project proposal titled Nation state, curriculum and the fabrication of national-minded citizens.

The European Picture: Christian Protestant Ideals and Curriculum Reforms

The Transformation of Christian Missions to Educational Colonization, or Motives of Speaking and Listening in the One-Sided Euro-American-Asian Dialogue

Daniel Tröhler

Introduction

Towards the end of the year 1723, there was a real scandal in the young and uprising Kingdom of Prussia when the great star of German philosophy, Christian Wolff, was personally expelled from the country by King Frederick William I of Prussia on 8 November under threat of the death penalty. Wolff, who had been given exactly 48 h to comply with the order, immediately travelled to the Landgraviate of Hesse-Kassel and accepted the chair of philosophy that had been offered to him by the University of Marburg some time before. But what had happened to bring about this widely discussed scandalous event?

The immediate occasion was actually an ordinary university ritual at the Prussian University of Halle to which Wolff had belonged since 1706. In 1720–21, Wolff served the university for one year as vice-principal and ended his term of office with a traditional vice-principal speech on July 12, 1721, which at the same time symbolized the handover of the office to his successor. Not really common, however, was the topic that Wolff dealt with in his speech—and also the title—, namely, the "Practical Philosophy of the Chinese," whereby "practical philosophy" had been, since Aristotle, understood to mean all those sub-disciplines that have something to do with human practice, i.e. ethics, philosophy of law and political philosophy. What did Wolff now say in his speech, that made parts of the audience so upset that they conspired against him and finally turned to the king residing in Berlin, who then drove Wolff out of the country?

What Wolff did in his speech was, based on the foundations of his own philosophy, analyze and judge Chinese philosophy. He began with Confucius (551 BC–479

D. Tröhler (✉)
Department of Education, University of Vienna, Vienna, Austria
e-mail: daniel.troehler@univie.ac.at

© The Author(s), under exclusive license to Springer Nature Singapore Pte Ltd. 2021
W. Zhao and D. Tröhler (eds.), *Euro-Asian Encounters on 21st-Century Competency-Based Curriculum Reforms*,
https://doi.org/10.1007/978-981-16-3009-5_2

BC), whom he assumed to be known to the public, and then moved on chronologically backwards to the Emperors Yao and Shun, who had been in power more than 2000 years BC and who had been so highly revered by Confucius himself (Wolff, 1726/1985, pp. 13–14). According to Wolff—he based this on Confucius' account—the Chinese people under these philosophical emperors had been politically very well led, i.e. had been virtuous and, in the end, happy. Confucius himself had been, Wolff says, a gift from God as he had been born at the time of China's disintegration, had renewed the old teachings of the emperors and had thus been able to restore the country through his work as a teacher of the people (pp. 15–19). According to Wolff, Confucius was for the Chinese what Moses was for Jews, Mohammed for Turks and Christ for Christians, insofar as one understands all of them as teachers and prophets.

Wolff used most of the speech to prove his thesis, which ultimately said that one can also live good and happy lives without Christianity. Methodically, he proceeded in such a way that he evaluated the principles of action of Chinese philosophy—after all, it was about practical philosophy—on the scale of what Wolff called the "nature of the human mind" (Wolff, 1726/1985, p. 23). Admittedly, he said that the ancient Chinese had not known the "Creator of the world" (the Christian God, of course), and had therefore also had no natural religion and certainly no testimonies of revelation, which is why they always had to limit themselves to what Wolff called "forces of nature" that were "free from any religion" (p. 27). By "forces of nature," Wolff meant strictly the peculiarities of the "human mind," which he interpreted in accordance with the rational thinking of the early Enlightenment; after all, Wolff was, in his way of thinking (about the world), a mathematician. This "human mind" was defined as the noblest part of the soul (nobler than emotions or the senses), which was understood as being given by God. But even if the human soul, and with it also its noblest part, the "human spirit," were indeed God-given, they were, as *human* artefacts, nevertheless imperfect. The great advantage of the Chinese philosophy was, Wolff says, that it had dealt less with this imperfection than with the question of how one could perfect the soul (pp. 27–29). This basic attitude, which Wolff recognized as in agreement with his own natural-law philosophy and that of his philosophical teacher Samuel von Pufendorf, is the basis of all virtue (Tröhler, 2017).

The precondition of human virtue was thus the exploration of the soul in general and the powers of the "human mind," as they provide the basis for the discovery of all "truths," in which no prejudices prevail, but only what is "true," what is sharply separated from the false (Wolff, 1726/1985, p. 29). Wolff's basic assumption was that any soul, while recognizing its own nature and truth, has a deep inclination to transfer the recognized true and good into human actions. Hence, knowledge of what is true and good is at the same time the trigger for action of what is recognized as good and true, that is of virtue. To Wolff, it was "generally known" that it belonged to the peculiarity of the soul "to desire only what it considers to be good and to detest only what it considers to be evil," so that in the end it was only about producing a correct assessment of things, i.e. to recognize the true; the good would then follow from this naturally (p. 31). In this view, acting badly is simply acting on the basis of a false insight in which the bad appears as the good.

Even if the ancient Chinese had by no means matured to perfection in this respect, Wolff states, they had lived and acted according to these principles and, above all, had recognized that the human soul had these two parts. The first part of the soul is the one of the senses, imaginations and feelings/temper (*Gemüt*), and the second part is the seat of the "pure mind" (*reiner Verstand*), reason (*Vernunft*) and free will (Wolff, 1726/1985, p. 35). Acting on the basis of the first part makes man no different from animals (p. 37). Against this background the human's duty is to train the mind towards the "clear knowledge of things," whereby reason then drives the doer to the realization of the good; he is determined by his "free will to good actions" and needs no further master: he is master of himself. "Whoever would have been better than the Chinese in training human morals, I do not know him indeed" (p. 37).

For this educational purpose, the ancient Chinese, under the wise rule of the two emperors, erected two types of schools. The first type was the "school of the younger ones," which would have focused on the lower parts of the soul and to which all children, regardless of their social background, between the ages of 8 and 15 had to attend. And the second was the "school of the adults," which would have concentrated on the nobler part of the soul and to which only the children of the emperor, kings, noblemen and the highly gifted of the normal people would have had access (Wolff, 1726/1985, pp. 37–39). In other words, the ancient Chinese had, according to Wolff, absolutely right philosophical insights, ones appropriate to the worthy human nature that distinguishes them from animals, and correspondingly right institutions.

This was, at least for a part of the audience, too much, because in their opinion a non-Christian people could have neither truth nor virtue, and they began to scheme against Wolff, to dissect his writings in order to demonstrate his godlessness and then they turned (successfully) to the king with the request of expelling this "dangerous man" from Prussia. That Wolff was non-Christian is of course nonsense, and he belonged, like his critics, to German Protestantism, that is, to Lutheranism. But the two parties to the dispute were, so to speak, at the opposite ends of the spectrum in which one could be Lutheran. Hence, the story with Wolff's expulsion represents what can be called the struggle for the supremacy of (one's own) understanding of the good life and the right social order via the lenses of Lutherans, that is, religious lenses in assessing the "right" social and political order.

The role of this inner-Lutheran aspect in the history of Wolff's expulsion is central, but it somewhat obscures the global view because the cause of the dispute was the confrontation of Northern German, that is Lutheran, philosophy with a non-Christian philosophy or religion, with what could have been called "Far Eastern culture." If one restricts oneself to this dispute only, the question of why and how one acquired knowledge about "foreign cultures" in the first place, and why the transfer of knowledge did not take place in the same way in both directions, disappears. Of course, people in China knew something about Europe, mostly about Christianity, but the gatekeepers of information were, in both ways of communication and knowledge transfer, European, usually missionaries and traders; hence, the mutual transfer of knowledge was one-sided and guided by European interests.

In this chapter, I would like to take both aspects of this dispute in Halle as an opportunity to reflect on the question of how strongly global dialogues have to do with motives of imperial hegemony, both then and now. The fact that large parts of East Asia have not been sustainably Christianized could lead one to speak of failure. The thesis is that, in this case, the "will to power," to use a *topos* by Friedrich Nietzsche in his *Thus Spoke Zarathustra*[1] (1883), is underestimated, and that it is easily overlooked that there are other forms and means of adapting or submitting "others" to one's own values and norms. In other words, the thesis is therefore that the will to global power, which has characterized Christianized Europe, partly failed in matters of missionary work but eventually triumphed at least in matters of education, as will be seen in the submission of Asian education policy to the regime of the international assessment culture in general and the OECD in particular. However, it is not so much their subordination to the PISA regime as such that bears witness to its triumph, but rather the adoption of a thoroughly educationalized culture in which large scale assessments currently appear to be the most efficient means of performing it. This is because it alignes most closely and submissively with the normal political power structures which stem from the conviction of a very specific Protestant church order, Presbyterianism.

Knowing well that 300 or more years of history cannot be dealt with in 15 pages, I would nevertheless like to take four thought-steps which, if they do not prove the thesis, can at least make it plausible. I will first contextualize the dispute in religious questions related to the political power, Lutheran Prussia, and then indicate the European and American Protestant rivalries and their educational aspirations in the educationalization of the world. In a third step, I will show which of these competing educational aspirations won in the wake of Sputnik and, subsequently, demonstrate how this became an enterprise of global colonialization and mission. The outlook reflects on the mutual flows of power ambitions and on meaningful research agendas in this difficult and complex setting.

Mission, Knowledge Transfer and Battlefields of Re-interpretation

It had begun, of course, with missionary work. Christian Wolff himself had never been in China, but had based his considerations on the translations of the French-Belgian Jesuit, François Noël (1651–1729), who from 1684 to 1708 had been active as a missionary in China and who also tried, like many other Jesuits, to justify an accommodation of Catholic teachings to the Confucian rites in order to avoid that Chinese conversion to Christianity would be separated from their traditional culture. Jesuits knew that missionizing the non-Christian Chinese was an undertaking that required a broad understanding of Chinese history and culture. In the course of his engagement with the great Chinese thinkers, Noël began efforts to translate the Chinese classics into Latin, the common language of European scholars. He was not the first to translate, for example, Confucius, but he did so with more objectivity than,

---

[1] Zarathustra was a Persian spiritual leader and founder of religion, who lived ca. 1000 BC.

for example, the Italian Jesuit missionary to the Qing Empire, Prospero Intorcetta, in his translation from 1687, *Confucius Sinarum Philosophus* (Liščák, 2015); even though he, Noël, made it clear that only Christianity, that is, Roman Catholicism, was the only true religion. In 1711, Noël first published a study of Chinese philosophy and simultaneously edited a translation of the great Chinese philosophical masterpieces in six volumes, the *Sinensis Imperii Libri Classici Sex* [The Six Classic Books of the Chinese Empire]; and it was this translation that had been the source of Wolff's vice-rectorate speech in 1721.[2]

Against this background one can guess what made the audience so angry when Wolff gave his speech in Halle on July 12, 1721. But what *exactly* disturbed them and why? Of course, the old story could be told here, according to which the Enlightenment or Enlightenment philosophy had to assert itself against religion in general and against the Church and theology in particular in order to give human understanding or human reason the leading charge in the shaping of social life. Wolff would thus be a representative of the rational Enlightenment, free of religious assumptions, and his critics and enemies would then be assigned the roles of reactionary actors of an authoritarian Christian state. And indeed, as mentioned above, anti-Christianity had been the accusation against Wolff. This criticism was made by a group of colleagues who belonged to a very active reform movement of German Protestantism (Lutheranism), and who called themselves Pietists. The name "Pietism" refers almost automatically to the program of this reform movement, namely to promote the *pietas* (Latin for piety) and thus to complete the work of the German reformer, Martin Luther. Halle was a European focal point of Pietism during this period, not least because it fitted in perfectly with the king's plans to make Prussia a leading Protestant monarchy in Europe, which, in alliance with the Calvinist Dutch Republic and moderately reformed Protestant England, aimed at being a counterweight to the major Catholic powers of France and Austria. Prussia's Frederick William I (king from 1713–1740) laid the foundations for this, and his son Frederick II (king from 1740 to 1786)—later called Frederick the Great, who pardoned Christian Wolff and brought him back to Halle as early as 1740—completed this plan. Within less than 70 years, Prussia had become a primarily militaristic great power, whose rulers liked to meet philosophers, such as Voltaire, and who ensured that the country was efficiently administered in terms of domestic politics. And that had a lot to do with education.

---

[2]Noël's translation was later paraphrased in detail in the encyclopedic work *Description géographique, chronologique, politique et physique de l'empire de la Chine et de la Tartarie chinoise* (Geographical, chronological, political and physical description of the Empire of China and the Chinese Tartaric Empire) by the French Jesuit, Jean-Baptiste Du Halde (Paris, 1735, vol. 2). This publication was, since it was written in French, available to many thinkers of the eighteenth century. Confucian thought became, for example, an important source of inspiration for the founder of modern economics (economic cycle), François Quesnay (1694–1774), and for David Hume (1711–1776), who is considered one of Scotland's leading philosophers. François Noël was thereby one of the most important cultural mediators between China and Europe in the early eighteenth century, when he inspired those thinkers who renounced theological interpretations and drew the picture of a philosophy that understood itself freely of God and Church (Elisseeff-Poisle, 1991; Mungello, 1991).

In contrast to England, with its comparatively weak institutionalized state and cities and the need for private associations of wealthy contemporaries to take care of the education of the less privileged younger generations, and in contrast to the Dutch Republic, with its highly established forms of republican urban self-government, Lutheran Prussia aimed at a strong monarchy with little self-government but with educated yet nevertheless obedient subjects. Pietism, which is latently anti-institutional, i.e. predominantly inward-thinking and pious, was suitable for this cooperation with a strong monarchical state that aimed at being an agent of controlled progress, strength and power. This strategy asked for a particular kind of education that promised, at the same time, both subservient Christian loyalty and individual empowerment (Horlacher, 2021). In this context, the Pietist, August Hermann Francke, became the figurehead of this ultimately state-driven desire. Francke arguably represents the most impressive model of what is called the educationalization of social problems and ultimately of the whole world in his time, a basic attitude according to which not only all kinds of (non-educational) problems and challenges can be solved by education but also the self, the world and the future as a whole fundamentally depend on education (Tröhler, 2016). What helped Francke in his aggression against Wolff after the vice-rectorate speech in 1721 was his tight relationship with the king, who hoped Francke would provide him with the right educated personnel to build up his Prussian power base.

The headquarters of this reform were to be in Halle, where the university was founded in 1694 by Frederick I (who would become the first King in Prussia in 1701, followed in 1713 by Frederick William I) and would become the *alma mater* of Christian Wolff in 1706. The university was founded to supply the booming city with professional power, and the city expanded not least because of the French Calvinist Protestants who had to flee France after the French absolutist King Louis XIV revoked the Edict of Nantes (1598) in 1685, which had given the French Protestants modest religious freedoms for almost a hundred years. In 1698, Francke, professor of Greek and theology at the University of Halle, founded an orphanage affiliated with the university. However, the orphanage was not only an orphanage but also comprised a *Paedagogium Regium* (boarding school for the sons of nobility as an annex to the university), a seminary for training elementary school teachers (*Seminarium Praeceptorum*) and an institution for women organized in different sections according to the women's social classes. This orphanage was what Francke called a *Universal-Einrichtung*, a universal facility for "universal improvement of all classes ... not only in Germany and Europe but in all other parts of the world" by virtue of Pietist education (1704/1962, p. 154).[3] In this way, it aimed at strengthening administratively the expanding Prussian monarchy by contributing to the "bureaucratization of daily

---

[3] By order of the Lutheran Danish King Frederick IV, in 1706, two theologians trained by Francke established a mission station in the Danish trading colony of Tranquebar on the south-east coast of India. The missionaries founded social institutions and schools based on the Halle model; a later result of these endeavors was the foundation of the Tamil Evangelical Lutheran Church (TELC) in 1919. On the "other" side of the world, Francke's contacts with the British colonies in North America led to priests from Halle travelling to North America in 1733 to assist the Protestant Salzburg emigrants in Georgia, from where the Lutheran Church of North America developed.

life and the creation of a 'police-state' in Prussia" via educating the poor to become teachers, who in turn were allowed to enter the university and through that "were helping territorial leaders to construct a meritocracy" within the expanding Prussian state (Whitmer, 2015, p. 9). Poverty was seen as a resource for the expanding Prussian state and its need for loyal administration and education was its pledge; and at the same time, Prussia was seen as a state to expand Lutheranism in the interpretation of Pietism (Tröhler, 2020a).

Now it becomes more understandable what upset the audience of Wolff's speech in 1721 and why they succeeded in getting the King of Prussia to expel Wolff in 1723. Wolff was not simply a purely rational thinker (if such a thing exists), or if he was, then he was within the framework of traditional Lutheran thought, according to which a strictly dualistic worldview assumed an inside and an outside and gave absolute preference to the former. Above all, in Wolff's interpretation there was no religious institution like that of the Catholic Church, which saw itself as holy and which assumed that the individual experience of salvation was only possible within its organizational structure. Wolff had thus taken the Catholic (Jesuit) motivation of missionizing the Chinese as the starting point for a strictly rational Lutheran interpretation of Chinese practical philosophy. With that, he failed, but not because he made this transfer at all, but because, in the eyes of the Pietists, he made it far too rational and not radical enough. For them, there was a primacy of (religious) emotional attitude, of piety, and an absolute pre-eminence of Christian revelation in the interpretation of Martin Luther. So how could one ascribe truth and virtue to a non-Christian or at least pre-Christian people like the ancient Chinese? If it was—as Wolff had done—inward rational philosophy that allowed for this assessment, then it simply had to be wrong and therefore dangerous.

The contrast that became apparent between the Pietists and "the Enlighteners" was, however, far less clear than the dispute would suggest. It was Christian Thomasius, the spiritual founding father of the University of Halle, who had advocated Francke's vocation even though he, like Wolff, belonged to the rationalists. After 1750, the contrasts between the two Lutheran strands could hardly be clearly identified anymore, and one can certainly read Immanuel Kant's philosophy as a synthesis of the two. This amalgam applies in particular to education. Based on his idea that the (inward) human mind has the disposition (and the task!) to perfect itself, Wolff had developed an implicit education (Tröhler, 2001), which was discussed in parallel to the educational aspirations by Pietism perhaps until the mid-eighteenth century. Yet, around 1750, the idea of perfection (of the inward soul) underwent an aesthetic transformation and emerged then as the German theory of *Bildung* (Tröhler, 2017), which then took on a deep nationalist connotation, especially after the collapse of the Holy Roman Empire of the German Nation by Napoleon's troops and the occupation of Berlin in 1806 (Horlacher, 2016).

So, the scandal we can see in the years 1721–23 is an expression of a somewhat highly stylized dispute within the same Protestant denomination, Lutheranism. They both argued internally, thus focusing on the soul (but did not attach equal importance to the different elements or parts), and thus had an ultimately a-political focus, which, precisely because it argued psycho-anthropologically, was cosmopolitan in its aspiration: the aspirational world of Prussia was, politically, liberal or pietistically, always the whole of humanity and the whole globe. No wonder, then, that in 1800 there were no questions of educating the future *citizens* in Germany, as compared to France or the United States, but always only of the *human being as such*. "Human education" (*Menschenbildung*) was—and to a large degree still is—the magic German word with which the Prussian-Lutheran heritage was imperially extrapolated (Tröhler, 2018).

Protestant Rivalries and Their Educational Aspirations

In the field of education, at least, there has been too little reflection on the fact that the Reformation (of the Christian Church, which eventually lead to a schism between Roman-Catholics and Protestants) in the sixteenth century was an extremely diverse movement with many local actors which had only been reduced to two or three "schools" over the course of the decades, not least because these had been supported by the respective political powers: Luther was protected by several German landgraves, Zwingli by the city of Zurich and Calvin by the city of Geneva. Since the two Swiss Reformation centers had converged theologically in the seventeenth century, it can be roughly simplistically said that there is a German Protestantism of Lutheranism, or Evangelical Protestantism, and a Swiss Protestantism of Zwinglianism and Calvinism, or Reformed Protestantism. The latter differs from the former in many theological questions, but the political dimension is more important here. While Lutheranism, with its almost exclusive orientation towards the inner world, largely refrained from political questions and accepted the absolute power of monarchs, even if they ruled unjustly, Reformed Protestantism was more strongly influenced by civic humanism and aimed to change the world; in principle it oriented towards free self-government of the citizens, i.e. it was republican (Tröhler, 2011).

These two denominations were already very skeptical about each other in the sixteenth century, as Luther's correspondence with Zwingli shows (Glöde, 1973). And from both emerged, not only different visions of political and social order, which were very sustainable, but also different educational languages or discourses which, from the eighteenth century at the latest, led to clearly distinguishable educational theory models. The differences between these are still effective today, even if they seem invisible: they are powerful modes of perceiving the educational world that strongly affect how people think, talk and act in education (Tröhler, 2011).

How strongly religion and politics are interwoven can probably best be shown by the extraordinarily bloody history of England in the wake of King Henry VIII († 1547), which was somewhat pacified only with the Glorious Revolution of 1688–89. This event indicates the deposition and replacement of the converted Catholic, James II, as the ruler of England, Scotland and Ireland by his Protestant daughter from his first marriage, Mary II, together with her husband, James II's nephew, the Dutch Calvinist King William III of Orange. The Anglican Church, which emerged from this history, was theologically moderately Protestant, but retained the strictly hierarchical church structure of Catholicism, however, with the king or queen at the top (Supreme head) rather than a church person (the Pope). It was this strong state centering and hierarchy, but also the only moderate Protestant theology, that forced the orthodox community or congregation-centered Reformed Protestants—denigrated as "Puritans"—to cross the Atlantic Ocean to the British colonies in America to build their "City Upon the Hill," the Kingdom of God on earth. From this institution-skeptical ideology of these Puritans, known as Congregationists, who envisaged flat hierarchies and the widest possible cooperation of the devoted and virtuous citizens for the good of God, the philosophy of pragmatism emerged at the end of the nineteenth century, which aimed precisely at creating, sometimes literally, the Kingdom of God in the United States with a kind of education that would meet the challenges of the times, that is big industry, capitalism, big cities and mass immigration (Tröhler, 2006).

Around 1900, the basic assumptions of the philosophy and education of pragmatism, especially those of John Dewey, quickly shaped American educational philosophy, the dominant doctrines of teacher education and thus the imaginary world of teachers and teachers' unions. The intellectual, educational and pedagogical attractiveness of pragmatism is unique in the world, it has led to countless dissertations as well as authored and edited research books. One is of course inclined to speak of a global influence of American pragmatism in general or of John Dewey in particular, but more detailed studies show that the local respective receptions treated John Dewey as an "indigenous foreigner" (Popkewitz, 2005) and took out of pragmatism that which somehow fitted into the local contexts. Thus, Dewey's pedagogy, not necessarily his philosophy, was able to gain a foothold in South America (Bruno-Jofré & Jover, 2012), and so, in this way, one can also speak of a *Chinese Dewey* (Schulte, 2012, see also Qi, 2005).

The great sympathy that educational research seems to share with the ideas of pragmatism has had its downsides, however, because it largely overlooked that, after 1900, another type of educational research had developed, which also came from a Protestant milieu, but from a different denomination. It may be considered ironic that, after 1904—when John Dewey moved from Chicago to Columbia University in New York—, the headquarters of the two dominant educational doctrines were separated by only one street, 120th Street, which was long called "the widest street in the world" ("Education", 1954, p. 64) because the intellectual preferences between Columbia University and Teachers College were so far apart, even though the two institutions were and are linked, albeit in rather complex ways. This divide was about what then developed as behaviorism in the latter institution, a field of educational research that made psychology the starting point for educational research rather than philosophy. And this had to do with a rival Protestant denomination that had emerged, in their journeys across the Western World, basically from the same roots: Calvinism. The later denomination, Presbyterianism, did not come to America via England, however, but via Scotland and Northern Ireland, which made an important difference precisely because of the different political conditions.

Teachers College had originally developed from an initiative by the daughter of William E. Dodge, Jr., the Presbyterian president of the Evangelical Alliance and of the National Temperance Society and vice-president of the American Sunday

School Union, Grace Hoadley Dodge. Facing the tremendous problems of immigration and (poorer) immigrants, in 1880, Dodge established a "kitchen garden" school on Manhattan Island to teach poor immigrant women lessons in cooking, sewing, hygiene and other practical arts. As the efforts took shape, Dodge realized that a new kind of pedagogy had emerged out of these activities—orderly teaching that reflected an understanding of the learners' background and that reflected how to present material in a relevant and meaningful way. In other words, social engagement or social work became educationalized (Eisenmann, 1998, pp. 134–135). That these efforts could also be institutionalized at a higher level was due to Columbia philosophy professor, Nicholas Murray Butler, whose grandfather had been president of the American Presbyterians. With his help as president of the Industrial Education Association (that had replaced the Kitchen Garden Association) and with the money donated by industrialist, George Vanderbilt, for a property on West 120th Street, a school for teacher training opened in 1887. Subsequently, and against the will of Columbia University's board of trustees, Butler succeeded, in 1892, in reorganizing the "Teachers College" into a largely independent institution affiliated with Columbia University (McCaughey, 2003, pp. 190–192). While Columbia University taught, among other academic fields, philosophy, which could include education—John Dewey had been appointed in 1904—the neighboring Teachers College was concerned with practical matters in education, such as efficient teaching and school administration.

For this purpose, Butler made two central personnel decisions in 1891. He appointed James Earl Russell as a dean, a Presbyterian who had studied in Germany with Rein and Wundt and had received his doctorate from the latter; and he hired James McKeen Cattel, professor of psychology and son of a Presbyterian minister of Scottish origin who had also received his doctorate from Wilhelm Wundt in Leipzig. Together with James McKeen's former doctoral student and new colleague, Edward Lee Thorndike, son of a Methodist Minister, Teachers College built up a broad, test-psychology-based expertise for efficiency in teaching and school administration, which quickly became a worldwide hub for school reform(ers) (Takayama, 2018). Hence, even if research—especially historical research—preferred to deal with John Dewey and pragmatism out of sympathy and step-mothered early test psychology, the educational principles of "social efficiency" had already begun to overtake pragmatism in importance by the late nineteenth century (Labaree, 2010).

At around 1900, the three dominant schools of Protestantism had created three academic educational ideologies: the Lutheran-based *geisteswissenschaftliche Pädagogik* centered around the notion of *Bildung* in Germany; the Congregational-based philosophy of education centered around the notions of democratic cooperation and interaction in the United States; and the Presbyterian-based technology of education centered around the notions of efficiency and evidence, equally based in the United States (Tröhler, 2020b). They all shared the belief that the world is indeed in its very fundament an educational project, and that education is always the empowerment to participate in the change of the world ("development"), but that in the end it is always about being a good person, whether as an inward man, or a virtuous or efficient citizen.

Educational Antagonism, the Cold War and the Final Victory of Test Psychology

When one says that the United States is in its basic culture WASP, then it refers to two different Protestant traditions of Anglo-Saxon Protestantism: the Congregational Protestantism developed in England and Presbyterianism developed in Scotland. Both shared the same roots and had similar theologies, but differed strongly with regard to the organizational principles of their respective churches. These different principles were also applied to the realm of the state, which in turn was quite directly reflected in their different educational convictions.

Both dominant Reformed churches, the Congregational (often together with the Baptists) and the Presbyterian (often together with the Methodists), originated from the Swiss Reformation and shared an understanding of organization that was independent from the political state. The Congregationalists in England had developed a deep skepticism towards centralized state power and the idea of a community-based church that was directly answerable to God, while the Presbyterians, because of Scotland's weakness in the face of complex successions and denomination, had built up their church organization virtually in place of the political state (Ryrie, 2006).

Congregationalism, as the name suggests, is based on the idea of the Christian congregational constitution, in which the autonomy of the individual church congregations has the highest priority, and the members of these congregations, as believers, are on an equal footing amongst each other and therefore have to manage their affairs together and cooperatively. Presbyterianism, on the other hand, derives its name from the Presbyterian form of church administration, which is hierarchically led by representative assemblies of elders. The Presbyterian church had replaced the previous Catholic episcopal hierarchy with a system of ecclesiastical authorities, which in its entirety was to constitute a national church, and with the decisions of the highest authority being binding to all parishes.

This juxtaposition was reflected in a direct way in the various concepts of education, which the eminent American educational historian, David Tyack, aptly termed in the one case as "administrative progressives," and in the other as pedagogical progressives (Tyack, 1974, pp. 126–129). Both movements were unsatisfied with how the traditional school had been dealing with the multitude of social challenges that were brought about with what can be labeled "modernity," but both followed different priorities. Whereas the pedagogical progressives of American pragmatism asked for a much closer cooperation between the learning environment of the family, the community, the Church, the playground and the school, and headed pedagogically for more cooperation in learning as problem-solving as a basis of a sound democracy, the administrative progressives attacked the traditional methods of decision-making and school politics by ridiculing "'the exceedingly democratic idea that all are equal' and urged that schooling be adapted to social stratification" (p. 126). Both educational priorities reflected the respective church organizations of the two different Protestant churches.

While the pedagogical progressives—in accordance with their own church organization—put the formal organization of the school on hold in favor of cooperative interaction between learners, the administrative progressives—in accordance with their church organization—aimed at efficient governance from above, whereby these "superiors" needed information (data) on the basis of which they could make their binding decisions. Accordingly, to Thorndike, schooling is about good teaching and good teaching meant simply to apply the right stimuli in order to achieve conformity with a particular moral dignity that was meant to dominate American culture: "The school must prepare for efficiency in the serious business of life as well as for the refined enjoyment of its leisure" (Thorndike, 1906, p. 5). Hence, teaching meant controlling and regulating human nature, "to produce and to prevent changes in human beings; to preserve and increase the desirable qualities of body, intellect and character and to get rid of the undesirable" (p. 7). Evidently, "to thus control human nature, the teacher needs to know it" (p. 7), and this was the task of (test) psychology, but efficiency and the appropriate behavior stimuli needed exact data, which was to be gained in the "scientific study of teaching," and this in turn indicated the need for "testing the results of teaching" (p. 257).

Given that public education in the United States is not national, but organized on a state and even local level, it is not surprising that these two educational movements coexisted for half a century with rather little reference to each other. This fragile peaceful coexistence was shaken, however, when the national government introduced the National Defense Education Act by Congress in 1958. The name of this law refers to the global and military motivation of the very first national school legislation in the United States and shows that Washington interfered with constituent state sovereignty precisely because America's political and economic elite feared that their Cold War arch-enemy, the Soviet Union, had developed frightening military advantages—which had become evident with the launch of Sputnik in 1957—which they attributed to the efficient school system of the USSR. The Cold War had become educationalized (Tröhler, 2013), and accordingly, national political pressure on the school increased, with the conviction that the "fight for education" had become "too important to be left solely to the educators," as the economist, Walter Heller, the then economic advisor to the President of the United States, said on the occasion of the very first OECD conference in Washington in 1961 (OECD, 1961, p. 35). Four years later, U.S. Secretary of Education, Francis Keppel, repeated this credo which was depicted on the front page of TIME magazine on 15 October 1965.

What followed in the United States was a massive accusation against teachers and their sympathy for pragmatism, which at that time was called "life adjustment education" and which had put real life skills like health, decency and citizenship at the center of the school. This was now, under cold governmental (ir)rationality, considered a serious problem. What followed was that Washington gave money to the country's generally underfunded schools, which increasingly turned to teaching mathematics, natural sciences and foreign languages; but the problem was that the schools, protected by central control, often used the money for quite different purposes. As a result, Washington began to examine the evidence of school effort through performance measurement, and, in 1964, an assessment agency, the National

Assessment of Educational Progress (NAEP), was established: Money from the federal government was to be given only to those schools that were able to account for their efforts in improved teaching of mathematics, natural sciences and foreign languages through improved performance. The founders of the Teachers College would of course have rejoiced, the country's general teaching staff, however, was appalled: school policy based on test-psychology evidence was now considered a central pillar in the defense of the Western world of individualism, freedom and democracy against the Cold War enemy.

This was essentially the national school policy of a country that believed that its (supposed) military inferiority was due to a bad school, but which was not allowed to pursue a direct school policy itself: What remained were incentives and control through performance measurement, basically a carrot-and-stick policy. How the United States then managed to make its own school policy a pattern to be imitated by the world through the OECD has been studied in broad outlines, at least enough to understand how, for example, PISA has been conceived, the test logic of which was based on the first NAEP studies of 1969. The success story of PISA now shows what global governance can mean. There is no need for missionaries (in the classical sense), and not even capitalism has managed to overcome nationalism, less and less so even today, not to mention that the United Nations or the UN Security Council become paralyzed by the veto of one of the victorious powers of the Second World War: the United States, Russia, France, England and China. It was the educationalization of the world that has become globalized, and it is prominently reflected in the triumph of PISA and other large-scale assessments providing data for policy makers. This shows the triumphal procession of Presbyterian control through the back door of education policy, so to speak.

The Educationalization of the World, Its Beneficiaries and Ambivalent Global Governance

Both expansions—or aggressions—of Europe, missionary work and colonization,[4] often working hand in hand with each other, have achieved rather mixed success. Although the Philippines and East Timor have remained Catholic countries, Papua New Guinea both Catholic and Protestant and South Korea partly Protestant (and Malaysia and Indonesia predominantly Islamic), in other countries, the popular Folk religions, Buddhism and Taoism, have maintained the upper hand or regained it; and the former colonies mainly have the effect that they still suffer under colonial rule, which usually terminated in the twenty years after the end of the Second World War. China is a prime example of the cooperation between economy and mission.

---

[4]It should by no means be claimed here that only the Western powers founded colonies; if we were talking about the complete colonial history of the world, we would also have to mention Japan (Taiwan, Korea and wider areas) or China, which, however, colonized foreign territories often less in the classical sense than incorporated them into their empire (for instance Tibet).

Its Protestant—more exactly: Presbyterian—mission, started in 1807, was led by the Presbyterian preacher Robert Morrison, who was employed by the East India Company (since 1711 in Guangzhou), a free-enterprise quasi-colony with governmental approval. Morrison translated the Bible into Chinese, but he also translated Chinese works into English and published an English-speaking Chinese grammar and an English-Chinese dictionary in order to facilitate the mission activity for later missionaries (Morrison, 1812, 1815a, 1815–1823). Those remained, however, with regard to confession and faith, relatively without consequence (Daily, 2013).

Neither the economy, nor religion, nor politics nor armies have succeeded, despite all attempts, in creating a harmonized global empire that is capable of bringing the different value systems of the world and their normative conceptions of a "right" social order in line. On the contrary, we are currently experiencing a renaissance of aggressive nationalism, reflected in the tension between (mostly a-religious) China and the (mostly Protestant) "West": economically with the United States and politically—in the case of Hong Kong—with the United Kingdom (and other European countries). These tensions may be real or stylized as electoral tactics, but they also direct attention away from the triumph of an idea that has been slowly and steadily spreading over the last 450 years, and the heart of this idea is that the present and future problems and challenges of life (or those "recognized" as such) can or actually should be solved through educational measures. While for the countries that have been described as developing countries, it is above all UNESCO that has been involved, for the other countries, it is foremost the transnational organization of the OECD that has developed into a forum in which PISA is used to determine what constitutes a "good" school. Its favored instrument in both detecting and improving the quality of a good school goes back to the Presbyterian activists around the Teachers College. This instrument was sanctioned by the American central government during the Cold War and has been increasingly disseminated globally through the OECD and PISA. Against this background, it is not surprising that the OECD's motto is "Better policies for better lives." But who has the power to define what a "better life" is? And who has the certainty of having the "better policies" for it?

A brief overview of the countries participating in PISA already gives a first indication of answers to these questions. In 2000, 34 countries participated in addition to most European countries: (former) Commonwealth countries, such as New Zealand, Australia, Hong Kong, Canada; the United States; Israel; and then Japan; Thailand; Brazil; Chile; Argentina; and Mexico as well as the Russian Federation. Three years later new countries joined in (and a few some dropped out), Tunisia, Macao-China, Turkey and Uruguay. Another three years later, in 2006, Azerbaijan joined, Indonesia, Qatar, Kyrgyzstan, Chinese Taipei, and Jordan, too; and in 2009, Costa Rica, Dubai, Georgia, India, the Kyrgyz Republic, Malaysia, Mauritius, Miranda (state of Venezuela), Panama, Peru, Shanghai (China), Singapore, Trinidad and Tobago, and the United Arab Emirates (except Dubai). In 2012, Vietnam followed;

in 2015, China (People's Republic of), who supplemented Shanghai with Beijing, Jiangsu and Guangdong,[5] and Lebanon; and in 2018, Morocco, Belarus and Brunei.

You can twist and turn it any way you like, but this is a unique victory story. PISA does not simply measure learning outcomes, but rather measures learning outcomes based on its own normative preferences, which affect learning content, learning methods and, above all, school policy. The program itself is an expression of the kind of school policy that the United States has been pursuing since 1960: evidence- and data-based. Not surprisingly, PISA has created its own consulting teams that advise countries to become better, i.e. to perform better in PISA on the occasion of the next test, or, in other words, to conform better to the normative preferences that PISA contains and expresses for itself. The incentive is clear: if you are behaving well, you will be ranked before your neighbors. Ironically, national vanity then becomes the motivating force in the global harmonization of a model[6] that has managed, especially in the OECD, to wash its religious-ideological origins beyond recognition.

Of course, the participating countries also play with these agencies of international assessments and use them for their own national purposes (Piattoeva et al., 2019), but still they do everything they can to do better. This can easily be seen in the example of Japan's shocked reaction to the declined PISA-results in 2004 (as compared to 2001), which eventually lead to a new education act and curricular reform in 2008, "to train children to be responsible for the new society, to live autonomously, prospering their future profession and life" (Tasaki, 2017, p. 151). The lens of the reform was, however, to a large degree that of the traditional values and norms to which global reform recipes had to be adapted in such a way that international success and confession of one's own tradition did not, as far as possible, exclude each other. That is, in fact, the principle that the Jesuits around 1700 had called "accommodation"; accommodation of the Catholic teachings to the Confucian rites, which was then forbidden for them to do by Pope Clemens XI in 1704 (and reaffirmed in 1715), thus leading Emperor Yongzheng to forbid Christianity in China in 1724 (Mungello et al., 1995). In contrast to 300 years ago, the global agitators of the West today have a much easier game: the thoroughly educationalized cultures of the world are now trying to create this "accommodation" themselves. A prime example is Shanghai, which "illustrates the symbiotic relationship between PISA … and the domestic education system that is characterized by both dependence and independence" (Tan, 2019, p. 391).

---

[5] The OECD calls the four participating regions of the Republic of China "participating economies" (OECD, 2016, p. 3).

[6] This was quite intentional, as can be seen from an early OECD seminar in 1964, where the instructor, Princeton economics professor, Frederick H. Harbison, explained to the ongoing strategists in national education policy that exactly because the different countries were "at different stages of modernization," comparative data were essential precisely by virtue of their comparability: "But from the standpoint of practical politics, the consideration that really influences policy-makers and even the people as well, is comparison with other countries. In this respect, nations resemble individuals—they want to keep up with the Joneses. And this is true of all countries, including the United States" (Harbison, 1966, p. 54).

In this view, China is again a prime example. In 2009 and 2012, it only had the PISA tests carried out in Shanghai, from whose school system the less gifted students had been removed. Shanghai subsequently scored very well, although data collected outside Shanghai, which were never published, revealed far lower results and great educational inequality, especially in rural areas (Schulte, 2019, p. 177). The Chinese did, however, not necessarily want to take part in PISA forever, but participated primarily in order to learn the technology of measuring school performance and to then develop a *Chinese version* of PISA. This Chinese-PISA only evaluates 10% of the actual test results and above all takes into account so-called "green indicators," for example, attitudes towards learning, moral behavior, mental and physical health, individual development, identification with the school, teaching methods, school management skills and the correlation between socio-economic background and student performance (p. 178). This reads almost like the catalog of competences of American life adjustment education—only less Congregational-reformed and thus less focused on a democratic republic with its virtuous citizens—which was put under pressure by the very movement from which PISA was to emerge. Yet, China does not want to look only at itself, but—for the first time in history?—it wants to become a model that can be copied and implemented all around the world (pp. 180–181).

Outlook

China's current global self-confidence is not primarily related to the excellent Shanghai PISA-data, which should not be taken at its face value, although other countries have also cheated on the respective composition of the cohort tested by PISA. This self-confidence is initially based on recent economic growth and military strength, which, however, has resulted in an increased demand for a significantly higher qualified workforce. Yet, the above-mentioned "green indicators" of China refer to national and cultural values that are more obvious and less hidden than the ones of PISA and are, therefore, precisely less suited for global dissemination. As much as "the West" was impressed by Shanghai's results (as it was once impressed by the Finnish)—the British sent their Minister of Education, Elizabeth Truss, to Shanghai and, in the wake of her visit, invited Shanghai teachers to the United Kingdom so that local teachers could learn from their teaching methods (Moss & Goldstein, 2014)—, "the West" is ideologically very well equipped to refuse to follow Asia in general and China in particular. They have better results? That's just a result of their almost inhuman treatment of children by the Asian *Tiger Mother* who drills her child to learn (Chua, 2011).

In fact, missionary work has almost always been a "Western" undertaking, especially if one generously includes Islam, which emerged in the Middle East. There were no Taoist or Buddhist missionaries in Europe in the same sense as for the Jesuits and various Protestant churches, and the Dalai Lama would still be in Tibet if he was allowed to practice his religion there. There were no Chinese trading companies in Europe that behaved like colonialists and certainly no colonies in Europe as was the case in the East Asian South Pacific; Albania has, as a matter of fact, largely depended on China since 1961, but it was no colony as there were no Albanian goods China was in need of or from which they could make money. This has had fundamental epistemological consequences. If Asian countries have better results than those in the West, it cannot be the result of better education (or of the stupidity of the testing apparatus), but a result of drilling, breeding, and inhuman ambition, and for that there are the wonderful national or racial prejudices that make it so obvious why the West should not follow "others" who do better on its own tests. This is cheeky!

So, the problem with PISA and comparable large-scale tests is not about testing at all. It is about deeply ingrained values and norms, which usually have religious roots and thus mostly implicit ideas of salvation and which have found their institutionalized form in the nation states; and all of them are convinced that they are "the right ones." That was probably already believed by the ancient Chinese before they were visited by the Jesuits; that is what the Jesuits believed and later the Protestants who did missionary work; that is what Wolff believed when he spoke about practical philosophy on the basis of Jesuit cultural mediation; and that is what Wolff's critics, who drove him out of Prussia, the Pietists, all believed—even up through the scientific community, not least including education. The founding president of Johns Hopkins University, Daniel Coit Gilman, said that "American universities should be more than theistic; they may and should be avowedly Christian—not in a narrow or sectarian sense—but in the broad, open and inspiring sense of the Gospels" (Gilman, cited in Hart, 1992, p. 107); the founding president of the University of Chicago, William Rainey Harper, said that "the history of civilization has been synchronous with the development of a pure and true conception of God, and of his relation to man" (Harper, 1904, p. 175); and Nicholas Murray Butler, the founding president of Teachers College, said that the United States was "the first moral power in the world" (Butler, 1914, p. 17). Beyond denominational differences among the Reformed Protestant churches, they would have all agreed with Harper, "in this work of educating humanity to understand God and itself, America is the training-school for teachers" (Harper, 1904, p. 184).

Of course, the easily identifiable religious terminology disappeared in the course of the twentieth century, but the language, understood as discourse (*langue*), remained. It is about being right, about mission, about power, and if these endeavors are not working, about war, politics or economy, and then the original Protestant field of indirect missionary work remains, namely education. As a cultural conviction, it can, above all, look to already old educational conceptions, transform the jealous nationalism of wanting to be right into the logics of numbers, and in this way set a global educational colonialization in motion that is only less obviously missionary than the old Jesuits. It remains to be seen whether the world will become a better place under its governance, as the OECD promises in its logo, and for whom.

In the meantime, international research, especially in the field of education, could emancipate itself from its obsession with PISA and its consequences—if the PISA makers received only one dollar per publication dealing with them and their consequences, they would probably all be millionaires—and understand PISA better as the expression of an ideology that has very old historical roots and has been moving along a long and complex path through time and space. It has made education socially acceptable, raised it to the status of an ambition of modern nation states and made the field of academic reflection and research in this field possible, that is, us. Perhaps, in this epistemological sense, it would be a good idea to reflect on ourselves, if only so that "the other" may not appear only as the "deviant" who is to be missionized, colonized and educated just because we are—even if we know nothing about it? Yet, yes, self-reflection is a profoundly Protestant credo, but at least one that calls for modesty and humility, which have not yet reached their full bloom in Western dominated science.

References

Bruno-Jofré, R., & Jover, G. (2012). The readings of John Dewey and the intersection of Catholicism. In R. Bruno-Jofré, & J. Schriewer (Eds.), *The global reception of John Dewey's thought. Multiple refractions through time and space* (pp. 23–42). Routledge.
Butler, N. M. (1914). *The United States of Europe. An interview with Nicholas Murray Butler by Edward Marshall. Reprinted from The New York Times of October 28, 1914*. Carnegie Endowment for International Peace.
Chua, A. (2011). *Battle Hymn of the tiger mother*. Penguin Press.
Daily, C. A. (2013). *Robert Morrison and the protestant plan for China*. Hong Kong University Press.
Du Halde, J.-B. (1735). *Description géographique, chronologique, politique et physique de l'empire de la Chine et de la Tartarie chinoise*. Chez P. G. Lemercier.
Education. (1954). In *TIME magazine*, 3 May 1954, pp. 63–64.
Eisenmann, L. (Ed.). (1998). *Historical dictionary of women's education in the United States*. Greenwood Press.
Elisseeff-Poisle, D. (1991). Chinese influence in France, sixteenth to eighteenth centuries. In T. H. C. Lee (Ed.), *China and Europe: Images and influences in sixteenth to eighteenth centuries* (pp. 151–164). Chinese University Press.
Francke, A. H. (1962). *August Herman Franckes Schrift über eine Reform des Erziehungs- und Bildungswesens als Ausgangspunkt einer geistlichen und sozialen Neuordnung: Der große Aufsatz [1704]* (O. Podczeck, Ed.). Akademie-Verlag. (Original work published 1704).
Glöde, G. (Ed.). (1973). *Reformatorenbriefe. Luther, Zwingli, Calvin*. Evangelische Verlagsanstalt.
Harbison, F. H. (1966). Strategies for human resources development (1). In OECD (Ed.), *Human resources development. Training course. Lectures and methodological essays on educational planning. Bergneustadt, 6–24 July 1964* (pp. 39–54). OECD Publishing.
Harper, W. R. (1904). America as a missionary field. In W. R. Harper (Ed.), *Religion and the higher life: Talks to students* (pp. 173–184). Oxford University Press.
Hart, D. G. (1992). Faith and learning in the age of the university: The academic ministry of Daniel Coit Gilman. In G. M. Marsden, & B. J. Longfield (Eds.), *The secularization of the academy* (pp. 107–145). Oxford University Press.
Horlacher, R. (2016). *The educated subject and the German concept of Bildung. A comparative cultural history*. Routledge.
Horlacher, R. (2021). German educational thought: Religion, rationalism, philanthropinism and Bildung. In M. Laverty, & D. Hansen (Eds.), *A history of western philosophy of education. A history of Western philosophy of education in the age of enlightenment (1550–1850)* (Vol. 3) (pp. 125-149). Bloomsbury.

Labaree, D. (2010). How Dewy lost. The victory of David Snedden and social efficiency in the reform of American education. In D. Tröhler, T. Schlag, & F. Osterwalder (Eds.), *Pragmatism and modernities* (pp. 163–188). Sense Publishers.
Liščák, V. (2015). François Noël and his Latin translations of Confucian classical books published in Prague in 1711. *Anthropologia Integra, 6*(2), 45–52.
McCaughey, R. A. (2003). *Stand, Columbia: A history of Columbia University in the city of New York, 1754–2004*. Columbia University Press.
Morrison, R. (1812). *Horae Sinicae: Translations from the popular literature of the Chinese*. Black and Parry.
Morrison, R. (1815). *Grammar of the Chinese language*. Mission Press.
Morrison, R. (1815–1823). *A Dictionary of the Chinese language, in three parts*. East India Company's Press.
Moss, G., & Goldstein, H. (2014). Epilogue. *Comparative Education, 50*(3), 374–377.
Mungello, D. E. (1991). Confucianism in the enlightenment: Antagonism and collaboration between the Jesuits and the Philosophes. In T. H. C. Lee (Ed.), *China and Europe: Images and influences in sixteenth to eighteenth centuries* (pp. 99–128). Chinese University Press.
Mungello, D. E., Spence, J. D., Zürcher, R., & Malatesta, E. J. (Eds.). (1994). *The Chinese rites controversy: Its history and meaning*. Steyler Verlagsbuchhandlung.
Nietzsche, F. (1883). *Also sprach Zarathustra. Ein Buch für Alle und Keinen*. Ernst Schmeitzner.
Noël, F. (Ed.). (1711). *Sinensis Imperii Libri Classici Sex* [The Six Classic Books of the Chinese Empire]. Charles-Ferdinand University Press.
Organisation for Economic Co-operation and Development (OECD). (1961). *Policy conference on economic growth and investment in Education. Washington 16th–20th October 1961*. OECD Publishing.
Organisation for Economic Co-operation and Development (OECD). (2016). *Education in China. A snapshot*. OECD Publishing.
Piattoeva, N., Tröhler, D., Cowen, R., Acosta, F., Valero, P., Zhao, W., Lingard, B., Grek, S., Silova, I., & Auld, E. D. (2019). Nations and numbers. The banal nationalism of education performance data. *Bildungsgeschichte. International Journal for the Historiography of Education, 9*(2), 244–279.
Popkewitz, T. S. (2005). *Inventing the modern self and John Dewey. Modernities and the traveling of pragmatism in education*. Palgrave Macmillan.
Qi, J. (2005). A history of the present: Chinese intellectuals, Confucianism and pragmatism. In T. S. Popkewitz (Ed.), *Inventing the modern self and John Dewey. Modernities and the traveling of pragmatism in education* (pp. 255–277). Palgrave Macmillan.
Ryrie, A. (2006). *The origins of the Scottish reformation*. Manchester University Press.
Schulte, B. (2012). The Chinese Dewey: Friend, fiend, and flagship. In R. Bruno-Jofré, & J. Schriewer (Eds.), *The global reception of John Dewey's thought. Multiple refractions through time and space* (pp. 83–115). Routledge.
Schulte, B. (2019). Curse or blessing? Chinese academic responses to China's PISA performance. In G. Steiner-Khamsi, & F. Waldow (Eds.), *Understanding PISA's attractiveness: Critical analyses in comparative policy studies* (pp. 177–197). Bloomsbury.
Takayama, K. (2018). Beyond comforting histories: The colonial/imperial entanglements of the international institute, Paul Monroe, and Isaac L. Kandel at Teachers College, Columbia University. *Comparative Education Review, 62*(4), 459–481.
Tan, C. (2019). PISA and education reform in Shanghai. *Critical Studies in Education, 60*(3), 391–406.
Tasaki, N. (2017). The impact of OECD-PISA results on Japanese educational policy. *European Journal of Education, 52*(1), 145–153.
Thorndike, E. L. (1906). *The principles of teaching based on psychology*. A. B. Seiler.
Tröhler, D. (2001). Christian Wolff und Johann Georg Sulzer – Eigenart und Problem rationaler Ethik und Pädagogik. In D. Jedan, & C. Lüth (Eds.), *Moral philosophy and education in the enlightenment* (pp. 118–142). Winkler.

Tröhler, D. (2006). The 'Kingdom of God on Earth' and early Chicago Pragmatism. *Educational Theory, 56*(1), 89–105.

Tröhler, D. (2011). *Languages of education. Protestant legacies, national identities, and global aspirations*. Routledge.

Tröhler, D. (2013). The OECD and cold war culture: thinking historically about PISA. In: H.-D. Meyer, & A. Benavot (Eds.), *PISA, power, and policy. The Emergence of global educational governance* (pp. 141–161). Symposium books.

Tröhler, D. (2016). Educationalization of social problems and the educationalization of the modern world. In M. A. Peters (Ed.), *Encyclopedia of educational philosophy and theory* [on-line]. https://doi.org/10.1007/978-981-287-532-7_8-1

Tröhler, D. (2017). Progressivism. In G. W. Noblit (Ed.), *Oxford research encyclopedias: Education* [on-line]. https://doi.org/10.1093/acrefore/9780190264093.013.111

Tröhler, D. (2018). Internationale Provokationen an nationale Denkstile in der Erziehungswissenschaft: Perspektiven Allgemeiner Pädagogik (Antrittsvorlesung Universität Wien). *International Journal for the Historiography of Education (IJHE), 8*(2), 173–189.

Tröhler, D. (2020a). Learning, progress, and the taming of change: The educational aspirations of the age of enlightenment. In D. Tröhler (Ed.), *A cultural history of education in the age of enlightenment* (pp. 1–23). Bloomsbury.

Tröhler, D. (2020b). The lasting legacy of the European Reformation of the 16th century: The dignity of Protestant souls or salvation through education. *Journal of Beliefs & Values. Studies in Religion & Education* (41). https://doi.org/10.1080/13617672.2020.1818934

Tyack, D. (1974). *The one best system: A history of American urban education*. Harvard University Press.

Whitmer, K. J. (2015). *The Halle orphanage as scientific community: Observation, eclecticism, and Pietism in the early enlightenment*. University of Chicago Press.

Wolff, C. (1985). *Oratio de Sinarum philosophia practica. Rede über die praktische Philosophie der Chinesen* (translated and edited by M. Albrecht). Felix Meiner Verlag. (Original work published 1726).

Daniel Tröhler is Professor of Foundations of Education at the University of Vienna since 2017 and Visiting Professor at the University of Oslo since 2018. His research interests lie in the international and transnational developments of the last 250 years with a focus around 1800s and the Cold War. In doing so, he relates the history of modern ideas to the history of institutions in the context of a broader cultural history by focusing on (educational) political and educational ideas and their materialization in school laws, curricula and textbooks, comparing different national and regional developments and investigating their possible mutual influences. He has published or edited over 50 books, 100 journal articles and some 150 book chapters in seven languages. For the book *Languages of Education: Protestant Legacies, National Identities, and Global Aspirations* (Routledge 2011) he was awarded the Outstanding Book of the Year Award of the American Education Research Association AERA in 2012. He is currently working on the development of an ERC project proposal titled Nation state, curriculum and the fabrication of national-minded citizens.

From Knowledge and *Bildung* Toward Competences and Skills in Finnish Curriculum Policy?: Some Theoretical, Historical, and Current Observations Related to Finland

Tero Autio

Introduction

In this chapter I will make an effort to characterize the Finnish case of education reforms and the construction of the Finnish welfare society by *Bildung*. Finland was thrust into the limelight of the world of education in 2001 when the results of the first international PISA test was issued. The coincidental timing of the result according to which the Finnish comprehensive school *Peruskoulu* was the best in the world assessed by how the students are able to apply in 'every day contexts' their learning in mathematics, science and literacy among the 15 years old students could have hardly been more dramatic (see Autio, 2017). *Peruskoulu*, the Finnish Comprehensive School that covers the grades from 1 to 9, from age seven to sixteen, was criticized since its first blueprints in the 1960's by the political right and subject teachers and from the 1980's onwards the critique was intensified by the representatives of the economy and industry, the Education Committee of the Confederation of Finnish Industries and Employers (CIE). For this "noisy minority", the Finnish *Peruskoulu*—that was considered among middle-class parents and the media in a typical modest Finnish style "good enough, but far from excellent"—was seen as a catastrophe. The timing of the irony of history couldn't have been more perfect:

> Just two weeks before the publication of the first report, PISA 2000, on 24 November 2001, the influential and powerful Confederation of Finnish Industries and Employers (CIE), which has been fiercely criticizing *Peruskoulu* since the early 1980's, organized an autumn seminar at one of Helsinki's main conference venues, Finlandia Hall. Key players in business and industry once again criticized Finnish comprehensive schools for their mediocrity and ineffectiveness, with reference to international evaluations of their quality and efficiency. This time they argued in particular for more competition and better conditions for private schools. Following the first PISA report the CIE became completely mute about *Peruskoulu* and all traces from the seminar quickly vanished (Simola, 2015, xiv).

T. Autio (✉)
Tampere University, Tampere, Finland

International PISA was the first national systematic test in the history in Finland. Finnish basic education system lacks altogether externally mandated tests and exams as a 'Finnish exceptionalism' in basic education on the global scene: no inspecting, no testing and no ranking. All tests are teacher-driven. There was a silent and consensual antipathy among teachers, their unions and education administration to issues, which particularly in English speaking countries, are "implemented" as "quality assurance and evaluation" (QAE) measures. Even the language of "implementation" and "quality assurance" are lacking in Finnish educational discourse despite some random efforts to introduce it. Finnish-Australian education policy analyst Pasi Sahlberg wrote ten years later, in 2011, *Finnish Lessons: What Can the World Learn from Educational Change in Finland* to unravel the "mysterious success" that perhaps amazed Finns themselves the most who on the basis of their own school experiences never regarded Finnish education as something special. On the contrary in documented memoirs of many, the incidences at school are recalled as the worst experiences in their lives! Despite the preference set for social mobility at the very outset, education is intrinsically not related to competition, ranking and assessment—echoing the old Finnish folk witticism: 'real winners do not compete'. The book became an immediate hit in Canada, United States and beyond, and first print was sold out in three days. This far the two editions, third one due January 2021, have been translated to almost 30 languages, including Finnish, Farsi, Azeri, Vietnamese and Thai. Unfortunately, the book does not specify the decisive theoretical and political contrasts between the Anglo-American Curriculum and the German *Bildung/Didaktik* tradition and their distinctive reception in Finland.

The book's enthusiastic reception was an index not only of the surprising international achievement of the small Nordic country per se but particularly of the distinctively contrastive yet unintended ways against the Anglophone US and UK grain on how education and curriculum was understood and organized in Finland.

> Ironically, Finland is the one country in the world that most distinctly deviates from the OECD's standard reform package. *Finland succeeds not by following the policies recommended by the OECD, but by ignoring them* (Meyer & Benavot, 2013, p. 15).

The perception of "by ignoring them" is arguably a precise but unrecognizably expressed perception of the Finnish version of the originally German *Bildung*-theoretical (in Finnish: *sivistysteoria*) tradition that renders decisive contrasts to the American/OECD instrumentalist concept of education as well as the latter's tacit but seamlessly recognizable connection to the American psychologized Curriculum. *Bildung - Didaktik* as 'the operative core' of *Bildung*—affected the Finnish curriculum thinking, design and teacher education from the nineteenth century till the end of World War Two. Apart from the Finnish difference to the American psychologized concept of education and curriculum, there is also a decisive distinction between German and Finnish concept of *Bildung*. Finns took in the nineteenth century so to say literally the double gesture inherent in the German concept of *allgemeine Bildung* that is interpretable both in political terms of the "*allgemeine*", "meant for all", and in curriculum terms of a "comprehensive coverage". The implication of the "meant for all" as an embodiment of the principle of social inclusiveness regardless of one's ethnicity, cultural, social or socioeconomic background rendered the cornerstone of *Peruskoulu* to be materialized as a free (of charge) access to schooling from the first grade on to the PhD level. The structural equality in this revolutionary education reform was complemented by emphasizing the comprehensive content coverage of the curriculum as an indispensable, subjective precondition for "*the Educated Subject*" (Horlacher, 2016) in strict contrast to the universalized, impersonal American notion of "*the Learner*".

While defying the sense of simplistic learning theories in creating the sustainable education system, this suggestion of the complexity of the Finnish educational DNA with key drivers of social equality and a structural, universal opportunity for actualizing one's potential may also make a *democratic difference* with the German original ideals of *Bildung*. Reforging the German *Bildung* in the Finnish context, the dynamics between social reconstruction and subjective transformation underscore the historically shaped, complicated yet consistent democratic flavour in Finnish education. These democratic features might also explain the utmost significance of trust as a key characteristic of society, one decisive index of which is trust in teachers and their action with students without fears of excessive external interference.

The Finnish historical emphasis on democracy and inclusive equality as a means for nation building has remained unarticulated but subtly present like a DNA of education in Finland. The DNA of Finnish *Bildung* is largely left unrecognized in the international reception of the Finnish case—also among Finnish education scientists drawing on empiricism in sociology and psychology alike, university teacher educators and education policy analysts. The obvious reason for the omission is the insufficient awareness of the European and American alternatives for 'curriculum theory' among Finnish education scholarship after the reactionary, unreflective adoption of US instrumentalist learning theories and educational psychology. Former educational and ideological connections to Germany decisively weakened after the War due to emerging local ideological complexities of world politics between Finland, Germany, the Soviet Union, and the US. Next, I will do a short excursion to the turbulent evolution of Finland as a Nordic welfare society.

A Historical Glimpse into the Evolution of Finnish Welfare Society as a Springboard for Finnish Education Reforms

On many accounts, all Nordic countries, Denmark, Finland, Iceland, Norway and Sweden, are lumped together and often for good reasons, yet there are distinctive dissimilarities between them. Currently, all those countries are advanced and full democracies despite their differing models of governance. Except Finland and Iceland, the rest three are monarchic democracies ceremonially run by the King (Norway and Sweden) or Queen (Denmark) but the political power is in the hands of the democratically voted Parliament and the Government representing the power relations of parties in the Parliament. Finland deviates from other Nordic countries in ethnic and particularly linguistic terms; Finnish language is totally different in terms of grammar and vocabulary to Danish, Icelandic, Norwegian and Swedish, yet Swedish as the legacy of history is the second official language in Finland and the recognized minority languages are Lappish Sámi languages, and Finnish and Finnish-Swedish sign languages for deaf people. The northern third of Finland lies within the Arctic Circle. For long as an area of Swedish–Russian rivalry, Finland was ceded to Russia in 1809, becoming an independent republic after the Russian Revolution in 1917. Wars with the Soviet Union were fought in 1939–40 and 1941–44. Finland joined the European Union in 1995.

Finland largely remained an agrarian country until the 1950s. After World War II, the country rapidly industrialised and developed an advanced economy, while building an extensive welfare state based on the Nordic Model, resulting in widespread prosperity and a high per capita income. Finland joined the United Nations in 1955 and adopted an official policy of neutrality and it joined the OECD in 1969.

The development of the country since the dearly sought-after independence in 1917 has been swift. Life had required a constant readiness in front of contingencies and dangers of the Nordic nature as well as the perpetual political tensions between the medieval Sweden-Finland and Russia, between Sweden, the Czarist Russia, and the Czarist Grand Duchy of Finland from 1809 till 1917 when Finland gained a sovereign independence. The 1918 bloody Civil War and the long-lasting World War Two 1939–1944 with heavy sacrifices and, despite the subsequent formal reconciliations, political uncertainties with the Eastern neighbour of Russia is lurking beneath the surface; all that accumulation of internal and external experiences and threats has irreversibly tainted the Finnish collective consciousness and rendered the complex dynamics for the construction of the Finnish society.

> History has left its mark on Finnish society, which – controversial as it may be – could be described as archaic, authoritarian and obedient. However, another side of this coin is the very quick and fundamental change to a post-industrial and late-modern culture that is apparent in society, science and technology in particular. The late process of industrialisation and the simultaneous growth of the service sector brought exceptionally rapid structural change. The transition from an agricultural to an industrial society, and further to a post-industrial society, took place within such a short period of time that *one could almost say the three societies currently coexist in a very special way in the country. The Finnish welfare state could be seen as a product of this historical turbulence: on the one hand industrial and individualist, and on another agrarian and collectivist* (Simola et al., 2017).

The Finnish historian Eino Jutikkala, in his studies on the development of democracy in Finland, pays attention to the unique status of the Finnish peasant in Europe. *For him, private ownership as a characteristic of Finnish society shaped the landowning peasant as the most important actor as an expression of the development of Finnish society*. Private ownership was for him not only a more traditional and popular form of ownership compared to co-ownership associated with socialist society, but also the key to outlining the birth and founding of Finnish society. In Jutikkala's conception of history, feudal society was an arbitrary phenomenon of the *ancien régime* that paralyzed development, as well as a threat to a relatively independent

Finnish peasant society. Jutikkala understood feudal society as a whole, where an individual did not receive the necessary reward in his life despite his possible efforts. The separation of Nordic, and especially Finnish society, from Eastern feudalism became more important during the twentieth century. The lack of feudalism distinguished the histories of Finland and the other Nordic countries in this respect positively from the history of the rest of the Western world. Indeed, from the Middle Ages to the eighteenth century, feudalism was an umbrella concept that structured society globally, with the exception of the Nordic countries. This view is based on the historical dimension of the free peasant, which is essential in Jutikkala's conception of history and society, *combining the dimensions of the independent peasant, economic individualism, constitutional society and European cultural history, particularly that of Bildung* (Norring, 2016).

Also Bo Stråth and Øystein Sørensen (in Kettunen, 2019, 5–6) argue that the Nordic Enlightenment "ironically and paradoxically enough had the peasant as its foremost symbol". The Nordic peasant was a figure of non-utopian pragmatic rationality, a figure that stamped its particular label on the Nordic Enlightenment and Nordic Romanticism as well as on Nordic democracy and the Nordic welfare state. The oldest reference to Nordic democracy can be found in the idealised figure of the free Nordic peasant (*"the Lutheran peasant Enlightenment"*) and the heritage of local, rural self-government: a peasant from time immemorial in Sweden-Finland had had full ownership of his land.

The Finnish peasant land-and-forest owner did not become an English-style landowner who leases his land onwards, but an employer engaged in productive activities for the economic well-being of the nation. The relative economic independence of the peasant contributed through the marriage institution positively to the rise of gender equality as well. Marriage was not dependent merely on 'pure love' but, as an economic and productive unit, it was rendering a basic dynamics for a functional, democratic society. Significant in terms of education was that Lutheranism combined education with the economic and erotic structure of an evolving society with a pastorally tested literacy of religious texts. Finnish women enfranchised in 1906. In New Zealand women got the rights to vote in 1893, but in Finland the female parliament members has the right to "run the office", to act as a Minister, from the very beginning. Today, somehow consistently, Finland has the Government consisting of Social Democratic Party as Prime Minister Party, Ms Sanna Marin as PM, Center Party, Green Party, Swedish People's Party of Finland, and Left Alliance. All the current Government parties are led by women.

According to Kettunen (2019, 4–5),

> The Reformation of the sixteenth and seventeenth centuries had set in motion the making of the centralised state, inseparably intertwined with the Lutheran Church and its message of conformity, while Lutheran Christianity at the same time stressed an immediate individual relationship to God. All this resulted, …, in a social democratic welfare state (…). *The strong state came to be oriented to securing individual autonomy and individual resources. Social solidarity was realised through high taxes, public systems of social security and vast public services for health, care and education that helped to liberate people from personal relations of subordination, especially those in the family*; as part of the efforts to achieve full employment, women became doubly dependent on the welfare state, both on public-sector

jobs and the services that facilitated combining motherhood and employment outside the home.

All world religions are concerned about alleviating human suffering. In Finnish context, secularizing Lutheranism, religion 'reasoned' rather than of revelation, was instrumental to translating the inarticulate suffering to

> social policy reforms that shaped the Nordic welfare state … aimed at breaking away from the paternalist structures of personal subordination and control that had been characteristic of rural households and communities and their Lutheran justification, including the humiliating practices of poor relief (Kettunen, 2019, 7).

While making efforts of turning 'vicious', suffering-inducing circles to 'virtuous' ones, society became conceived of as an actor implementing its own normative standards, as a framework of solidarities and conflicts, and as a target of criticism, knowledge and politics. The interplay between these different "societies" came to be important in the making of the welfare state. *The virtuous circle included something more than just organised economic interests promoting each other. It was also a virtuous circle between equality, efficiency and solidarity,* which, in a sense, can be seen as being based on three different ideological strains of the Nordic modernisation processes: (1) *the idealised heritage of the free, independent peasant,* (2) *the spirit of capitalism* and (3) *the utopia of socialism.* The virtuous circle was supposed to be achieved through compromises between conflicting organised interests and with the support of social planning within national society (Kettunen, 2019, 10).

Characteristically to Finland, the paradoxical blend of contrastive ideologies and histories provided society with a comprehensive mixture of consensual and antagonistic resources for the contingent and shifting dynamics as the normative standards of society. "The normative standards of society were not only moral rules, but also rules for the most rational functioning and rationalisation of society by turning vicious circles to virtuous ones in tackling the real and imaginable uncertainties. They were also rules for how the productive capacities of individuals could be released as well as rules concerning the contents of those capacities, such as self-disciplined citizenship. *In the ideational framework of a modernising nation-state society, the perspectives of economic rationalisation and social integration intersected*" (ibid., my emphasis).

Virtuous circles contained the code for society's future change and reform and, thus, the normative standards for assessing the present. This implied an idea of *immanent critique*: the normative standards of a society served as the criteria by which society could be criticised. Conformity that Lutheran tradition advocated by no means implied an absence of class conflicts and class consciousness. Rather, the construction of the nation as an "imagined community" offered a normative code against which socially subordinated groups could contrast their individual and local experiences of suppression and injustice, and generalise from these experiences to form a political class consciousness. The idea of a society being able to anticipate, criticise and revise itself was then, already in the 1930s, promoted by the class compromises between workers, farmers and the bourgeoisie, and by the agenda-setting power of reformist socialism (Kettunen, 2019, 11–12).

Bildung *and the Nation Building—"Democracy Without* Bildung *Is an Empty Shell"*

It may be said with good reasons that the idea of Finnish education was employing the turbulence of history and the immanent critique of society in which the turbulence provides a driving force to turn vicious circles to virtuous one as a dynamic platform for education reforms.

The Hegelian Johan Vilhelm Snellman (1806–1881), the national Finnish philosopher, in his influential lectures in education in 1861 (http://snellman.kootutteokset.fi), "argued that the country had to be built up *from the inside* with the means of *Bildung*". "*From the inside*" has a double reference that would combine subjective transformation with social and economic reforms in the historical continuity of a nation. For Snellman, *Bildung* was united by the ideals of classical humanism, a human being aspiring toward autonomy and independence through cognitive development, aesthetic refinement and moral edification in the holistic process of becoming of "*the Educated Subject*" (Horlacher, 2016) as a vital subjective counterpart in the social and economic reconstruction of society.

In Snellman's thought, *education was not a particularly nationalist idea that would have involved the idea of the superiority of one nation over another*. Rather, it was a belief in progress that is common in Enlightenment thinking, an effort to shape a better world. Snellman laid the foundation for Finnish-language culture and folk education—without forgetting the preconditions of Finnish-language high culture. He developed Hegel's obscure philosophy into Finnish conditions in a creative and aptly critical way. Snellman's theoretical influence is still recognizable in the spirit of Finnish basic education, *Peruskoulu,* which cherishes democracy, autonomy and freedom of teachers and students alike. Unlike Hegel, in his main work *Läran om Staten* ('the Idea of State') (1842), Snellman shifted the emphasis from a strict state control to a 'freer' civil society. He also emphasized the development of the nation's own public consciousness, its own cultural heritage, and its own individual thinking and moral consideration against ahistorical and abstact formal methods of education and teaching. Unlike the politically cautious Hegel, Snellman wanted to act more strongly as a social reformer, and according to him, education had to play a key role in building a free and democratic Finnish civil society (http://snellman.kootutteokset.fi).

This comprehensive complex, in essence, is a crucial part of a historical explanation of why Finns esteems education so highly—the very birth of the nation is interwoven with the concept of *Bildung* and the rise of the own Finnish language: paradoxically, the most eager advocates of Finnishness, as Snellman himself, speak Swedish as mother tongue.

> This journey of *Bildung* and schooling is also a story of the stepwise development of the Finnish language into the main language in Finland, in addition to Swedish, which today are the national languages of the bilingual country. Teacher education and the educational sciences in Finland have been much more geared towards the German tradition especially, compared to Norway and Sweden, who were more oriented towards the USA, especially after 1945 (Uljens & Nyman, 2013, 36).

Yet there are important reservations to be taken into account while talking about *Bildung* in the Finnish context. The adoption of *Bildung* in Finland as the guiding beacon for education had at academic levels quite intense relations to Germany and Switzerland; however, those intellectual ideals were suffused in Finland in a democratic sense with down-to-earth and material necessities in mind to tackle poverty and neediness of the quite primitive, agrarian society. Due to the still immature economic development, the aversion of the twentieth century affluent advocates of German *Bildung* to materialism, capitalism, and democracy, exemplified by the Nobel Literature laureates Thomas Mann and Rudolph Eucken, never met full resonance in Finland.

> Germany was already the leading economic power in Europe at the time of the First World War. Nevertheless, only the states to the West were reproached with materialism. This discrepancy between German economic prosperity and German ideology, or between matter and *Geist*, was not, however, due to a lack of knowledge about Germany's national economic potency. Instead, the contradiction was consciously nullified by a further dualism, inward purity and outward corruption ... Eucken acknowledges that Germany – like France, England, or America – had experienced tremendous economic growth in the nineteenth century. The crucial difference according to Eucken, however, is that this development did not corrupt the Germans' true character: "Have we then fallen away from our own selves when we turned to the visible world, when we developed our forces on land and water, when we took the lead in industry and technology? Have we thus denied our true, inner nature?" Eucken asks, only to respond, "No and once again no!" (Tröhler, 2003, 764).

However, the early German reservation about materialism and capitalism for the 'purity of the soul' is feebly traceable in Finnish mentality as well, particularly as a longstanding effect of Lutheranism that worked in tandem with *Bildung* to creating a Finnish kind of modest people. The Finnish *Bildung* and its connection to material well-being and autonomy were oriented towards the fight against poverty and the simultaneous independence of mind and spirit historically embodied in the politically free and economically independent landowner, the Lutheran Finnish peasant. Human or spiritual 'growth' and striving for reasonable material well-being—without sacrificing the purity of the soul for crude materialism and capitalism in accordance to the German model—was intertwined as a core in the Finnish variant of *Bildung*—'*Bildung* and the national railways belong together!' was one of the argument Snellman raised for the infrastructural needs of the democratizing Finnish society. The virtuous circle Snellman already envisioned in his comprehensive *Bildung* concept came to engage social equalization, economic growth and widening democracy.

The complementary comprehensiveness of the Finnish *Bildung* concept between the balance of the Material and *Geist* made it at the very outset at odds with the vulgarized capitalist description of the 'virtuous circle' between growing consumption and growing production—arguably a tacit background premise in the false proven trickle down economy to combat inequality and poverty in the OECD education policy recommendations. The Nordic and Finnish way of creating an effective virtuous circle takes place more directly where economic interests are not severed from social and educational issues in the wishful, ineffective and the social fabric violating trickle down economy thinking. *In the logic of the virtuous circle of welfare thinking, the promotion of social equality was held to be the means of releasing human productive capacities and thus the means of promoting economic effectiveness, which, in turn, was seen as a fundamental precondition for achieving social equality.* Education is a key in this virtuous circle, conceived of as a complex interplay between subjective transformation and social reconstruction in the spirit of *Bildung* as open-ended processes that defy the simplistic efforts of standardization and external control of massive international assessment systems as an index of 'quality education'.

Trust, Autonomy and Democracy as Preconditions for Sustainable Teaching and Curriculum

Social equality, trust and autonomy as vital characteristics of a democratic society and their embodiment in the practice of teaching and curriculum arguably make the Finnish education system tick in genuine educational terms. The autonomy and trust shown by society and experienced by teachers themselves are key issues for the democratic, sustainable functioning and efficiency of the education system—and as an index of the attractiveness of the teaching profession. Finland's immediate neighbours, Sweden and Estonia, as former *Bildung* states, have both been adopting a neoliberal education policy according to the US and OECD model: Sweden after the decades-long Nordic social democratic welfare state, Estonia as a fascinating Western novelty after the Communist regime. As a matter of fact, the Estonian leap to the neoliberal camp is not so long: the German social theorist Ulrich Beck (1999, 22) refers to the shared affiliation between the respective totalitarian ideologies: "… *ironically the neoliberal and original Marxist positions share the same basic assumptions*".

According to the 2013 TALIS report, after the Swedish version of American corporate/charter schools *(fri skolor)* was introduced in Sweden since the 1990's, one consequence of which is that five (5%) per cent of teachers perceive their profession to be valued in society. Somehow consistently, the lack of competent teachers in a relatively small country is assessed to grow to 45 000 in fifteen years (https://www.thelocal.se/20191210/swedish-education-agency-warns-of-major-teacher-shortage). The problem is exacerbated by the inequality between schools in privileged and disadvantaged areas that is one result of the increasing privatization/inequality of basic schooling in Sweden à la the neoliberal US/OECD model. In Estonia, the corresponding valuation indicator is 14 per cent. Finland's exceptionalism in the democratic *Bildung* spirit, as bucking the OECD trend and stubbornly holding on public schooling, comprehensive, broad-based curricula defying the PISA shrinkage of the curriculum to the "*core curriculum*", the lack of external testing and the professional autonomy of teachers, is evidenced - in spite of neoliberal bite—by the 59 per cent public support in the same TALIS report (Autio, 2017, 55).

Autonomy and trust has been a prevailing democratic principle throughout the whole system of Finnish basic education. Arguably, devoid of professional autonomy is related to the issue of the democracy of society at large. Pinar's alarming account of the accountability policies of American basic education as a form of neo-fascism is signalling the serious devoid of democracy. In this context, Pinar (2011a, xiv) suggests "it is time to again to selectively incorporate German concepts in North American practices of education":

> Despite its displacement in some countries by traditional US curriculum theory, in recent years, *Bildung* has enjoyed something of a revival, thanks in part *due its wedding with democratization* (...). *Without Bildung*, Karsten Schnack asserts, *democracy is an "empty shell, a procedure or form of government"* (italics added). Commitment to inner development and social democracy are juxtaposed in my conception of curriculum as lived experience: *currere*. (Pinar, 2011a, 4–5, my italics).

In another context, Pinar unintentionally but succinctly captured this image and mood of curriculum, teaching, and learning preferred in the Finnish *Bildung* conception since the introduction of the reformed basic schooling (*Peruskoulu*):

> ... school curriculum guidelines must never be more than guidelines. Subjectively situated, historically attuned teachers must be free to follow wherever their imaginations and instincts lead them, acutely aware of the disciplinary knowledge which structures their ongoing inquiry and testimony. ... The teacher is in this sense an artist and complicated conversation is the teacher's medium ... It might be helpful to the teacher to reflect on what her or his intentions are, but "objectives" are hardly primary concerns. What matters is how complicated the conversation becomes. ... what students make of such knowledge, a fate hardly removed from the province of the teacher but never definitively dependent on the teacher. Even the most creative and provocative lessons can fall flat, as anyone knows. Attempting to force students' engagement (let alone learning) becomes autocratic if not mediated by the subjective knowledge teachers have of the individuals in their classroom. Moreover, what students make of their study may not be known, and then only by the students themselves, for years (Pinar, 2011b).

The moral and aesthetic dimensions of curriculum—together as a comprehensive 'big picture' and ultimate motivation of teaching activity is traditionally accented in *Bildung* theories already present in J. F. Herbart's argument of *'the aesthetic representation of the world as the main business of education'* (Herbart, 1804/1986). Art and aesthetics have their own epistemic and ontological regimes that do not definitely acknowledge the notion of progress and control as is the case with scientific positivist knowledge as 'the main business' of the mainstream of the American/Western education, *'to see in order to predict and control'*. Interestingly, the same tension that prevails between *Bildung* and the US/OECD education has its parallel in the Chinese current tensions between the traditional Confucian culture and *suyang*, *'going global'* when China makes efforts to "hopefully and proactively keep Chinese students and talents globally competitive" (Zhao, 2019, 36). In both respective cases, unique and idiosyncratic as they are, moral and aesthetic 'regimes' are indispensable in the field of education as a 'non-scientific sphere of science' that makes education educative and provide for education an 'open source' for political, moral and aesthetic critique, corrective and transformation.

Art and aesthetics has a tradition of recognition in Finland particularly among professors from J. W. Snellman to the twentieth century's philosophically oriented professors Juho August Hollo, Erik Ahlman, J. E. Salomaa and Reijo Wilenius who advocated in their teaching of student teachers the invaluable contribution the imagination and creativity can have as a complementary or corrective to the 'scientific' elements of teachers' work. Viewing of the teacher as an artist as well underscores the professional autonomy of the profession in Finland. When I studied to become a teacher, our lecturers humorously congratulated us telling that in the profession we can combine a steady, index-bound petty bourgeois salary with a freedom of an artist. As a matter of fact, the features of "pedagogical artistry" (Henderson, 2015), freedom and autonomy between the interplay of (academic) knowledge and subjective preferences can render teaching an interesting, intellectually complex and demanding, aesthetic, ethical and practical activity that appeal to many of the most 'enlightened' and talented among young generations and make the profession in Finland a 'competitive' match with more instrumental professions of lawyer and medical doctor. The *Bildung*-theories' stress on freedom and self-determination intellectually legitimate the teacher's professional opportunities for subjective yet knowledgeable moral judgments and aesthetic options. These kinds of parameters of teaching are instrumental to shaping of the conditions and contexts by the mutual recognition of the value of (test-) free, democratic communication between teachers and students, ideally benefitting all the participants. These ideals of pedagogical practice only as ideals make them real latest in the teachers' resistance of external interference in teaching often stamped by undemocratic or bureaucratic interests, for example, focusing on teaching merely in terms of raising the test scores. These kinds of views in teaching and curriculum may partly explain the "Finnish hostility and antipathy toward rankings", "publish or perish" attitudes and other artificial competitive means to understand life and education in terms of the politicized and fabricated Darwinism. In the real test of Darwinism, on collective scale, living in the initially poor and primitive, now affluent welfare North wouldn't have been possible without non-competitive cooperation, creating sustainable conditions for personal and social trust, knowledge acquisition and education, individual and group creativity, turning personal and collective vicious circles to virtuous ones, often in harsh circumstances where there can be very few if any standardized solutions.

The positioning of the teacher arguably signals the overall educational characteristics and sustainability of the system. Juxtaposing the Finnish experience, "successful basic schooling must depend on those who implement every school reform, in other words the teachers" (Simola et al., 2017, 129) with the respective US practice, "teachers are always the invisible agents of the system, seen as "animated" and directed *by* the system, and not as sources of animation *for* the system" (Westbury, 2000, 21) discloses the most dramatic difference in viewpoint between Finnish and American/OECD ideas of education and curriculum—and of social trust and democracy! A related further significant point is the contrast between theories of science undergirding the respective notions of the curriculum: a positivist conception of science and curriculum in the US reception versus a hermeneutic notion of science and curriculum in the *Bildung* tradition. The charting below employing of Ian Westbury's account between *Didaktik* and Curriculum (1998, 2000), adapted here to the Finnish context, summarizes these contrastive distinctions: they represent "two very different intellectual systems developed out of very different starting points, and seek to do very different kinds of intellectual and practical work" (Westbury, 1998, 48).

The Ideal Image of the Teacher and Curriculum in the OECD/Anglo-American Tradition

- Teacher's role as the intellectually passive "agent of the system" (Westbury, 2000, 21)
- Teacher-proof curricula;"existing teachers are a (if not **the**) major brake on the innovation, change and reform that the schools always seem to require" (Westbury, 2000, 21)
- Curriculum-as-manual; a very limited space for professional autonomy, freedom and judgment
- Teaching essentially means teaching to the test.

The Ideal Image of the Teacher and Curriculum in the Finnish *Bildung* Tradition

- Curriculum is an organizational and ***intellectual*** centerpiece of education.
- "An autonomous professional teacher ... has complete freedom within the framework of the curriculum to develop her or his own approaches to teaching" (Westbury, 2000, 17).
- This relationship btw the curriculum and the teacher; teacher as **the** curriculum theorist and practitioner.
- High trust in well-educated teachers.
- Tests are not externally mandated but teacher-driven securing a relaxed and task-oriented atmosphere in classrooms instead of competitive, stressful and test-driven classroom.

Yet, instructively, the trust so manifestly present in current teacher autonomy in Finland, has historically been far from self-evident: Finnish professor Hannu Simola's doctoral dissertation traced

> all 'state educational discourse' since the establishment of primary schooling in Finland from 1863 to 1995. *With two minor exceptions, he found no trace of trust or appreciation of the work of classroom teachers between the 1960s and the 1990s.* (Simola et al., 2017, 90).

The blueprint for *Peruskoulu* was far-sightedly linked to *the creation of social trust* as a glue in the rising post-industrial, individualizing democracy after the authoritarian-agrarian, industrial and monocultural past. The *Peruskoulu* ideology should be inclusive to many kinds of people, aiming to provide equal access to opportunities and resources for people who might otherwise be excluded or marginalized on the basis of their socio-economic, ethnic or cultural background, or having mental or physical disabilities or belonging to other marginalized groups. Social trust is hard to achieve and easy to lose. In the Finnish case, the creation of social trust and the sustaining political will has been a long and complex historical process that is permanently vulnerable and unfinished—in the constant process of becoming, construction and deconstruction like the concept and phenomenon of *Bildung* itself as an open-ended interplay between subjective transformation and social reconstruction.

Social trust as an indispensable condition for the autonomy and democracy throughout the whole chain of the Finnish education system, from teachers to municipalities and state governance of education, is consistently supported by promoting local self-government and the modernization of municipal services.

> Since 2001, the municipalities are no longer merely education providers executing top-down, national-level decisions; they are real political actors with their own agenda. This gives them a vast amount of *Spielraum* in this peculiar twofold system in which the nation-state and the municipalities are the main actors driving education policy (Simola et al., 2017, 64).
>
> …
>
> *It could be concluded that, thus far, Finnish antipathy towards ranking, combined with a bureaucratic tradition and a developmental approach to QAE strengthened by radical municipal autonomy, have represented embedded policies that have been rather effective in resisting transnational policies of testing and ranking.* It is significant, however, that they are curious combinations of conscious, unintended and contingent factors. *Therefore, it also seems evident that the articulated unity is rather fragile given the exogenous trends and paradigm convergence in global reforms of education politics.* (ibid., 66-67).

One of the "exogenous trends" in global education reforms is the PISA for Schools comparisons of local performance that is actively promoted by the OECD. Its aim is to create commensurate spaces of comparison and governance, enabling the OECD to reach into school-level spaces and directly influence local educational practices. Its actively promoted comparisons of local performance occur predominantly through the competence- and skills-based framings of education, an emphasis that largely marginalizes other possible renderings of school effectiveness (Lewis et al., 2015). Despite the OECD's insistence that education policy based on the above pictured extension of the US/OECD positivist image of teaching and curriculum has the greatest capacity to influence variations in student performance, Finland's case is a strong counterargument. A successful schooling system is significantly mediated by local historical and cultural factors *in addition to policy settings* instead of the obsolete OECD advocated positivist and antidemocratic one-size-fits-all "evidenced-based" competence and skills policy as an educational embodiment of the commodified political authoritarianism.

Contrary to the "evidence-based" transnational policies, and due to long and strenuous efforts to build a democratic educational system worth of its name,

> the professionalism of Finnish teachers is above all some kind of self-image that does not seem to be endangered. The volume of applicants for teacher education appears very stable year on year, and even if our PISA fame diminishes over the years, it is hardly logical to claim that the globally praised Finnish teacher has suddenly deteriorated (Simola et al., 2017, 124)

It is tempting to fantasize the *Peruskoulu* as a remote Nordic incarnation of the great political and educational ideas embodied respectively in the French Enlightenment and German late Enlightenment; *liberty, equality* and *solidarity*, and *allgemeine Bildung;* inclusive, equitable, 'meant-for-all' education, welded together as a dynamic political and educational complex for socially, psychologically, and economically sound society.

The mutually reinforcing effect of adopted curriculum theory and practiced education policy depends crucially on how the teacher is positioned in the education system: as an autonomous, comprehensively educated professional trusted by her/his society like in (Finnish) *Bildung* or as a subordinated "conduit", "cipher" or "agent" of the System (Westbury, 2000, 21) with a very restricted professional freedom in the pressure of the prescribed curriculum by externally mandated control and testing business. The OECD has seamlessly adopted this distorted and undemocratic concept of education and curriculum in its suggestions and recommendations to improve education by "evidence-based" attempts to raise the test scores as the main business of education in the creation of the *Homo Economicus*. As rendering of education and in the light of all what we know about education, the twenty first-century *Competences* arguably signal many steps backwards for education. Just an attempt to discard "knowledge" by replacing it by "competence" in the vocabulary of education may imply we lose touch with traditional conceptions of truth, justifications of one's beliefs and opinions and other vital (epistemic) criteria indispensably related to education and worthwhile life: what is true, just, good and beautiful. By just this one ill-informed manoeuvre, as we can already witness, OECD may have an authoritative, subtle partisan role in contributing to the rise of political populism, 'alternative truths' and social pathologies blended with a kind of academic populism where higher education is transformed to vocational training of skills and competences. Obsessive building of external assessment system as an index of 'educational quality' that has reached Finnish universities as well is proved detrimental to trust, demoralizing devoted spirits in universities, increasing the sense of psychological and social pathology of these reforms, feeding unhealthy and ritualistic competition resulting even in cheating and corruption as a mode of *educational doping*, all phenomena that were very marginal before the global 'soft power reforms' recommended by the OECD.

There would be an urgent need to turn vicious circles to virtuous ones on a global scale what took place on the national level in the history of the poverty and misery ridden Finland in the past:

> Economic globalization has exacerbated social inequalities and deepened social gaps and income disparities both internationally and within nations. There is an extreme dichotomy in the world between those who can enjoy new cultural goods and services, such as higher education and its benefits on a world market scale, and those who are victims of nomadic capital in the global economy. The dichotomy between the globally rich and the place-bound poor may never have been as massive, visible, and sharp as it is today and the same is true of educational capital (Rinne & Simola, 2015, 201, my translation from Finnish).

Due to the void of the concept of knowledge and *Bildung*, it is hard to find any informed OECD response to the emergence of urgent global vicious circles of pandemics, ecological disaster, glaring racism, 'white supremacy', worsening poverty and inequality. In its presently documented intellectual and political capacity and 'competence', it seems evident, there may not be much more relevant analysis to be expected beyond the simplistic, a-theoretical and ahistorical suggestions of *'Competences and Skills'* in the OECD's contribution to our existential task to turn our global vicious circles to virtuous ones. After the 60 years since the foundation of the OECD, maybe time is ripe for *Bilanz*. Then the main concern of the founders was that education is too important to be left for educationists; now after the sixty years of experience of the OECD impact on education, it seems evident that education is definitely too important to be left for economists.

The Finnish long-built, context-specific, yet internationally informed recipe for the successful basic schooling is overtly simple and commonsensical but hard to duplicate or export; every nation has to find her own way to scrutinize the complex of political, cultural, subjective, scientific, economic, educational and international forces that was and is making us as us.

> What, if anything, can the world learn from educational change in Finland? We can readily agree with Sahlberg's (2011) three final conclusions. First, successful basic schooling must depend on those who implement every school reform, in other words the teachers. From this perspective, humiliating school inspections, standardised curricula and naming-and-shaming ranking lists are more than questionable. Second, efforts must be made to preserve a relaxed and fear-free learning environment for pupils by keeping testing to the absolute minimum, as well as by creating a caring and demanding ethos in the learning community. Finally, enhancing trust within educational systems is *de rigueur* for sustainable success. This means putting responsibility before accountability, and 'good enough' before excellence, and coming up with an adept combination of embedded national traditions and international insights. (Simola et al., 2017, 129–130).

Acknowledgements I am very thankful to Daniel Tröhler and Weili Zhao for their insightful comments on the drafts of this chapter.

References

Autio, T. (2017). Johdanto: Kansainvälistyvä opetussuunnitelmatutkimus kansallisen koulutuspolitiikan ja opetussuunnitelmareformien älyllisenä ja poliittisena resurssina (Introduction: International curriculum research as an intellectual and political resource for national education policy and curriculum reforms). In T. Autio, L. Hakala, & T. Kujala (Eds.), *Opetussuunnitelmatutkimus: keskustelunavauksia suomalaiseen kouluun ja opettajankoulutukseen* (*Curriculum research: An invitation for discussions of Finnish schools and teacher education*). Tampere University Press.
Beck, U. (1999). *What is globalization?* Polity Press.
Henderson, J. (Ed.). (2015). *Reconceptualizing curriculum development: Inspiring and informing action.* Routledge.
Herbart, J. F. (1804/1986). Über die ästhetische Darstellung der Welt als das Hauptgeschäft der Erziehung [On the aesthetic representation of the world as the main business of education]. In J. F. Herbart (Ed.), *Systematische Pädagogik* (introduced, selected, edited and interpreted by Dietrich Benner, pp. 59–70). Klett-Cotta.

Horlacher, R. (2016). *The educated subject and the german concept of Bildung*. Routledge.
Kettunen, P. (2019). The concept of society in the making of the Nordic welfare state. In S. Kuhnle, P. Selle, & Sven E. O. Hort (Eds.) *Globalizing welfare: An evoking Asian European dialogue* (pp. 143–161). Edward Elgar Publishing.
Lewis, S., Sellar, S., & Lingard, B. (2015). *PISA for schools: Topological rationality and new spaces of the OECD's global educational governance*. Published by: The University of Chicago Press on behalf of the Comparative and International Education Society.
Meyer, H.-D, & Benavot, A. (2013). Introduction. PISA and the globalization of education governance: Some puzzles and problems. In H.-D. Meyer, & Benavot (Eds.), A *PISA, power, and policy: The emergence of global educational governance* (pp. 9–26). Symposium Books.
Norring, P. (2016). *Eino Jutikkala and social change in the history of agriculture* (Trans. from Finnish). https://www.ennenjanyt.net/2016/05/eino-jutikkala-ja-yhteiskunnallinen-muutos
Pinar W. (2011a). *The character of curriculum studies: Bildung, Currere, and the recurring question of the subject*. Palgrave Macmillan.
Pinar, W. (2011b). *Allegories of the present: Curriculum development in a culture of Narcissism and Presentism*. Paper presented at the University of Tallinn, Estonia, on August 22, 2011.
Rinne, R., & Simola, H. (2015). Yliopistojen uusi hallinta (New university governance). In H. Simola, (Ed.) *Koulutusihmeen paradoksit: esseitä suomalaisesta koulutuspolitiikasta (Paradoxes of the miracle of education: Essays on Finnish education policy)* (pp. 178–212). Vastapaino.
Sahlberg, P. (2011). *Finnish lessons: What can the world learn from educational change in Finland*. Teachers College Press.
Simola. H. (2015). *The Finnish education mystery*. Routledge.
Simola, H., Kauko, J., Varjo, J., Kalalahti, M., & Sahlström, F. (Eds.). (2017). *Dynamics in education politics: Understanding and explaining the Finnish case*. Routledge.
Snellman, J. W. (2005). http://snellman.kootutteokset.fi
Tröhler, D. (2003). The discourse of German *Geisteswissenschaftliche Pädagogik* – A contextual reconstruction. *Paedagogica Historica, 39*(6), 759–778.
Uljens, M., & Nyman, C. (2013). Educational leadership in Finland or building a Nation with *Bildung*. In L. Moos (Ed.), *Transnational influences on values and practices in Nordic educational leadership: Is there a Nordic model*? (pp. 31–48). Springer.
Westbury, I. (2000). Teaching as a reflective practice: What might Didaktik teach curriculum? In I. Westbury, S. Hopmann, & K. Riquarts (Eds.), *Teaching as a reflective practice: The German Didaktik tradition* (pp. 15–39). Lawrence Erlbaum.
Westbury, I. (1998). Didaktik and curriculum studies. In B. B. Gundem, & S. Hopmann (Eds.), *Didaktik and/or curriculum: An international dialogue* (pp. 47–77). Peter Lang.
Zhao, W. (2019). *China's education, curriculum knowledge and cultural inscriptions: Dancing with the wind*. Routledge.

Tero Autio has worked in his career as classroom teacher in Finnish comprehensive schools, special teacher at the child and youth psychiatric ward in the university hospital, teacher educator in the vocational teacher education college and senior lecturer at university. He has served as full professor of curriculum studies and teacher education at Tampere University, Finland and invited international professor of curriculum theory, funded by the European Union, at Tallinn University, Estonia. His research interests cover curriculum theories and histories, education policies and their effects on teachers' work; political theories; Eastern, Southern and Western theories of subjectivity. He has done and is doing research and consultancy on curriculum issues and education reforms with colleagues in North and South America, Europe, South Korea, mainland China, Hong Kong, Japan, Saudi Arabia, and Turkey.

Historical Trajectories of the Contract-School Model in Norway

Kirsten Sivesind

By situating the analysis in cultural studies of education history, this chapter explores how school authorities in Norway have promoted a school system that reflects historical reform trajectories influenced by both national and international reform ideas. Most of the school reforms in Norway have built on the contract-school model, which began as a Lutheran project in Northern and Central Europe during the early eighteenth century. This chapter presents this model, focusing on how it developed in Scandinavia and Norway and how complementary ideas and power-relations emerged and contested the old legacy of this model during the nineteenth and twentieth century.

Introduction

Evidence-informed policy has recently emerged as a global trend driving change in educational curricula and assessment systems. Among the key narratives currently attracting considerable attention in reform-making processes are twenty first-century skills, which emphasise students' learning and well-being in a knowledge-based society. Moreover, knowledge within and across scientific disciplines have been declared necessary for each student within a lifelong perspective and for the future of the society. A core question is whether this emphasis on competence as an emerging theme transforms national school reforms by contesting older trajectories and reform models dating back to the origin of public schooling.

K. Sivesind (✉)
Department of Education, University of Oslo, Oslo, Norway
e-mail: kirsten.sivesind@iped.uio.no

This chapter uses an analytical narrative approach, where I examine the ways key reformists and experts have developed new ideas and proposed historical trajectories, decisive for curriculum reform within and across national contexts. I review relevant documents, academic literature and draw on a series of interviews I have conducted with Norwegian reform makers about the formation of a particular governance model; the so called contract-school model. By drawing on Popkewitz's (2013), I apply two reasoning styles: a retrospective approach that searches for social and cultural patterns in the past and a prospective approach that historicises the present by applying social and cultural theories to interpret current reform initiatives. In the first case, Tröhler's (2014) recognition of the Protestant denominations that developed into Lutheran-pietistic reasoning in the early eighteenth century serves as a backdrop for understanding the cultural foundation of curriculum reforms. In the second case, I refer to research studies and documents on national reform efforts in Norway, and argue that pietism as an ideological movement has interplayed with alternative sources of legitimization, such a philanthropy that stimulated to intellectual developments and a renewed pedagogy during the early nineteenth century. Moreover, current reform trajectories are influenced by global and international competence policies that contest the contract school model by emphasising scientific reasoning as the raison d'être for pursuing reform within the twenty-first century. The next three sections present how the interplay of various ideas and movements evolved during three centuries.

Pietistic Rationales and the Contract-School Movement (1736–1813)

Ideas of how to strengthen the younger generation's literacy are not new within the Norwegian reform context, as they have been featured in reform policies for centuries. The first attempt to provide public schooling in Norway was in the early eighteenth century due to Dane-Norwegian King Christian the 6th's desire to establish a contract school and thus increase literacy and spread Lutheran-protestant ideas. This kind of school drew on Western reform ideas from ancient Greece and Rome, where a new alphabet was developed in the eighth century BCE (Thomas, 2009, p. 346), about one thousand years after reading and writing were taught in national and local schools during the Shang Dynasty in China (Wang et al., 2009, p. 394).

In Northern and Central Europe, literacy, as a core focus of teaching and learning, was strengthened through Lutheran reform efforts, including the establishment of public schooling that prepared adherents for Christian confirmation in the early eighteenth century CE. In this region of Europe, the teaching of literacy skills is associated with the contract school and the Lutheran ways of practicing public schooling in homes and churches in the early eighteenth century. The Lutheran Reformation challenged the Pope's power as the man closest to God and the person of highest rank who represented the will of God. Martin Luther, who is the forefather and the main reformist in this movement, contested both the position of the Pope and the language of the church. He suggested replacing Latin with the mother tongue in church and in schools, which, at the turn of sixteenth century, were part of the same establishment. Monasteries and cathedral schools, later called Latin-schools, provided education for work in the Church and allowed entrance into universities. Luther's idea was that the state should replace the church role in areas of schooling (Myhre, 1976: 133–134). Although Luther did not argue for a secular curriculum, he was aware of two horizons for the definition of schooling: learning the word of God and acknowledging the world itself (Luther, 1529/2007). This distinction led to a new model called the *contract-school* model, which integrated the mother tongue into the curriculum (Hopmann, 2000).

The main idea of this chapter is to characterize how this contract model was made into a state-organized system based on pietistic rationales, successively established and reformed throughout the nineteenth century in Norway. After the mid-nineteenth century, schooling took place primarily in small schoolhouses. The core ideas that inspired this project were political actions and cultural dispositions that benefited individuals by developing inner harmony for the salvation of their souls (Tröhler, 2014). Religious aims were of utmost concern to school reformers. King Christian the 6th, was a Christian, who have learned about pietism from his teachers, demanded the peasants and the church to arrange education based on pietistic rationales in the rural areas of Norway, which was declared by law. He sought to create a moral and religious population by unifying separate regions and interests (Tveit, 1991, p. 22).

Combining state interests and religious motives was however not of Danish-Norwegian origin. A state-pietistic rationale for reform had already succeeded in Prussia, a state within the German empire. The pietistic movement was initiated and supported by theologians, who challenged the Orthodox priesthood of the Lutheran church. Philipp Jakob Spener (1635–1705), who claimed to be the 'second reformer' of the state Lutheran church, and his friend and follower Hermann Franke (1663–1727) were forerunners to the pietistic movement (Hermansen, 2003). Under the motto 'pray, work, and passion', people sought spiritual renewal. Private meetings, so-called *conventicles*, gathered people in their homes for worship and prayer. The devotion of the heart rather than the intellect and living one's life in wholeness, purity, and piety according to God's will were keystones of their practicing theology, which developed further within the Lutheran church. An orientation to both practical and religious experiences was the core of this movement. Rasmussen (2004, p. 33) characterises this rationale as 'enlightened pietism,' as the intellectual orientation should be replaced by an interest in experience and enlightenment.

Although the movement was not popular among Orthodox Lutherans, it became a supporting element in the government of the state and the regulation of public schooling in both Prussia and Denmark-Norway. The combination of state and religious concerns can be explained by the success of reform activity and school development in Halle. First, the reform university in Halle became one of the most prestigious and influential universities at the turn of the eighteenth century. In cooperation with King Friedrich Wilhelm the 1st of Prussia and private sponsors, Franke also organised schooling for poor children, which, over several decades, became organised into an establishment of many buildings and departments called the 'school-cum-orphanage complex' (*Armenschule, Paedagogium, and Anstalten*) (Payne, 1998). The system of schooling that subsequently arose became widely recognised for its hard-working students and exemplary teaching. It offered poor children the opportunity to attend school with the help of funding to pay for further education at the university. The success of this system, however disciplined, ascetic and autocratic, explains why pietistic schooling served as a model within the government regime of the time.

The schooling enterprise of Franke and the pietistic movement legitimised interest in 'real' things within the boundary of schooling. In contrast to Spener who preferred to work for a loosely coupled network of *conventicles*, Franke implemented a more militancy school system that aimed at transforming both the church and the social order of the society (Gawthrop, 1993, p. 150). Students of Halle learned to be loyal to authorities and disciplined about their life and work based on an absolutism of how to comply with the law and thereby God. Their aspirations of doing practical work rather than merely contemplating their inner beliefs and reflections closely matched the ideals of state governance and radical ideas of reordering the world.

The educational embodiment of this rationale was the *Realschule*, based on *Realien*, which means to be engaged in 'real things' or science. As Brubacher (1966, p. 113) confirms, pietistic schooling inspired new interest in a realistic orientation to schooling, which later developed into a scientific curriculum movement in Germany in subsequent decades. However, pietistic scholars did not ascribe to an empiricist orientation to the *Realien*, which was important to Christian Freiherr von Wolff (1679–1754), who later became a leading intellectual in Halle. His principles were incorporated into a curriculum system at universities in Prussia and Denmark at the turn of the eighteenth century and focused on an empiricist view of knowledge where principles were deduced through mathematical, logical reasoning, based on the values of science and God (Clausen, 1896; Koch, 2003).

After studying in Halle, many students were employed in offices and services, such as the military, the church, and schools. More importantly, primary schooling in Prussia was based on the model of the *Anstalten* in Halle after the *Decree of 1717*, which made public schooling mandatory at the primary level for all children living within the vicinity of a school. It was based on "a general call to grace" and according to Gawthrop (1993, p. 152) rejecting any form of predestination. A school for all would spread the word of God and save the souls from corruption so far *the teaching estate* (Lehrstand) enabled the mediation of God's word. This approach to curriculum was exemplary within its contemporary time and context. And therefore, this architecture that implied particular form of governance, also became the model for the Dane-Norwegian King, which, through the *School Ordinance of 1739* and *Decree of 1741*, made pietistic schooling mandatory in rural areas across Denmark and Norway.

Despite international influences, early attempts to regulate a public school system in Denmark-Norway are considered successful, particularly within a comparative perspective. As summarised by Val de Rust (1989, p. 31), because of its home-schooling tradition, Sweden adopted its first regulation for public schooling in 1842, about one hundred years later than Norway. In Great Britain, elementary schooling became compulsory in 1880. Even France, known for egalitarian rationales of education, formalised public schooling as late as 1791 and adopted further regulations in 1882. Based on this background, the *School Ordinance of 1739,* designed to regulate urban schooling in Norway, was, from a European perspective, a brave and early attempt to create a local public school system for people in disparate districts.

However, organising public schooling within a sparsely populated and vast country was not a straightforward task, especially given the historical and demographic conditions of Norway (Gundem, 1993b). Civil servants, independent farmers, and peasants were powerful groups across Norway, and they did not necessarily obey new laws without first demanding their rights. According to Tveit (1991), the introduction of an autocracy in 1660 gave all formal power to the King, but in reality, it created a powerful bureaucracy of civil servants. Norwegian farmers and peasants had become powerful groups due to the taxes they paid to the Norwegian state as well. By not paying the taxes, they could, in principle, play a sanctioning role according to new directives. Moreover, they were as Lauglo (1982) puts it, promoted through free-holding farming, 'freeing farmers from diffuse dependence on upper-class landlords. A mismatch between expectations of the state and the rural population can be explained by long distances between the lawmakers and the rural population. Moreover, the authors of the School Ordinance from Denmark, who originally formulated the curriculum instruction, were not informed about the local conditions for organizing schooling in the districts of Norway. They imagined a well-organised school similar to a model that developed in *Slesvig and Holstein,* very different from what could be accomplished within outlying districts in Denmark-Norway (Tveit, 1991).

The solution was to develop different decrees (*Plakat*) adjusted to regional circumstances (Decree, 1741). These decrees, one each for Denmark and Norway, would be followed up with local school plans or foundation documents (*Fundas*) within the districts. This system of decrees and local school plans represents the first systematic attempt to create formal curriculum documents across Norway; however, it cannot be considered a national system, which is an invention of the late nineteenth century (Engelsen, 2003; Gundem, 1993a, 1993b). The main change resulting from the new *Decree of 1741* was to place responsibility for public schooling on the districts. According to this *Decree of 1741,* taxes should be paid, but there were no fixed or general taxes imposed, which meant that the local districts decided how to solve funding problems and decide how much money they would spend on establishing and maintaining primary schools. Schools could be built in the local district (*fastskoler*) and used primarily for education, or it could take place in homes or elsewhere (*omgangsskoler*) and the location used temporarily for teaching and prayer. Certainly, ambulatory schools were much cheaper alternative and more practical for peasants in the districts. In practice, it was similar to what was institutionalized as home-schooling in Sweden (Tveit, 1991).

The physical equipment varied depending on what the peasants could afford with the donations and offerings (*almisse*) received. All inhabitants with a regular income should, in principle, pay for the establishment of primary schooling (Decree, 1741). Hence, home-schooling became a model for many districts, which meant that Norway and Sweden ended up with a similar model of schooling despite differences in centralized regulations. Administratively, the local school commission was in charge of the organisation of schooling, as well as its content. This commission should, according to the decree, consist of the four most knowledgeable men in the parish besides the vassal (*lensmann*), his curates (*kapellaner*), and the parsons (*sogneprest*). This commission was charged with formulating the local school plan (*fundas*) to regulate both the content and organisation of schooling within the parish. Many districts in both Southern and Eastern Norway completed this task in a relatively short time. Two-thirds of the districts in Eastern Norway drafted their school plans (*fundas*) within a year as they were instructed to do so by the state. Within three years, almost 95% of the districts had organised their own school commission (Tveit, 1991: 53). Half of the rural population in Southern Norway was offered public schooling by 1744, and it increased to 89% in 1750 (Tveit, 2004). In Northern Norway, Sami schools were introduced a decade earlier than those for non-Sami students.

In the selection of content, the main goal was that students would learn to read the Bible and understand the Lutheran Catechism. This aim prolonged a local tradition established by the church, which was formalised with the *Ordinance of 1739*. Additionally, parents could decide whether a teacher would teach their children writing and arithmetic, and both of these skills were considered part of the secular aims of schooling. The skill-set of the 'three R's' included a fourth: religion, reading, writing and 'rithmetic' (arithmetic). Although religion and reading were mandatory, writing and arithmetic were left to the parents' discretion and their ability to pay for the educational material (Johnsen, 2002; Markussen, 1990). However, most children were sent to school to learn what was considered necessary: learning to read and preparing for Christian Confirmation. This rite was mandatory for everyone, as proclaimed by the *Law of 1736;* Confirmation not only marked a youth's membership in the Lutheran Church and was a statement of faith, it was also considered important for civic reasons (Ordinance, 1736). Christian confirmation provided access to civil services, including getting married, joining the military, getting a proper job, and acquiring land and other property. The tradition and formalisation of Confirmation explain the high number of people who participated, and it remained a driving force in public schooling for the next 100 years (Tveit, 1991).

An interesting dimension of the reform trajectory that developed during this century is the distribution of responsibilities between the church and the school as two different systems. According to conceptual differentiations made according to the law, teaching and schooling were defined on their own terms after 1739. The awareness of what sets teaching and schooling apart from other interests is exemplified by the texts. Principles of teaching were incorporated into drafts of the *Decree of the Confirmation* as early as 1736. Although this decree did not reflect a comprehensive theory of teaching, it addressed how the Church should train young people for Confirmation and thereby reflected a conceptual distinction between teaching and 'Confirmation, examination, and assessment' (*prøvelse*). In 1736, both activities were organised during Sunday church services (Ordinance, 1736). However, after the school ordinance of 1739, the formal role of the Church was to supervise the education of youngsters, and teaching became a matter of schooling (Instruction,

1739; Ordinance, 1739). The order of *Ordinance and Instruction* maintained that Christian Confirmation and the Catechesis were the missions of the priest, and the clerk should teach the text of the Catechis.

When the confirmation was organised in terms of a catechesis during Sunday services, the priest asked the youngsters to recall what was written in the Lutheran Catechism; the process was ritually organised and included a series of questions and answers that had been reformulated and edited by Pontoppidan (1737/1787). This text, referred to as *Sannhet til Gudfryktighet: Forklaring over Dr. M. Luther's Lille Katekisme* [From Truth to the Fear of God: Explanation of Dr. M. Luther's Small Catechism] was a shortened version of Spener's text, further confirming the impact of the pietistic movement since Spener, as mentioned, was one of its forefathers (Jensen, 2007a). The Norwegian Instruction of 1739, based on an *Aristotelian-Thomistic* view that implied to see the word of God from the perspective of the learner. Creating understanding was therefore as important as reproducing knowledge, which also meant that a particular sequence of teaching should consider the student's capability to develop understanding:

> He (the teacher) shall with all his diligence, teach the children within the Dr. Martin Luther's Small Catechism, so as they first, rightly understand the meaning of each part and thereafter teach them to recall word by word; and subsequently he ought to teach them the common explana*tion to the Cat*echism. Whereas he is not going train them to recall by memory, to be bound to the words, but time and again change the questions directed to them, since it is better that they can put in plain words (gjøre Forreede) for the Meaning, than just read the words, without a sense of what they mean (utden at forstaae dem). (Instruction, 1739: Section 2)

The Catechesis of the Church followed a similar scheme of practices but was based on the Church's approval of what was to be learned. During services, students were placed in a group led by a teacher who was most often the clerk. When the bishop visited the church, students were divided into classes based on the level they had achieved. Only students who *understood* the main parts would be asked to recall the Catechisms from memory; if they were well prepared, they would also be asked to explain the answers. Despite all historical accounts confirming the opposite, the priest should have, according to the law, ensured that students were not embarrassed or overwhelmed during the rehearsal process (Rasmussen, 2004). Young children were required to recall the Ten Commandments, the Creed, the Lord's Prayer and, in some cases, the Sacraments of the Alter from memory; in principle, however, these texts were expected to have been taught at home.

A second point to be made is that Luther viewed schooling through the lens of man's immortal destiny, but he also argued for secular aims concerning both practical knowledge and moral issues. Thus, religious and secular aims supported the idea of organising schooling for *all*, which, during the early eighteenth century, became a leading idea in the state-pietistic movement. However, viewing nature as having value in itself was not shaped by Lutheran *pedagogy*. This idea developed from naturalistic philosophy in the early seventeenth century and was incorporated into a philosophy of education by Johan Amos Comenius (1592–1670). This philosophy was then mediated by pietistic reformers, including Spener and Franke. The naturalistic approach to understanding the world stressed the value of education in accordance with nature and teaching based on the principle of 'learning through the senses' (Comenius, 1658, p. 115). Pietists who followed Comenius' strand of thought were against any rationalisation of religion and instead sought validation of their inner faith through an external educational expression of learning and new sensory experiences. They argued against the view that the structure of the content itself defines what is significant to learn. Using the senses according to experiences of the world was, therefore, an invention of Comenius and at the core of *pietism*.

Democratisation Processes and the Academic Elite of Civil Servants (1814–1890)

During the nineteenth century, the pietistic efforts to develop education across the nation evolved into a school system that was governed by state administrative bodies. The rise of a central public bureaucracy occurred when Norway became a centralised state in 1814, when Denmark relinquished the Province of Norway to Sweden (Christensen, 2005, pp. 721–722). In other countries, such as England, national assemblies were organised into different chambers and divided according to class and status. In Norway however, there were few feudal elites who expected to be honoured with powerful positions (Elster, 1988, p. 11). The assembly in Norway, *the Storting*, consisted therefore of an elected group, who represented different geographical regions and institutions: the peasants, the church and the military. Due to long geographical distances, people from the Northern part of Norway was however, not represented.

The Danish prince Christian Frederik (1786–1848) formulated a public letter that requested a national election and he asked the parishes to appoint two electives who then organized elections within the parishes. These elections are regarded as reflecting one of the most democratic systems in Europe at this point in history, and it resulted in a governance form, representing a pre-party state that dominated until 1884 when the national assembly gained authority over executive politics. After 1884, the parliament *the Storting* had formally the ruling power over the ministerial government (Christensen, 2003), that is, manifested parliamentarism that developed into the particular model of governance that characterized Norwegian politics and governance throughout the twentieth century.

Nonetheless, in the nineteenth century, the school reforms and renewals were not demanded by any nobility. Neither the Danish prince Christian Frederik, who was appointed as he Norwegian King in 1814 for five months, nor the Swedish King, Kong Carl 13th and his adopted French son, Prince Carl Johan,[1] who had served as a Marshal of France during the Napoleon wars, demanded for any school reform. Rather, the enthusiasts for reforms were a group of intellectuals who strived for independence and the establishment of national institutions. They were all devoted to ideas of national self-awareness, defended the rights and interests of the rural population, and were acquainted with traditions and knowledge from abroad since many were educated in Denmark. This *intellectual drive* is equal to the *Enlightenment* movement in Prussia, although the rationales of schooling and administration were respectively different. Jacob Nicolai Wilse (1736–1801) was among the first *Enlightenment* professors who worked for the renewal of the school system. He was greatly inspired by Comenius' *Orbus Pictus*, which he read in school (Høverstad, 1918, p. 37). At the same time, the farmers can be considered an ultra-conservative force in religious and social matters and were not agents of reforms, as they challenged their way of life. According to Sirevåg (1986), the early rise of a public school system in Denmark-Norway and the establishment of Latin schools in the sixteenth century created a climate for modernisation, which explains why Norwegians were at the forefront of modernisation in Europe.

Niels Treschow (1751–1833) serves as an illustrative example of how intellectuals became involved in administrative positions during the early nineteenth century. He advocated rationales from abroad while defending a national orientation to schooling and reform that guaranteed the private rights of peasants. Treschow had participated in the Augustenborg reform programme at the Christiania Cathedral School, where he was a principal from 1789–1803; thus, he was experienced and well-acquainted with education and curriculum development. Although he did not view comprehensive schooling reform as his primary objective, a Dane-Norwegian model of reform became a *Leitbild*, a guiding composition of principles for the renewal of general schooling that influenced the law-making process during the early nineteenth century. A strand of thought, philanthropy, was formally institutionalised through a process developed by the establishment of a School Commission between 1875 and 1905. It was named: Instructional Committee: the Direction for Learned Schools, and the University (*Komité for Opplysningsfaget*), where Trehschow participated. Some members of this commission had opposing viewpoints, particularly about questions concerning the *Learned Schools* and curriculum. Some individuals on the commission defended a neo-humanistic and classical view, along with Prussian ideas, while Treschow essentially defended a philanthropic approach.

In 1815, the Direction for Learned Schools was integrated into the Ministry, which became a Government-College (*Regerings-Collegium*) with full responsibility for school matters, and Treschow became the first minister (Riksarkivet, 2007c). According to this new body, the minister was only in a position to give advice to the national assembly, as the Swedish King could favour suggestions given by the parliament. When Treschow commented on the new law proposition published in 1816, he only gave advice on how to organize reforms for elementary schooling within rural districts. Law proposals were prepared by committees, approved by the national assembly, and thereafter supported by the King. In cases where different committees prepared the same reforms, some representatives met and prepared a joint draft, which was eventually discussed by the national assembly (Sirevåg, 1986: 136). A hierarchy of committees constituted the system for creating reforms during the nineteenth century. When giving advice about new law revisions prepared in 1816, Treschow clearly expressed his viewpoints in favour of pietistic rationales that considered private commitments significant to the organisation of schooling.

The idea that 'parents should have the prime mandate to take care of children's upbringing and education' (The Law-committee, 1814–1830: § 1) seems to have been decisive in the new law proposition. In the amendment process, another distinction between two types of obligations was made: public schooling established by parishes and the education of children in general (*skoleplikt vs. opplæringsplikt*) (Sirevåg, 1986, p. 142). The law committee also decided that methods of instruction should be included in new instructions for teachers and developed by each parish (The Law-committee, 1814–1830: §24).

Preparations for the law revision went on for years; it was developed by committees, discussed within the national assembly, and finally approved by the Swedish King. The School Act of 1827, which finally became decisive for rural schooling at the primary level, shows the results of committee work and a course of decision-making that involved different parties (Lov, 1827). The law mandated a new system to go along with an established tradition of local curriculum planning and the pietistic reform ideals from 1739–1742. However, certain points were emphasised and clarified (§ 14). Subjects were divided into (a) reading, combined with reasoning exercises (*forstandsøvelser*), (b) religion and bible history to accommodate instructional texts, (c) singing from the hymn book, and (d) writing and arithmetic. Compared to the School Ordinance of 1739, there was a greater emphasis on writing and arithmetic (Jensen, 2007b). The reasoning exercises referred to looking up keywords in the textbook, which were in an appendix containing up to 800 words (Jensen, 2007b). These changes can be looked upon as a modernization of the reform trajectory, influenced by philanthropic ideas.

Local parishes were also ordered to provide a local teaching plan and a decree that described the duties of the teachers (§ 26). The bishop had the overall responsibility for making a plan, which should, by law, not hinder the course of teaching; instead, it should ensure that schooling was organised according to the above-mentioned paragraph (§ 14). Moreover, this plan and the instructional plan for teachers had to be approved by the Ministry of Ecclesiastical Affairs and the school system. This system of curriculum-making, as well as reading material, such as the ABC for learning the alphabet, and religious texts, provides narratives of a national unification and a formalisation of curriculum-making for general schooling in the early nineteenth century. Although textbooks were not approved by the ministry before the period of 1889–1908, instructional texts were nonetheless considered exemplars of subject matter, as both parents and teachers used them consistently in the schools (§ 14) (Skjelbred, 2000).

A survey of the teaching material produced between 1779 and 1842 reveals that ideas of what should be taught reflected Enlightenment ideas, as well as advice on teaching children, for example, reading (The oldest Norwegian ABC-books, 2007). Preparation books in religion, also used for exercises in reading, expressed a philantropic rationale of what to teach. For example, the *Book of Grøgaard* covered Bible stories (about 60%). In addition to Christian church history, Islamic faith (*Mahomet*), and Norse mythology (*Odin*), a short introduction to philological questions was included (Grøgaard, 1821, pp. 117–118). In many ways, this book reflected enlightenment in terms of philanthropic ideas as a curriculum rationale, including knowledge about various cultures and life-views. Moreover, it was intended for elementary education. The author also recommended teaching methods that differed somewhat form traditional pietism. For example, Grøgaard states that the teaching of children should start with subject matter that is the easiest and most comprehensible. One (the teacher) should not choose to start teaching pupils with the highest wisdom of the religion. Chilrden should not start by learning anything other than what they can accomplish through reason (*end hvad de kunne tænke noget ved*). In this way, boredom and habits of laziness are avoided (Grøgaard, 1815, p. 2).

This idea is not entirely novel since a pietistic reform also preferred a realistic orientation to content. However, in this period, the use of reason was emphasised to a greater extent and further strengthened by Enlightenment ideas (Brubacher, 1966). Johnsen (2017) has reviewed literature about Grøgaard's position, not merely as one of the elected representatives in the national assembly in 1814, but as an educator and an enlightenment scholar being aa distinguished author of school books at this moment in history. B. E. Johnsen argues that Grøgaard's widely used schoolbooks: the ABC, published in 1815, and a reader, published in 1816 were highly inspired by Danish rationalism, at first influenced by the Swiss-French philosopher Jean-Jacques Rousseau (1712–1788) with the work Émile: *Ou de l'Education* from 176nd 2, thereafter by Philanthropy and the work of Basedow through the Danish reformist, Friedrich Eberhard von Rochow (1734–1805). Rochow authored a reading book for ordinary people in Denmark, the *Child Friend* (*Børnevennen*) that was published in eleventh editions, and also widespread in Norway. It is important to mention that the Danish reform trajectories at the turn of the nineteenth century did not contest pietism and Lutheran ideas as such, but aimed at challenging superstition within the population. Thus, reading books became oriented to scientific knowledge about the laws of nature, and towards moral guidelines more than upbringing in Christian faith. Rather than executing corporal punishment as a disciplinary device, philanthropism advocated to tell stories for children for an educational purpose, and as Rochow argued, through moral upraising, the need for punishment would diminish by itself (Johnsen, 2017, p. 150).

Although Bible stories and the catechism were traditionally the core of what should be learnt at school and what tested through the catechetic of the church, the new textbooks extended the curriculum to cover small poems, fairy tales, and general history and geography. The catechetic method, in the form of a question-answer pattern, was replaced. Most of the books consisted of exercises and showing children how to put letters together to spell words. However, the most interesting characteristic is the content. The ABC-book of Knutzen, for example, showed pictures of animals from all over the world as well as from the Nothern part of Europe (see Fig. 1). These pictures were considered objects that should develop children's knowledge and understanding of nature, as well as the characteristics of different species (Knutzen, 1836). In the preface, Knutzen claims that Latin was excluded and that the pictures replaced Danish ones because, according to his viewpoint, they did not give an accurate representation of nature. This textbook expresses a naturalistic approach to content through pictures, tales, and stories, which was legitimised by paragraph 14 of the new law. A similar textbook, published in 1837, also includes knowledge about

Fig. 1 The tiger, the wolf and the wild boar. Page 19–20 in *The newest Picture-ABC* for adolescents (Knutzen, 1836)

history and geography. Although educational ideas, as well as the overall governance of the education system, continued along pietistic reform trajectories, this textbook depicts images consistent with what was typical at this point in history. The catechetic method is not used; instead, the book focuses on ways of teaching children to read and learn certain subject matter.

National school authorities formulated an official curriculum in 1834 already (Plan, 1834). This curriculum did not conflict with the above-mentioned rationale, except for the monitorial[2] method. This method of instruction that involved a group of pupils being taught to instruct younger students, as a form of peer turoring, gained worldwide recognition during the nineteenth century (Hopmann, 1990, p. 13). However, in Norway, conditions for organising education within the districts, with a sparsely populated country, did not allow for this movement to survive. Rather, the enacted curriculum was more in line with educational principles introduced during 1739, along with pietistic rationales. Therefore, pietistic reasoning continued as a justification for public schooling in the nineteenth century, while discussions within the national assembly touched upon the question of how a modern curriculum for Norwegian schooling should be developed for the purpose of establishing a comprehensive education system.

For example, Frederik Moltke Bugge (1806–1853), who served as a member of a national board for reforming secondary schools, argued for reforming schooling into a comprehensive education system. In the first stage of the work of this board, Bugge visited the states and provinces of Germany[3] and France to study their school systems. He spent one and a half year on this task and wrote a report for the commission that covered 1144 pages and filled three volumes (Bugge, 1839: I–III). The national school authorities distributed this report to all schools in Norway at no cost, and the same year, Bugge launched a programme for creating a comprehensive education system (Roos, 2019). The resistance to a comprehensive curriculum system was however, considerable due to disagreements within the national assembly, as well as within local communities. Both the upper and middle classes residing in cities were a rather small group compared to the peasantry in the rural districts, and national politics were influenced by those living in regional areas. They represented a '*demokratisch prägendend Kraft*,' [a democratic oriented force], as Werler (2004: 215) characterises this moment in history.

Nonetheless, due to the need for central support at the school district, municipal, and regional levels and the smooth modernisation regulated by the Ministry of Education, popular ideas of social movements were not opposed in principle. This was, above all, a problem in Denmark, where the state and bureaucracy lacked legitimacy among the peasants, particularly after their loss of Holstein to Germany in 1864 (Korsgaard & Wiborg, 2006). In Denmark, Korsgaard (2003) claims that the creation of central regulations challenged the ideas of the schooling tradition of Grundvigians, known as promoters from *Folk-Bildung*, who were, in principle, against state-ruled institutions and favoured local control of schools and the parents' right to choose between alternative schools with different pedagogical and social profiles; thus, Grundvigians were not a driving force for developing a public school system (Lauglo, 1982). The establishment of a comprehensive public school system was therefore developed in opposition to the Grundvigian movement.[4]

Thus, the peasants' attitudes towards a state-governed school system in Norway differed from those in Denmark, where conservatives were in charge of the national government at the turn of the twentieth century. This meant that the government in Denmark allowed the establishment of alternative schools free for parents to choose between, in addition to public schooling, although not necessarily founded on Grundvigian ideas, while local demands were supported in Norwegian state educational politics, guaranteeing the rights of the rural population until centralisation was considered reasonable. This need evolved throughout the nineteenth century, and a significant step towards educational administration at the central level occurred when the department appointed the first secretary general for school affairs in 1856. The position was first held by a theologian until 1863 and thereafter by the educator Hartvig Nissen (1815–1874), who argued for a differentiated system of central and local administrations providing for the organisation of a comprehensive educational system in Norway (Gundem, 1993a: 28). Nissen, who had been a student of Bugge, worked to make the system similar to the Prussian model in accordance with the suggestions put forward by Bugge. However, Nissen was far more progressive in terms of the content of the reforms. Here, Nissen prolonged the contract school idea of Luther: 'schooling must always start with the mother tongue, given its fundamental connection to any people. The purpose of all teaching is, as Nissen sees it, at every stage of the school's formation' (Roos, 2019).

Meanwhile, there were signs of adjustments to a Prussian model in Norway during the establishment of a national curriculum for the secondary level. The 1858 'normal plan' for the integrated Latin grammar and 'real' or science school represents an emergent step in the development of a national upper secondary school in Norway. According to this reform, the upper secondary school should prepare students for both academic and vocational studies and seek to differentiate teaching material according to pupils' interests. As claimed by Bjørg B. Gundem, this curriculum prepared the first step for a nationally prescribed curriculum or a 'normal plan' for secondary schooling and strengthened the realistic dimension of the contract-school movement. The national curriculum was probably heavily inspired by the Prussian curriculum, *'Normalplan für Gymnasien* of 1816', which is now widely considered a German invention (Gundem, 1993b: 255, 264). In this curriculum, content descriptions were of primary significance.

The governance of public institutions differed between Denmark and Norway. Neither Danish nor Norwegian reform efforts became legitimised according to Grundvigian ideas in this matter (Korsgaard & Wiborg, 2006). Differences between Denmark and Norway might shed light on the underlying model of curriculum governance that was established in this period. Korsgaard and Wiborg conclude that the countries' education governance aligned with two different reform models (Korsgaard & Wiborg, 2006). At this point, they draw on Slagstad's (2001) book, *The National Strategists [De Nasjonale Strateger]*. Slagstad claims that the Norwegians modelled their reforms based on the Prussian model, where the term *folkelighet* [popuaristic] reflected the German concept of *Volkstum* [ethnicity]. These two concepts differed in their substantive foundation, specifically where the *reform-compromise* is considered a characteristic trait of the Norwegian alternative: equally evaluating cultural ideals and popular requests. Slagstad views this compromise as inspired by both German romanticism and French-English rationalism, or what can be considered both expressive and instrumental in its orientation to public concerns. The pietistic trajectory was thereby contested and adjusted ideologically.

There was certainly political interest in increasing the wealth of the people according to political requests, as Nissen proclaimed in his political programme for education reform (Thuen, 2004). One might agree that the Norwegian curriculum model placed more authority and responsibility in the State's governing bodies, where intellectuals participated, and where the state held a more profound role more like in Prussia and unlike England, for example. In the Norwegian and German contexts, a tradition of 'reform from above' was established. With a focus on the state, the elites were identified with state initiative and expansion, unlike elites within the English laissez-fair-system (Slagstad, 2001, p. 151). Thus, one might conclude that the Danish government corresponded with the British liberal governance tradition of John Locke and the French tradition of Jean-Jacques Rousseau (1712–1778) giving the private domain and, in this case, parents overall authority for their children's upbringing and teaching. In comparison, the Norwegian model adjusted its reform trajectory to the Prussian model of reform, encapsulating traditional *Didaktik* [didactics] as a normative and connecting link between public politics and local schooling.

However, such a view undermines the changes in rationale that developed from below, where ordinary teachers and principals cooperated with laymen and others who worked for the establishment of a professional discourse. This tradition was not German in origin. Rather, this Dane-Norwegian tradition was established through pietistic and partly philanthropic inspired reform, which sought to combine principles of instruction with instructional principles of moral character that had implications for re-presenting the content in for example text books. Furthermore, it was informed by popular requests and very different from the tradition in England, where the curricula tradition became focused on methods without concern for the purposes and principles of the overall enterprise of education (Reid, 1997, p. 679). Norwegian reform work aimed for a coherent approach and sought to bring together means with aims, which was not accomplished in England to the same extent. Nevertheless, Korsgaard and Wiborg (2006) identify similarities between the Norwegian system and the Prussian model both in church and school politics. They claim that state-oriented pietists had a greater impact in Norway than in Denmark, with a 'clearly visible line running from state pietism to social democrats, different from an anti-state ideology based on Grundvigian rationales in Denmark' (Korsgaard & Wiborg, 2006, p. 376).

However, a formal decision that reflects a modernizing trend in Norway was made in 1889, when local school boards were no longer in the hands of the church and the parishes since the church no longer had a supervising role in school matters (Gundem, 1993b). This event resulted in a renewed demand for curriculum to be based on secular and popular purposes, inclusive of encyclopaedic content and methodological advice. Although content was formed into a predefined subject matter (*stoff*), local and popular demands for schooling were, however, strengthened, politically, through the Liberal Party, which increased in importance during the coming years.

A curriculum for the primary levels appeared in 1890. Additionally, regional school directors appointed in each county instigated a centralisation of curriculum-making by creating the first regional plan in 1874 (Gundem, 1993b). Their work resulted in an overall plan for the creation of local school plans. Although one could argue that the regional school directors represented a conservative class at that time (Telhaug & Mediås, 2003), they were served as a bridge between the central authorities, local elected boards, and teachers in this system. Earlier plans, entitled *Instruction for the Teachers*, were aimed at the individual schoolteacher, who was responsible for his own administration and teaching (Gundem, 1993b). The new plan, entitled 'teaching plan', pointed towards an impending school system that was equipped with school buildings and teaching material. This plan contained not only bodies of prescribed content to be taught but also entailed the purposes of each subject, as well as axioms of methods for teaching specific subjects (Gundem, 1993a: 32). It was devised as a guideline, which referred to the Primary Education Act of 1860 (Lov, 1860).

Therefore, one might question whether educational reform initiatives in Prussia and Denmark-Norway shaped bureaucratic institutions into a centralised system ruled from the top, as indicated by Slagstad (2001). This is a two-fold issue: (1) how the Prussian system did not necessarily function as a top-down project, and (2) how the establishment of the Norwegian schooling system addressed political, professional, and to some extent private interests differently than education systems in other countries, such as in Germany. Moreover, one might also discuss whether a pietistic tradition resulted in an instrumental rationality, as claimed by Weber (1930/2001), and if so, whether it worked as a foundation for curriculum control during the next century, which is a theme that will be addressed in the next section.

Modernising School Reforms: Based on Scientific Rationales? (1890–1997)

Following the School Act of 1889 (Lov, 1889), the state's power to sanction municipalities with regard to the preparation and planning of the school curriculum was limited. In the 1920s, this power distribution began to change, as the government started to see the need for state control over curriculum matters. A parliamentary decision in 1920 provided a new system of funding intended to extend general schooling from five to seven years. The parliament decided to allocate money only to continuation schools (middelskoler) that were based on a seven-year programme. The 1936 law stated that every child should be given the same economic and cultural opportunities and have equal access to a unified school system that provided an equally high level of quality and prepared students for both vocational and academic studies. Although political parties spanned the political spectrum, party leaders reached an agreement about centralised education, and a unified system was established. Thus, the establishment of a unified school system served as a common programme and fulfilled the goals of different parties.

A substantive body of literature underscores the empirical orientation in the field of education of the 1930s (Dale, 1999, 2005; Helsvig, 2005; Lønnå, 2002). A cluster of principles, which changed the traditional concept of allmenndannelse [general education], was considered in light of psychologically-oriented theories (Bakken, 1971, pp. 9–15). The idea of what to teach became a question of what could be learned. This idea was investigated through empirical methods and experiments. Psychological education theories were discussed at Nordic school conferences as early as 1900 and were also written about in volumes of the teacher journal Skolebladet, which was more radical than the older and more conservative journal Norsk Skoletidende (Harbo, 1969, p. 202). Quantitative studies paved the way for new considerations of what and how to teach, always according to practical perspectives on schooling that provided a fundamental foreground for the reformists, who were well-educated intellectuals.

It is obvious that the empirical report published during the initial phase of the reform process in 1936 was based on a pedagogical-psychological approach, as indicated in the title: The teaching plans in the Folk-school—a pedagogical-psychological preparation of the new plans for social studies (Ribsskog & Aall, 1936). The report evaluated student outcomes in different grades and subjects, from the second grade of the folk school to adult education levels. However, due to the limitations of this kind of research, wise judgements about what could and should be achieved could not be outlined on an aggregated level that matched the conditions of the education systems across countries. Thus, teachers' knowledge and experiences were considered a more appropriate source to formulate the curricula, which resulted in the two 'normal plans' in 1939, one for rural and another for urban schooling. Similar plans developed during the period from 1890 to the Normalplans of 1939 pawed the way for national curricula. However, these plans, such as the Normalplan curricula from 1922 and 1925, based on classical and realistic ideas, more or less continuing the pietistic reform trajectory. During the 1930s, empirical rationales evolved through nation-wide reforms, and contested the old rationales, now through a centralized reform, subsidised and funded by the state and evolving along with continuous economic growth, which throughout the century made Norway a rich nation (Østerud, 2005).

Modernization during the twentieth century implied a restructuration of industrial transformation that aimed at creating equal opportunities for various parts of the population across the country. An overall aim was to achieve equality between urban and rural areas, rich and poor, men and women, and the majority and minorities, which became a political issue in the 1970s. These optimistic trends, as well as the need for creating structured and planned development of welfare services, justified empirical research, scientific enquiry, and experimentation (Gundem, 1995). This empirical orientation was decisive for political action and critical curriculum theorising, along with ideas brought forward by Habermas' Technik und Wissenschaft als Ideologie [Technology and Science as Ideology] (Habermas, 1968). Slagstad (2004, p. 74) claims that the scientific vocabulary that developed during this period pursued a 'new way of putting knowledge into practice'. Scientific rationales were decisive in reorganising the compulsory school system in 1969. Parliament had already decided that compulsory education (grunnskole) would be extended from seven to nine years (The School Act of 13 June 1969). The Public School Act of 1959 had motivated the newly established National Council for Innovation in Education, which was responsible for different research projects during the 1950s and 1960s, to create a provisional plan called the 1960 Curriculum, which was used to guide a new nine-year compulsory school model (Forsøksrådet for Skoleverket, 1960).

Equality, in terms of accepting diversity or a multitude of cultural orientations, was approached in the curriculum reform efforts throughout the 1970s and 1980s, however, without constraining teaching to merely focus on competence and which resulted in two national curricula, one for the nine-year school in 1972 which was conditional type of curriculum that provided long lists of content in the school subjects and which outlined cross-disciplinary themes every teacher should take into account in cross-disciplinary projects or in each subject. Adapting education to individual interests referred meant to broaden the content in terms of variety of subjects and requirements rather than focussing on competence in terms of individual or aggregated outcomes. The new concept of suitably adapted education [tilpasset opplæring] turned into a practical approach during the 1970s. Teachers cared for individual self-determination by referencing the formal mandate for education and they secured quality through a pedagogy from below. Moreover, the reform did not advocate for equality in outcomes, as public enquiries and researchers would still argue for, but rather in terms of meeting interests of different kinds, corporative associations at the state level, and the students and their families within the context of schooling at the local level. Thus, the reforms followed what is typically considered a Norwegian model where a unitary State oriented its decisions towards the citizens' needs by combining a pluralistic and consensual government style, both by governance at the national and local level (Kickert & European Group of Public, 1997) and through pedagogy pursued by teachers in schools.

The emphasis on local development work was reflected in national and international development projects throughout the 1980s as well and in the national curricula. In 1985 the formal curriculum of 1974 was replaced first with a provisional curriculum (M85) and later with a final version (M87). In the 1980's, curriculum guidelines for the first time made centralised aims compulsory for all students between the ages of 7 and 16. It is therefore considered a major break with established traditions from the 1970's. However, the breakthrough ideas, which after all might be considered as resulting in a bright new curriculum, is the The Core Curriculum from 1993 (L93) and the Curriculum guidelines for compulsory school (L97), which were followed by the Knowledge promotion curriculum in 2006 (LK06) and a renewed national curriculum in 2020 (LK20). An interesting fact is that during the 1990s, empirical research on learning outcomes neither guided decision-makers responsible for curriculum reforms, nor inspired educational researchers to advocate new models for curriculum reforms. This problem turned into a headache for Gudmund Hernes, one of the authors of the public enquiry reports about result quality from the 1970s (NOU, 1976), when he became the Minister of Education.

The systemic reform this minister of education initiated, resulted in Curriculum 1993 (a general curriculum for primary, secondary and adult education that outlined the purpose of education based on four legal mandates) and Curriculum 1997, which covered both Curriculum 1993 and a set of principles and guidelines for organising education alongside the traditional school curricula for primary and lower secondary education. Among the source documents for this reform, I have found a note referring to an international survey conducted by the IEA and one reference to a national research report about the inefficiency of teaching with implications for students' learning outcomes. The Minister of Education, who formulated parts of the curriculum framework and served as the chair of several conferences and meetings within the reform processes, denied in my interview with him that there were empirical studies that exerted a valid influence on the reform work in this period. He claimed that no empirical evidence could at this point legitimise the policy decisions that had been made due to the extent and quality of the empirical research about the Norwegian school system at that time. Yet, at that time, there were signs of a national orientation towards literacy; in addition, some committee members who were involved in writing curriculum documents in English for example, and international experts with experience in conducting IEA studies, confirmed that there was a tendency to adopt conceptions of competence and literacy within the curriculum making process.

Policymakers working within the ministry considered the minister the inventor of this curriculum and the most influential actor in its formulation because he developed the general part of the curriculum after being in contact with three advisory groups. The ministry composed three committees tasked with providing ideas and drafts for the general and middle parts, consisting of the principles and guidelines. However, Hernes, the Minister of Education at the time, finally decided to write the first draft of the general curriculum and half of the middle part, which were finally integrated into a 'blue book' with hard binders in 1996. Both texts were however, subjected to public hearings and revisions as well as comments from officers within the Ministry of Education.

The first text, published in 1993, was authorised by the parliament to become the general part of the curriculum for primary, secondary, and adult education in Norway. Notably, this part of the curriculum was translated into languages other than Norwegian for the first time, and interviews with several officers within the Ministry of Education, are helpful in understanding why it was translated and in which languages. From interviews with the minister and his colleagues, it seems clear that the core ambition was to write a curriculum that teachers and all individuals involved in the Norwegian education system could be proud of using. The minister preferred a text that was stimulating to read, not at least for parents, and therefore aimed at writing a curriculum, characterised by fluency, suppleness, and rhythm. In the general part, the Minister of Education also aimed to formulate a text that integrated theories about education and its relation to society. Thus, the curriculum was designed as a social contract between the state authorities, the local school, and the surrounding communities, where the school collaborated with organisations, and the pupils participated in their leisure time and with the families in particular. This idea continued old reform traditions, in which parents were considered primarily responsible for raising their children, the Minister confirms in the interview. It developed core ideas that was in particular important for the national curriculum from 1939.

Formally, the main themes found in the National School Act provided the bases for the structures of the curriculum and its sections: 'The Spiritual Human Being', 'The Creative Human Being', 'The Working Human Being', 'The Liberally Educated Human Being', 'The Social Human Being', 'The Environmentally Aware Human Being', and 'The Complete Human Being' (L93). These categories were approved by a group of ministry officers but were more or less a result of how the Minister of Education decided to formulate the curriculum. The contents refer to a broad spectrum of questions and the challenges and tasks faced by teachers and students today. There is an emphasis on classical content to be taught in schools and important knowledge to learn for life. In addition, there are photographs of arts and crafts, as well as technological inventions illustrating classical and realistic perspectives on culture and knowledge. However, both the contents and the visual documentation make this curriculum a different type of text compared to the previous curricula in both the national and international contexts. The new rationales that brought together systems of reasoning draw on various knowledge sources, including American reform ideas. According to some informants, the minister was inspired by American sociological research, which he learned about during his visits and scholarships as a professor in one of the prestigious universities in the United States. A rationale that grew out of this interest consisted of pedagogical challenges and solutions that take young students as a whole, childhood, and youth cohorts into consideration when formulating the curriculum. From this sociology of research viewpoint, traditional schooling was criticised, and as one of our informants claimed, 'we need[ed] to find other approaches, pedagogically' (R1).

This critique may have stimulated the focus on a common set of values and norms that everyone should endorse and incorporate into educational practices. The minister also referred to the American scholar Hirsch (1983), who argued for a return of cultural literacy to bring about more heterogeneity within the global cultures. Few experts within the Norwegian curriculum context were familiar with this approach that built on pure scientific rationales rather than a pragmatic approach. Thus, Hernes introduced scientific reform ideas that to some extent differed from the Nordic curriculum tradition by emphasising that teachers are not merely going to teach what is written in the curriculum or the textbooks and adapt this to the individual student, but should even more concentrate on what the students need to learn and master for the sake of their own life and society. Thus, the development of literacy became a major theme in the first part of this reform project. A few public enquiries also emphasised the importance of competence-based reform, and by drawing on one such enquiry, competence-based objectives were included in the curricula for upper secondary education (Reform 94). Hernes also included the word competence in one paragraph in the general curriculum (L93).

However, after completing the work on the curriculum for upper secondary education, the minister rejected the use of competence as the overall approach and purpose of general education. This decision indicates that, for example, IEA studies, which introduced the concept of scientific literacy during the 1980s in Norway, were not really a core inspiration for the Minister of Education. Interestingly, the general part was highly inspired by the Lutheran tradition despite the recognition of scientific rationales, as illustrated by the education clause presented in the first part of the curriculum:

> Primary and lower secondary education shall, with the understanding of and in cooperation with the home, assist in providing students with a Christian and ethical upbringing, develop their mental and physical abilities, and give them a broad general education so that they can become useful and independent persons in their private lives and in society. (The Royal Ministry of Education Research and Church Affairs, 1993)

The curriculum text focuses on, among various themes, the role of Christian and human values, but national and global concerns are also considered:

> Christian and humanistic values both demand and foster tolerance, providing room for other cultures and customs. They buttress the rule of law and the democratic state as the framework

for equal political participation and debate. They emphasise charity, brotherhood and hope, promote progress through criticism, reason and research; and they recognise that humans themselves are a part of nature by their bodies, their needs and their senses. (The Royal Ministry of Education Research and Church Affairs, 1993)

Narratives and images reflecting the government's interest in presenting the core curriculum as both traditional and modernised brought national images into the global discourse by focusing on particular and, one may claim, national values, but the theories and epistemologies attached to these narratives created another frame that also made sense in other cultural settings. This part of the historical trajectory is amazing compared to common sense expectations. Several informants remembered how the Minister of Education presented the general part of the curriculum in other countries, such as Russia, where the ministry distributed thousands of copies of the curriculum translated into Russian. One informant stated that Russian bookshops asked for translations, and the minister regarded this event as creating an opportunity to put the national Norwegian curriculum on the world map. Interviews with curriculum makers close to the minister confirmed that this national curriculum achieved popularity internationally. The Curriculum was translated into English, French and Chinese. One even confirmed that the text was used directly, not only as an information source, but as a blueprint in another European country, where a new state-based curriculum was underway. As one informant claims: "They felt that this document was equally relevant for them as it was for us, and it doesn't matter because it is a good text". (R2)

Between 1999 and 2003, experts from Norway participated in projects run by the OECD, which became a decisive global actor in defining and conceptualising cross-curricula competencies and skills for being used in national policy projects (Sivesind, 2019). A new curriculum in 2006 manifested this policy through a core focus on competencies. However, this curriculum did not replace the new overall curriculum guideline. The general part published in 1993 was replaced by a new visionary document in 2017 and adopted in 2020. This document was not subject for any discussions within the parliament, but draw on public enquiries and white papers that set the agenda for the 2020 reform. According to information I obtained from interviewing officers within the Ministry of Education in 2019, the new overall curriculum was developed through collaboration with academic researchers and representatives from various associations, such as the teachers' union within the country. Interestingly, the structure of this new curriculum entirely copied the structure of the education clause formally authorised in 2008. According to the appointed leader of the public enquiry team that prepared this law, this clause created openness towards society by emphasising human rights and societal values. The wording and structuring of the new curriculum show that the school's mandate is both far and deep as it concerns identity development and learning in several fields. Values, learning, and knowledge development are both essential aspects and cultural heritages, which imply nationalisation of reform processes.

Reform Trajectories Within the Twenty-First Century

The new national curriculum in Norway, that are implemented in Norwegian schools from the school year 2020–21, aims to improve learning by actively involving teachers, schools, and the society in the training and upraising of young students (The Royal Ministry of Education and Research, 2017, p. 2). On this backdrop, representatives of the nation state (e.g. ministers, scientists, or officers) both implement global policies by recognizing individual rights and human values and by advocating for the re-contextualisation of global reform initiatives within the context of a national school system. Does this reform project contest the legacy of the contract-school model?

This study confirms what Zhao and Tröhler claim in the introduction chapter: 'Education and curriculum are never a neutral knowledge (re)production system but always a contested site where multi-layered power relations are (re)produced and effectuated through the play-with and play-against of varying mechanisms in history' (Chapter "Euro-Asia Encounters on 21st-Century Competency-Based Curriculum Reforms: A Historical and Cultural (Re)Turn"). Thus, there is no guarantee that the contract-school model will develop along the same lines as in earlier centuries. In the present chapter, I explored state governance in the field of education and reform and the ideas and legacies underpinning the school plans and national curricula in Norway since the early eighteenth century. In particular, I focused on the role of the state and used examples to illustrate how curriculum developed as a reform project, both as a receptor of international ideas throughout the three centuries and even as a provider of international ideas in the 1990s.

During all the periods covered by this chapter, there are signs of a cultural-educational impact of historical legacies. The Lutheran contract-school model evolved in both Central and Northern Europe during the nineteenth century and is by itself not national in its origin. The model developed through history and made curriculum reforms more or less centralised and open to realistic world views and enlightening rationales. As I have described, in Norway, the pietistic trajectory developed into a model that was legitimised and organised through a collaboration between representatives from the state and local school boards with formal responsibility for education in the districts. Moreover, civil servants and intellectuals, educated at Universities in Denmark and Germany contributed significantly, and proactively put their own national fingerprints on the school reforms while being involved in reform-making processes. Philanthropic ideas were decisive for revising the catechetic method during the first decades of the nineteenth century.

A pietistic reform trajectory that influenced curriculum reforms in Norway, were combined with both philanthropic and empirical rationales during the nineteenth and twentieth centuries, however, without changing the contract school model that governed education by law and simultaneously through the semantic of schooling. This semantic emphasised principles for teaching and grading, and viewed formal education from an inside-out perspective, but without necessarily situating the school content in a national context restrained by a particular culture (Klafki, 2000, p. 89).

Representing the outside world through texts and also focusing on practical and moral purposes, is a typical trait of philanthropic reform known within Scandinavian countries (Sivesind, 2008). Ideas that renewed pietistic reforms originated in this case through text book production that had substantial impact on reading literacy within the population.

Therefore, one cannot think of curriculum reform initiatives in Norway as beginning as a top-down effort in terms of universal reforms, or even serving as a form of centralized implementation of national reform during the nineteenth and twentieth century. Rather, one should consider curriculum-making a public project and an innovative practice that created space for both political and practical developments. I have characterised this institutional arrangement as a top-bottom-up model (Sivesind, 2008), and which contrasts reform work in many other countries, often portrayed as either top-down or bottom-up (Smith & O'Day, 1990).

After the parliamentary system was introduced in Norway in the 1880s, political decisions became involved in regulating schooling for children in urban areas. Political control was accomplished by law, which however, restricted the positive use of political power through formal decrees and allocation of money and thereby allowed for local control and professionalization of teachers. The parliament could discuss and approve decisions in some areas of curriculum reform, but the decision-making processes on how to formulate curriculum guidelines were handed over to committees. Nearly all reforms during the twentieth century based on practical reasoning and knowledge within subject matter areas. Although researchers prioritised psychometric research during the 1950s and 1960s, the curricula were primarily formulated by professionals and authorized by the state and for some parts, the parliament [Stortinget].

During the 1970s, critical sociology created a new era in curriculum theorising, and intellectuals promoted universal values as crucial in restructuring the Protestant contract-school model. Societal change and critical-rational reasoning made society highly secularised, a process that evolved from the mid-nineteenth century in Denmark and Norway (Markussen, 1990). Currently, empirical evidence justifies competence and skills as a scientific invention. An empiricist view on the twenty-first century skills contests the contract-school model that was, despite Lutheran ideas of making the reformation universal, a highly contextualized project from the beginning. Today, content-based curricula are replaced by a futuristic oriented pedagogy that focuses on generic skills. The contract-school model is thereby challenged. However, Tröhler (2017) argues that declining legacies provide an opportunity to regard the historiography of reform as an expression of change that is configured differently across time and space, both institutionally and intellectually. For this reason, historical interpretation of national trajectories of education systems and the way we reflect on education are important, as they both stimulate to rethink traditions and enlighten the intellectual debate about curriculum and competence within the twenty-first century.

Notes

1. His original name was Jean Baptiste Bernadotte.

2. The monitorial method originated at the Military Male Orphan Asylum, Egmore, near Madras, India, where Andrew Bell (1753–1832) served as an army chaplain. The method was described in a brief article published in 1797. At first, this system did not gain any public support. Joseph Lancaster (1778–1838), a Quaker living in London, found the method to be useful in his education of poor children in the slum quarter, and developed a similar method, which gained success in mass-schooling institutions. This method was introduced in the new curriculum for national schooling in Norway in 1934, but without any success since schooling in Norway was mainly organized within districts and with only a few students at a time.
3. Bugge visited Bayern, Sachsen, and Württemberg.
4. Contradictions were also visible in disputes about how to establish Folk high schools in Norway, which, after discussions in the parliament, resulted in a system equal to the Prussian model (Korsgaard, 2003). This is the reason why the Folk high school lost its status and became an optional or alternative school in Norway, comparable to a state-owned public education system.

References

Bakken, J. (1971). *Synet på verdien av lærestoffet kontra arbeidsmåten i norsk folkeskole i vårt århundre* [The view and value of the teaching material versus the working method in Norwegian primary and lower secondary schools in our century]. University of Oslo.

Brubacher, J. S. (1966). *A history of the problems of education*. McGraw-Hill Book Company.

Bugge, F. M. (1839). *Det offentlige skolevæsens forfatning i adskillige tydske stater, tilligemed ideer til en reorganisation af det offentlige skolevæsen i Kongeriget Norge: En indberetning, afgiven til den Kgl. Norske Regjerings Departement for Kirke- og Undervisningsvæsenet, ifølge Kgl. Naadigst Resolution af 23de Juni 1836* [The constitution of public schools in several German states, along with ideas for the reorganization of public schools in the Kingdom of Norway: A report submitted to the Royal Norwegian Government, Department of Church and Education, according to Kgl. most gracious Resolution of 23rd June 1836]. Christiania, Norway: Chr. Grøndahl.

Christensen, T. (2003). Narratives of Norwegian governance: Elaborating the strong state tradition. *Public Administration, 81*(1), 163–190.

Christensen, T. (2005). The Norwegian state transformed? *West European Politics, 28*(4), 721–739.

Clausen, J. (1896). *Frederik Christian, hertug af Augustenborg (1765–1814): En monografisk skildring* [Frederik Christian, Duke of Augustenborg (1765–1814): A monographic depiction]. Det Schubotheske Forlag.

Comenius, J. A. (1658). *Orbis sensualium pictus*. Retrieved from Bibliotecha Latina http://www.grexlat.com/biblio/comenius/index.html

Dale, E. L. (1999). *De strategiske pedagoger* [The strategic educators]. Ad Notam Gyldendal.

Dale, E. L. (2005). *Kunnskapsregimer i pedagogikk og utdanningsvitenskap* [Knowledge regimes in pedagogy and educational science]. Abstrakt Forlag.

Decree. (1741). *Placat og nærmere Anordning angaaende Skolerne paa landet i Norge: Christiansborg Slot udi Kiøbenhavn den 5te Maji 1741* [Poster and further arrangement regarding the schools in the countryside in Norway: Christiansborg Castle in Copenhagen on the 5th of May 1741]. Retrieved from http://fagsider.nla.no/kirkehistorie/lover/1741_placat.htm

Elster, J. (1988). Introduction. In J. Elster, & R. Slagstad (Eds.), *Constitutionalism and democracy* (pp. 1–17). Cambridge University Press.
Engelsen, B. U. (2003). *Ideer som formet vår skole? Læreplanen som idébærer—Et historisk perspektiv* [Ideas that shaped our school? The curriculum as a bearer of ideas—A historical perspective]. Gyldendal-Akademisk.
Forsøksrådet for Skoleverket. (1960). *Læreplan for forsøk med 9-årig skole. Forsøk og reform i skolen nr 5.* [Curriculum for experiments with 9-year school and experiments and reform in school no. 5]. I Kommisjon hos Aschehoug.
Gawthrop, R. L. (1993). *Pietism and the making of eighteenth century Prussia.* Cambridge University Press.
Grøgaard, H. J. (1815). ABC. *De umistelige bøger. Sogneprest til Vestremoland. Christiansand* [The inalienable books. Parish priest to Vestremoland. Christiansand]. H. Th. Bachruds Enke. Retrieved from http://www-bib.hive.no/tekster/umistelige/17-1815/01.html
Grøgaard, H. J. (1821). *Læsebog for børn, en forberedelse til religionsunderviisningen, især i Norges omgangsskoledistrikter. Tredie rettede og forøgede udgave. Sogneprcest til Nykirken i Bergen. Trykt paa forfatterens forlag hos Chr. Dahl, R. S.* [Reading book for children, a preparation for religious education, especially in Norway's community school districts. Third corrected and augmented Edition. Parish priest for Nykirken in Bergen. Printed at Forfatterens Forlag hos Chr. Dahl, R. S.). Retrieved from https://www.nb.no/items/88a30087b7f72b12673d6 3c02210eae0?page=123&searchText=L%C3%A6sebog%20for%20B%C3%B8rn,%20en%20F orberedelse%20til%20Religionsunderviisningen,%20is%C3%A6r%20i%20Norges%20Omga ngsskoledistrikter
Gundem, B. B. (1993a). *Mot en ny skolevirkelighet? Læreplanen i et sentraliserings- og desentraliseringspersektiv* [Towards a new school reality? The curriculum in a centralization and decentralization perspective]. Ad Notam Gyldendal.
Gundem, B. B. (1993b). Rise, development and changing conceptions of curriculum administration and curriculum guidelines in Norway: The national-local dilemma. *Journal of Curriculum Studies, 25*(3), 251–266.
Gundem, B. B. (1995). The role of didactics in curriculum in Scandinavia. *Journal of Curriculum and Supervision, 10*(4), 302–316.
Habermas, J. (1968). *Technik und Wissenschaft als Ideologie* [Technology and Science as Ideology]. Suhrkamp.
Harbo, T. (1969). *Teori og praksis i den pedagogiske utdannelse. Studier i norsk pedagogikk 1818–1922* [Theory and practice in pedagogical education. Studies in Norwegian pedagogy 1818–1922]. Universitetsforlaget.
Helsvig, K. (2005). *Pedagogikkens grenser: Kampen om norsk pedagogikk ved Pedagogisk forskningsinstitutt 1938–1980* [The boundaries of pedagogy: The struggle for Norwegian pedagogy at the Pedagogical Research Institute 1938–1980]. Abstrakt forl.
Hermansen, K. (2003). *Kirken, kongen og enevælden—En undersøgelse af det danske bispeembede 1660–1746* [The church, the king and the autocracy—A study of the Danish episcopate 1660–1746]. Doctoral thesis, University of Southern Denmark, Odense, Denmark.
Hirsch, E. (1983). Cultural literacy. *The American Scholar, 52*(2), 159–169. Retrieved December 18, 2020, from http://www.jstor.org/stable/41211231
Hopmann, S. T. (1990). Case studies in curriculum administration history. In H. Haft, & S. Hopmann (Eds.), *Case studies in curriculum administration history* (pp. 23–31). The Falmer Press.
Hopmann, S. T. (2000). *Didaktikkens didaktikk* [Didactic didactics]. Unpublished manuscript. Norwegian University of Science and Technology.
Høverstad, T. (1918). *Norsk skulesoga. Det store interregnum 1739–1827* [Norsk skulesoga. The great interregnum 1739–1827]. Kristiania.
Instruction. (1739). *Instruction for Degne, Klokkere og Skoleholdere paa Landet i Norge: Friderichsberg den 23. januar. Anno 1739.* [Instruction]. Retrieved from http://www.fagsider.no/kir kehistorie/lover/indexlover.htm

Jensen, O. J. (2007a). *Katekismeforklaringer i Norge* [Catechism explanations in Norway]. Retrieved from http://fagsider.nla.no/kirkehistorie/tabell/katekismeforklaring.htm

Jensen, O. J. (2007b). *Lov, angaaende Almue-Skolevæsenet paa Landet* [Law concerning the peasant school system in the country] Stockholm Slot den 14 July 1827. Retrieved from http://fagsider.nla.no/kirkehistorie/lover/1827_skole.htm

Johnsen, B. H. (2002). Traditions and ideas underlying 'the school for all' or 'the inclusive school'. In K. Nes, T. O. Engen, & M. Strømstad (Eds.), *Unitary school—Inclusive school. A conference report*. Høgskolen i Hedmark. Rapport nr. 9: Elverum.

Johnsen, B. E. (2017). «Fornøielig uden Skjenden, Hug og Slag» Abc-og lesebokforfatteren Hans Jacob Grøgaard–en pioner i sin tid. [*«Enjoyable without Violation, Warning and Percussion» Abc and reading book author Hans Jacob Grøgaard—a pioneer in his time*] *Heimen*, 54(02), 145–165.

Kickert, W. J. M., & European Group of Public. (1997). *Public management and administrative reform in Western Europe*. Edward Elgar.

Klafki, W. (2000). The significance of classical theories of bildung for a contemporary concept of allgemeinbildung. In I. Westbury, S. Hopmann, & K. Riquarts (Eds.), *Teaching as a reflective practice. The German didaktik tradition* (pp. 85–107). Lawrence Erlbaum Associates, Publishers.

Knutzen, K. O. (1836). *Nyeste Billed-ABC for den Norske ungdom (papirutgave)* [Latest Picture ABC for the Norwegian youth (paper edition)]. Retrieved from http://www-bib.hive.no/tekster/umistelige/20/20-01.htm

Koch, C. H. (2003). *Dansk Oplysningsfilosofi: 1700–1800* [Danish Enlightenment Philosophy: 1700–1800]. Gyldendal.

Korsgaard, O. (2003). Den store krigsdans om kirke og folk [The great war dance about church and people]. In L. Løvlie, R. Slagstad, & O. Korsgaard (Eds.), *Dannelsens forvandlinger* [The transformations of formation] (pp. 53–71). Pax.

Korsgaard, O., & Wiborg, S. (2006). Grundtvig—The key to Danish education? *Scandinavian Journal of Educational Research, July 50*(3), 361–382.

Lauglo, J. (1982). Rural primary school teachers as potential community leaders? Contrasting historical cases in Western countires. *Comparative Education, 18*(3), 233–255.

Lov. (1827). Lov angående Almue-Skolevæsenet paa Landet : Stockholms Slot den 14de Juli 1827. Retrieved from http://fagsider.nla.no/kirkehistorie/lover/1827_skole.htm#pp14

Lov. (1860). Lov om Skolevæsenet paa Landet: Stockholms Slot den 16de Mai 1860. Christiania. Retrieved from Norsk lærerakademi. Kirkiehistorisk arkiv http://fagsider.nla.no/kirkehistorie/lover/1860_skole.htm#d1. Retrieved 26.06.07 Norsk lærerakademi. Kirkiehistorisk arkiv http://fagsider.nla.no/kirkehistorie/lover/1860_skole.htm#d1

Lov. (1889). *Lov om Folkeskolen paa Landet.: Stockholms Slot den 26de Juni 1889. Kristiania. P.T. Mallings Boghandels Forlag*. Retrieved from Høyskolen i Vestfold http://www-bib.hive.no/tekster/skolehistorie/lover/1889/side04.html. Retrieved 12.03,08 Høyskolen i Vestfold http://www-bib.hive.no/tekster/skolehistorie/lover/1889/side04.html

Luther, M. (1529/2007). *The small catechism*. Retrieved from http://www.bookofconcord.org/smallcatechism.html

Lønnå, E. (2002). *Helga Eng. Psykolog og pedagog i barnets århundre* [Helga Eng. Psychologist and educator in the child's century]. Fagbokforlaget.

Markussen, I. (1990). Curriculum and literacy: The 18th century Danish case. In G. Genovesi, B. B. Gundem, M. Heinemann, J. Herbst, T. Harbo, & S. Tønnes (Eds.), *History of elementary school teaching* (pp. 27–36). Edition Bildung und Wissenschaft.

Myhre, R. (1976). *Pedagogisk idéhistorie fra oldtiden til 1850* [Pedagogical history of ideas from antiquity to 1850] (3rd ed.). Fabritius.

NOU (1976). *Utdanning og ulikhet* [Education and inequality]. Official Norwegian Report, Oslo.

Ordinance. (1736). *Kong Christian den Siettes II. Forordning. Angaaende den tilvoxende ungdoms confirmation og bekreftælse udi deres daabes naade* [King Christian the Siettes II. Ordinance concerning the confirmation and confirmation of the growing youth in the grace of their baptism]. Retrieved from http://fagsider.nla.no/kirkehistorie/lover/1739_skole.htm#pp0

Ordinance. (1739). *Forordning, om skolerne paa landet i Norge, og hvad klokkerne og skoleholderne derfor maa nyde* [Ordinance on the schools in the country in Norway, and what the bells and the schoolmasters must therefore enjoy]. Retrieved from http://fagsider.nla.no/kirkehistorie/lover/ 1739_skole.htm#pp0

Østerud, Ø. (2005). Introduction: The peculiarities of Norway. *West European Politics, 28*(4), 705–720.

Payne, J. (1998). *Halle pietism: Religious compromise and Prussian social transformation.* Retrieved from http://www.geocities.com/Athens/Aegean/7023/pietism.html

Plan. (1834). *Plan, hvorefter underviisningen og disciplinen i almueskolerne paa landet ... skal indrettes, approberet ved høieste resoliution af 22 de Juni 1834* [Plan, according to which the teaching and discipline of the peasant schools in the country ... must be arranged, approved by the highest resolution of 22 June 1834].

Pontoppidan, E. (1737/1987). *Sannhet til gudfryktighet: forklaring over Dr. M. Luthers lille katekisme* [Truth to Godliness: Explanation of Dr. M. Luther's little catechism]. Det Evangeliske-Lutherske Kirkesamfunn.

Popkewitz, T. S. (2013). Styles of reason: historicism, historicizing, and the history of education. In T. S. Popkewitz (Ed.), *Rethinking the history of education. Transnational perspectives on its questions, methods, and knowledge* (pp. 1–26). Pagrave Macmillan.

Rasmussen, T. (2004). Erik Pontoppidan: Opplyst pietisme [Erik Pontoppidan: Enlightened pietism]. In H. Thuenog, & S. Vaage (Eds.) *Pedagogiske profiler. Norsk utdanningstenkning fra Holberg til Hernes* [Educational profiles. Norwegian educational thinking from Holberg to Hernes] (pp. 33–43). Abstrakt forl.

Reid, W. A. (1997). Principle and pragmatism in English curriculum making 1868–1918. *Journal of Curriculum Studies, 29*(6), 667–682.

Ribsskog, B., & Aall, A. (1936). *Undervisningsplanene i folkeskolen: Et pedagogisk-psykologisk forarbeide til nye planer for orienteringsfagene* [The curricula in primary and lower secondary school: A pedagogical-psychological preparation for new plans for the orientation subjects]. Gyldendal.

Riksarkivet. (2007c). *Kommisjonen Og Direksjonen for Universitetet og de Lærde Skoler* [The Commission and the Executive Board of the University and the Scholarly Schools]. Retrieved from http://www.arkivverket.no/arkivverket/publikasjoner/nett/handbok-ra/sentralinst/kommisjon.html

Roos, M. (2019). *Hartvig Nissen og NFS Grundtvig. Grundtvigianske aspekter i norsk skoletenkning rundt midten av 1800-tallet. Polemikken mellom Hartvig Nissen og Frederik Bugge i Morgenbladet 1845* [Hartvig Nissen and NFS Grundtvig. Grundtvigian aspects in Norwegian school thinking around the middle of the 19th century. The controversy between Hartvig Nissen and Frederik Bugge in Morgenbladet 1845].

Rust, V. D. (1989). *The democratic tradition and the evolution of schooling in Norway.* Greenwood Press.

Sirevåg, T. (1986). *Niels Threschow: Skolemann med reformprogram - det frie Norges første kirkestatsråd. Ved aktstykker opplyst* [Niels Threschow: Schoolboy with reform program—The free Norway's first church council. In case of documents stated]. Selskapet for norsk skolehistorie.

Sivesind, K. (2008). *Reformulating Reform. Curriculum history revisited.* Avhandling for Dr. Phil graden: Det utdanningsvitenskapelige fakultet. University of Oslo.

Sivesind, K. (2019). Nordic reference societies in school reforms in Norway: An examination of Finland and the use of international large-scale assessments. In F. Waldow, & G. Steiner-Khamsi (Eds.), *Understanding PISA's attractiveness. Critical analyses in comparative policy studies.* Bloomsbury Academic.

Skjelbred, D. (2000). *Norske ABC-bøker 1777–1997. Rapport Høgskolen i Vestfold: 2: Tønsberg* [Norwegian ABC books 1777–1997. Report Vestfold University College: 2: Tønsberg].

Slagstad, R. (2001). *De nasjonale strateger* [The national strategists]. Pax.

Slagstad, R. (2004). Shifting knowledge regimes: The metamorphoses of Norwegian reformism. *Thesis Eleven, May*(77), 65–83.

Smith, M. S., & O'Day, J. (1990). Systemic school reform. In S. H. Fuhrman & B. Malen (Eds.), *The politics of curriculum and testing. Yearbook of the politics of education association* (pp. 233–267). Falmer Press.

Telhaug, A. O., & Mediås, O. A. (2003). *Grunnskolen som nasjonsbygger. Fra statpietisme til nyliberalisme* [Primary school as a nation builder. From state pietism to neoliberalism]. Abstrakt Forlag as.

The Law-committee. (1814–1830). *The draft to the Law-committee made by the Minister Niels Treschow*. Riksarkivet, pk 13. Reprinted in Sirevåg (1986) (pp. 230–240).

The Ministry of Education and Research. (2017). *Core curriculum—values and principles for primary and secondary education*. Retrieved 09.06.21, from https://www.regjeringen.no/en/dok umenter/verdier-og-prinsipper-for-grunnopplaringen---overordnet-del-av-lareplanverket/id2570 003/

The oldest Norwegian ABC-books. (2007). *ABC-books*. Retrieved from http://www-bib.hive.no/ tekster/hveskrift/rapport/2000-02/index.html

The Royal Ministry of Education Research and Church Affairs. (1993). *Core curriculum for primary, secondary and adult education*. Oslo.

Thomas, R. (2009). The origins of western literacy. In D. R. Olson, & N. Torrance (Eds.), *The Cambridge handbook of literacy* (pp. 346–361). Cambridge.

Thuen, H. (2004). Hartvig Nissen: 'Den politiske pædagogik' [Hartvig Nissen: 'The political pedagogy']. In H. Thuen, & S. Vaage (Eds.), *Pedagogiske profiler. Norsk utdanningstenkning fra Holberg til Hernes* [Educational profiles. Norwegian educational thinking from Holberg to Hernes] (pp. 65–80). Abstrakt forlag.

Tröhler, D. (2014). The construction of society and conceptions of education. In T. S. Popkewitz (Ed.), *The 'reason' of schooling. Historisizing curriculum studies, pedagogy and teacher education* (pp. 21–39). Routledge.

Tröhler, D. (2017). Tracking the educationalization of the world: Prospects for an emancipated history of education. *Pedagogika, 67*(4).

Tveit, K. (1991). *Allmugeskolen på austlandsbygdene 1730–1830* [Schooling for the rural population in the eastern parishes]. Rådet for samfunnsvitenskapelig forskning NAVF. Universitetsforlaget.

Tveit, K. (2004). Skolen i Nord-Noreg på 1700-tallet. In S. Skolen (Ed.), *Årbok for norsk utdanningshistorie* [The yearbook for Norwegian education history] (pp. 35–63). Notodden.

Wang, F., Tsai, Y., & Wang, W. S. (2009). Chinese literacy. In D. R. Olson, & N. Torrance (Eds.), *The Cambridge handbook of literacy* (pp. 386–417). Cambridge.

Weber, M. (1930/2001). *The Protestant ethic and the spirit of capitalism*. Routledge.

Werler, T. (2004). *Nation, gemeinschaft, bildung: Die evolution des modernen Skandinavischen wohlfahrtsstaates und das schulsystem* [Nation, community, education: The evolution of the modern Scandinavian welfare state and the school system]. Schneider Verlag Hohengehren.

Dr. Philos. Kirsten Sivesind is Associate Professor at the Department of Education at the University of Oslo, where she received her Ph.D. in 2008. Beyond her academic discipline of curriculum theory, her research focuses on comparative policy analysis and the history of knowledge and education. Currently, she is the Principle Investigator for the five-country study "Policy Knowledge and Lesson Drawing in Nordic School Reform in an Era of International Comparison," funded by the National Research Council in Norway. During the past several years, she has served as an associate editor for the Journal of Curriculum Studies and an executive editor for the European Educational Research Journal.

Globalization and Localization in the Shaping of the Danish Public Education System: Recontextualization Processes in Four Historical Educational Reforms

Christian Ydesen

Introduction

The contemporary role of international organizations in shaping education globally has been widely explored by researchers from various fields (e.g. Auld et al., 2019; Grek, 2020; Kulnazarova & Ydesen, 2018; Mahon & McBride, 2009; Martens & Jakobi, 2010; Wiseman & Taylor, 2017). A key concern is understanding the gearing between globalization and localization processes, that is, the interactions, influences, and struggles between agendas, agents, technologies, and institutions in complex spaces (Mundy et al., 2016; Tröhler & Lenz, 2015).

This chapter contributes to this line of research by offering a historical analysis of which cultural-hegemonic values travel to Denmark and how they are implemented in the cultural ideals of the Danish public education system. A historical approach allows for contextual identification of the trajectories and path dependencies inherent in diachronic developments and sheds light on the various mechanisms in the shaping of education systems. Additionally, historical analysis offers a platform for critical reflection and awareness of lost alternatives of the past and thus holds the potential to emancipate the present through problematization of the contemporary situation.

Denmark joined the OECD as a founding member in 1961 and even delivered the organization's first secretary-general, the economist and Liberal-Conservative politician Thorkil Kristensen (1899–1989), in office between 1961 and 1969. Since then, Denmark has been working closely with the OECD in the field of education. However, the role and significance of OECD-driven and OECD-adopted discourses in Danish education reforms have never been fully explored historically.[1] This chapter aims to remedy this omission by analysing the discursive contexts of the preparatory work of the four major educational reforms of 1975, 1993, 2006, and 2014.

C. Ydesen (✉)
Department of Culture and Learning, Aalborg University, Aalborg, Denmark
e-mail: cy@learning.aau.dk

© The Author(s), under exclusive license to Springer Nature Singapore Pte Ltd. 2021
W. Zhao and D. Tröhler (eds.), *Euro-Asian Encounters on 21st-Century Competency-Based Curriculum Reforms*,
https://doi.org/10.1007/978-981-16-3009-5_5

These reforms have all significantly contributed to the development of the Danish education system and must be understood against the backdrop of important societal currents and trends, such as the rise of the universal welfare state, the oil crises, neoliberal reforms, and the emergence of the competitive state (De Coninck-Smith et al., 2013). However, at the same time, the Danish educational authorities actively participated in funding and shaping OECD programmes, and Danish experts and representatives served in OECD bodies, working in education, testifying to the reciprocity of OECD–Denmark relations.[2]

Methodology, Theory and Chapter Structure

To provide the knowledge required to engage with the research focus, the chapter is primarily based on archival sources of the Danish National Archives and the OECD Archives in Paris. But to a minor extent, the chapter also draws on anonymized interviews with high-level officials and politicians in the Danish Ministry of Education. The material consists of all hearing responses involved in the four reforms. This material allows for the characterization of the political discursive landscape surrounding the four reforms. The chapter approaches the discursive landscape using a Fairclough inspired Critical Discourse Analysis (CDA) approach. As described by Anderson and Holloway (2018),

> CDA in education policy research is (…) concerned with how power and related relations (e.g. ideologies) in the real world are reflected, reproduced, or resisted in micro-textual sites such as policy documents, often focusing on issues of control (p. 5).

CDA thus becomes a lens for constructing and problematizing the discursive landscapes in keeping with the aforementioned emancipatory aspect of historical research. CDA offers a toolbox for deciphering the normativity of policy formulations and policy enactments in general and lay bare the cultural ideals of the Danish public education system in particular.

Concretely, it means that the hearing responses are understood as discourses on the role and purpose of education in society as reflected in the agendas and viewpoints promoted in the texts. In other words, the policy formulations of the hearing responses are seen as reflections of the underlying cultural, ideological, and value-based meaning making of stakeholders attempting to discursively impose concepts, relations, categories, and classifications upon the world and legitimize them. To maintain this focus, the analysis is delimited to responses addressing the content of education, and omits responses concerning organizational and administrative issues.

The second analytical operation consists in juxtaposing the Danish political discourses and the discourses of the relevant OECD educational agendas allowing the exploration of recontextualization and reassembly processes. The focus of this part of the analysis is to determine which cultural-hegemonic values travelled to Denmark. This operation will draw on the links and connections between the Danish educational field, the OECD Education Committee, and the OECD Centre for Educational Research and Innovation (CERI). This step of the analysis is based on the archival correspondence between the Danish Ministry of Education and the OECD, as evident in both archives.[3] The use of both archives for this purpose allows for a deeper inquiry, because the material also contains the internal correspondence at both ends and, thus, a glimpse into the reception history. However, the connection underpinning the recontextualization and reassembly processes cannot be made only by juxtaposition. Instead, the connections are qualified using contextual and chronological analysis, as well as the source criticism procedures of historical research (Ifversen, 2003).

The chapter starts with a brief history of OECD discourses on education, to establish an interpretative framework. Chronological analyses of the four reforms. The concluding discussion will present the trajectories and path dependencies identified in terms of cultural-hegemonic values and the contextual shaping of the Danish public education system.

A Brief History of OECD Discourses in Education from the 1970s to 2010s

The OECD underwent significant organizational changes in 1970, allowing it to focus more on the interrelated aspects of economic policy (Spring, 2015). In the field of education, the Committee for Scientific and Technical Personnel (CSTP), founded in 1958 under the Organisation for European Economic Co-operation, became the Education Committee. The Education Committee worked with education policy and was populated by officials from member countries, while CERI, which was financed by the Ford Foundation and Royal Dutch Shell between 1968 and 1971, was an autonomous and academic body dedicated to innovation in education (Vejleskov, 1979).

From a discursive perspective, the connection between CERI and the Ford foundation is relevant because the foundation was guided by a particular cultural thesis about ordering society based on 'a scientific-rationalistic approach towards education based on the paradigms of economic growth, productivity and technological advancement' (Elfert & Ydesen, 2020, p. 77; see also Berman, 1983). This cultural dimension came to shape the OECD approach to education which was built on systemic planning and output governance (Bürgi, 2016).[4]

Within the OECD, education took a role of functioning as a bridge between economic and social concerns (Bürgi, 2015; Morgan, 2009). For instance, OECD programmes in education paid close attention to the labour market, the issues of equal access and recurrent education, and the publication of country reports (Papadopoulos, 1994). In the 1960s and much of the 1970s, the centre of gravity for the OECD's discourse on education was the state, i.e. how states could optimise manpower investments to improve economic growth and how mathematical models could be developed to forecast these needs (Grek & Ydesen, 2021). In line with the systemic planning discourse, the OECD launched its work on the development of indicators in education because such an undertaking was seen as necessary to fulfil the cultural ambitions of developing and improving, essentially ordering, the world.

Around 1980, the OECD began to reorient its centre of gravity from the state to the individual, as evidenced by the increase in new public management recommendations. Lundgren (2011) contends that, as a general characteristic of this decade, 'education became the arena for consultants with ambitions to increase efficiency and restructure management' (p. 21). These changes indicate a shift towards a more market-oriented approach to education (Kallo, 2020). In terms of discourses, it is possible to identify a shift from manpower planning and forecasting in the 1960s to a more encompassing approach covering social concerns in the 1970s to a more hardcore human capital approach in the 1980 (Heynemann, 2019).

Within CERI, these discursive shifts were not easy. CERI came under severe pressure from the United States to develop international comparative output indicators, since studies by the International Association for the Evaluation of Educational Achievement (IEA) had shown the United States lagging behind the other participating nations in terms of performance (Morgan, 2009). The US Department of Education raised questions about the quality of the indicators hitherto used. Henry et al. (2001), drawing on interview data, reveal how President Reagan's administration drove the OECD to launch a programme aimed at improving the international indicators of education to make transnational comparisons more reliable and valid.

The end of the Cold War meant that many Western organizations and countries increasingly pursued market-driven economic policies of privatization and governance through incentives. The OECD was no exception. Martens (2007) has argued the emergence of a 'comparative turn' around this time. Discursively, education was positioned as an economic production factor tasked with providing human capital to sustain national economic competitiveness in an emerging knowledge economy (Xiaomin & Auld, 2020). Participation in international large-scale assessment programmes such as the Programme for International Student Assessment (PISA) and the Teaching and Learning International Survey (TALIS) was presented as a guarantee of being on the right track in the global competition race and in terms of education quality assurance (Rasmussen & Ydesen, 2020).

A look across the four decades covered in this brief historical characteristic of OECD discourses in education from the 1970s to the 2010s reveals that the OECD has been consistent in retaining an economic outlook in its approach to education. Even so, agendas, priorities, and approaches have shifted over the decades. Development, progress, and welfare have been recurring points of orientation for the economic outlook. In this sense, key policy programmes have sought to achieve efficiency, optimization, and investment in education and the provision of skills matching identified or projected labour market needs. These values and styles of reasoning testify to the inherent cultural dimensions of the OECD's approach to education. As we shall see, these neoliberal cultural dimensions came to be joined by more national conservative cultural values emphasizing the nation in general and the nation's cultural legacies in particular.

The 1975 Education Reform in Denmark

The 1975 education reform had been in the pipeline for several years. Shifting governments had attempted to pass a bill, but the efforts had come to nothing, because of acrimonious ideological and political debates (De Coninck-Smith et al., 2013; Ydesen & Buchardt, 2020). In 1975, however, the newly appointed Social Democratic minister of education (MoE), Ritt Bjerregaard, managed to pass the bill with the support of 119 members of parliament out of 179.[5]

Some big discursive debates in the political negotiations were the use of streaming, grades, and exams. Being staunch architects and supporters of the universal welfare state model, the Social Democrats sought to introduce comprehensive schooling with no streaming (except for special cases that could be decided locally). The right-wing Liberal Party, on the other hand, maintained a commitment to catering for the needs of the labour market. For this reason, the party wanted some degree of streaming in math, English, and German in forms 8–10 and in physics/chemistry in forms 9 and 10, as well as two course levels, basic and expanded, between which the students should be allowed to choose.

Following the same discursive lines, the Social Democrats wanted to abolish all grades and exams in order to promote equality and comprehensive schooling for as long as possible, while the Liberal Party wanted to have grades from form 7 onward and to keep examinations in all main subjects.[6] The end result was essentially a compromise featuring the implementation of streaming according to the Liberal Party (but with the possibility of local exemptions) and grades from form 8 on. The Social Democrats also agreed to keep examinations, on the condition that they also encompass practical subjects (e.g. sloyd, home economics), testifying to a discourse of giving equal status to both practical and academic subjects.

An important reason for the success in passing the bill was Bjerregaard's use of the bill proposed by the former right-wing government (which had had a Liberal Party MoE) as a template, adding only a few Social Democratic fingerprints, such as using education as a vehicle to level socioeconomic differences and promote the equality of status between practical and academic subjects. In terms of culture in the public education system, the 1975 reform placed increasing emphasis on schooling in democracy and equal participation, and a significant feature was the introduction of 10 years of almost undivided comprehensive schooling, which, in principle at least, provided all students with access to upper secondary education and thus to higher education. This was an old dream coming true for many progressive educationalists who had advocated such measures since the interwar years (Nørgaard, 1977).

The Hearing Responses

In the preparatory phase, the Ministry of Education received 79 hearing responses from a long list of organizations, interest groups, and individuals,[7] none of which referred directly to the OECD. Most hearing responses reflected the desire to promote specific agendas. For instance, the Danish Women's Council argued for stronger promotion of gender equality in education, and the Norden Association wanted to strengthen the Nordic dimension in education by integrating Nordic language learning into the curriculum.[8] Other hearing responses dealt explicitly with the promotion of subjects such as physical education, Esperanto, biology, and German, and, more broadly, room for creative subjects.[9] These responses were closely linked with particular interest groups arguing either the potential advantages of adopting their agendas or the problems of not doing so. None of these agendas could be specifically attributed to any connection to OECD agendas.

In terms of discourses, the Danish High School Student Association produced one of the most critical responses, mainly arguing that the bill failed to ensure coherence in a 12-year school system. The association found that the bill inadequately addressed the main problems of education, such as 30% of student cohorts not getting into higher education and students' weariness of school attendance. These problems, the association argued, could only be solved within the public education system itself, with its 'antiquated structure and obsolete content and teaching methods which do not support the students' engagement with education.'[10] Generally, the discourse is ripe with youth rebellion and a desire to tear down the establishment, but, interestingly, the response also contains a distinct orientation towards the labour market and the lifelong learning agenda:

> There is a growing need in society today for better and longer basic education. Technical and scientific progress has decidedly changed the conditions for the individual citizen. While you might expect to work in the profession you were once trained in, we see today how more than half of all employees are employed in a profession that did not exist at the turn of the century. The requirements for the individual are therefore a question of greater flexibility in the labour market, so that one can adapt to new jobs without major difficulties and incorporate the latest knowledge and technology into his work. It requires basic training to ensure that everyone has such thorough knowledge and skills that the individual will have a solid foundation of knowledge and skills to continue their further education and employment. (p. 2.)

In order to approach the discourse promoted by the association, it is worth noting that the OECD had engaged with leaders of the 1968 youth rebellion—even at the secretary-general level—to identify problems of modern society. According to director of CERI, Ron Gass, Kristensen even put the analysis ensuing from the dialogue with the youth rebellion leaders before the OECD council.[11] A key point of orientation in the OECD's work in the 1970s was the recurrent education agenda that arose from the problems of the labour markets' inability to absorb increasing numbers of higher education candidates (Centeno, 2017; Elfert, 2018). According to Papadopoulos (1994), the core issue was the kind of education needed:

> Under modern conditions of rapid social, economic and technological change; the framework of general education within which specialisation should be developed so as to avoid highly

qualified 'morons', as the student activists would call them; what were the needs for life-long learning to combat the obsolescence of high-level skills, and what were the respective roles of industry and the educational systems in these matters. (p. 68)

The discursive similarities are uncanny as we do see the same cultural ideals about the cultivation and long-term development of human capital as a key purpose of education in society.

The Role and Significance of OECD-Driven and OECD-Adopted Discourses

But perhaps we can undertake an even deeper approach to the presence of OECD-driven and OECD-adopted discourses in Danish education in the 1970s. In the wake of the 1975 reform, Bjerregaard tasked the Danish Central Education Council with a comprehensive analysis of education and a framework for the entire education system until 1990. This work yielded the report 'U90: Danish Educational Planning and Policy in a Social Context at the End of the Twentieth Century' (Ministry of Education, 1978). In 1977, the OECD was asked to contribute to the external input by appointing a team of examiners to critique the plan in provisional form and subsequently review the Danish educational system, using as a point of entry the final version of U90 (OECD, 1977). The U90 report was translated into English and circulated among the OECD Education Committee.

According to the foreword of the Danish translation of the OECD report published in the ministerial journal *Uddannelse* in 1979, the 'examiners' report contains so many interesting and provocative views and evaluations of the standards of Danish education that a Danish translation should be made public in the first volume of the journal upon the release of the report' (Anonymous, 1979, p. 387). In its report, the OECD demonstrates a rather balanced view of education and refrains from presenting distinct policy advice. Nevertheless, the report does contain critical points.

For instance, the OECD examiners found the education research landscape in Denmark to be weak and diffuse. Domestic education researchers had only lent limited assistance over the two-year gestation period of the U90 report. For this reason, the OECD called for more applied research and suggested the formation of a 'policy research and analysis agency within the compass of the Ministry of Education and reporting directly to the minister.'[12] As a discourse, this idea about education research reflects an ideal about policies based on applied research; not least because the report also contains criticism of 'remote, academic researchers' with unclear implications for the 'real world'.[13]

Another criticism was the inability of the Danish education system to adequately handle the so-called residual group, that is, 'those who live in geographically isolated areas, the considerable number of adults who have received inadequate schooling (defined as seven years of initial education), and the handicapped', in spite of the strong egalitarian ideals and tone of the report, which the OECD viewed as offering little concreteness in terms of policy. In fact, the inspection team found that the U90 report took '(…) the notion of equality too far for practical policy purposes.'[14] This discourse goes hand in hand with a third criticism identifying a too limited concern with individual demands for education and lifelong learning.[15] In this sense, the OECD report captures some of the same criticisms as the Danish High School Student Association, although more subtly, and it may also be interpreted as expressions of the same cultural dimensions as the ones prevalent in the OECD centred on economic growth, productivity and technological development.

A wider search for the explicit presence of OECD-driven or OECD-adopted discourses prior to 1975 has been a meagre undertaking. Nevertheless, the Ministry of Education points out that Danish education, policy, and development have benefitted significantly from participation in OECD educational activities.[16] Prior to the 1975 reform, the Teacher and Educational Change Studies programme (OECD, 1974) was emphasized as having had an impact on Danish education. In 1974, one of its high-level evaluation conferences, organized by CERI and held in Rungsted, Denmark, witnessed the participation of teachers from all stages of the educational system (Papadopoulos, 1994). In its response, the ministry points out that

> The studies and the outcome of the seminar have since been distributed to and used by teacher training colleges. Thanks to the OECD studies, the expertise of consultants has become available to the Danish authorities. This would otherwise not have been the case.[17]

Finally, it should be observed that the OECD programme Educational Investment and Planning, launched in 1962, led to the establishment of a statistics section in the Danish Ministry of Education (Ydesen & Grek, 2019). In that sense, the OECD influenced the organizational setup of the Danish Ministry of Education, as well as what was considered valuable in the planning of education policies.

The 1993 Education Reform

In January 1993, Ole Vig Jensen (1936–2016) of the Social Liberal Party took office as MoE. Jensen replaced the right-wing liberal Bertel Haarder (1944–). As with the 1975 act, the 1993 reform was built on a bill instituted by Jensen's predecessor (Juul, 2006).

The key components of the new act were increased interdisciplinarity, earlier language learning, and the abolition of the last remnants of streaming, replaced by differentiated teaching (De Coninck-Smith et al., 2013). Even though the reform was made under a centre-left government, the 1993 reform largely epitomized a shift towards marketization. The gradual shift is clearly expressed since the early 1990s, with the introduction of free school choice and 'taximeter regulation', which meant that funding to institutions follows the students. According to Imsen et al. (2017), the reform transformed the purpose of education from comprehensive, democratic *Bildung* to education for employability.

Strong neoliberal discourses permeated the Danish Ministry of Education prior to the passage of the 1993 education reform, reflected, among other places, in Haarder's speech at the OECD conference of ministers on 'high quality education and training for all', held in Paris in November 1990:

> The free choice among educational institutions is crucial to the competition among them, hence to efficiency and quality.... Detailed control is to be replaced with framework control and market control, centralization to be replaced by decentralization and responsibility at local level.[18]

Haarder was quite an ideological minister, with very clear opinions about the direction of public education. Upon his accession in 1982, he closed the Central Education Council, because he found U90 to be essentially a Social Democratic document with too much focus on equality.

As part of the framework control, the 1993 reform meant new authority for the Ministry of Education to define final statutory objectives within the various subjects. In this sense, the 1993 act gave rise to the curriculum's centralization, compared to the reform of 1975, which only laid down a single statutory central knowledge area in Christian studies (Sorensen, 2011). At the same time, however, the reform increased the autonomy and jurisdiction of local authorities and schools. In this sense, the 1993 reform could be seen as an example of what Verger et al. (2019) have called school autonomy with accountability reforms aiming to modernize education systems and strengthen their performance.

In terms of discourses, the sources provide a very revealing glimpse into the struggles. In the preparatory work of the 1993 reform, the ministerial civil servants presented Haarder a draft requesting his comments before the bill was finalized and sent to hearings. The draft is based on the judgements of civil servants, input from interest groups, and other political parties' wishes. The idea was to create a bill that would feasibly survive the hearing process. The document contains the minister's handwritten comments in the margins. It is clear that Haarder stood firm on the existing framework of grades and examinations. For instance, on a formulation creating the possibility to retake the school leaving examination, Haarder commented with a blunt, 'No, there is no repetition'.[19]

The Hearing Responses

In the hearing phase, the ministry received 80 hearing responses, plus 21 that were submitted too late.[20] Unsurprisingly, a great number of responses promoted specific agendas and subjects. For instance, two German teachers promoted the status of German language learning, Amnesty International and the Danish Institute for Human Rights promoted human rights, and the Norden Association promoted the Nordic dimension.

A centrepiece of the political struggles was the preamble stipulating the purpose of public education. In a ministerial note after the hearing, the civil servants reflected on the new preamble as follows:

> The rewording of public school's purpose means an increased emphasis on cultural conditions and personal insight, drive and action and the interaction with nature. The proposed wording clarifies that the school and the parents are not the only ones responsible for the students developing their abilities and personality. The individual student has a responsibility/obligation to contribute to this development. As something new, the purpose clause states that students have a right to become familiar with Danish culture, just as the school must promote students' knowledge of other cultures through its teaching. In addition, the purpose clause has stated that an understanding of human interaction with nature must be imparted to pupils.[21]

In this sense, the revised preamble reflects an emphatic discursive amalgamation between individualism and national culture in the context of surrounding cultures and nature. In the coming years this amalgamation would prove increasingly unstable.

There was particular disagreement over the individualistic turn reflected in the draft bill concerning the preamble. The Danish Confederation of Trade Unions (*Landsorganisationen i Danmark*, or LO) wrote,

> The current preamble refers to sympathy and participation, the acquisition of skills, etc., which contribute to the diverse development of the individual pupil. LO does not want these concepts replaced by others, such as personal development, responsibility and duty. Children and young people need a broad and comprehensive level of action. They need to learn cooperation and democratic agency. They do not need a narrow personal qualification, as proposed in the bill. A dignified human life is based on the opportunity to acquire many and versatile skills in order to be a flexible person who can use these skills both in the work situation and in their leisure time in a constructive, active and forward-looking manner for the benefit of themselves and the community ....
>
> The proposal for a preamble aims at individualists (personal development) who know the responsibilities and duties of a people's government (parliament). The old preamble aims at versatile, active, independent democratic (with participation at all levels of society) young people. LO therefore wishes the old purpose clause to be preserved, only supplemented by the requirement of cultural knowledge and an understanding of nature.[22]

LO's response reflects deep concern that the new preamble expresses a reductionist understanding of human life in general and the role of education in particular. The discursive struggle can be boiled down to a disagreement over the very purpose of education. Should education serve the purpose of creating responsible agents able to competently navigate the demands of the economy and be firmly rooted in national culture or should education serve the growth and development of democratic citizens in all aspects of human life? The end result indicates that the Liberal Party was successful in promoting individualism in the preamble by using the phrase 'the students' versatile personal development', while the left-wing parties had to settle for the compromise of *equal status*, rather than *equal opportunity*.

The Role and Significance of OECD-Driven and OECD-Adopted Discourses

The juxtaposition of these developments with the OECD-driven and OECD-adopted discourses in education in the 1980s reveals distinct similarities. Most prominent is the focus on the individual and new public management approaches to education governance. The shared concern was the labour market's problems with high levels of youth unemployment.

Denmark was a keen participant in OECD activities in education in the 1980s, including the review of 'Adolescents and Comprehensive Schooling', published in 1987; 'The Changing Role of Vocational and Technical Education and Training'; 'Overcoming Disadvantage and Improving Access to Education and Training'; 'The Condition of Teaching'; and 'Higher Education and Employment'.[23] Additionally, Denmark was an active participant in CERI's International Education Indicators Project (INES), launched in 1988, a precursor of PISA. In its comments on the project, the Danish MoE wrote,

> There is every indication that the INES project will make progress compared to existing international educational indicators. The project is joined by all countries of direct interest to Denmark in an international framework, including the Nordic countries and the EEC [European Economic Community] countries.[24]

In 1989, Haarder announced that the Danish public education system was the most expensive among OECD countries and raised serious doubts about whether it was the best system (De Coninck-Smith et al., 2013). Thus, in May 1991, Denmark requested the OECD review its education system, which had not been done since 1979. The review was conducted in May and September 1993 and focused specifically on standards and quality in youth education.[25] In its 1991 country report titled 'The Effectiveness of Schooling and of Educational Training', the OECD applies a very economistic approach to education, emphasizing effectiveness and evaluation practices as necessary conditions for a well-functioning education system:

> Obviously, a well-functioning educational system is one of the most important conditions for the competitiveness of the Danish economy in an international context. Evaluation and innovation therefore constitute indispensable elements in education if Denmark is to meet the demands of a modern society from a global perspective.[26]

When the review came out in 1994, there was a distinct focus on the steering and control of the education system. On this note, the OECD reviewers set up a dichotomy between government control and market-led models. For instance, they write,

> The drive for higher economy, efficiency and effectiveness through competition, choice and other market mechanisms is impeded by central government's retention of detailed statutory rules and collectively agreed upon, highly specific conditions for staff salaries, working hours, and formal competences.[27]

However, in 1994, Denmark had a centre-left government unwilling to uncritically follow the agenda of globalization and international competition in education.

Even so, there are very strong similarities and connections between the OECD and Denmark in education prior to and after the 1993 reform. Due to its particular genesis, the reform was not only a distinct step towards increased marketization and new public management, but also a platform for increased emphasis on national culture. As we shall see, both trends would be significantly strengthened in the new millennium, at least partly promoted by the OECD's greater influence in defining the global education field.

The 2006 Education Reform

In 2001, a right-wing government with Anders Fogh Rasmussen (1953–) as prime minister, took office. Within the first couple of years, the new government took education policy in a more neoliberal direction. Rasmussen's speech at the parliamentary opening in 2003 confronted the traditionally strong progressive education approach in Danish education by saying, 'It is like learning of academic skills has been de-emphasized in favour of sitting in a circle on the floor and asking: "What do you think?"' (cited and translated in Gustafsson, 2012, p. 185). The same year, common national objectives for all subjects in forms 0 to 10 were introduced.

In 2005, Haarder returned to office as MoE, carrying through the 2006 reform. According to the explanatory memorandum distributed in the hearing process, the bill was explicitly made in response to the OECD's recommendation to strengthen the evaluation culture in the Danish public education system in general and the 2003 PISA result that 16.5% of Danish 15-year olds were insufficiently proficient in reading.[28] In accordance with the new line of policies, the 2006 reform meant increased focus on academic knowledge, the introduction of national tests, mandatory school leaving exams, municipal quality reports, individual student plans, and a canon in history and Danish. In the same year, teachers' education was changed to ensure that all teachers were familiar with fundamental democratic values and the Danish modes of government and could pass on these values to the next generation (De Coninck-Smith et al., 2013; Juul, 2006; Sorensen, 2011).

The Hearing Responses

The MoE received 68 hearing responses altogether. The big bones of contention were the strengthened position of examinations and the introduction of national tests. The government received wide support from the business world, as well as a host of agencies at lower echelons and managerial levels, such as the Confederation of Danish Industry, the Danish Evaluation Institute, the Organisation for Municipal Managers, and the Association of Head Teachers.[29] Opposing discourses are mostly found in the responses from the Danish Teachers' Union, teachers, and bodies dedicated to safeguarding the lives and well-being of children. For instance, the National Council for Children shared,

> ... the desire of the conciliation parties and the government to increase the pupils' benefits from education and absolutely supports initiatives to strengthen the ongoing internal evaluation in public school. Professional knowledge and skills are welcome targets for an evaluation. However, they need to be seen in a wider context based on children's curiosity and desire to acquire and test new knowledge. Here, knowledge becomes personally entrenched, and not just the results of superficial learning.
>
> Professional insight cannot be reduced to test results. The wording of the proposal confuses student tests with evaluations. A complete picture of the overall competence environment of schools requires the evaluation of far more elements of school life, including teacher training and development. In addition, the bill focuses exclusively on the pupils' professional benefits from teaching and has no interest in the development and learning of social skills, which can be assumed to be fundamental prerequisites for the learning of academic knowledge.[30]

In this response, we see some of the same dichotomies as in the discursive landscape of the 1993 reform, such as a focus solely on academic proficiency versus a holistic focus on the role of education and the school in also addressing the softer areas of human life. Nevertheless, the discourse tries to connect with the government's agenda on academic knowledge by presenting the conditions of what could be called deeper learning.

The Danish Teachers' Union authored a response along some of the same lines, finding it

> Regrettable that a strengthened evaluation culture in the submitted bill is so closely linked to the application of national tests. As shown by PISA 2003, the use of national tests has no documented impact on student outcomes .... In its report on primary schools, the OECD highlighted the commitment of teachers. The Danish Teachers' Union believes that an enhanced evaluation culture should continue to be based on job satisfaction, commitment, democratic tradition and quality that the OECD noted of Danish teachers. The Danish Teachers' Union sees the proposal for national tests as one of several proposals that provide for further central control of public school. The union considers that the proposal risks weakening the responsibility and commitment of the individual school and teacher. The Danish Teachers' Union must strongly warn against the imposition of a series of untested tests on the Danish public school. The experiences of England and Norway are frightening. The results of the English School Effectiveness Programme show that teaching and ongoing evaluation are confined to the areas being tested, while the problems and frustrations that have followed in the wake of the Norwegian test programme are well known.[31]

It is worth noting how the Teachers' Union explicitly uses the OECD in its argumentation. It does not critique the OECD, but, rather, emphasizes other aspects of the OECD report than those highlighted by the government. Discursively, the argument is an attempt to fight fire with fire, by proposing a critique of the Danish authorities' interpretation of the 2004 OECD report.

The Role and Significance of OECD-Driven and OECD-Adopted Discourses

In terms of discourses, the 2006 reform is interesting, because the links to OECD educational recommendations are so explicit. In the spring of 2003, Denmark was offered by the OECD to participate in a pilot review of its compulsory school system. The new format meant stronger emphasis on international comparisons, compared to the earlier country review model. The review was published in 2004, and the review team found a significant number of weaknesses in the Danish education system:

> The weaknesses we found in the system include a marked lack of achievement of the expected learning goals, lack of a strong tradition of pupil evaluation and consequent inadequate feedback, the absence of self-assessment in schools and too little joint use of good practice, inadequate recognition of early reading problems, failure to compensate for the impact of adverse conditions at home, an ambivalent attitude towards school management, inadequate initial and teacher training, an overly restrictive teacher agreement, rising expectations of the role of teachers in relation to, say, prevention and child rearing; communication difficulties between different staff groups, insufficient support for pupils in need of special education; and inadequate support for bilingual pupils (Ekholm, 2004, p. 65f.).

Based on this diagnosis, the OECD presented a comprehensive catalogue of 35 recommendations. One of the most significant was the formation of an evaluation culture:

> Since a large part of Danish society seems to have taken the success of the school system for granted, and the assessment of its capacity in comparison with other systems has only been possible in rare cases, it is clear that it will be difficult to establish a new evaluation culture. However, this is probably the single change that is most important to achieve if other initiatives are to be introduced so that they take effect and standards can be raised (Ekholm, 2004, p. 129).

As Sorensen (2011) argues, the term *evaluation culture* had become endemic as the main rationale for the imposition of systems of accountability in education governance (Sorensen, 2011). It is striking how explicit and critical the OECD evaluation and policy recommendations are compared to earlier evaluations in 1979 and 1994, not least centred on the explicit articulation of standards and results as being the indispensable ingredients in education. Nevertheless, it is interesting that the introduction of national tests in effect had been decided prior to the publication of the OECD review. Uffe Toudal Pedersen, a high-level official in the MoE, was a leading proponent in introducing national tests. In fact, Peter Mortimore, who was head of the OECD inspection team, strongly advised against the introduction of national tests if they would be used to produce rankings of schools.[32]

Apparently, Denmark now had a government with the will and intent to adopt and enact the OECD's views and recommendations in support of its own political agenda, even if it meant going beyond the actual recommendations. The top-down enforcement of changed cultural ideals for the Danish public education system were indeed a priority for the government and the OECD discourse based on data and international knowledge was used as a supporting act.

The 2014 Education Reform

In 2011, a new centre-left government took office and the Social Democrat Christine Antorini (1965–) took office as MoE. In August 2012, Antorini launched the New Nordic School project, inviting institutions from the educational sector (from pre-primary education to upper secondary education) to participate. The New Nordic School project was part of the ideological basis of later school reform. The reform had three overall goals for public schools: to challenge all pupils to reach their fullest potential, to close the attainment gap, and to enhance trust in public school and pupils' well-being by showing respect for professional knowledge and practice. These goals were to be accomplished through concrete changes, such as longer school days, earlier foreign language learning, 45 min of exercise daily, homework assistance in 'homework cafés', and more lessons in Danish and math (Reder & Ydesen, 2021).[33]

The 2014 reform proved to be one of the most controversial and hotly debated political reforms in recent Danish history. The reform itself was very much in line with the policies of the previous government, which had launched the so-called 'Schools' Travelling Team', tasked with examining the needs for a reform of the public school system. In 2010, the team concluded that teachers, on average, were teaching 40% of their total working time, and that there were large differences between municipalities in terms of local working time agreements. Therefore, the political background of the reform was an understanding among the main political parties, the municipalities, and the business world that Danish schoolchildren do not learn enough because teachers spend too much time on activities other than being present in the classroom together with students. In this sense, the reform, by its very nature, implied a clear conflict area with the Teachers' Union, which strongly opposed taking away time for teaching preparation, parental cooperation, and other activities alongside classroom classes. The price for teachers spending more time in the classroom was a cut in their preparation time and historically acquired flexibility in terms of home office time. The change in teachers' working conditions resulted in conflict and a 25-day strike of approximately 67,000 teachers in April 2013. Finally, the government intervened and ended the conflict, which fundamentally changed the working conditions of the teachers.

The Hearing Responses

Of the 66 parties invited to give a hearing response, only 34 replied. Many hearing responses clearly reflect the towering position of the OECD in education. PISA and the OECD's recommendations became the centre of gravity for both proponents and critics of the new bill. A key area of dispute was again the purpose of public school. In 2006, the independent think tank Sophia was established, dedicated to critical analysis of education with a humanistic foundation. Sophia's hearing response stands out in the discursive landscape because it problematizes the inherent cultural assumptions of the policies pursued in education since at least the turn of the millennium:

> The overall proposal for reform of the public school system continues the process of shrinking the purpose of the school in recent years and replacing it with a number of politically defined and operational objectives for pupils' learning. This is a final cementing of the work begun in 2000 with the introduction of clear objectives, later to become common objectives. Thus, the primary school reform can be seen as the final push for the shift that has taken place from a school that legitimized itself through its purpose to a school that legitimizes itself through its goals. It is also in light of this shift that, despite a few positive moments (such as strengthening language teaching), learning can now be seen as reduced to technical skills, which, by their visibility and demonstrability, define teaching as involving the selection of appropriate, obvious methods of achieving this or that competence, skill or knowledge. The problem is that human education, pedagogy, teaching, knowledge, or learning cannot and should not be understood as being as simple as that.[34]

The critique largely reflects the criticisms raised of PISA in international educational scholarship (e.g. Hopmann, 2007; Zhao, 2020), but, as Hopmann argues, the OECD-driven discourse in education revolving around PISA seems to be largely immune to criticism. In discursive terms the response points to the big cultural contrast between the legitimization of public education in the 1970s as the forum for the development of critically reflective, democratic citizens of the welfare state to an essentially employable citizen in the 2000s (Ydesen & Buchardt, 2020).

The Role and Significance of OECD-Driven and OECD-Adopted Discourses

In 2011, the OECD published an evaluation of Danish education (Shewbridge et al., 2011). Compared to the reviews prior to 2000, the report is very clear and direct in diagnosing and promulgating policy recommendations. The evaluation explicitly builds on the 2004 report and assesses the initiatives of the Danish authorities in response to it. Looking at the most central OECD policy documents in the process leading up to the 2014 reform, the entire PISA 2009 document complex stands central. The same holds true of the OECD's 2010 Education at a Glance Report (Reder & Ydesen, 2021).

According to a high-level official in the Danish Ministry of Education, the OECD documents were often used to diagnose the education system, 'serving as the basis of improvement.'[35] On the same note, a high-level politician explains how

> The OECD reports and Education at a Glance and the PISA consortium actually provided some very nuanced country evaluations that could be used as inspiration for what might work well in our context. And they also pointed to some of the challenges in the Danish school system.[36]

The quote is an indication that the OECD influenced the mindset and constituency surrounding the reform process. A key point of orientation is the knowledge brokers between the OECD and the Danish education field, who can be found in the shifting consortia tasked with conducting the PISA surveys (Ydesen et al., 2021). Then long-time chairperson of the PISA consortium, Niels Egelund of the Danish School of Education, was behind the report 'Danish Youth in International Comparison' [*Danske unge i en international sammenligning*], on the results of PISA 2009. Egelund was also a member of the Agency for the Quality Development of the Public School established in 2006. Another leading figure was Lars Qvortrup, then dean of the Danish School of Education and who worked closely with Egelund. In an interview, the high-level politician emphasizes,

> You see, someone like Lars Qvortrup, he has studied the education revolution – if I may put it like that – in Singapore, but he also looked at what happened in Ontario …. Qvortrup was very vocal in trying to bring international agendas into what we ought to work with in a Danish school context.[37]

It is striking that Egelund, Qvortrup, and their colleagues Jens Rasmussen and Andreas Rasch-Christensen, head of research at VIA University College, appear on a number of ministerial committees and institutions surrounding the reform. Generally, these four prominent agents, who command considerable influence in the Danish field of education, have been very vocal and visible in the entire reform process, right from the preparatory work to the evaluation of the reform (Ydesen et al., 2021).

The discursive positions surrounding the 2014 reform reveal a rather acrimonious environment. The above-mentioned researchers associated with OECD policy instruments and the development of education policy constitute one camp, whereas a host of critical researchers make up another camp. Notably, in his 2017 Ph.D. dissertation, titled 'Down to the Ground—Didactics in the Teaching Profession?' [*I bund og grund—lærerprofessionens didaktik?*], Keld Skovmand (2017) claims that the 2014 education reform is grounded in neither evidence nor knowledge. These debates are still ongoing, more than six years after the reform. Thus, it is fair to say that Danish education research often finds itself in a very toxic environment, with significant antagonism between at least two main clusters, one being a discourse on the role of education research as being the evidence-based what works type of research and the other discourse understanding education research as something adhering to pedagogical ideals about *Bildung* and emancipation, as well as a notion of pedagogy being a unique field, with its own values and contributions (Rømer, 2017).

Concluding Discussion: Looking Across the Reforms

The historical trajectories of the four education reforms analysed clearly indicate some key processes in the interplay between globalization and localization mechanisms. From a diachronic perspective, the analysis reveals the increasing influence of globally driven reforms and, on the other hand, the rising presence of Danish values and culture. For instance, the revision of the preamble in the 1993 reform reflects an amalgamation of individualism and national culture in the context of surrounding cultures and nature.

Across the decades, Denmark has clearly followed a path of neoliberal reforms, with accountability and marketization as some of the hallmarks. A clear example is a shift from addressing issues at the societal level in the 1970s to holding school leaders, teachers, parents, and students responsible for performance in the 2010s. Another example is the changed governance structure revolving around the concept of 'framework control' which entered the scene with the 1993 reform. However, these developments blend with a strong nationalist tone rooted in a resurgence of a national conservative focus on Danish culture, as reflected in the implementation of national canons in the early 2000s.

Overall a picture can be drawn of Danish education policies in the 1970s and 1990s following the same styles of reasoning found in the OECD shifting its centre of gravity from the state to the individual. In other words, a movement from a traditional social democratic focus on the welfare state to a neoliberal focus on economic globalization. In the 2000s, the globalization optimism was joined—and to some extent challenged—by a strand of national conservative cultural values emphasizing the nation in general and the nation's cultural legacies in particular. As an example, this cultural strand is visible in the launch of the New Nordic School project as part of the ideological basis of the 2014 school reform.

Under the lens of recontextualization and reassembly, the Danish reforms can best be described as ambiguous processes where cultural, ideological, and value-based agendas promoted by different agents and governance instruments serve as arbiters and gatekeepers for the implementation of globalized education policies. Indeed, the education system is a marked field of contestation. As seen, some key debates have been over assessment, accountability, streaming, centralization/decentralization and, not least, the very role and purpose of education. For instance, the process surrounding the 2006 reform clearly shows a discursive dichotomy between a focus on academic proficiency and an encompassing focus on the role of education and the school in also addressing the softer areas of human life. At the same time, however, the governance of education at the national level is strongly influenced by who is in government. The ideological preferences of shifting governments have been a key factor in understanding the recontextualization and reassembly processes, even if there has been a strong tradition for consensus and not discarding preparatory reform work when a new government takes office. Shifting ministers of education have downplayed certain aspects of OECD policy documents and emphasized others according to their ideological preferences. Cultural idiosyncrasies remain important and have a defining role in terms of which cultural-hegemonic values travelled to Denmark and how they were implemented in the cultural ideals of the Danish public education system. But generally, we do see a shift from the development of critically reflective, democratic citizens of the welfare state in the 1970s to an essentially employable citizen in the 2000s.

Throughout the period covered here, the OECD has served as a partner for testing proposed education policies through evaluations and, with increasing intensity, also policy recommendations as a legitimating factor. In this sense, the OECD has served as a joint think tank and consultancy of the member states. In the 1970s, though, this role was not as developed as it has subsequently become. In the first decades, the OECD served more as a meeting place where actors from different countries could assemble for seminars and projects (Andreasen et al., 2013). This observation falls in line with Papadopoulos (1994), who contends that the OECD's influence in education in this period must be understood as a *catalytic* role that relates to identifying major policy issues and facilitating policymaking, programme planning, and implementation. Indeed, Danish agents were inspired through their interactions with the OECD. Generally speaking, the OECD has gone from being a forum of exchange to a hard-line think tank wielding considerable capital in advancing its programmes and agendas. But it is important to note that the recontextualization and reassembly of OECD-driven and OECD-adopted policies since the 2000s has been strongly supported by the establishment of national partner consortia affiliated with PISA. These consortia play a role in defining what is up and down to the larger education constituency in Denmark. In this sense, the analysis clearly demonstrates the OECD's increasingly visible role in Danish education. It is striking how both proponents and opponents of the 2006 and 2014 reforms used OECD reports and data to support the arguments. The OECD has gradually become an inescapable and towering frame of reference in most of the Danish educational field.

However, in understanding the recontextualization and reassembly of globalized education policies in Denmark, it is crucial to note that Danish agents—civil servants and MoEs—also played a role in defining and developing OECD education policy programmes. We have seen how Danish agents played an active role in OECD fora and cherished the exchange and outcomes of OECD programmes. Throughout the period covered in this chapter, Danish officials have held the OECD's work in education in high regard.[38] In the first decades, the OECD impact on Danish education is not so palpable, but it is nevertheless important to note that the OECD is not an entirely external agent in defining what is up and down in education. Member states and, in this case, Denmark play a role in defining objects of focus, and, in this sense, the OECD can be an active partner in creating leverage for those in power to promote political reforms in the domestic context. This vital aspect in the gearing between globalization and localization processes is sustained by the great flexibility in the OECD's modus operandi which means that member states can opt in and out of programmes and even contribute to the development of programmes to fulfil national demands in general and demands of decision-makers in particular.

Notes

1. Although not covering education, the most important work exploring the significance of the OECD in Danish policymaking is a volume in *The Danish Democracy and Power Study* (Marcussen, 2005).
2. For instance, Kaj Aage Spelling (1915–1994), a former educational psychologist and professor at the Royal Danish School of Education, was a member of the CERI governing board in the 1970s. He was replaced by his colleague, professor Hans Vejleskov (1935-) in 1977. The Danish esteem for CERI's work is reflected, among other places, in the ministerial will to continue the funding of CERI programmes. For instance, in 1981, Denmark opposed the cuts

of CERI's budget proposed by the United States (correspondence regarding the Danish position on potential cuts to OECD educational work, May 1981, Danish Ministry of Education, 8-41-04-1/81, Danish National Archives).
3. The analysis draws on a searchable database of OECD archival documents consisting of 2027 documents on various programmes and activities in education between 1961 and 2014.
4. For example, see the background paper 'Changing Standards of Performance and the Quality of Education', written by John Keeves, Centre for the Study of Higher Education, University of Melbourne, Australia, for the OECD Directorate for Social Affairs, Labour and Education in the summer of 1986.
5. In the Danish history of education, reforms of the public education system have traditionally involved broad cross-party compromises to secure political continuity and broad support from stakeholders to secure involvement (De Coninck-Smith et al., 2013).
6. Note about differences between the Social Democratic Party's and the Liberal Party's views on the new education act, 14 October 1975, Ministry of Education, records [*journalsager*], The first 12 education years (1974–1980), box no. 758, Danish National Archives.
7. Draft report on the Education Bill, June 1975, Education Committee, Second assembly, Ministry of Education, records [*journalsager*], The first 12 education years (1974–1980), journal number 1974-212-1, box no. 758, Danish National Archives (this document contains a complete list of all hearing responses).
8. Hearing response from the Danish Women's Council, April 1975, Ministry of Education, records [*journalsager*], The first 12 education years (1974–1980), journal number 1974-212-1, box no. 758, Danish National Archives. Hearing response from the Norden Association, 24 April 1975, The first 12 education years (1974–1980), journal number 1974-212-1, box no. 758, Danish National Archives.
9. Letter to the MoE from the chair of the State Music Council, 23 September 1975, Ministry of Education, records [*journalsager*], The first 12 education years (1974–1980), journal number 1974-212-1, box no. 758, Danish National Archives. This concern was also raised by the Association of History Teachers.
10. Hearing response from the Danish High School Student Association [*Danske Gymnasieelevers Sammenslutning*], Ministry of Education, records [*journalsager*], The first 12 education years (1974–1980), journal number 1974-212-1, box no. 758, Danish National Archives. All translations from Danish into English are by the author unless stated otherwise.
11. Interview with Ron Gass conducted in Paris, 22 August 2017, by Maren Elfert and PhD fellow Trine Juul Reder. The data was collected under the auspices of the Global History of the OECD project, hosted by Aalborg University, Denmark, with Christian Ydesen as the principal investigator.
12. Education Committee, Review of Educational Policy in Denmark, Examiners' Report and Questions, May 1979, ED(79)4, OECD Archives, Paris, p. 54.
13. Ibid. p. 53.
14. Ibid., p. 7.

15. Education Committee, Country Educational Policy Reviews, Denmark: Phase I, September 1977, ED(77)10, OECD Archives, Paris.
16. Education Committee, Governing Board, Review and Forward Planning of OECD Educational Activities—Country Responses, Denmark, May 1980, ED(80)10/05; CERI/CD(80)14/05, OECD Archives, Paris.
17. Education Committee, Governing Board, Review and Forward Planning of OECD Educational Activities—Country Responses, Denmark, May 1980, ED(80)10/05; CERI/CD(80)14/05, OECD Archives, Paris, p. 1.
18. Meeting of the Education Committee at Ministerial Level, Item 4, National Statement, Denmark, 19 November 1990, ED/MIN(90)5/05, Ministry of Education, Denmark, OECD Archives, Paris, p. 3. These changes are also reflected in the 1991 country report 'The Effectiveness of Schooling and of Educational Resource Management' for the OECD Education Committee, SME/ED/WD(91)21, OECD Archives, Paris.
19. Note for the minister about suggestions for a bill changing the Public Education Act, 10 October 1991, Ministry of Education, Department of Public School, box 1649, Danish National Archives, p. 12.
20. Høringsliste, March 1993, 1987–1994 *Journalsager*, Ministry of Education, Department of Public School, box 1649, Danish National Archives; *Høringssvar fra dels for sent indkomne og dels ikke høringsberettigede*, 22 January 1992, 987-1994 *Journalsager*, Ministry of Education, Department of Public School, box 1649, Danish National Archives. The fact that so many responses came in late can be explained by the very short response time. The hearing was initiated 4 December 1991 and the deadline for submitting responses was 10 January 1992.
21. Ministerial note after the hearing, 22 January 1992, Ministry of Education, Department of Public School, box 100, Danish National Archives.
22. Response from LO to the Ministry of Education, 7 January 1992, Ministry of Education, Department of Public School, box 100, Danish National Archives, pp. 1 and 3.
23. Review of Youth Education Policy in Denmark, 4 March 1994, DEELSA/ED(94)2, OECD Archives, Paris.
24. General Assembly on International Education Indicators, Countries' Comments, September 1991, CERI/INES(91)23/ANN, OECD Archives, Paris. In a recent e-mail correspondence, Haarder describes his relationship with the director of CERI, Tom Alexander (1941–2012), as close (E-mail from Bertel Haarder to research assistant Nanna Ramsing Enemark, 8 July 2020, private archives).
25. Education Policy Review Denmark, 18 March 1993, DEELSA/ED(93)4, OECD Archives, Paris.
26. The Effectiveness of Schooling and of Educational Training, Country Reports, Denmark, November 1991, SME/ED/WD(91)21, OECD Archives, Paris.
27. Review of Youth Education Policy in Denmark, 4 March 1994, DEELSA/ED(94)2, OECD Archives, Paris, p. 12.

28. Hearing response from the Danish Teachers Union, 31 October 2005, available at https://www.ft.dk/samling/20051/lovforslag/L170/index.htm.
29. See https://www.ft.dk/samling/20051/lovforslag/L170/bilag.htm (accessed 3 July 2020).
30. Hearing response from the National Council for Children, 1 November 2005, available at https://www.ft.dk/samling/20051/lovforslag/L170/bilag.htm (accessed 3 July 2020).
31. Hearing response from the Danish Teachers' Union, 31 October 2005, available at https://www.ft.dk/samling/20051/lovforslag/L170/bilag.htm (accessed 3 July 2020).
32. Memorandum from the think Tank Sophia, 20 November 2007, available at https://www.ft.dk/samling/20072/almdel/udu/bilag/8/407055.pdf (accessed 22 December 2020).
33. The analysis of this reform draws on some of the Danish partnership work undertaken by PhD fellow Trine Juul Reder and Christian Ydesen in the project Policy Knowledge and Lesson Drawing in Nordic School Reform in an Era of International Comparison, hosted at the University of Oslo.
34. Hearing response from the think tank Sophia, 24 January 2014, available at https://www.ft.dk/samling/20051/lovforslag/L170/bilag.htm (accessed 3 July 2020), p. 2.
35. Interview by Trine Juul Reder with a high-level Ministry of Education official, 23 May 2019.
36. Interview by Trine Juul Reder with a high-level politician, 23 May 2019.
37. Interview by Trine Juul Reder with a high-level politician, 23 May 2019.
38. For instance, in its country response in 1980, the Danish Ministry of Education wrote the following about CERI: 'The quality of the work undertaken has always been very high. It should especially be underlined that the secretariat over the years has had great ability to select consultants and experts of excellence. This ability is part of the OECD success in the field of education and it is highly regrettable that the resources for employing these consultants and experts have been severely reduced over the last years' (Education Committee, Governing Board, Review and Forward Planning of OECD Educational Activities—Country Responses, Denmark, May 1980, ED(80)10/05; CERI/CD(80)14/05, OECD Archives, Paris.

References

Anderson, K. T., & Holloway, J. (2018). Discourse analysis as theory, method, and epistemology in studies of education policy. *Journal of Education Policy, 35*(2), 188–221. https://doi.org/10.1080/02680939.2018.1552992

Andreasen, K. E., Rasmussen, P., & Ydesen, C. (2013). Den diskrete internationalisering: Danske uddannelser i international kontekst 1968–1982 [The discrete internationalization: Danish education in international context 1968–1982]. *Uddannelseshistorie, 47,* 36–59.

Anonymous. (1979). På vej mod 1990—OECD's bedømmelse af U 90 samt problemstillinger og udviklingstendenser i dansk uddannelsespolitik. [Towards 1990—ECD's assessment of U90 and problems and developments in Danish education policy] *Uddannelse, 7*, 387–469.

Auld, E., Rappleye, J., & Morris, P. (2019) PISA for development: How the OECD and World Bank shaped education governance post-2015. *Comparative Education, 55*(2), 197–219. https://doi.org//10.1080/03050068.2018.1538635

Berman, E. H. (1983). *The influence of the Carnegie, ford, and Rockefeller foundations on American foreign policy: The ideology of philanthropy.* State University of New York Press.

Bürgi, R. (2015). *Geplante Bildung für die freie Welt. Die OECD und die Entstehung einer technokratischen Bildungsexpertise.* Doctoral Dissertation, University of Luxembourg. Retrieved from http://orbilu.uni.lu/handle/10993/22041

Bürgi, R. (2016). Systemic management of schools: The OECD's professionalisation and dissemination of output governance in the 1960s. *Paedagogica Historica, 52*(4), 408–422. https://doi.org//10.1080/00309230.2016.1178780

Centeno, V. G. (2017). *The OECD's educational agendas: Framed from above, fed from below, determined in an interaction: A study on the recurrent education agenda.* Peter Lang Verlag.

De Coninck-Smith, N., Rasmussen, L. R., & Vyff, I. (2013). Da skolen blev alles—Tiden efter 1970. In N. De Coninck-Smith, & C. Appel (Eds.), *Dansk skolehistorie: hverdag, vilkår og visioner gennem 500 år* [Schools in Denmark: A history of everyday life, conditions, and visions over 500 years], (Vol. 5). Aarhus University Press.

Ekholm, M. (2004). *OECD-rapport om grundskolen i Danmark—2004* [OECD report about the elementary school in Denmark—2004]. Ministry of Education.

Elfert, M. (2018). *UNESCO's utopia of lifelong learning: An intellectual history.* Routledge, Taylor and Francis Group.

Elfert, M., & Ydesen, C. (2020). The rise of global governance in education: The OEEC and UNESCO, 1945–1960. In K. Gram-Skjoldager, H. A. Ikonomou, & T. Kahlert (Eds.) *Organizing the world—International organization and the emergence of international public administration 1920–1960* (pp. 73–89). Bloomsbury.

Grek, S. (2020). Prophets, saviours and saints: Symbolic governance and the rise of a transnational metrological field. *International Review of Education.* https://doi.org/10.1007/s11159-020-09844-z.

Grek, S., & Ydesen, C. (2021) Where science met policy; Governing by indicators and the OECD's INES Programme. *Globalization, Societies and Education,* (forthcoming).

Gustafsson, L. R. (2012). *What did you learn in school today? How ideas mattered for policy changes in Danish and Swedish schools 1990–2011.* Doctoral dissertation, Arhus University.

Henry, M., Lingard, B., Rizvi, F., & Taylor, S. (2001). *The OECD, globalisation, and education policy.* Pergamon Press.

Heynemann, S. (2019). *World Bank, rates of return & education development,* FreshEd [Audio podcast], no. 155, May 20. http://www.freshedpodcast.com/heyneman/

Hopmann, S. T. (Ed.). (2007). *PISA zufolge PISA =: PISA according to PISA ; hält PISA, was es verspricht?* Lit Verlag.

Ifversen, J. (2003). Text, discourse, concept: Approaches to textual analysis. *Kontur, 7*, 60–69.

Imsen, G., Blossing, U., & Moos, L. (2017). Reshaping the Nordic education model in an era of efficiency. Changes in the comprehensive school project in Denmark, Norway, and Sweden since the millennium. *Scandinavian Journal of Educational Research, 61*(5), 568–583. https://doi.org/10.1080/00313831.2016.1172502

Juul, I. (2006). Den danske velfærdsstat og uddannelsespolitikken [The Danish welfare state and education policy]. *Uddannelseshistorie 40*, 72–100.

Kallo, J. (2020). The epistemic culture of the OECD and its agenda for higher education. *Journal of Education Policy*, 1–22. https://doi.org/10.1080/02680939.2020.1745897

Kulnazarova, A., & Ydesen, C. (2018). *UNESCO without borders: Educational campaigns for international understanding.* Palgrave.

Lundgren, U. P. (2011). PISA as a political instrument. One history behind the formulating of the PISA Programme. In M. E. Pereyra, H.-G. Kotthoff, & R. Cowen (Eds.), *PISA under examination. Changing knowledge, changing tests, and changing schools* (pp. 17–30). Sense Publishers.

Mahon, R., & McBride, S. (2009). *The OECD and transnational governance*. UBC Press.

Marcussen, M. (2005). *OECD og idéspillet—Game over?* [OECD and the game of ideas—Game over?] Hans Reitzel.

Martens, K. (2007). How to become an influential actor—The 'comparative turn' in OECD education policy. In K. Martens, A. Rusconi, & K. Leuze, K. (Eds.), *New arenas of education governance: The impact of international organizations and markets on educational policy making* (pp. 40–56). Palgrave Macmillan.

Martens, K., & Jakobi, A. P. (Eds.). (2010). *Mechanisms of OECD governance: International incentives for national policy-making?* Oxford University Press.

Ministry of Education. (1978). *U90: Samlet uddannelsesplanlægning frem til 90'erne* ['U90: Comprehensive educational planning towards the 90 s']. Ministry of Education.

Morgan, C. (2009). *The OECD programme for international student assessment: Unravelling a knowledge network*. VDM Verlag.

Mundy, K., Green, A., Lingard, B., & Verger, A. (2016). Introduction: The globalization of education policy—Key approaches and debates. In K. Mundy, A. Green, B. Lingard, & A. Verger (Eds.), *The handbook of global education policy* (pp. 1–20). Wiley https://doi.org/10.1002/9781118468005.ch0

Nørgaard, E. (1977). *Lille barn, hvis er du? En skolehistorisk undersøgelse over reformbestræbelser inden for den danske folkeskole i mellemkrigstiden* [Little child, whose art thou? An educational history investigation of reform attempts in the Danish public school system in the interwar years]. Gyldendals Pædagogiske Bibliotek.

Organisation for Economic Co-operation and Development. (1974). *The teacher and educational change: A new role*. (Vol. I, General Report). OECD.

Organisation for Economic Co-operation and Development. (1977). Denmark: A long-term plan for education. In *Innovation in Education* (Vol. 16) (June). OECD.

Papadopoulos, G. S. (1994). *Education 1960–1990: The OECD perspective*. OECD.

Rasmussen, A., & Ydesen, C. (2020). *Cultivating excellence in education: A critical policy study on talent*. Educational Governance Research, Springer Nature, Cham.

Reder, T., & Ydesen, C. (2021). Policy borrowing and evidence in Danish education policy preparation—The case of the Danish public school reform of 2013. In B. Karseth, K. Sivesind, & G. Steiner-Khamsi (Eds.), *Evidence and expertise in Nordic education policies: A comparative network analysis from the Nordic region*. Palgrave (forthcoming).

Rømer, T. A. (2017). Pure and impure pedagogy. Report from an educational controversy in Denmark. *Paideutika—Quaderni Di Formazione e Cultura [Notebooks on Education and Culture], 13*(25), 45–55.

Shewbridge, C., Jang, E., Matthews, P., & Santiago, P. (Eds.). (2011). *OECD reviews of evaluation and assessment in education: Denmark 2011*. OECD Publishing.

Skovmand, K. (2017). *I bund og grund—lærerprofessionens didaktik?* [Down to the Ground—Didactics in the Teaching Profession?]. Doctoral dissertation, Danmarks Institut for Pædagogik og Uddannelse, Aarhus University.

Sorensen, T. B. (2011). *The bias of markets: A comparative study of the market form and identity politics in English and Danish compulsory education*. Copenhagen Studies in Bilingualism (Vol. 60). University of Copenhagen.

Spring, J. H. (2015). *Economization of education: Human capital, global corporations, skills-based schooling*. Routledge, Taylor and Francis Group.

Tröhler, D., & Lenz, T. (2015). *Trajectories in the development of modern school systems*. Routledge, Taylor and Francis Group.

Vejleskov, H. (1979). CERI/OECD's arbejde på uddannelsesområdet [CERI/OECD's work in education]. *Uddannelse, 4*, 194–200.

Verger, A., Fontdevila, C., & Parcerisa, L. (2019). Constructing school autonomy with accountability as a global policy model: A focus on OECD's governance mechanisms. In C. Ydesen (Ed.), *The OECD's historical rise in education: The formation of a global governing complex* (pp. 219–243). Springer International Publishing. https://doi.org/10.1007/978-3-030-33799-5_11

Wiseman, A. W., & Taylor, C. S. (Eds.). (2017). *The impact of the OECD on education worldwide* (International Perspectives on Education and Society, Vol. 31), Emerald Publishing Limited.

Xiaomin, L., & Auld, E. (2020). A historical perspective on the OECD's 'humanitarian turn': PISA for development and the learning framework 2030. *Comparative Education, 56*(4), 503–521. https://doi.org/10.1080/03050068.2020.1781397

Ydesen, C., & Buchardt, M. (2020). Citizen ideals and education in Nordic welfare state school reforms. *Oxford Research Encyclopedia of Education.* Retrieved 3 Nov. 2020, from https://oxfordre.com/education/view/10.1093/acrefore/9780190264093.001.0001/acrefore-9780190264093-e-1450

Ydesen, C., & Grek, S. (2019) Securing organisational survival: a historical inquiry into the OECD's work in education during the 1960 s. *Paedagogica Historica, 56*(3), 412–427. https://doi.org/10.1080/00309230.2019.1604774. https://www.tandfonline.com/doi/full/10.1080/00309230.2019.1604774

Ydesen, C., Kauko, J., & Magnúsdóttir, B. R. (2021). The organization for economic cooperation and development—A field analysis of knowledge brokers in Denmark, Finland, and Iceland. In B. Karseth, K. Sivesind, & G. Steiner-Khamsi, *Evidence and expertise in Nordic education policies: A comparative network analysis from the Nordic region.* Palgrave (forthcoming).

Zhao, Y. (2020). Two decades of havoc: A synthesis of criticism against PISA. *Journal of Educational Change, 21*(2), 245–266. https://doi.org/10.1007/s10833-019-09367-x

Christian Ydesen is a professor (WSR) at the Department of Culture and Learning, Aalborg University, Denmark. He is the PI of the project 'The Global History of the OECD in education' funded by the Aalborg University talent programme and the project 'Education Access under the Reign of Testing and Inclusion' funded by the Independent Research Fund Denmark. He has been a visiting scholar at the Edinburg University (2008–2009, 2016), the Birmingham University (2013) Oxford University (2019), and Milan University (2021) and published several chapters and articles on topics such as educational testing, international organisations, accountability, educational psychology and diversity in education from historical and international perspectives. He currently serves as an executive editor of the European Educational Research Journal.

Fixing the Future: Public Discourse on the Implementation of Education Standards in Austria

Bernadette Hörmann

Introduction

Like many other countries, Austria has implemented a competency-based curriculum reform subsumed under the term 'education standards' (*Bildungsstandards*) as a consequence of its results in the Programme for International Student Assessment (PISA). Over the decades, Austrians have been proud of their school system, which they considered to be of high quality and reputable. The results of the PISA study, especially in 2003, were a deep disappointment to Austrian people who expected first-rate results. The crisis marked the birth of some reform projects that were all based on a specific 'set of terms' (Tröhler, 2019) such as 'standards', 'competencies', 'performance', or 'outputs', which originated from an international discourse on education and permeated the education language. Besides concepts such as all-day-schooling, a comprehensive school system, a standardised graduation exam at the end of twelfth grade, and a structural reform of teacher education, competency-based curricula in combination with education standards were an often-demanded reform that was finally implemented in 2008–2009. The implementation process and the consequences of the reform have been investigated and followed up by research in recent years (e.g. Altrichter and Posch, 2007; George et al., 2019; Greiner et al., 2020; Koch and Beer, 2010; Specht and Lucyshyn, 2008; Stamm, 2008). In general, these research endeavours assumed that the idea of standards emerged after the disappointing performance of Austrian students in PISA and other assessment studies. Some authors attributed this emergence to the preceding promotion of school autonomy and quality management in schools (Wiesner et al., 2020); however, it is not yet clear why and how standards arose as a reform idea or why they were considered an appropriate solution to particular problems (cf. Steiner-Khamsi, 2012).

B. Hörmann (✉)
Department of Education, University of Oslo, Oslo, Norway
e-mail: bernadette.hormann@iped.uio.no

Investigating the local policy context contributes not only to a deeper understanding of the education system in nation states, but also to a more differentiated picture of developments on a global scale (Sivesind and Wahlström, 2016). From a cultural-historical perspective, faith in education standards can be regarded as originating from an American-Presbyterian milieu at the very beginning of the twentieth century (Tröhler, 2019; Tröhler and Maricic, 2021). Promoted by international agencies like the Organisation for Economic Co-operation and Development (OECD), standardised curricula and testing spread globally and have been implemented in many countries for different reasons, with different manifestations and representations, and for varying purposes (EACEA P9 Eurydice, 2009; Sivesind, 2013). Following up this interesting empirical observation, my research examined the recontextualisation of standards in the local, cultural-historical policy context of Austria, which today is a small nation state built on a powerful history rooted in monarchic-aristocratic traditions and Roman Catholic culture. By investigating the public discourse that led to the actual implementation of standards in 2009, the chapter's research examined how the global idea of standards became relevant and how it has been recontextualised in a nation state with a heritage shaped by its Catholic and monarchical past. In which respects were education standards regarded as an appropriate reform measure within public discourse in Austria, what were the local reform needs, what kinds of educational problems did the public perceive, and why did standards appear as a reasonable solution to these problems?

In Austria, the implementation of education standards and their testing was accompanied by extensive discussions and concentrated public attention. Assuming that public discussion reflects a stock of knowledge regarding education standards, this research investigated the public discourse in Austrian newspapers before the standards were implemented. By mapping media statements from experts, practitioners, parents, students, and other stakeholders, the research investigated the knowledge that laid the foundation for the implementation of education standards in Austria. By drawing on the 'sociology of knowledge approach to discourse' (SKAD; Keller, 2011; Keller et al., 2018), the analysis focused on the conceptualisation of education standards in the collective discourse. It was of interest to determine which local problems were prevalent in the discourse, how these problems were conceptualised, and why standards were considered a meaningful reform in Austria.

This chapter will first introduce the cultural-historical context of Austria and briefly describe the emergence of the idea of implementing standardised curricula in section two. In the third section, I will explain how analysing public discourse can contribute to the exploration of the recontextualisation of global standards at a national level. Section four presents the dataset and the applied method and is followed by section five which describes the analysis. The final section summarises the findings of the discourse analysis and discusses them from a broader perspective.

Global Ideas and Their Recontextualisation: The Case of Austria

Terms like competencies, standards, testing, performance, and outputs have permeated the education language in many European countries, mostly in relation to the publication of the PISA results in 2000 and the OECD's subsequent recommendations to each member country. Regardless of their actual PISA rankings, many participating countries turned their results into crisis stories. Resembling Nordin's description of the legitimating effect of a story of crisis, PISA results became an important point of reference for different reform suggestions in the participating countries (Nordin, 2014; Ringarp, 2016; Tröhler, 2019). By referring to external data, results, concepts, or ideas such as those mentioned above, nation states tried to solve their internal problems, often producing a 'salutary effect' (i.e. external points of reference experienced as 'neutral' solutions to gridlock problems that have remained unsolved for long periods; Steiner-Khamsi, 2013; Steiner-Khamsi and Waldow, 2012).

The case of Austria and its adoption of global ideas and terms provided an especially interesting research opportunity because of the country's cultural, historical, and constitutional framework. Despite its current role as a relatively small nation in the geographical centre of Europe, it is built on a powerful history. Its predecessors, the Austrian Empire and the later Austro-Hungarian Empire, were *the* dominant powers in Central Europe from the late Middle Ages to 1918. During the nineteenth century, several attempts to unify all German-speaking people failed, leaving Austria outside the newly created German Empire. When the Austro-Hungarian Empire dissolved in 1918 after the First World War, Austria shrank to its German-speaking core with an oversized capital, and people doubted whether the small Republic was actually viable. Thus, one could find supporters of a unification with Germany in all political parties. All of this made the development of an Austrian identity or idea of an individual nation (as cultural basis for an autonomous nation-state of Austria, as it had been recommended by the victorious powers after the First World War) difficult. The young democracy failed, and so did an authoritarian counter project to fascist Nazi Germany, eventually leading to Austria's annexation by Nazi Germany in 1938, which was welcomed by many people. After the devastating atrocities of the National Socialists and a disastrous World War II, the 'Second Democratic Republic of Austria' was founded. In search of a national identity, several myths were born: a glorified remembrance of monarchic Habsburg times, success in ski sports, and the establishment of Austria as a 'cultural nation'. The former monarchy in fact influenced the later Republic, not only in terms of what is labelled a 'culture of remembrance', but also in the form of laws and institutions, many of which have continued to this day. As a consequence of its history, Austria's post-war politics were mainly built on the collaboration of the two main parties—the Social Democratic Party and the People's Party—which have governed the country for many decades.

From a cultural-historical perspective, the Republic relied on structures and mental frameworks originating from a hierarchical aristocratic regency with powerful institutions, formal regulation of social life, a hierarchically determined society, and conservative attitudes. These structures can be explained by the great influence of the Roman Catholic Church throughout the history of the country and the tight, formal ties between the Austrian emperors and the Pope in the Holy Roman Empire. Even though large parts of Austria became Protestant during the Reformation until its end in 1620, Catholic influence has predominated for hundreds of years. Institutional thinking and a God-given hierarchical order among the people permeated the structures during the monarchy and have shaped the nation's culture to a certain extent ever since, including its current form as a democratic nation state. Possibly its most obvious manifestation is the structure of Austria's school system, which is segregated after the first four years of primary school. At the lower secondary level, students and their parents can choose, based on certain criteria, between a vocationally oriented school *(Mittelschule)* and an academically oriented school called a *Gymnasium*. Founded originally by the Catholic congregation of the Jesuits in 1554 and later followed by knights' academies founded by the aristocracy (Engelbrecht, 1984), *Gymnasiums* still have an exclusive and rather conservative image. A common belief in Austrian society is that the ideal education (i.e. the most desirable school trajectory) is a *Gymnasium* education, which eventually grants access to university. The ideas of education standards and international student assessment, however, originated from Protestant-Presbyterian milieus in the United States (US), where education is focused on individual development regardless of collective structural orders, on the empowerment of the individual and how it can fulfil its calling and thus contribute to the realisation of God's empire. Unlike in Catholic-dominated cultures, institutions in the US are in the background, and individuals are expected to rely on their own efforts to achieve good lives (Tröhler, 2011; Markussen, 1995). Correspondingly, the US constitutional mindset strives to protect individuals from the misuse of institutional power and considers the rights of the individuals as givens, while individuals' rights are constituted and limited by law in Austrian and Prussian mindsets. Institutions in, for instance, Austrian mindsets set the boundaries for social and individual life, and individuals are thus embedded in a certain order within the legislation (Hopmann, 2008), in turn belonging to a hierarchically structured whole (Tröhler, 2011). Considering these different cultural foundations, it was intriguing to consider how the pragmatic, Protestant-shaped, and globalised model of standards was adopted, legitimated, and reshaped by a nation state that is deeply rooted in Catholic and aristocratic structures.

However, historically, Austria's segregated school system has been disputed. It is, in fact, a rather longstanding, unsolved political dispute which first began in 1848, and later gained traction in 1922, when the socio-democratic reformer Otto Glöckel initiated trial models for a comprehensive school system at the lower secondary level. In line with Protestant-oriented ideas, the Social Democratic Party has always aimed for a comprehensive school system with only one type of school for compulsory education, while the Conservative party (the Austrian People's Party) has continued to support the diversified system with two different school types at the lower secondary level. Each faction interpreted the PISA results (PISA 2000 results were around the OECD average and ranked between 8 and 11, and PISA 2003 results were slightly below OECD average and ranked between 15 and 20) in favour of its own ideology, perpetuating the same disputes (Bozkurt et al., 2007). Only when references to the PISA winner (Finland) were made did potential solutions to the crisis come up in media discourse, including education standards. In 2003, the idea of standards was presented by a commission called the Future Commission, which was mandated to suggest solutions to the education crisis. Among further measures, it recommended that competence standards should 'systematically improve the school system', orient endeavours towards the outputs of learning, and assure the quality of education (Haider et al., 2005 p. 11ff). Literature on the history of standards has revealed that these measures were hailed as a reasonable, new mode of governance that would introduce autonomy and promote quality management in Austrian schools (Eder and Altrichter, 2009; Wiesner et al., 2020). Simultaneously, those who were involved in the development, implementation, and evaluation of the standards conceded that the discussions of standards mostly concerned how they would be applied, instead of why they were needed (Freudenthaler and Specht, 2006).

Although the discussion on the structure of the school system remained on the agenda and was eventually translated into an effective reform via a school trial in 2008, education standards suddenly became an interesting alternative that was appreciated in the public discussion. In line with this, the Future Commission proclaimed 'quality development before structure reform' (Haider et al., 2005, p. 12) as its reform strategy and focused on teaching and performance rather than changing the structure of the school system (ibid.).

The Future Commission's report did not contain explicit references to education standard models in other countries (Haider et al., 2005), even though the Klieme-Expertise played a significant role in the process, since Germany was the most important reference country for Austrian policymaking (Klieme, 2003; Wiesner et al., 2020). Instead of referring to already existing models, the Future Commission's report introduced the idea of education standards as an innovation without legitimising them. Their quality-improving effect seemed to be obvious, without any need for explanation (Haider et al., 2005). The term 'standards' might have had the same effect as Lundahl and Waldow described in the context of 'quick languages': by reducing complexity, the term 'standards' 'offers a shared medium of communication and facilitates dialogue within the educational system' (Lundahl and Waldow, 2009; Waldow, 2012, p. 420), meaning that the term itself had legitimising power because of its discursive omnipresence.

Investigating the process of recontextualisation offers insight not only into national values, characteristics, and priorities, but also into the process of legitimisation and reasoning for school reforms. It therefore appeared to be a promising way to discover the 'why' of implementing standards and its embeddedness in the Catholic-conservative cultural context of Austria.

Externalisation in Public Discourse

The process of externalisation has already been described in various publications (Schriewer, 1992; Steiner-Khamsi and Waldow, 2012). The term refers to Luhmann's systems theory, which referred to different sub-systems that fulfil different functions in society. The sub-systems are internally linked communications that act autonomously and seek to maintain themselves (autopoiesis). However, systems can be irritated by external communications. An irritation is processed by the system or sub-system trying to integrate and make meaning of the new input (the principle of operative closure), which explains the core of the externalisation process. By using external points of reference, education systems can legitimate and process unresolved issues, and in so doing, restore their self-referentiality. External points of reference can be many systems, situations, organisations, or values. In the case of communication regarding reform needs in education systems, important points of reference can be systems of science, certain values (such as those provided by religious systems or political parties), highly trusted organisations like the OECD, national actors like interest groups or institutions, or so-called 'world situations' (Schriewer, 1992). Such a world situation can, for instance, entail a critical number of nation states referring to a similar reform concept by participating in discourse on, in the case at hand, education standards. According to Steiner-Khamsi, externalisation to world situations often happens, not for rational reasons, but for political or economic ones (Steiner-Khamsi, 2012, 2013). In protracted policy conflicts, international data and ideas provide seemingly neutral solutions that parties can accept without breaching their values and commitments. Simultaneously, the specific issue at hand that is processed within the education (political) system of a nation state is redefined to fit the international 'solution' (Steiner-Khamsi, 2013).

The local policy context as a research field often focuses on the investigation of specific stages of policy processes, such as policy formulation, formal processes of reform design, and the final documentation of reforms and their implementation. This kind of research offers important and extensive insight into these processes; however, a blind spot in the research regarding the local policy context is public discourse in terms of reactions to reform suggestions by people who are not officially involved in the reform process, but who are, as citizens, professionals, parents, or students, concerned about the reform. Theory on school reform has demonstrated that curriculum work occurs on different levels and is an aggregate of multiple layers in which public discourse has a prominent place (Hopmann, 1991). In democratic nation states, reforms are not only prepared for the public, but need to be legitimised by the public and become subject to public deliberations. The segmentation of the levels of discourse in curriculum reform is an essential component that ensures a democratic process—not in the sense of a participative approach, but in the sense that the subject matter is part of public and transparent deliberation by different groups that balance different arguments, take different aspects and perspectives into consideration, and give precise reasons for what they are demanding and claiming. Different sectors of society that are concerned about the reform acquire an arena where they can be included in the process—formally and informally—such as by contributing to media discourse. A historical analysis of curriculum reforms in Prussia revealed that reforms failed if different interests were not considered in the reform process:

> All attempts to proceed without such a discourse segmentation failed. If the entire process of curriculum making was handed over to a single body like, for example, academic institutes or general commissions on school reform, the administration's two direct counterparts in the deliberation process, i.e. the public and the practioners (sic) from local or school levels, felt pushed aside and made the administration feel that its legitimation capacity would not be sufficient to overcome their combined intervention. This is exactly why some of the major West German curriculum revision projects of the 1960s and 70s were closed down. (Hopmann, 1991, p. 61)

Accordingly, Haft and Hopmann developed a model of formal linkages in curriculum making (Fig. 1), in which the school, the administration, and the public contributed to curriculum discourse. Even though the recently increasing inclusion of experts and expert commissions might introduce new aspects to the picture (Seifert, 2012; Weingart, 2003), the model describes the reform processes in an accurate way and holds true for both general educational reforms and curriculum reforms in particular (which both apply in the case of the implementation of education standards in Austria). The model described public discourse as an 'external force' that contributes to curriculum discourse, in which problems are defined and implementation is provided (Hopmann, 1991, p. 65).

People who are not officially involved in the reform process can contribute their opinions, statements, suggestions, and demands through 'regular channels of public debate', such as, for example, via hearings, informal talks, and cooperation with people and powers in the administration (ibid.). People can also make use of the media to mobilise others, point to hitherto unfamiliar or unmentioned topics and, in so doing, participate in collective struggles over the definitions of situations. Paying attention to media debates and their role in policy making is not only rewarding because they are part of the legitimatisation of politics and play an essential role in the endeavours of the welfare state (cf. Enli et al., 2018), but also because they have an important impact on collective stocks of knowledge by structuring and distributing knowledge in society (Keller et al., 2018). This analysis therefore focused on the order of knowledge presented within media discourse. More precisely, it investigated newspaper articles that expressed the views of citizens in the form of debate articles, chronicle articles, editorials, and letters to the editors. In so doing, it provided a description of one of the multiple layers of curriculum reform.

Data and Method

The data for the study were collected from a media database called APA-DeFacto (https://www.defacto.at/wissenswelt/home.htm), accessed during May and June 2020. APA stands for Austrian Press Agency, and the database provides national and some international newspaper articles dating back to 1990 and press agency releases

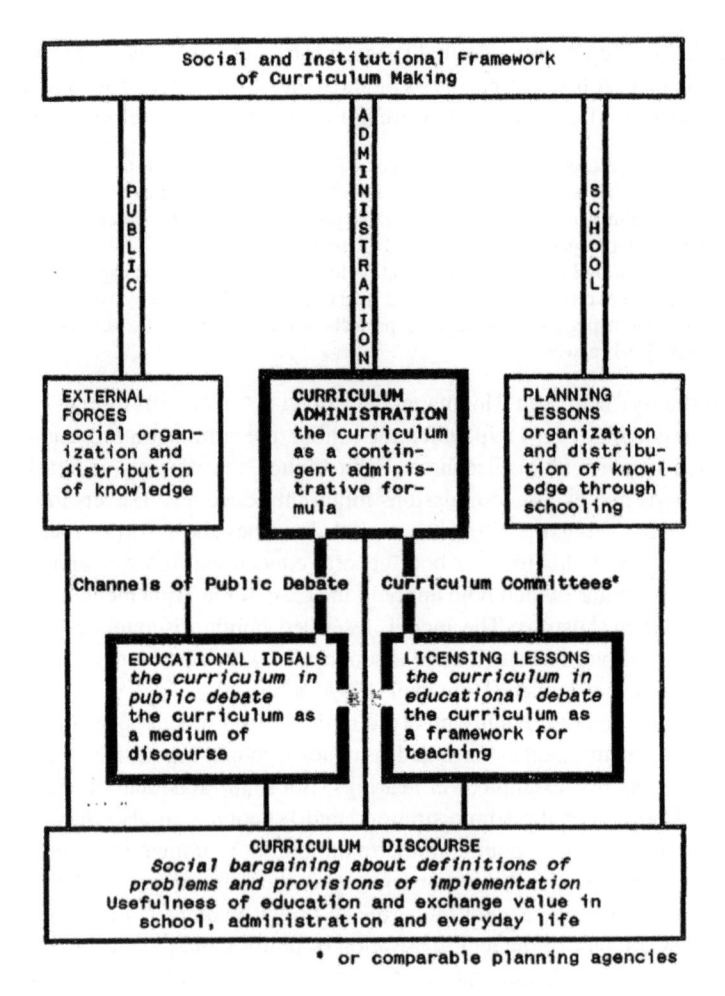

Fig. 1 The formal linkages of curriculum making (Hopmann, 1991, p. 65). The figure reveals public discourse as an external force that contributes to curriculum making, together with discourse in administration and schools

from 1955 to date. From a database comprising about 130 million articles from more than 800 different media, I searched for the term *Bildungsstandards* (education standards) in national, daily, and weekly newspapers. This is the most common term used for the school reform, and it also covers competency descriptions for curricula and national standardised tests. In 198 newspapers, 1807 articles published between 1 January 2000 and 31 December 2010 contained the term *Bildungsstandards*. Since my research interest was directed towards articles that presented opinions and arguments (chronicle articles), I selected only those articles that fulfilled this criterion. I included not only chronicle articles, but also editorials and letters to the editors, because they also expressed the opinions of Austrian citizens and therefore represented public discourse. This led to a dataset of 72 items.

Statements in the media can be regarded as a representation of the social knowledge of social agents who aim to gain legitimacy and recognition of their own interpretations of the world. By bringing themselves into the discourse, the agents hope to obtain coalitions, support, and attention for their positions within the struggle for the definition of situations (Keller, 2018). By applying the 'sociology of knowledge approach to discourse' (SKAD; Keller, 2018), my analysis focused on the reconstruction of knowledge orders and relations (i.e. how the discourse on education standards was constructed in Austrian newspapers). How were standards conceptualised and legitimised? What kind of definitions did the discourse use in collective struggles for education standards and with what effects? And who was allowed to speak and define the matter at hand? (ibid.) One important caveat with regard to the sample was that it was affected by social bias. In most cases, only people with a certain background have the opportunity to publish their comments in the media, and only a specific group of people writes letters to newspapers. It requires a certain amount of language proficiency and the ability to formulate arguments and opinions in a way that matches the expectations of newspapers. The data was therefore not representative of the public as a whole, but rather represented a well-informed and engaged group of people: journalists, representatives of occupational groups, researchers, pupil and student representatives, parents, teachers, headmasters, officials from the education administration, and representatives of the Catholic Church were among those who discussed standards in newspapers in the given period.

The SKAD methodology builds both on socio-constructivist concepts of knowledge (Berger and Luckmann, 1966) and Foucault's concepts of discourse and knowledge regimes (Foucault, 1966, 1969; all cited in Keller et al., 2018). It aims to overcome the individualistic approach of a single person's utterances by focusing on the discursive processes by which collective stocks of knowledge are produced, circulated, and manifested. The analysis therefore concerned, not the expressions of single contributors, but how the collective stock of knowledge was structured and situated in relation to the temporal, social, and geographical space (ibid.).

Education standards in Austria were introduced on the premise that the level of student performance was unsatisfactory and that the quality of the school system needed to be improved (Haider et al., 2005). This was the official justification for the reform measures. By investigating public discourse regarding the implementation of education standards, my analysis complemented the existing picture by making visible how citizens conceptualised the suggested reforms and on what basis they built their arguments. Officially involved policy actors often draw on international language and global ideas because they are confronted with them in their reform work. Simultaneously, people who are not officially involved in the reform process are obliged to draw more on their own local experience in the meaning-making process when defining the situation. In some cases, they react to reform suggestions that they can support, complement with new arguments, or criticise. In other cases, they present arguments on related topics and refer to reform suggestions as supporting evidence. In formulating their arguments, they draw on their previous stocks of experience, which differ from those of people who are officially mandated to develop the reform. Different systems of relevance explain the different approaches, which, according to SKAD, should be regarded as a collective discourse.

The analysis aimed to reveal the unfolding structuration of meaning in the public discourse on standards in Austria. I was interested in discovering what kinds of definitions were used in the collective struggle for standards and with what effects. More precisely, the research questions for the analysis were:

(1) How is the global idea of education standards conceptualised in local public discourse?
(2) Which local problems that should be solved by standards can be identified in the discourse?
(3) Why can standards be regarded as a meaningful reform in the local policy context of Austria?

Analysis

The SKAD (Keller, 2007, 2011, 2018) suggests five different categories that orient the analysis of discourses, out of which four were considered relevant for the analysis. Firstly, different social and collective meanings and action-organising schemes that are transmitted via discourses can be identified. I was interested in identifying which knowledge patterns certain groups of people established to interpret and deal with specific life situations. These *interpretative schemes* are a result of the social construction of reality and play an essential role in allowing us to master our daily lives, because they help us to identify and distinguish different typical situations from others and give us ideas about what to do and how to react in certain situations. In the case of statements on education standards in the Austrian media, it was of interest to learn how meaning regarding education standards was made, how the standards were conceptualised, and as responses to which situations. I also aimed to determine the expectations of standards and what problems they were considered to solve. Secondly, by identifying *argumentation clusters*, different types of arguments within a discourse can be made visible. Thirdly, *phenomenal structures* deal with the way in which phenomena are constituted within concrete discourses. Discourse participants refer to the topic from different angles and address its various dimensions. Chronicle articles can be based on sarcasm, present arguments, dramatise current conditions, present narratives, be data- and fact-oriented, and much more. Also, the knowledge constructed within discursive meaning-making can refer to different forms of evidence, such as scientific, moral, religious, or political evidence. Given that these structures can easily change over time, their reconstruction is especially interesting when compared to similar reconstructions over time. Fourthly, the *narrative structures* of a discourse map the way statements and discourse are narrated. This is a configurative act that relates signs and statements in the form of narratives by establishing categories for the analysis (interpretive schemes, classifications, and dimensions of the phenomenal structure) in relation to each other. In the case of education standards discussed in the Austrian media, it was of interest to understand how the knowledge on standards was presented in the media and what kinds of stories were told about them (ibid.). The fifth category, *classifications,* deals with the visualisation of 'highly effective forms of social typification processes' (Keller, 2018, p. 33), which establish an order with clear consequences for action. The data featured reasoning and arguments and were rather theoretically oriented; hence, since identifying classifications was not applicable and there were no clear consequences for action, this category was excluded from the subsequent analysis.

The data were analysed using typical methods drawn from grounded theory, such as theory-oriented sampling, minimum and maximum contrasting, and axial coding. Following the four categories presented above, my analysis identified interpretative schemes with respect to (1) the conceptualisation of education standards and (2) their legitimation. Thereafter, (3) argumentation clusters were identified and (4) the phenomenal and narrative structures of the discourse were determined.

(1)   Interpretative schemes: the conceptualisation of education standards

The discourse on standards in the media was quite polarised. The authors of the articles argued either for or against standards and rarely took a differentiated position. Of course, some authors suggested directions and changes for the implementation and emphasised a need for various types of action, but no article suggested alternative ways of measuring school quality and student performance (which, in fact, was suggested by the prominent researcher Werner Specht; see Wiesner et al., 2020), or discussed possible collateral damages. The core collective meaning that emerged within the articles was that standards were a means to objectify not only student and teacher performance, but also the performance of the whole school system. The articles revealed a deep longing for a more just school system, with student performance comparable across different schools. This became especially relevant in the fourth grade, when pupils had to decide whether to attend an academically oriented school type (a *Gymnasium*) or a grammar school (a *Mittelschule or Hauptschule*). This decision was not irreversible, but constituted a high-stakes decision that determined the students' futures to a large extent. Standards, so the authors believed, would ensure that the decisions would be based on objective data and no longer depend on teachers' 'subjective grading of performance' (Article 15). In other words, the imagined ideal was that every pupil should end up in a school that matched his or her actual level of talent:

> There is one principle that must be followed: those who are proficient enough for a *Gymnasium*, should go to a *Gymnasium* [...] But what does it mean nowadays to be proficient enough for a *Gymnasium*? Good grades received as a gift? It is necessary to find more objective criteria to remove the pressure from the primary school teachers. This happens now with education standards. This insight came late. Very late. (Article 66)

The overall firm belief in the objectivity of standards was not only evident in the context of student performance, but also in the context of teacher performance and school quality in general, and some articles argued that standards would be an appropriate way to ensure quality in the event of the school system being changed to a comprehensive school system. The concept of education standards was also interpreted as a means to improve student performance and the school system in general by documenting the students' knowledge and making the school system more competitive. Throughout the articles, there was a pervasive fear of falling even further behind in the international competition, which was argued by referring to other, successful countries. In the example below, the author proclaimed that Austria was finally about to implement standards, but ...

> ...even before they [the standards] were on the table (where are they?), the Ministry has put on the breaks and assured us that the results will in no case be used competitively and that it will not be permitted to communicate the results in the form of public rankings. Quality checks as privatissimum. Once more, it is worth looking to the avant-garde north. If a school ranks top in a subject matter in Finland, the PR-gurus of the school promote it with brochures. If a school scores below average, the school board calls for a conference with the teachers concerned and discusses measures to address the deficits. This ranges from additional teaching in the afternoons to splitting classrooms and additional seminars for the teachers. (Article 16)

The counter-discourse on education standards was comparatively small, based on the number of articles: only ten out of 72 articles argued against standards. The discourse was quite fragmented and based on different arguments. A common conceptualisation was that standards were an insufficient, narrow means of measuring education, which was vaguely depicted as something different and more comprehensive than the standards tested. Further arguments presented in the articles were that it was impossible to lift all students' performances to the same level; that standards would lead to manipulation and undesirable competition, rewards those with good performances; and that science was being misused to support other interests.

(2) Interpretative schemes: the legitimation of education standards

The common reason for supporting education standards was, in fact, a conviction that the school system was in dire need of reform. This was asserted with no justification in most of the articles. Only limited exceptions referred to PISA results as the reason for the school system needing to be reformed. The implementation of standards was also presented as a means to make school performance comparable. The different levels of mastery in different schools were experienced as an injustice, and equal education opportunities were demanded for all students. Equal education opportunities were predominantly mentioned in the context of access to the *Gymnasiums* (i.e. the academic school type that opens the way to higher education). The argument was that all students who are talented enough should be given the opportunity to attend an academic secondary school.

A further, important way of legitimating standards concerned quality assurance. Standards, so the argument went, would ensure quality in the event of a comprehensive school system being implemented in Austria. This was a prominent argument in the protracted policy conflict regarding comprehensive schooling, because one of the main arguments of its opponents was that a common school system from the first to eighth grades would lead to a downgrading of the quality level. One article argued that the quality of a vital reform of the curriculum for Islamic religious education could be assured by standards, thus contributing to new curricula that would be better aligned with the conditions of a democratic nation state (Article 12).

International references were rarely used to justify standards. Some cases mentioned Finland as a positive example for dealing with standards and as an argument for increasing the standardised test results. Only twice were the average reading performance results of Austrian pupils in PISA used as a reason for demanding education standards. One article referred to an unspecified OECD study proving that Austrian schools and teachers were seldom or never evaluated externally. The author therefore demanded the implementation of education standards and a general reform of the teacher education system (Article 64).

The anti-standards discourse based its arguments mainly on test critiques (standards cannot measure education or prepare students for the future) and a critique of the standards' underlying conception of education.

(3) Argumentation clusters

The different discourse strands among those who argued for education standards could be assigned to specific clusters, which in many cases overlapped. The most comprehensive cluster concerned arguments that promoted competition, following an economically market-based notion of growth and ambition. Student performance, school quality, and teaching quality were supposed to become better and higher, resulting in better performance in international comparative studies. A further cluster dealt with equity in education, demanding equal opportunities for all students. This overlapped with a cluster of arguments stemming from parents' need for reliable expectations: 'Will my child receive adequate education at the school we have decided on?' Pedagogical modes of reasoning followed two different strands. One was based on the idea of progress, claiming that each student should advance in her or his learning and that additional support needs should be detected as early as possible. The other argued for a more comprehensive understanding of education and results which definitely rejected the idea of standards. The final cluster stemmed from a legal discourse strand and proclaimed the right of citizens to know how public resources are used in schools and with what degree of success.

(4) Phenomenal and narrative structures

The discourse arguing for education standards was relatively coherent and unambivalent. The articles and their way of conceptualising and discussing the need for standards were compatible with each other and followed a common narrative. The only variation within the discourse concerned the level of the standards, with some articles arguing that the current suggestions were too lenient. The overall narrative reflected the uncertainty people experienced with schooling and the future in general: everybody hoped that their children would be successful. Merits that were perceived as being distributed in a non-objective way, arbitrarily, and limiting the freedom of school choice led to a longing for a school system that would deliver what it promised. Standards were regarded as such 'promises', and as an effort to set up precise goals for education that could lead to desired success. The whole pro-standards discourse told the story of how standards could easily fix a wide variety of problems in Austrian schools and at the same time restore a feeling of security and control to the people.

The discourse arguing against standards was, firstly, small and inhomogeneous. It adopted a protective attitude towards a comprehensive understanding of education and the students' role in learning. Education should not comprise only the mere learning of facts, but should also encompass social skills and holistic human development. The narrative concerned school as a place for holistic learning without any pressure, where the students would be inspired by a wide range of content matter. This discourse drew on the traditional German concept of *Bildung*, which refers to a holistic form of education that exceeds the narrow conception of education in the case of education standards.

Summary

The analysis aimed to reveal how standards were conceptualised in the public discourse, which local problems should be solved by them, and why they appeared as a meaningful solution.

Firstly, the polarised discourse revealed a firm belief in the objectivity of standards and their potential to end the perceived injustice within the school system. They were regarded as a means to improve student performance and school quality by documenting the students' knowledge and making the school system more competitive. However, the discourse arguing against standards emphasised the narrow understanding of education that underpins the concept of standards and competence, warning against a focus on competition.

Like discourse at the political and administrative level, standards were rarely justified by arguments that went beyond the mere use of catchwords in public discourse. In general, standards appeared to be a self-evident measure for responding to some problems in Austrian schools. In particular, they were referred to as a means of making school performance more comparable and providing equal opportunities for all students. These 'equal opportunities' were coded in terms of access to the academic strand of secondary education—the so-called *Gymnasium*. One further relevant point in the reasoning was the demand for quality assurance, which was often mentioned as a solution to the protracted policy conflict regarding the school structure. By implementing standards, so the argument went, a comprehensive school system could assure high quality and avoid a levelling of performance, as predicted by the opponents of a comprehensive school system.

Externalisation (i.e. references to PISA studies or other countries' school systems) played a minor role, but was nevertheless part of the discourse. References to PISA served mostly to legitimate the education crisis proclaimed in the discourse, with Finland mentioned as a best-practice example for the implementation of standards. Those who argued for higher stakes in relation to standards usually referred to Finland.

The standards were praised as a solution to problems associated with the uncertainty that people experienced with regard to the future and to the effectiveness of education and learning. The most apparent local problem people perceived was that of the arbitrary grading of students. 'Subjective' forms of grading made people unsure about the students' actual performance and could jeopardise future opportunities. Standards, however, seemed to promise information on students' real performance and were therefore perceived as more just. One further local problem was the impression that the Austrian school system was of lower quality than expected, at least according to the PISA results in 2000 and, especially, in 2003, when Austria was ranked lower than Germany—an important reference country for Austria. People wondered whether their children or students would learn enough at school to be successful in their later lives. Before the Austrian system was diagnosed as not being good enough, people had to trust the schools they were provided with and probably assumed that the state would ensure the necessary quality, enabling their children and students to make their way into the future. Education standards were presented as a means to stimulate learning progress and to document the schools' work; thus, they were perceived as a guarantee of improved quality in schools and, as a whole nation, competitiveness in international testing.

Discussion: Standards As a Means of Placing Students

The discourse analysis of newspaper articles on education standards in Austria revealed that the knowledge presented in public discourse was based on a serious concern about the younger generation's future opportunities. It conceptualised standards as a tool for providing realistic and reliable expectations and giving people and the administration objective data and clear goals for achievement. The social problem of the uncertainty of social advancement has always been regarded as a main driving force for schools, but the data for this article made it clear, on the one hand, how serious this concern was and, on the other hand, the extent to which the concern motivated the development of amplified educational solutions for dealing with an undefined future (Tröhler, 2016).

According to Tröhler, the idea of education standards emerged from a Presbyterian/Methodist milieu in the US, where experimental psychologists laid the ground for a modern empirical education science (Tröhler, 2019; Tröhler and Maricic, in press). Standards were considered a means to support individuals in finding their way into their future lives. Education, according to a Protestant mindset, deals with an individual's soul, which is supposed to be empowered and prepared to make a contribution to society (or, in other terms, realise God's empire) (Tröhler, 2011, 2019; Markussen, 1995). As my analysis revealed, whenever people in Austria argued for education standards, they referred to them as a means to determine students' levels of mastery, which should in turn determine the students' further education opportunities. Standards were conceptualised as a 'quick fix' for determining the students' placement in the education system: are they proficient enough to attend an academically oriented G*ymnasium* school or does their level of proficiency correspond better with the demands of a vocationally oriented *Hauptschule*? Similarly, on the system level, standards were expected to ensure that a comprehensive school system could deliver adequate, high-quality education according to each student's personal needs. This corresponded with a Catholic mode of thinking that regarded each individual as belonging to a hierarchically structured society (see section two above). Education within this tradition focuses on each individual finding their place in the collective order, and schooling contributes to this search by its placement function. Schools as crucial societal institutions constitute an authority that leads students to their place within the societal order by applying appropriate pedagogical strategies and methods and establishing a more or less transparent meritocratic framework for how to succeed. From this perspective, education standards appeared as an appropriate and 'objective' means to define who is granted which type of education. The contributions in the Austrian media I analysed clearly revealed a longing for objective ways of defining a student's level of mastery, because it eased the burden of unjust and highly life-affecting decisions, leaving them to the seemingly objective outcomes of standardised tests.

People's expectation that standards might also ensure the quality of a comprehensive school reform was another interesting result of my analysis. The struggle over Austria's school structure has been ongoing for about a century with the two main political parties—the Social Democratic Party and the Austrian People's Party (the conservatives)—locked into fixed positions. While the Social Democratic Party has always aimed for an equal society, the Austrian People's Party has instead argued for a structure in which efforts and success are rewarded. In different periods of time and in different parts of Austria, one or the other ideology has been at the forefront of discourse, arguing for either an elitist or an egalitarian paradigm. Drawing on the concept of standards, some conservative politicians were suddenly willing to discuss a comprehensive school system, provided that education standards ensured the quality of schooling. To them, standards appeared to be a means to control students' development, ensuring that each individual would receive appropriate teaching. This could also be regarded as reflecting a Catholic mindset that perceives institutions as providing the means and structures to guarantee that students will find their places in the societal order. A protracted policy conflict (Steiner-Khamsi, 2013) led to a temporary solution in the form of several school reform trials; however, ironically, Austria's (culturally determined) reform has eventually ended up as a reform of the vocationally oriented *Hauptschule* that still exists next to the academically oriented *Gymnasium*. Austria's school system is therefore effectively segregated to this day.

The global idea of education standards was as a paradigmatic change that could potentially fix some social problems and unify quite contradictory political positions and world views. One year before their implementation in 2009, the director of the Austrian institute responsible for the implementation of the standards talked about a 'real paradigmatic change for teachers', because it would be 'output oriented' and teachers would no longer 'teach the students content', but rather 'develop their competencies' (derstandard.at, 2020). Ten years later, a study on the effect of standards recognised that standards had fallen short of expectations. Data-based decision-making rarely takes place and has only a very limited impact on school and teaching development (Zuber et al., 2018). A further often-mentioned political ambition was to develop a more equitable school system (Geppert et al., 2012; Hopmann et al.,

2010)—an ambition that has hitherto not become a reality. The expectation that standards can objectively decide the appropriate school type for an individual student can never be fulfilled, since standards are by definition not an individual measurement tool, but a tool that relies on, and is even legitimised by, aggregated data. People's high hopes of standards as expressed within the public discourse therefore contrasted with the standards' efficacy, and both politics and research could have been clearer about the limits and constraints of the new policy tool (cf. Tröhler, 2019).

This chapter has presented the public discourse regarding the implementation of education standards in the local policy context of Austria, informed by a Catholic-conservative history of culture. The recontextualisation of an originally Protestant idea of standards in a Catholic context illustrates the different manifestations of global concepts in different cultures, leading to the development of different meanings of terms such as 'equity', 'equality', 'fairness', 'future', and similar; for instance, discourses on equity are based on different images of a society, and discourses on students' futures can fundamentally vary from each other. What the different translations and meanings have in common, however, is people's desire to deal with the uncertainty of the future. Together with their expectations that standards give clear directions for decisions on the future and objective data on the proficiency of schools and their students, this desire poses important challenges and tasks for both research and politics. The extent to which standards can live up to expectations, and how far they are a justified answer to people's desires, should be clearly addressed and discussed.

Appendix: Overview of the Database

Art. no.	Date	Title of article	Newspaper
1	27.6.2009	Das Wichtigste fehlt noch	Salzburger Nachrichten
2	9.6.2008	Bildung: Her mit den Standards!	Die Presse
3	24.6.2008	Bildung: Wehret den Standards!	Die Presse
4	6.5.2009	Bildungspolitik, Bildungsforschung und Statistik	Die Presse
5	5.2.2009	Schüler und Lehrer brauchen mehr Qualitätskontrolle	Burgenländische Volkszeitung
6	8.5.2009	Das Schweigen der Lämmer	Die Presse
7	29.8.2007	Die Mär vom «Ernst des Lebens»	Die Presse
8	6.12.2007	Die Neue Mittelschule geht baden	Die Presse
9	8.8.2007	Es geht um Werte, nicht um Organisation	Wiener Zeitung

(continued)

(continued)

Art. no.	Date	Title of article	Newspaper
10	17.1.2006	Gleiche Bildungschancen. Zukunft trotz Herkunft	Die Furche
11	17.1.2006	Ideologische Sackgasse	Die Furche
12	1.2.2009	Scheitert Österreich, scheitert Europa	Die Presse
13	5.3.2008	Geheimniskrämerei als Reform	Die Presse
14	11.10.2007	Gesamtschule: Schöne Vision, schlechte Praxis	Die Presse
15	23.4.2008	Gleiches Unrecht für alle Schulpflichtigen	Der Standard
16	22.9.2004	Der große Reformstau	Kleine Zeitung
17	22.12.2004	Ohne Titel/no title	Kleine Zeitung
18	1.6.2005	Gerechtigkeit	Kleine Zeitung
19	3.8.2007	Debatte Leistungs-Schmiede Kindergarten	Kleine Zeitung
20	20.8.2007	Schritte in richtige Richtung	Kleine Zeitung
21	28.10.2007	Bildung in der Sackgasse	Kleine Zeitung
22	6.3.2008	Noten für Lehrer	Kleine Zeitung
23	30.4.2008	Prüfungsangst?	Kleine Zeitung
24	4.7.2008	Bildungsstandards einführen	Kleine Zeitung
25	26.7.2008	Neue Tests, alte Probleme	Kleine Zeitung
26	23.1.2009	Bildungsstandards: ein Qualitätssprung	Kleine Zeitung
27	13.2.2008	Krise der Schule, Krise der Schulpolitik	Die Presse
28	31.5.2008	Warum wehren sich die Lehrer gegen eine Beurteilung ihrer Leistung?	Kronen Zeitung
29	9.6.2008	Wie jedes Jahr um diese Zeit geht die Prüfungsangst um	Kronen Zeitung
30	20.4.2006	Lehrergewerkschaft: Bitte nicht stören!	Wiener Zeitung
31	17.12.2008	Naturwissenschaft wird vernachlässigt	Niederösterreichische Nachrichten
32	4.11.2009	Bildung steht im Wandel	Niederösterreichische Nachrichten
33	29.1.2009	Nur «Befriedigend» für Schüler—und Lehrer	Die Presse
34	1.12.2004	Ohne Titel/no title	OÖN
35	27.12.2004	Weit weg von PISA	OÖN
36	1.12.2007	Frühförderung	OÖN

(continued)

(continued)

Art. no.	Date	Title of article	Newspaper
37	6.9.2005	Noten in Österreich? Schall und Rauch	Die Presse
38	19.12.2005	Wie toll ist das Gegenteil von «Eintopf»?	Die Presse
39	10.9.2006	Bildungspolitiker im Bildungsnotstand	Die Presse
40	6.3.2007	Schulvisionen—braucht die SPÖ dafür einen Arzt?	Die Presse
41	13.2.2008	Noten-Lotterie	Neues Volksblatt
42	13.1.2009	Prüfstand	Neues Volksblatt
43	25.6.2010	Ziel aus den Augen verloren	Die Presse
44	13.2.2004	Feilschen um die Schulqualität	Die Presse
45	3.3.2004	Der lange Weg der Schulen ins 21. Jahrhundert	Die Presse
46	18.5.2004	Bildungsstandards führen zu Rankings	Die Presse
47	25.5.2004	Die Vorteile von E-Learning	Die Presse
48	25.5.2004	PISA ist ein schiefer Turm	Die Presse
49	8.6.2004	Das lange Warten auf die Schulreform	Die Presse
50	14.4.2005	33 Empfehlungen–und noch offene Fragen	Die Presse
51	3.5.2005	Eltern für klare Bildungsstandards	Die Presse
52	3.5.2005	Schüler: Unterricht oft «unaktuell»	Die Presse
53	3.5.2005	Die Gesamtschule lebt—in der schlechtesten Form	Die Presse
54	15.12.2008	Was ist los mit Österreichs Lehrern?	Die Presse
55	28.4.2008	Pädagogen auf dem Prüfstand	Die Presse
56	15.9.2009	Reform statt jonglieren mit Puzzlesteinen!	Die Presse
57	11.5.2004	Der Standpunkt	Salzburger Nachrichten
58	22.6.2004	Bildungs—NOTstandards	Salzburger Nachrichten
59	9.11.2006	Der Standpunkt	Salzburger Nachrichten
60	16.7.2007	Der Standpunkt	Salzburger Nachrichten
61	9.8.2007	Warum Intelligenztests auch dumm machen können	Salzburger Nachrichten
62	10.3.2009	Gleiche Preise für die Noten	Salzburger Nachrichten
63	6.5.2009	Überwachung der Bildung	Salzburger Nachrichten

(continued)

(continued)

Art. no.	Date	Title of article	Newspaper
64	27.6.2009	Das Wichtigste fehlt noch	Salzburger Nachrichten
65	15.2.2010	Leistungstests an den Schulen	Salzburger Nachrichten
66	21.1.2006	Schwach ist nicht schlecht	Tiroler Tageszeitung
67	13.6.2009	Unwissenheit ist Stärke	Vorarlberger Nachrichten
68	3.7.2010	Der begrenzte Horizont	Vorarlberger Nachrichten
69	13.3.2009	Wenn sie nur immer so streitbar wären	Der Standard
70	1.3.2009	Wie finde ich die richtige Schule?	Die Presse
71	2.7.2010	Tag der Wahrheit?	Wiener Zeitung
72	29.1.2008	Zahlen für eine bessere Schule?	Die Presse

References

Altrichter, H., & Posch, P. (2007). Analyse erster Erfahrungen mit der Implementierung von Bildungsstandards. *Erziehung und Unterricht, 157*(7–8).
Berger, P. L., & Luckmann, T. (1966). *The social construction of reality*. Anchor Books.
Bozkurt, D., Brinek, G., & Retzl, M. (2007). PISA in Österreich. Mediale Reaktionen, öffentliche Bewertungen und politische Konsequenzen. In *PISA zufolge Pisa—PISA According to PISA: Halt Pisa, was es verspricht?—Does PISA Keep What It Promises?* (pp. 321–362). Lit Verlag.
derstandard.at. (2020, March 6). *Bildungsstandards: "Ein Paradigmenwechsel für LehrerInnen"*. https://www.derstandard.at/story/3251386/bildungsstandards-ein-paradigmenwechsel-fuer-lehrerinnen
EACEA P9 Eurydice. (2009). *National testing of pupils in Europe: Objectives, organisation and use of results*. Retrieved from Education, Audiovisual and Culture Agency, P9 Eurydice. European Commission.
Eder, F., & Altrichter, H. (2009). Qualitätsentwicklung und Qualitätssicherung im österreichischen Schulwesen: Bilanz aus 15 Jahren Diskussion und Entwicklungsperspektiven für die Zukunft. In *Nationaler Bildungsbericht Österreich 2009. Band 2: Fokussierte Analysen bildungspolitischer Schwerpunktthemen*. Salzburg: Leykam.
Engelbrecht, H. (1984). *Geschichte des österreichischen Bildungswesens. Erziehung und Unterricht auf dem Boden Österreichs, Band 3, Von der frühen Aufklärung bis zum Vormärz*. Wien.
Enli, G., Syvertsen, T., & Mjøs, O. J. (2018). The welfare state and the media system. *Scandinavian Journal of History, 43*(5), 601–623.
Foucault, M. (1966). *The order of things: An archaeology of the human sciences*. Routledge.
Foucault, M. (1969). *The archaeology of knowledge and the discourse on language*. Vintage Books.
Freudenthaler, H. H., & Specht, W. (2006). *Bildungsstandards: der Implementationsprozess aus der Sicht der Praxis: Ergebnisse einer Fragebogen-Studie nach dem ersten Jahr der Pilotphase II*. Zentrum für Schulentwicklung, Abt. Evaluation und Schulforschung, Bundesministerium für Bildung, Wissenschaft und Kultur.
George, A. C., Schreiner, C., Wiesner, C., Pointinger, M., & Pacher, K. (2019). *Fünf Jahre flächendeckende Bildungsstandardüberprüfungen in Österreich: Vertiefende Analysen zum Zyklus 2012 bis 2016*. Waxmann Verlag.

Geppert, C., Bauer-Hofmann, S., & Hopmann, S. (2012). Policy reform efforts and equal opportunity—an evidence-based link? An analysis of current sector reforms in the Austrian school system. *CEPS Journal: Center for Educational Policy Studies Journal, 2*(2), 9–29.

Greiner, U., Hofmann, F., Schreiner, C., & Wiesner, C. (2020). *Bildungsstandards: Kompetenzorientierung, Aufgabenkultur und Qualitätsentwicklung im Schulsystem.* Waxmann Verlag GmbH.

Haider, G., Eder, F., Specht, W., Spiel, C., & Wimmer, M. (2005). *Abschlussbericht der Zukunftskomission an Frau Bundesministerin Elisabeth Gehrer.* Wien: Bundesministerium für Bildung, Wissenschaft und Kultur.

Hopmann, S. T. (1991). Retracing Curriculum History: Curriculum Administration as Symbolic Action. In B.B. Gundem, B.U. Engelsen & B. Karseth (eds.) *Curriculum Work and Curriculum Content, Theory and Practice: Contemporary and Historical Perspectives* (pp. 49–68). University of Oslo.

Hopmann, S. T. (2008). No child, no school, no state left behind: Schooling in the age of accountability. *Journal of Curriculum Studies, 40*(4), 417–456.

Hopmann, S. T., Bauer, S., & Geppert, C. (2010). *Bildungspolitik im Widerstreit. Metaanalyse aktueller österreichischer Bildungsprogramme.* (NOESIS Arbeitsbericht Nr. 2).

Keller, R. (2007). Diskurse und Dispositive analysieren: die wissenssoziologische Diskursanalyse als Beitrag zu einer wissensanalytischen Profilierung der Diskursforschung. *Forum Qualitative Sozialforschung, 8*(2), 73–107.

Keller, R. (2011). *Wissenssoziologische Diskursanalyse: Grundlegung eines Forschungsprogramms.* VS Verlag für Sozialwissenschaften.

Keller, R. (2018). The sociology of knowledge approach to discourse. An introduction. In *The sociology of knowledge approach to discourse. Investigating the politics of knowledge and meaning-making.* Routledge.

Keller, R., Hornidge, A.-K., & Schünemann, W. (2018). *The sociology of knowledge approach to discourse: Investigating the politics of knowledge and meaning-making.* Routledge.

Klieme, E. (2003). *Zur Entwicklung nationaler Bildungsstandards. Eine Expertise.* Deutsches Institut für Internationale Pädagogische Forschung.

Koch, C., & Beer, R. (2010). Schwerpunkt: Standards machen Schule. *Erziehung und Unterricht, 160*(3–4), 218–373.

Lundahl, C., & Waldow, F. (2009). Standardisation and 'quick languages': The shape-shifting of standardised measurement of pupil achievement in Sweden and Germany. *Comparative Education, 45*(3), 365–385.

Markussen, I. (1995). Den store læseplan. In K. Schnack (ed.), *Didaktiske studier: vol. 20. Læseplanstudier 3* (pp. 311–325). Danmarks Lærerhøjskole.

Nordin, A. (2014). Crisis as a discursive legitimation strategy in educational reforms: A critical policy analysis. *Education Inquiry, 5*(1), 24047.

Ringarp, J. (2016). PISA lends legitimacy: A study of education policy changes in Germany and Sweden after 2000. *European Educational Research Journal, 15*(4), 447–461.

Schriewer, J. (1992). The method of comparison and the need for externalization: Methodological criteria and sociological concepts. In J. Schriewer & B. Holmes (eds.), *Theories and methods in comparative education* (pp. 25–83). Peter Lang.

Seifert, M. (2012). *Politikberatung in Österreich. Diploma thesis.* University of Vienna, Vienna.

Sivesind, K. (2013). Mixed images and merging semantics in European curricula. *Journal of Curriculum Studies, 45*(1), 52–66.

Sivesind, K., & Wahlström, N. (2016). Curriculum on the European policy agenda: Global transitions and learning outcomes from transnational and national points of view. *European Educational Research Journal, 15*(3), 271–278.

Specht, W., & Lucyshyn, J. (2008). Einführung von Bildungsstandards in Österreich. Meilenstein für die Unterrichtsqualität? *Beiträge zur Lehrerinnen- und Lehrerbildung, 26*(3), 318–325.

Stamm, M. (2008). Bildungsstandardreform und Schulversagen. Aktuelle Diskussionslinien zu möglichen ungewollten Nebenwirkungen der Schulqualitätsdebatte. *Zeitschrift für Pädagogik,* 54(4), 481–497.

Steiner-Khamsi, G. (2012). Understanding policy borrowing and lending: Building comparative policy studies. In *policy borrowing and lending in education* (pp. 3–17). Routledge.

Steiner-Khamsi, G. (2013). What is wrong with the 'What-went-right' approach in educational policy? *European Educational Research Journal, 12*(1), 20–33.

Steiner-Khamsi, G., & Waldow, F. (2012). *Policy Borrowing and Lending in Education.* Routledge.

Tröhler, D. (2011). *Languages of education : protestant legacies, national identities, and global aspirations.* Routledge.

Tröhler, D. (2016). The grand narratives of modernity and the modern self: The Protestant Idea of the Soul and the Educationalization of the World. *Education Letter, 7*(2), 27–29.

Tröhler, D. (2019). Bildungsstandards oder die Neudefinition von Schule. In Julia Zuber, H. Altrichter, & M. Heinrich (Eds.), *Bildungsstandards zwischen Politik und schulischem Alltag* (pp. 3–24). Springer Fachmedien Wiesbaden.

Tröhler, D., Maricic, V. (2021). Data, trust and faith: The unheeded religious roots of modern education policy. *Globalisation, Societies and Education, 19*(2), 138–153. https://doi.org/10.1080/14767724.2021.1872371

Waldow, F. (2012). Standardisation and legitimacy: Two central concepts in research on educational borrowing and lending. In G. Steiner-Khamsi & F. Waldow (eds.), *Policy borrowing and lending in education. World yearbook of education 2012* (pp. 411–427). Routledge.

Weingart, P. (2003). Paradox of scientific advising. In G. Bechmann & I. Hronsky (eds.), *Expertise and its interfaces: The tense relationship of science and politics* (pp. 53–89). Edition Sigma.

Wiesner, C., Schreiner, C., Breit, S., & Schratz, M. (2020). Bildungsstandards—Einblicke in die Entwicklung in Österreich. Eine historische Betrachtung. In *Bildungsstandards. Kompetenzorientierung, Aufgabenkultur und Qualitätsentwicklung im Schulsystem.* (pp. 25–72). Waxmann.

Zuber, J., Altrichter, H., & Heinrich, M. (2018). *Bildungsstandards zwischen Politik und schulischem Alltag.* Springer Fachmedien Wiesbaden.

Bernadette Hörmann PhD (2015, University of Vienna), postdoctoral fellow at the University of Oslo. Her postdoctoral research project is a comparative study about externalization in curriculum-making processes in Austria and Norway. Her research interests are school reforms in an international and comparative perspective, education policy, as well as school and curriculum theory in general. She is co-author of an article in the Nordic Journal of Studies in Educational Policy (2018).

A Critical Review of the Competency-Based Curriculum in Spain

Ana Sánchez-Bello

The rise in competency-based approaches to education has come about in concert with policy reforms at all levels of the education system. As we know, education policy frequently seeks to impose an ideological agenda beyond its educational objectives, since it is here that social models and people's roles in society are determined. This raises the question of whether the purpose of the competency-based model being promoted in Spain is to create critical, autonomous, compassionate, engaged citizens or to produce efficient man- and woman-power for the more technical, complex and demanding labour market of the future. Historically, Spanish governments on each side of the social, political and economic divide have tended to promote one of these sets of objectives or the other.

While sharing the overall spirit of competency-based education, countries vary in terms of their individual understanding and implementation of competency-based curricula according to their particular history and characteristics. In Spain, for example, the effects of forty years of dictatorship (1936–1975) are still present today (Fusi et al., 2005; González, 2018; Pérez and Sanz, 2015). After the Spanish Civil War (1936–1939), citizens had not the privilege of free elections again until 1977, and this democratic lag is mirrored—at least from the perspective of an almost linear developmental epistemology shared and imposed by the United States and Spain's northern neighbours—in the country's considerable social, economic and cultural underdevelopment. In education, these unresolved tensions are reflected in the ongoing debate over the place of religion in schools and the teaching of Education for Citizenship.

Since its entry into the European Union (EU) in 1986, Spain has undergone a gradual process of adaptation of its legislation to EU recommendations to member states regarding the creation of a common education policy (Lorente and Torres,

---

A. Sánchez-Bello (✉)
University of A Coruña, A Coruña, Spain
e-mail: ana.sanchez.bello@udc.es

© The Author(s), under exclusive license to Springer Nature Singapore Pte Ltd. 2021
W. Zhao and D. Tröhler (eds.), *Euro-Asian Encounters on 21st-Century Competency-Based Curriculum Reforms*,
https://doi.org/10.1007/978-981-16-3009-5_7

2010). The Education Act (LOE) passed in 2006 provided explicitly for competency-based learning as a compulsory and necessary part of the primary and secondary school curricula. However, the progressive assimilation of EU education policies must be viewed in relation to the history of education in Spain and its effect on the perception and implementation of competency-based teaching and learning.

The concept of 'competence' is confusing because it contains a large variety of meanings (Weinert, 1999). The use of the term in the context of Spain is complicated even further by the history of education reform during the years of the dictatorship. Under Franco, children were streamed from the age of ten into two tracks: those destined for university, and those destined for the workforce. According to this binary and consequently unequal system, competencies were clearly bracketed as part of the vocational training curriculum.

The long period of dictatorship in Spain has embedded the association between curricular competencies and a type of education that prioritises employment and economic interests over humanistic values, such as freedom, social rights self-fulfilment, or well-being. Unsurprisingly, education reform during the dictatorship was particularly active in relation to secondary education, since this was when children were segregated into academic and vocational learners. Within this divisive and unequal dichotomy, the term 'competency' features frequently in relation to vocational training, but much less so in relation to studies leading to university entrance. One of the most significant reforms of the period was the 'propaedeutical' 1955 Industrial Vocational Training Act, the purpose of which was to prepare pupils to meet Spain's growing industrial workforce needs following the Civil War. The 1955 act, which defines vocational training in the first chapter as 'the section of education whose central purpose is the preparation of skilled workers for the different areas of industry', thus filled the gap left by the 1938 Secondary Education Act, which provided only for secondary studies leading to university entrance (Martínez, 2015). In doing so, however, the new reform marked the end of the liberal tradition of considering secondary education as a prolongation of primary, whose only purpose was the acquisition of knowledge for ends other than the needs of industry (Puelles, 2000).

The education system in Spain was not subjected to major reform until 1970, five years before Franco's death. The General Education Act (1970), which included the principles of universal access to education and free compulsory education until the age of fourteen, signalled the most ambitious overhaul of the system since the Moyano Act in 1857. Its aim was to bring Spain into step with the rest of Europe at a time of global social and economic change.

Despite the inclusion of far-reaching reforms such as universal access, the 1970 act was mainly focused on educating pupils for the world of work, reflecting a behaviourist view of education redolent of Pavlov (1927), Skinner (1938) and Watson (1913), in which the process of teaching and learning is made subordinate to the result. With the restoration of democracy in Spain, education resumed its role as an equalising force in society. The 1990 General Organisation of the Education System Act (LOGSE) confirmed the change in direction by attempting to replace the behaviourist model with more constructivist approaches, in line with the humanistic reorientation of education by progressive teachers' movements away from the needs and demands of the labour market (Sánchez-Bello, 2016).

The decades-long association in the Spanish educational context between competency and meeting the needs of industry has made it very difficult for teachers and education stakeholders to define exactly what we mean when we talk about 'competence' in a formal education context. This confusion is epitomised by the fact that even the most unconditional supporters of competency-based education seem unable to offer a clear definition of what the model consists of (Gimeno, 2008).

Another reason for the difficulty in establishing a precise definition of competency is the two opposing rationales represented by the EU and the OECD regarding the function and purpose of competency-based learning and assessment. The aim for the EU is to develop a set of common, supra-national standards in an attempt to harmonise the quality of education across Europe and allow mutual recognition of degrees and other qualifications between member states (European Union, 2006, 2010). For the OECD, on the other hand, competencies represent standardised educational outcomes with standardised outcome variables, which may be compared nationally and internationally to account for the relative success or failure of each system (Carabaña, 2015, 2016; Gimeno, 2008; OECD, 2001). Despite the different principles and priorities pursued by each, however, it is the OECD model that is seen as the standard in educational practice.

As regards the efficacy of multiple choice testing as a means of assessing competency-based learning, subjects such as maths, science and technology are undoubtedly more susceptible to measurement than, for example, civic skills or the ability to learn. The shift towards standardised testing thus reflects a growing bias towards certain competencies over others. In parallel with EU recommendations to member states regarding the acquisition of key competencies as one of the main aims of general compulsory education, the OECD has established a framework of international key competency assessment through its DeSeCo programme; two projects premised on the same concept, but for very different ends. While the EU is concerned with curriculum design and development in each member state, the OECD is more interested in identifying and testing learning outcome indicators to measure the comparative success or failure of the education system in each country. The OECD does not, therefore, issue direct recommendations with regard to curriculum development, but it does influence educational content, organisation and practices indirectly, as we will see (Bolívar, 2008; Gimeno, 2008).

This divergence of perspectives is clearly reflected in the disjunction between education legislation and educational practice in Spain, with the former influenced by the priorities and recommendations proposed by the EU, and the latter more focused on meeting the performance benchmarks set by the OECD:

> The inclusion of key competencies in the curriculum has a number of different objectives: firstly, to combine different types of formal (subjects and subject areas), informal and non-formal learning; secondly, to allow students to assimilate their learning experiences, relate them to different types of content, and apply them effectively as needed in a range of situations and contexts; and thirdly, to steer education in a new direction by identifying essential content and assessment criteria, and inform decision-making in relation to the teaching and learning

process. (Royal Decrees 1513/2006 and 1631/2006, regulating minimum requirements for primary and secondary education, respectively)

As we will see in the next section, the result of this has been the bureaucratisation of the teaching and learning process, with teaching reduced to the search for strategies to raise student performance in competency testing and thus avoid being 'named and shamed' in the national and international rankings.

Competency-Based Education or Competency Assessment-Based Education?

In the clash of conflicting conceptualisations of competency, the PISA model of standardised assessment has won the day. Extensive media coverage has made PISA a household name in Spain, surfacing in conversations everywhere from the family dinner table to the supermarket checkout. While this familiarity does not mean that people actually understand what it is that PISA measures, it does illustrate how the logic of standardisation has taken root among the general public.

Despite the growing trend in Spain towards external assessment (Álvarez, 2008; Carabaña, 2016; Tiana, 2014), it is clear that most people's understanding of the system is too incomplete to allow them to reflect on the situation critically, which has, in turn, led to its acceptance as something normal, obvious and necessary. It is an example of Campbell's Law (1976), where the more any quantitative social indicator is used, the more subject it becomes to corruption pressures and the more likely to corrupt the processes it is intended to measure.

The reigning discourse is that of the need to quantify knowledge, despite a host of dissenting voices from a variety of settings and perspectives concerning the essence, implementation and effect of competency-based education on schools and educational practices (Conley, 2015; Gimeno, 2008; Hopfenbeck et al., 2015; Monarca and Rappoport, 2015; Pérez Gómez, 2014; Stobart, 2008; Turnipseed and Darling-Hammond, 2015). The culture of standardised testing has now permeated education systems all over the world, from the smallest village school to the largest city lycée (Apple, 2010; Díez, 2007; Mouffe, 2007; Torres, 2017; Rizvi and Lingard, 2010). One of the consequences of this is that education and the cultural values it transmits are treated as just another marketplace commodity. Under the current framework, priorities such as socialisation, citizenship, empathy and understanding have been relegated in favour of academic results.

The pressure of standardised external assessment forces teachers to adopt teaching methods in the classroom based on closed questions that elicit a single, pre-defined answer (Torres, 2017). This way of working makes reflection in action an almost fanciful notion, yet reflective thinking by teachers is an essential part of understanding their performance and strategies in the classroom (Marcelo, 1987; Esteve et al., 1995 Schön, 1983; Fullan and Hargreaves, 1996).

Rankings are a simple way of presenting information to the general public, but the PISA rankings present more than just statistics for experts to pore over. The PISA process contains an emotional component that makes ordinary people take the results of the report personally. So effective is its dissemination strategy that in Spain, every new education reform mentions the country's poor performance in the latest PISA study to justify its proposed changes to the system. The need to improve the country's PISA results is presented as a question of national pride: reforms no longer promise to improve teaching and learning practices, but to bring the country level with those higher up the table.

Notwithstanding the caveats of international education experts regarding the need for a more nuanced, contextualised reading of the results (letter to the OECD; in Carabaña, 2015), the OECD controls public opinion about the state and needs of education by controlling how the information in the report is expressed and delivered. For example, the average score in PISA is 500, with a standard deviation of 100. If one country has a score of 520 and the other a score of 521, it stands to reason to think that the two education systems must be very similar; however, the conclusion highlighted by the report is that one of the countries has a better education system than the other. A straightforward ranking system delivers simple, direct, easy-to-understand information, uncomplicated by reflection, analysis or more flexible conclusions—more soccer league than serious assessment.

The fact that PISA measures general competencies betrays the complex reality behind the simplified findings presented to the educational community. PISA does not measure the acquisition of subject-specific knowledge defined in the curriculum, but its application in alleged real life based on a broad understanding of key concepts (OECD, 2001). When assessing general competencies, however, it is impossible to establish whether they have been acquired at school or elsewhere. Children who are regularly taken to visit museums, lectures, exhibitions, concerts or dance events with their family, for example, will develop more abilities than children who are not exposed to the same kind of sociocultural interaction. For this reason, the data presented by PISA reveal very little about the effect of teaching on student performance and are much more concerned with proposals in relation to organisational issues, such as school autonomy, hiring practices, accountability, etc. This focus on political-ideological strategies rather than didactic concerns exposes the great contradiction at the heart of PISA, since what really needs to change in education in order to promote a broader understanding of key concepts and the development of skills such as the ability to communicate in one's own language, to explain natural phenomena or to deal with complex problems is, precisely, the model of teaching and learning. Nevertheless, the stubborn reality is that this change has not taken place and a concept-based learning curriculum in Spain remains a long way off, regardless of the country's position in the PISA rankings.

It is much easier, therefore, to represent Spain's performance relative to other countries as a source of national pride (or shame), and to use it as a pretext for political rather than educational change. This ideological imperative is reflected in the type of competencies prescribed by each new reform.

In 2006, for example, the following competency-based curriculum was established by a social democratic government in legislation regulating minimum requirements for primary education:

1. Language skills
2. Mathematical skills
3. Knowledge of and interaction with the world
4. Information management and digital skills
5. Social and citizenship skills
6. Cultural and artistic skills
7. Ability to learn how to learn
8. Personal autonomy and initiative

Nine years later, the list of competencies was modified by ministerial order by the new conservative government and reduced to seven:

1. Language skills
2. Mathematical skills and basic knowledge of science and technology
3. Digital competency
4. Ability to learn how to learn
5. Social and civic skills
6. Initiative and entrepreneurial spirit
7. Cultural awareness and expression

The most significant modifications introduced by the conservative revision of the legislation are the replacement of 'personal autonomy and initiative' by 'initiative and entrepreneurial spirit', and the change from 'social and citizenship skills' to 'social and civic skills'. The conceptual differences between citizenship education and civic education are reflected in the competencies included in the curriculum: whereas citizenship is associated with active, critical participation in society, civic competencies are more concerned with compliance with social norms (Ruiz and Chaux, 2005). Children who are taught citizenship values learn about the importance of active critical engagement with and responsibility for creating social norms, not just following them; purely civic instruction, on the other hand, teaches compliance with the democratic legal principles of acceptable social values.

An example of purely civic competency in action is the participation of parents in how schools are run, in accordance with their rights under Spanish law. Though active in issuing protests and demands from within their own organisations, families are much less inclined to extend their participation to the administrative and consultative bodies of the schools themselves. Ministry for Education figures show that only 12.5% of parents in public schools and 11.2% in private schools stand for representation on the boards of their children's schools. (Ministerio de Educación y Formación Profesional, 2020). They thus fulfil their social (civic) duty to be part of their children's schooling, but fail to assume an active (citizenship) role in deciding what that education should be. A curriculum for citizenship education should be based on critical thinking and argumentation, therefore. In recent decades, however, the restyling of citizens as consumers and technically competent workers has led instead to the progressive elimination of the humanities and philosophy from the curriculum (Torres, 2017).

As regards 'initiative and entrepreneurial spirit', it is not clear how this new key competency relates to the intellectual, moral and socio-emotional development of pupils at primary level, bearing in mind that primary education is designed to provide children with a sense of human dignity and a solid general foundation upon which to develop their ability to deal with the problems of everyday life. Competency in 'initiative and entrepreneurial spirit' seems more in keeping with economistic principles than humanistic educational ones.

What is at stake here is the type of education we want for our future citizens. Under the current globalised system of education, the legitimation and mandated assessment of certain types of knowledge has led to the delegitimation of the work teachers do and external oversight of their own assessment procedures.

Given the difficulty of comparing schools at even a regional or national level, it is hard to see how decontextualised international standardised testing can serve any educational purpose. Nevertheless, in Spain and elsewhere, external assessment has become a profitable business for the companies that create and administer tests, and offer test coaching and preparation to schools. A clear example of this is the company 2E Estudios, Evaluaciones e Investigación S.L., accredited by the OECD to implement its PISA for Schools programme in Spain.

The legislative changes, assessment pressures and strategic use of media by the OECD have resulted in teachers treating competency-based education as a merely technical innovation. They have been loaded with a responsibility for academic success that is not theirs to assume (owing to the multitude of factors affecting student performance), and left alone to explain to parents why the school's place in the external assessment rankings should not be taken as an automatic reflection of the quality of teaching provided there.

Schools cannot teach children everything they need to know about the complex world in which we live, but they must give them a foundation upon which to construct an informed, critical understanding of society in all its diversity. As it stands at present, education is more focused on transmitting instrumental knowledge with measurable, comparable indicators, than on teaching children the cultural principles they need in order to become good, active citizens.

The More Things Change: The Influence of the Catholic Church

In each new education reform, however minor, the role of the church and/or religion in education is always the biggest stumbling block to agreement. While the Roman Catholic church has always had a prominent place in Spanish life and politics, its unwavering support for Franco's military dictatorship was rewarded with unprecedented power and influence within the openly confessional new national Catholic state.[1] Catholicism was taught as a compulsory subject, from primary school right up to university level (Mayordomo, 1990; Blas Zabaleta, 2005; Puelles, 2007). Spain today is non-denominational but not secular: while there is no state religion, the only religion named in the constitution is Roman Catholicism, and the separation between church and state is blurred by the commitment in law to maintain relations of cooperation with the religious faiths in Spain (Spanish Constitution, Article 16.3; Puelles, 2007).[2]

Since the restoration of democracy, the Roman Catholic church has continued to enjoy a privileged position in education and knows how to use this privilege to its own advantage. The Concordat signed between the first democratically elected post-regime Spanish government and the Vatican in 1979 granted the Catholic church special rights in relation to education, establishing Catholicism as a compulsory subject and making the church hierarchy responsible for defining the contents of religion textbooks and any other educational materials used. Religion teachers, meanwhile, were paid by the state but appointed from a list of 'persons considered competent' presented by the bishop of each diocese (Castillejo, 2012; Díez de Velasco, 2016 Torres, 2017; Viñao, 2014). The terms of the 1979 Concordat remain in force today, with the only difference that while it is still compulsory for schools to offer Catholic religious instruction as a subject, it is no longer compulsory for pupils to choose it.[3] The removal of the obligation to study religion was welcomed as a sign of progress after decades of subservience to the Catholic church, but its success was only partial as the newly optional nature of the subject led to the segregation of pupils who choose to study religion and those who opt for the subject, Social and Civic Values (Tamayo 2007).[4] The fact that Social and Civic Values is not taught to all pupils means that some are not given the opportunity to think about questions related to citizenship, democracy, social and human rights, and the democratic organisation of society.

In a secular education system, moral competency is based on the values of constructive, peaceful coexistence in open, inclusive, plural societies, as embodied in the democratic constitution of the state and the Universal Declarations of Human Rights. Secular schools educate children in and for pluralism, teaching them to respect, experience and cultivate diversity in all of its religious, cultural and ideological forms. Secular education teaches pupils about the different moral, cultural and ideological ideas and orientations that make up our social reality, and about the importance of respecting opinions and beliefs different from their own and using critical, reflective thinking to make responsible decisions about them (Mayoral, 2016).

In the 1990s, the concept of citizenship became a way of mediating between liberalism and communitarianism, combining the idea of liberal justice and legitimacy and a sense of group social identity and common purpose (Cortina, 2009). Citizenship was used as the cornerstone for debates about what kind of society people wanted to build, and how to change social relations to ensure equitable representation for all groups of society.

Another essential aspect of democratic citizenship is the idea of participation beyond the right to vote. The emergence of alternative social movements is a symptom of the participation deficit within the current system and the need for greater public debate, discussion, decision-making and influence (Young, 2011). Good citizenship requires good citizenship education, however, and the only social institution with the undivided focus and capacity to instil in children the knowledge, skills, values and attitudes they need to work together for the common good is education.[5]

The end of the dictatorship in Spain left many issues unresolved. One of the most public and contentious of these was the question of who would now be responsible for setting the moral standard and ensuring the moral welfare of Spanish society: the state or the Catholic church? In education, the same debate asked whether church or state should be responsible for inculcating children with social values. The conflict between church and state intensified in 2006 with the passing of the Education Act (LOE), which introduced 'Education for Citizenship and Human Rights' as a compulsory subject that all pupils were required to take during one of their final years of primary school and one of the first three years of secondary.[6] As regards religion, far from disappearing under the new reform, the legal requirement to offer Catholic religious instruction as an optional subject (though not other forms of religious instruction) remained.

Despite the compulsory legal nature of the competencies defined by the 2006 reform, the implementation of Education for Citizenship and Human Rights, with a syllabus specifically designed to promote a freer, more tolerant society, was met with massive public criticism and obstruction (Fernández-Soria, 2008; Muñoz, 2016). The Roman Catholic hierarchy called on families to exercise their right to conscientious objection and withdraw their children from the subject. Many lodged appeals before the courts in defence of their right to conscientious objection on the grounds of indoctrination, while private religious organisations were also very active in their attempts to have parts of the syllabus removed.

The promotion of citizenship competence was dealt another blow in 2015 by the conservative government Improvement of the Quality of Education Act (LOMCE), which eliminated Education for Citizenship and Human Rights from the curriculum and replaced it with a new optional alternative to religious instruction, Social and Civic Values. The optional nature of even this diluted form of civic education means that not all children have the chance to learn about the principles of citizenship. Moral competence, understood as a kind of ideal or code of best practice (Dennett, 2015), should be taught to children as a function of their relationship with the world around them, not of their (constitutionally protected) faith in a supreme being.

Conclusions

The model of society that a country wishes to create is reflected in the type of education it offers its citizens. The general education goals and principles established in the national curriculum reveal whether that model is humanistic or economic. While a humanistic society requires an education based on values of diversity, inclusivity, tolerance and critical thinking, an economic society requires technical competence and efficiency.

In Spain, this division of perspectives has been particularly apparent in the way competency-based learning has been represented in educational discourse. The manipulation of language plays a vital role in shifting our perspective and moulding our thinking about society in general and education in particular. Real political agendas are obscured behind an easy rhetoric of concealment, falsifying reality using familiar terms and concepts that have been resignified and renamed to defuse their transformative potential or appropriate them for alternative ends (Pucciarelli, 2001; Torres, 2009).

The official discourse regarding the need for and benefits of competencies elides public debate around the philosophy and socio-educational implications of competency-based learning. News of education reform is generally presented in terms of improvement and progress, even though Spain's track record in this area has not always been one of positive change. The discourse around competencies is basically a way of rebranding the existing trend towards functional, useful, efficiency-based learning of various kinds that has more to do with economic developmentalism than with social and human progress.

The increasing bureaucratisation of the education system means that legislative reform rarely advances beyond a few changes in terminology and an earnest statement of principles in the preamble. Instead of real curriculum development, the ministry and departments of education seem more interested in ensuring teachers accept and adapt to the new terminology and system of competency-based learning, even to the detriment and neglect of other more pressing responsibilities and the fundamental purpose of education. With all of their efforts focused on attempting to decide which competencies to prioritise for each type of learner, teachers no longer have time or energy to think about transformative strategies to improve the quality of the teaching and learning process and reprioritise certain educational values. The speed of implementation of the competency-based model has left them with no choice but to assimilate its linguistic codes, and no time to reflect critically and constructively on the educational implications of the new system. With teachers otherwise occupied, the potential to transform educational practice by re-envisioning competencies to prioritise relevant learning experiences and the meaningful construction of knowledge remains untapped.

The tactic of focusing public debate on technical-bureaucratic issues is an effective way of deflecting attention and analysis away from the idea of a system of education based not only on transmitting knowledge (as if knowledge itself were a neutral, impartial concept), but also on helping children to acquire the attitudes and aptitudes necessary to think critically about all aspects of life and the world around them. Legislators on both sides of the political divide seem determined to reduce education to meeting the needs and interests of the capitalist system, regardless of their social value or purpose. As a consequence, the state at present is failing in its duty to provide citizens with the ethical education they need to live in accordance with the rights and responsibilities of a democratically constituted society (Díez, 2007; Rizvi and Lingard, 2010; Torres, 2001).

Competency-based curricula conceived in terms of technical principles and performance metrics make it very hard, if not impossible, to provide children with a humanistic education. One alternative to this approach is Nussbaum's (2012) work on capabilities and human functioning, which in turn grows of Sen's (1993) earlier analysis of well-being as the ability to function. Nussbaum's framework is intended as a way to measure quality of life and think collectively about the importance of social justice Nussbaum (2012).[7] This so-called 'capabilities approach' could be a starting-point from which to reassess the value and purpose of competency-based learning and give education the flexibility to adapt to and accommodate the great diversity of social, personal and educational contexts in which learning takes place. Diverse schools have diverse curricular needs, which cannot be met by plans based on uniformising standards. What is required is a shift in perception and priorities: to reconceptualise competencies in terms of principles like those of the 'educational revolution' called for by Robinson and Aronica (2015), and to focus on providing children with the opportunities and foundation to reach their full, complex potential for the good of society as a whole.

Notes

1. Opus Dei, founded in Madrid in 1928, is one of the most influential religious organisations in Spanish history. The organisation rose to prominence following its expansion to the rest of Spain after 1939 and played a key role in the social and political life of the country during the Francoist dictatorship. Nowadays, the more visible face of the church's influence in Spain is represented by Catholic parents', teachers' and cultural associations, many with strong ideological ties to Opus Dei.
2. 'Secularism' refers to a separation between church and state. As far as education is concerned, it means that religion should be taught at home or at the child's place of worship, and it is people's protected right to do so. Far from being at cross purposes with religion, therefore, secularism is tolerant of religious faith, guarantees neutrality towards the plurality of religions recognised by the state, and works with the different faiths to ensure citizens' right to practise their religion as a private matter (Tamayo, 2005, 2010). Religious belief is conceived of as a free, personal choice which may not be imposed explicitly or implicitly on any citizen (in contrast to what happens when religion is taught in schools).
3. The most recent figures provided by the Ministry of Education show that 64.8% of pupils choose religion over Social and Civic Values (Ministry of Education, 2020). The difference between public and private schools is significant, however. In Spain, most private schools are run by religious orders: here, take-up of religious instruction is 85% at primary level and 81.5% at secondary level.
4. Following the introduction of Education for Citizenship and Human Rights at secondary level in 2006, the Roman Catholic hierarchy called on families to exercise their right to conscientious objection and demand their children's exemption from the subject, arguing that the new education law was part of 'the alarming spread of secularism in our society' (Tamayo, 2007).

5. This article focuses on the role of education in the development of citizen consciousness, but of course education is not the only condition for the creation of a society of citizens. A sense of political membership of society also requires a level of economic well-being and equality that allows citizens to demand their rights and participate in public life. In her analysis of the concept of personal responsibility, Young (2011) criticises the false dichotomy in the writings of Lawrence Mead and Charles Murray between structural processes and personal responsibility in the creation of social injustice. Instead, Young proposes a model of combined responsibility that acknowledges both structural and individual causation, since structures are, at the end of the day, made up of individuals.
6. The syllabus for Education for Citizenship and Human Rights is provided in Royal Decree 1513/2006 (7 December) and Royal Decree 1631/2006 (29 December) for the regulation of minimum education requirements for primary education and secondary education, respectively.
7. Nussbaum's (2012) list of core capabilities for human functioning is as follows: Life, Bodily health, Bodily integrity, Senses, imagination and thoughst, Emotions, Practical reason, Affiliation, Other species, Play, and Control over one's environment.

References

Álvarez, J. M. (2008). *Evaluar el aprendizaje en una enseñanza centrada en las competencias*. Morata.
Apple, M. (2010). *Global crises, social justice and education*. Routledge.
Blas, P. (Coord.). (2005). *Laicidad, educación y democracia*. Biblioteca Nueva.
Bolívar, A. (2008). El discurso de las competencias en España: educación básica y educación superior. *REDU. Revista de Docencia Universitaria, 6*(2), 1–23.
Campbell, D. T. (1976). *Assessing the Impact of Planned Social Change*. The Public Affairs Center, Dartmouth College.
Carabaña, J. (2015). *La inutilidad de PISA para las escuelas*. Catarata.
Carabaña, J. (2016). El éxito de PISA y el poder de las clasificaciones. *Con-Ciencia Social, 20*, 157–163.
Castillejo, E. (2012). *La enseñanza de la religión católica en España desde la Transición*. Catarata.
Conley, D. (2015). A new era for educational assessment. *Education Policy Analysis Archives, 23*(8).
Cortina, A. (2009). *Ética de la razón cordial. Educar en la ciudadanía en el siglo XXI*. Nobel.
Dennett, D. (2015, July 24). Interview with Núria Jar. *SiNC—Servicio de Información y Noticias Científicas*. Retrieved from https://www.agenciasinc.es/Entrevistas/La-religion-no-es-el-motor-de-la-moral-sino-el-freno-que-ha-ralentizado-su-desarrollo
Díez, E. (2007). *La globalización neoliberal y sus repercusiones en la educación*. El Roure.
Díez de Velasco, F. (2016). La enseñanza de las religiones en la escuela en España: avatares del modelo de aula segregada. *Historia y Memoria de la Educación, 4*, 277–306.
Esteve, J., Franco, S., & Vera, J. (1995). *Los profesores ante el cambio social*. Anthropos.
European Union. (2006). *Recommendation of the European Parliament and of the Council on key competences for lifelong learning*. https://eur-lex.europa.eu/legal-content/EN/TXT/PDF/?uri=CELEX:32006H0962&from=EN

European Union. (2010). *Education & training 2010.* https://eur-lex.europa.eu/legal-content/EN/TXT/?uri=OJ%3AC%3A2004%3A104%3ATOC

Fernández-Soria, J. M. (2008). Educación para la Ciudadanía y los Derechos Humanos. Controversias en torno a una asignatura (o entre ética pública y ética privada). *Transatlántica de Educación, 4,* 45–64.

Fullan, M. & Hargreaves, A. (1996). *What's worth fighting for in your school?* (Revised edition). Teachers' College Press.

Fusi, J., García, J., Juiá, S., Malefakis, E., & Payne, S. (2005). *Franquismo: El juicio de la historia.* Booket.

Gimeno, J. (2008). *Educar por competencias, ¿qué hay de nuevo?* Morata.

González, T. (Ed.). (2018). *Entre el olvido y la memoria: educación, mitos y realidades.* Tirant Humanidades.

Hopfenbeck, T., Flórez Petour, M. T., & Tolo, A. (2015). Balancing tensions in educational policy reforms: large-scale implementation of Assessment for Learning in Norway. *Assessment in Education: Principles, Policy & Practice, 22*(1), 44–60.

Lorente, R., & Torres, M. (2010). Políticas de educación y formación en la unión europea: una historia de cambios y continuidades. *Revista Española de Educación Comparada, 16,* 159–183.

Marcelo, C. (1987). *El pensamiento del profesor.* CEAC.

Martínez, M. (2015). Consideraciones a una ley paradigmática en la historia de la formación profesional española: la Ley de Formación Profesional Industrial (FPI) de 1955. *Participación Educativa, 4*(6), 107–112.

Mayoral, V. (2016). *Escuela laica y sociedad democrática.* CIVES.

Mayordomo, A. (Ed.). (1990). *Historia de la educación en España V. Nacional-Catolicismo y educación en la España de posguerra.* Ministerio de Educación y Ciencia.

Ministerio de Educación y Formación Profesional. (2020). *Informe 2019 sobre el estado del sistema educativo 2016–17.* Retrieved from http://www.educacionyfp.gob.es/dam/jcr:4f35ae94-f996-4ceb-b3f0-21b2e421ec26/i19cee-informe.pdf

Monarca, H., & Rappoport, S. (2015). *Opinión del profesorado sobre evaluaciones externas.* GIPES-UAM.

Mouffe, C. (2007). *En torno a lo político.* Fondo de Cultura Económica.

Muñoz, A. (2016). ¿Qué ha sido de Educación para la Ciudadanía con el Partido Popular? *Foro de Educación, 14*(20), 105–128.

Nussbaum, Martha. (2012). *Crear capacidades. Propuesta para el desarrollo humano.* Paidós.

OECD. (2001). Conocimientos y aptitudes para la vida. Primeros resultados del programa internacional de evaluación de estudiantes (PISA) 2000 de la OCDE. Paris: Organisation for Economic Cooperation and Development.

Pavlov, I. P. (1927): *Conditioned reflexes.* Oxford University Press.

Pérez Gómez, Á. (2014). Evaluación externa en la LOMCE. Reválidas, exclusión y competitividad. *Revista Interuniversitaria de Formación del Profesorado, 81*(28.3), 59–71.

Pérez, L., & Sanz, I. (Eds.). (2015). *Del franquismo a la democracia 1936–2013.* Marcial Pons.

Puelles, M. (2000). Política y Educación: cien años de historia. *Revista de Educación,* special issue, 3–37.

Puelles, M. (2007). Religión y escuela pública en nuestra historia: antecedentes y procesos. *Bordón, 58*(4–5), 521–535.

Pucciarelli, A. (2001). El régimen político de las democracias excluyentes. El caso de la República Argentina. *Sociohistórica, 9–10,* 445–475.

Rizvi, F., & Lingard, B. (2010). *Globalizing education policy.* Routledge.

Robinson, K., & Aronica, L. (2015). *Creative schools: The grassroots revolution that's transforming education.* Viking Penguin.

Ruiz, A., & Chaux, E. (2005). *La formación de competencias ciudadanas.* Ascofade.

Sánchez-Bello, A. (2016). Gender studies in Spain: From theory to educational practice. In A. Darder, P. Mayo, & J. Paraskeva (Eds.), *International critical pedagogy reader* (pp. 39–45). Routledge.

Schön, D. (1983). *The reflective practitioner: How professionals think in action*. Basic Books.
Sen, A. (1993). Capability and well-being. In M. Nussbaum & A. Sen (Eds.), *The quality of life*. Clarendon Press.
Skinner, B. F. (1938). *The behavior of organisms: An experimental analysis*. B. F. Skinner Foundation.
Stobart, G. (2008). *Testing times: The uses and abuses of assessment*. Routledge.
Tamayo, J. J. (2005). *Desde la heterodoxia. Reflexiones sobre laicismo, política y religión*. El Laberinto.
Tamayo, J. J. (2007). Iglesia católica y estado laico. *Revista CIDOB Dáfers Internacionals, 77,* 1133–6595.
Tamayo, J. J. (2010). *En la frontera: cristianismo y laicidad*. Editorial Popular.
Tiana, A. (2014). Veinte años de políticas de evaluación general del sistema educativo en España. *Revista de evaluación de programas y políticas públicas, 2,* 1–21.
Torres, J. (2001). *Educación en tiempos de neoliberalismo*. Morata.
Torres, J. (2009). La mercantilización y despolitización de la educación. *Eskola publikoa, 42,* 8–13.
Torres, J. (2017). *Políticas educativas y construcción de personalidades neoliberales y neocolonialistas*. Morata.
Turnipseed, S., & Darling-Hammond, L. (2015). Accountability is more than a test score. *Education Policy Analysis Archives, 23*(11).
Viñao, A. (2014). *Religión en las aulas. Una materia controvertida*. Morata.
Watson, J. B. (1913). Psychology as the behaviorist views it. *Psychological Review, 20,* 158–177.
Weinert, F. E. (1999). *Definition and selection of competencies: Concepts of competence*. Max Planck Institute for Psychological Research.
Young, I. (2011). Responsibility for justice. Oxford University Press

Ana Sánchez-Bello is a Professor of Curriculum Studies at the Department of Curriculum Studies in Faculty of Education at the University of Coruna (Spain). She teaches graduate and undergraduate courses on educational leadership, critical discourses, and curriculum theory. Her interests centre on the analysis of educational policy, the role of women in science and several aspects of the critical curriculum. She is member of the Research Group GIE dedicated to the study of educational innovation and equality. She has participated in various research projects related to school policies and equity. She was responsible for establishing the university´s Office of Gender Equality.

Competence-Based Curriculum Reforms in the Context of University Engineering Education in the Post-Soviet Lithuania—Hope or Disappointment?

Rūta Petkutė

Universities across diverse cultural contexts in Europe have been pressured by supranational and national bodies to re-orient their traditional knowledge or input-based curricula so that the focus is on pre-specified outcomes and the development of competences that have job relevance. In Europe, the so-called 'progressive' competence-based curriculum model has gained prominence through knowledge economy policies as well as the Bologna process and its curriculum reforms in higher education. However, an increasing number of authors draw attention to the limitations of the standardized competence-based curriculum model and warn that, when implemented in practice, in particular contextual circumstances, it may have negative consequences that are related to its inclination to underplay the traditionally important role of knowledge in curriculum. In the context of the North-Continental Europe, this curriculum reform has meant a cultural change—moving away from the classical knowledge-centred Humboldtian (*Bildung*) idea of university towards the Anglo-American model that is focused on measuring and managing learning outcomes. This chapter seeks to explore, through the eyes of academics, how the globally pervasive competence framework is implemented and responded to in the specific cultural context of the post-soviet Lithuania and the disciplinary context of engineering. In doing so, it brings together the sociology of curriculum and curriculum studies, as well as uses academics' narratives that are drawn from the qualitative empirical study. Threading through the chapter is a concern about how this standardized curriculum model plays out when embedded within particular contextual circumstances.

R. Petkutė (✉)
Tallinn University, Tallinn, Estonia
e-mail: ruta.petkute@tlu.ee

Introduction

Since their earliest beginnings, universities in Europe placed knowledge—whether religious or secular—at the heart of their enterprise. The classical Humboldtian idea of a university (*Bildung*), which influenced or inspired educational systems in Continental Europe, despite its inherent elitism, suggested that the open pursuit of knowledge (culture), even if not fully realised in practice, is an important ideal to aspire (Ward, 2012: 4). Accordingly, the question 'Which knowledge is the most valuable?' was considered a starting point for developing the curriculum (Autio, 2016). Yet, as Tero Autio notes, in the light of German educational tradition, knowledge is not to be understood in narrow utilitarian terms but in a broad sense. As he puts it, curriculum content is to be interpreted as "large cultural and historical bodies of knowledge and human achievements often carrying a moral or rational flavor, like humanity, humankind, World, objectivity, general" (2007: 3).

The recent European policy narrative on 'knowledge economy and 'knowledge society', too, has been highlighting the knowledge function of universities; however, it seems to conceptualise knowledge in a narrower instrumental sense as the key driver of the European economy (European Commission, 2010). In order to tackle the employability issue and more general economic problem in Europe, the focus of the European policy has been placed on the development of employability-relevant competences and skills (European Commission, 2012). It is important to mention that the outcomes-based curriculum model, as stipulated around pre-specified generic employability competences and transferable skills, has been endorsed on the basis of 'soft law' (Magalhaes, 2010: 41). Since the inception of the Bologna process in 1999, the outcome-based curriculum has been universally pushed through the European Tuning project (Tuning Educational Structures in Europe, n.d.a, n.d.b.) as the most efficient curriculum model for all disciplines. It allegedly has "to offer more possibilities for employment" than the traditional input-based curriculum (Tuning, n.d.a: 20). As a result, this curriculum framework has been gaining prominence across national higher education systems in Europe, at least at the policy level. The countries outside Europe have also been enthusiastically borrowing the outcome-based curriculum model, along with other Bologna-initiated measures, to modernize their higher education systems (Crosier and Parveva, 2013). Hence, there seems to be an exponentially growing global trend towards homogenization of curriculum reform measures in higher education.

However, despite this global policy enthusiasm about competences, an increasing number of authors—especially the ones who come from the field of the sociology of curriculum and knowledge—express their concern about some serious challenges and problems that can possibly come along with the implementation of these outcome-based curriculum policies and reforms. To begin with, there are different understandings across different countries and contexts of the terms 'learning outcomes', 'competences', and 'skills' (Allais, 2012, 2014). What is more, these terms are often used interchangeably and have obscure relationships (Adam 2008; Allais, 2012, 2014). Although the European Tuning project (n.d.a., n.d.b) defines competence as "a dynamic combination of knowledge, understanding, skills and abilities" (Tuning n.d.b), a closer look at the European policy texts suggests that there is a lack of conceptual consistency in the use of this term. It is natural to assume that the conceptual ambiguity surrounding the term competence may hinder the implementation of the competence-based curriculum. Moreover, in Continental Europe, implementating the Bologna curriculum reform measures seems problematic as it involves a substantial cultural shift from the 'traditional' knowledge-based Humboldtian idea of education aiming at the aesthetic inward transformation labelled *Bildung* to the neoliberal Anglo-American outcome-oriented model. As Susan Braedley and Meg Luxton (2010: 7) point out, the key feature of neoliberal policies of the late twentieth century is that they "have brought the logic of the market to bear on seemingly every facet of social life, rather than just economic life". Chris Lorenz (2006) notes that the Bologna-related policy narrative avoids mentioning that Bologna-initiated reform measures inescapably involve this fundamental move. According to him, this is probably done "in order not to arouse national sensitivities". Furthermore, some authors (Wheelahan, 2010; Young, 2011; Lorenz, 2010; Allais, 2014) warn that the current policy shift towards standardized work-relevant competences runs the risk of trivialising the more traditional forms of academic knowledge which have other than economic value. It appears to ignore the significance of the traditional disciplinary academic knowledge in the university curriculum and to have a standardizing or 'de-differentiating' effect on knowledge (Muller and Young, 2014). Therefore, these authors conclude that the new curriculum model is more likely to have negative consequences. Finally, it is officially reported (Sursock, 2015) that there is a gap between official institutional and individual academic responses to the Bologna-related curriculum changes, whereby academics perceive the changes less positively than institutional leaders and administrators. Given this, there is a need for a closer examination of the way university academics—who are experts of their knowledge fields—respond to the introduced standardized competence-based curriculum model in their specific national and disciplinary contexts.

Introducing the Study

The present chapter seeks to look at how Lithuanian academic engineers respond to the globally pervasive, homogeneous competence-based curriculum policy trend against the specific cultural background of the German and Soviet-influenced Lithuanian academic tradition. It draws on the findings from Rūta Petkutė qualitative empirical study (ongoing) that investigates the way academics from four different disciplines make sense of and respond to the European outcome and competence-based reforms in the cultural context of Lithuania. The original study was based on qualitative interviews with twenty four academics and used a thematic narrative portrayal (a detailed individual case study) (Goodson, 2013)—the element of the narrative/life history research—as a tool to analyse and present qualitative data. The focus of this chapter is confined to the discipline of engineering. The reason for choosing this particular discipline to look at more closely the way the standardized competence-based curriculum scheme plays out in a specific educational context is its distinctively two-fold—scientific and professional-applied—nature. Even without the current heightened political pressure towards performativity and practical applicability of knowledge, engineering is a practice-oriented discipline that has a strong scientific basis. Given this, it can be assumed that, in the face of instrumental competence-based reforms, which emphasise the utilitarian, vocational purpose of higher education, this discipline struggles to maintain the necessary balance between the practical/instrumental and scientific/academic sides of its curriculum.

The present discussion draws on the empirical data from six interviews with Lithuanian academic engineers. However, according to the narrative/life history research methodology, only thematically the richest narratives are selected to present data in order to gain a more in-depth and systematic understanding of the case in question. In this chapter, Lukas and Alex—two academic engineers whose narratives were thematically most dense—are at the focus.

Given its contextual specificities, Lithuania is an interesting case to explore the before-discussed global trend towards the homogeneous culture of the curriculum. Lithuania is an Eastern European, post-Soviet country and a current member of the European Union, which underwent a fast-paced transition from the Communist system to the Western free-market capitalist economy that accompanied the restoration of independence in the 1990s. Historically, its higher education system was influenced by the German and Soviet educational cultures. For early-twentieth-century Lithuania and other German-influenced countries of Eastern and Central Europe, the German Humboldtian university model, "which placed 'knowledge' at the centre of the mission of the university" (Scott, 2002: 140–141), was a source of inspiration. The early-twentieth-century trend in Lithuania to look at Germany for academic innovations can be explained by the fact that German language was taught at Lithuanian schools and thus was the key for the Lithuanian academic community to understand German literature and ideas (Gieda, 2013: 75–78). Given this historical link between the Lithuanian and German cultures, it can be assumed that Lithuanian higher education system has been influenced by the German neo-humanist educational philosophy of *Bildung* (inward self-cultivation as opposed to 'useful' knowledge). In this period, university education in Lithuania was oriented towards broad intellectual development. Later on, the Soviet university model, which considered the preparation of narrow technocratic specialists for the soviet industry and planned economy to be the key function of the university, was imposed. While under soviet rule, the narrow focus on the instrumental purpose of the university determined the prioritization of engineering discipline in Soviet times. It is important to stress that both German and Soviet educational traditions were knowledge-oriented and teacher-centred, which explains why the Lithuanian academic culture has traditionally been input, rather than outcome, based. However, since Lithuania's accession to the European Bologna process in 1999, the Lithuanian higher education system has begun to follow the Bolognian outcome and competence-oriented curriculum framework. Thus, the politically endorsed new curriculum model seems to impose an alien curriculum culture on the Lithuanian academic tradition.

Cultural and Disciplinary Understandings of Curriculum as Expressed by Academics

What can be seen from the narratives is that academic engineers share a traditional, academic conception of the engineering discipline. More specifically, a common assumption that is threading through their narratives is that, although engineering has a strong orientation to profession, it is not reducible to its practical, instrumental side and also has a strong scientific, conceptual basis. In fact, academic engineers tend to underline precisely the scientific, conceptual basis, rather than professional-practical aspects, of their discipline because it is a prerequisite for fulfilling its social role and the commitment to the interests of the public. What can be understood from their narratives is that professional engineers have an important societal role and commitment to mediate the science-based knowledge to the world of practice and, in this way, improve society at large. This broad understanding of the social role of engineering and its knowledge is reflected in the comment of Lukas, one of the interviewed engineers, that the science and preparation of engineers *"shouldn't be understood as an element of the free market"*. He explicates that, even if the engineering knowledge is a *"necessary instrument"* to benefit the market, it *"shouldn't be all this"*. In order to illuminate broad societal implications of engineering, he likens the purposes of the science-based engineering knowledge and the knowledge of humanities, suggesting that, similarly to humanities, science and engineering have a broader agenda to improve society through creating and disseminating scientific knowledge to society. In a similar vein, Alex, another interviewed engineer, conceives engineering as a practical profession-oriented discipline, which, nonetheless, helps to address society's complex problems. He stresses that the scientific basis is what makes the university-based engineering knowledge qualitatively different from the vocational engineering knowledge which is utilized by engineering technicians. According to him, for a professional engineer, it is insufficient to have practical, skill-based knowledge because he or she is *"solving complicated problems"* and *"thinks—why?"*. In his view, in the university, the knowledge needed to solve complex societal problems is developed. This conceptualisation of the engineering discipline as having a two-fold nature resembles Bernstein's (2000) theoretical concept of 'regions' which refers to professional disciplines that are, by their nature, oriented both inwardly towards academic disciplines and outwardly towards the world of practice. According to Bernstein, 'regions' resulted from the growth and technologisation of knowledge in the late nineteenth and twenty centuries. In order to respond to practical exigencies of the world of work, traditional inward-looking academic disciplines (such as physics), which he calls 'singulars', have been re-contextualised to form larger outward-looking, professional, practice-oriented disciplines (such as engineering). As a result, Bernstein explains, new professional disciplines or 'regions' have become dominant forms of knowledge organisation, whereas 'singulars' or traditional academic disciplines have been increasingly being pushed to the sidelines (Bernstein, 2000: 9). In other words, traditional theoretical or conceptual disciplinary knowledge has started to give its place to professional knowledge increasingly.

Following this understanding of the nature and purpose of engineering, university engineers conceive disciplinary engineering knowledge to be both practical and theoretical. They see engineering as a complex knowledge field that is simultaneously oriented towards professional concerns and thus requiring the development of profession-related skills and procedures and relying on the array of theoretical knowledge of different fundamental disciplines, such as mathematics and physics. Given this two-fold orientation of engineering, it seems that the key feature and concern for organising knowledge and curriculum in this discipline is developing and transmitting broad and diverse knowledge systematically. The concern for the inner coherence of knowledge is always implicitly or explicitly present throughout their narratives. For example, Lukas highlights that the relations between scientific concepts within the engineering knowledge structure are "deterministic" and not arbitrary. His argument for 'deterministic' relations between engineering concepts and the systematicity of the engineering knowledge indirectly demonstrates his assumption that the engineering knowledge has objective value and cannot be reduced to individual's or students' personal beliefs. Alex, too, underlines that accuracy and reliability are important aspects in the disciplinary context of engineering. For him, the pursuit of objectively correct knowledge makes the discipline of engineering different from social sciences in which an individual or a student has more space for interpretation. The academics can tell from their own work experience in an industry that the systematicity of knowledge is a precondition for avoiding *"wrong decision"* in engineering. What this suggests is that striving for accurate and systematic knowledge in engineering is an engineer's professional responsibility.

What the academics' narratives importantly bring to light is the recent wider technologisation process of the engineering field, the result of which is that computers do more engineering thinking. According to them, this has not only positive but also negative effect on the development of engineering knowledge. Although they treat the rise of digital engineering as a beneficial thing, they think that the over-reliance on digital engineering tools leaves little room for nourishing systematic human thought and leads to a consumeristic, passive and fragmented approach to the development of engineering knowledge. Lukas stresses that *"computers are only tools"*, which are useful but, nonetheless, cannot replace engineer's thought entirely. For Alex, the most valuable thinking in engineering is the one that is independent of technology. He sheds light on the fact that, unlike today, earlier engineers used to rely on their own technology-independent professional knowledge. He is worried that today the knowledge of a younger generation of engineers is entirely dependent on digital tools and confined to instrumental technical skills. In general, engineers think that the university is where the technology-independent professional engineering knowledge and thinking are to be nourished and passed on to younger generations of engineers.

These broader assumptions that engineers make about engineering as a wider discipline are echoed in their expressed understanding of the engineering curriculum. What surface from the narratives is that academic engineers assume that the engineering curriculum, just like the disciplinary engineering knowledge itself, is a mixture of different kinds of theoretical and practical knowledge. Yet it is the development of theoretical or conceptual knowledge, rather than practical, instrumental skills that should be at the main focus of the university engineering curriculum. Engineers argue for the centrality of knowledge in the engineering curriculum and stress the priority of fundamental theoretical knowledge over practical knowledge and skills. They say that it is important to start with theory and only then proceed with its practical application. Alex underlines that the focus on the development of theoretical knowledge and understanding, rather than practical skills, makes university engineering education qualitatively different from technical education. As he explains, this is because the knowledge gained through university engineering education is deeply linked to solving complex practical engineering problems and adapting to different unexpected situations.

Moreover, according to Lukas, theory helps students transgress their segmental everyday practical knowledge and think more systematically. He suggests that it is important not only to introduce students to the theoretical or conceptual knowledge but also to show them the links between the concepts. This kind of systematic knowledge and understanding serve as a conceptual resource for engineers to think of engineering alternatives and create solutions to engineering problems. Lukas argues that the engineering curriculum needs to be coherently structured around broad but systematically connected knowledge of different relevant disciplines to reflect the complexity of engineering knowledge structure as a discipline. For him, the inner coherence of the engineering curriculum is a precondition for students to develop systematic knowledge and understanding. *"So this is what I want to say: you can't form the matrix here [points to his head], in a student's head, without teaching them different disciplines coherently."*

What also emerges from the narratives is that, besides teaching engineering students disciplinary knowledge, it is necessary to develop some general academic capacities, such as critical thinking and argumentation; however, their development should go along with teaching disciplinary engineering knowledge.

Negotiations Between Cultural and Disciplinary Understandings of Curriculum and the Neoliberal Competence-Based Logic

In general, academics engineers expressed a critical attitude to the recent curriculum trend towards competences and outcomes. *"But I'll tell you honestly—I don't like those reforms"*, Lukas says. Alex reiterates: *"Of course, personally, I'm always against it."* The way they see it, there was no educationally justifiable reason to change the traditional knowledge-based curriculum with the competence and outcome-based one. Lukas expresses his opinion: *"Essentially, I don't want this old system of learning to change. We had a good system, do you get my point?"*. What can be traced throughout the narratives is that there are several interrelated reasons for their critical responses to the curriculum restructuring.

To begin with, the academics oppose the new curriculum scheme and associated competence vocabulary because they perceive these reform measures as bureaucratic and hierarchically imposed on them, rather than voluntary or rising from genuine academic concerns.

What interestingly stood out from the narratives is that academics have been expected by university administration to implement the competence and outcome-based curriculum framework in practice without being properly familiarized with the curriculum reform's rationale and its wider context. Lukas comments: *"I've only heard these things in various presentations"* and *"Yes, I read them all the time [ironically]."* Alex, too, admits that he has heard the name of the Bologna but could not tell anything more about it. He often sees the new educational concepts in the formal descriptions of study programmes. *"We encounter them frequently"*, he says, adding: *"Every other day. It's been flying around everywhere, in papers, and here, too, everywhere... competences, competences."* The academics view the newly prescribed educational concepts of competences and learning outcomes as well as the rationale behind them as deriving from purely economic and image-building concerns and thus alien to their academic reality. Alex asks, irritated: *"And what is this competence, may I ask?"* According to him, the new educational language of competences and outcomes is *"just nice sounding phrases"* which exist only *"in papers"*. In his understanding, the deployment of the competence-based approach and the new competence discourse is endorsed only to make the curriculum seem more relevant for students-customers. For this reason, he finds the curriculum change and the associated educational vocabulary *"populist"*, rather than educationally justified. Lukas, too, sees the promoted standardized vocabulary of competences and the related curriculum change as bureaucratic and unsustainable. He hints about a 'copy-paste' manner of implementation of the reform: *"Yes, I read them all the time. I'm telling you, these are the key words"*. He adds: *"I'm telling you, the entire subject has changed, but only on paper"*. As Lukas notes, the competence-based curriculum framework requires too detailed, lengthy, and bureaucratic descriptions of learning objectives and outcomes, which over-burden academics. As he complains, *"they write these huge amounts now"*. The way he sees it, the vocabulary of competences is merely *"marketing stuff"*, which is used to attract more students to study programmes. As the new standardized educational concepts lack connection to the academic concerns of the engineering discipline, he ignores them in his own academic practice: *"You know, I am relatively deaf to these phrases and terms"*.

The other reason academics oppose the competence-based curriculum reform is that they are tired of perpetual, fast-paced, and radical educational reforms. Lukas is worried that a negative result of the relentless short-term educational reformations and changing demands is *"a lack of consistency"* in curriculum decisions and discontinuity with the existing curriculum culture. This, according to him, obstructs rather than benefits the educational process. He reflects, in an irritated tone: *"It's been reforms through my entire career. There's nothing stable, do you understand, it's jumping to the left, then to the right, and then somewhere else, it's a total mess"*. Similarly, Alex complains about the current political and institutional pressure to reform higher education and make changes in curriculum constantly. He is irritated that the need for curriculum change is often justified by some *"abstract talks"* that *"everything's bad to the bone, we need a revolution"*. Interestingly, the overly enthusiastic educational discourse that surrounds the competence and outcome-based curriculum reform unpleasantly reminds them of the Soviet times in Lithuania and the optimistic Communist talks. Lukas laughs: *"But I see a thing that we already had, the resulting process is like the plenums of the Young Communist League that we used to have in the past—pretty talks."* For Alex, too, the new educational language of competences and outcomes and of employability relevance of the engineering curriculum resembles the reality of the soviet-time Lithuania when the government gave people unrealistic promises.

In general, the academics seem to believe that the so-called 'progressive' standardized competence-based curriculum can have, and already has had, negative educational effects in the specific disciplinary context of engineering. Alex shares his opinion:

> I, as an engineer, want some concreteness in this case […] What's it gonna give us, is it really gonna give us something? Or is it just a revolution with no direction, just as it was with [pauses] atomic bomb, right, when the foreseen results were foggy, unknown, so… But it can change some things, and, instead of getting a positive, we can get a negative result.

More specifically, the academic engineers are worried that, in the context of employability-oriented, competence-based reforms, it becomes difficult to justify developing the traditional foundational scientific knowledge, which, as they assume, is of the utmost importance in university education for engineers. In this reform context, the traditional knowledge-oriented curriculum is systematically criticised for being outdated and irrelevant to students and the labour market. Alex constantly hears growing public complaints that university engineering graduates lack practical knowledge and thus are not properly prepared for jobs. One can often hear that *"[…] having graduated from university, they have basic theory, a lot of theory and no practice."* The current reform discourse, he says, creates an illusion that *"it was different before, for many years, people used to leave university and stay jobless. But now everything's changed."* However, Alex argues that the traditional engineering curriculum has had employability relevance even without the current policy focus on employability. University engineering graduates are valuable to the industry because they have cognitive tools for *"solving complicated problems"*. Therefore, he sees the current efforts to focus the engineering curriculum towards employability purpose and re-stipulate it according to the ever-changing demands of the market as redundant. He notes that *"earlier people also got employed"* and *"engineering students, they're the ones that are wanted […]"*. As he insists, *"Fundamental things must be kept, knowledge remains…"* In a similar vein, Lukas argues that the development of the foundational knowledge needs to remain the primary goal of the engineering curriculum, and only later a more practical orientation and specialisation should follow. *"The basic things need to be what they are—basic [accentuates]. You have specialisations after that—play your games there [accentuates] […]. But the basic subjects—that's it! Keep your hands away from it. Without this knowledge, they…"*

He goes on to stress that developing traditional knowledge is a necessary condition for developing practical judgement: *"After that you can show all the latest innovations to them. But then they're going to assess them based on these mechanisms they already own."*

Also, what is important to note is that, although the academics acknowledge the importance of teaching critical and logical thinking, as well as computer literacy skills, they do assume that they should not be taught separately from the disciplinary knowledge. Contrary to the new competence-based approach, they do not consider them generic or transferable competences that can be taught separately from specific knowledge content. Even more, the academics seem to treat them as traditional general academic capacities that have been long developed in the university along with the acquisition of knowledge. Alex accentuates: *"They should be in the modules themselves. It should be more as a certain spirit....teachers...should develop them along with knowledge"*.

What emerges from the narratives is that the current pressure towards instrumental competences and skills in engineering manifests itself most strongly through the new curriculum focus on instrumental computer literacy competences as related to mastering digital engineering. While the academics are not dismissive of the importance of technical competences, they draw attention to the fact that the current heightened focus on them tends to marginalise the fundamental scientific knowledge in the engineering curriculum. Alex warns: *"A part might be lost that way..."* According to Lukas observations, the recent restless curriculum reforms have negatively affected the structure of the engineering curriculum, which, as he unpacks, has also inevitably affected students' development of knowledge and understanding. He explicates that the structure of the curriculum has been changed to give more room for the externally prescribed generic agenda, e.g. developing students' technical skills related to using digital construction and communication competences, while undermining the importance of foundational knowledge. Lukas comments on the recent changes in the curriculum structure: *"So, I'm telling you, they've turned this grid into a tragedy"*. He points to an ironic paradox that the more *"the wrapping"* of the engineering curriculum is being *"polished"* in the context of the curriculum reform, the more its educational content is *"getting worse"*. Lukas shares a concern that the current curriculum over-emphasis on mastering digital engineering runs the risk of becoming dependent on technology and developing an overly consumeristic relationship to knowledge. *"So, what, after the graduation, they're going to click the button "Where's my house at?" They're going to ask the computer, is that it? Or— "How do I build a house?" Of course, the computer will do it for them somehow, but whether it'll do it in the right way—it depends on what's been entered into it."* Also, according to his observations, the over-reliance on computer tools obstructs students' development of systematic knowledge and independent thinking. As he puts it, *"If their abilities here [points to his head] are diminishing. It could be that their abilities to make all sorts of presentations, advertisements are growing"*. He continues: *"And now, when I talk to young people, they don't have this matrix"*. What is more, they demonstrate *"detachment from any theory"* and an over-reliance *"on what they know from practice"*, the result of this is fragmented, *"market-type thinking*". If students do not develop the foundational knowledge and conceptual understanding, Lukas explains, "*they're guessing*", rather than trying to systematically and critically think on their own. Both Alex and Lukas believe that the labour market and the economy at large will not benefit from the current curriculum focus on instrumental employability competences because engineering graduates—lacking the systematic knowledge— cannot solve complex problems and think of alternative solutions. Given these limitations of the competence-based curriculum, academic engineers are largely critical of the current political and institutional rush to abandon the traditional knowledge-based curriculum.

The competence-based curriculum trend described by academic engineers reflects the emergence of what Bernstein (2000) terms generic modes of knowledge organisation or 'genericism', which is the more recent and radical form of the technocratisation and professionalisation of knowledge. According to Bernstein, while traditional professional knowledge or what he calls 'regions' of knowledge are oriented towards both scientific/academic and professional/instrumental concerns, the new generic forms of knowledge shift the focus away from academic concerns exclusively to "extra-school experiences: work and life". As he maintains, the problem with these currently prevailing instrumental modes of knowledge is that rather than focusing on learner's "capacity to project him/herself *meaningfully*", they are narrowly focused on the development of relevant "flexible performances" through "the concept of trainability" (ibid.: 53–62). What can be inferred from academic engineers' narratives is that, in the context of the current competence-based curriculum reforms, standard generic, work-related competences and skills are emphasized at the expense of disciplinary content and thus has a flattening effect on curricula.

Conclusions

This chapter has suggested that the competence-based higher education reform in Lithuania should be understood as part of the global-wide homogeneous educational reform processes, which introduce a hegemonic curriculum culture that is focused on externally pre-defined learning outcomes and efficiency. The restructuring of the higher education curriculum is conceptualised as integral to the global neoliberal knowledge economy policy discourse underpinned by the economically-driven logic. Also, what can be learned from the interviews with academic engineers is that the recent policy shift from the traditional disciplinary academic knowledge towards pre-specified outcomes and generic employability competences is a result of the growing technocratisation and commercialisation of knowledge. It has been argued that the globally dominant competence-based curriculum reforms with their emphasis on standard generic employability competences are indicative of the emergence of generic modes of knowledge, which itself is a response to instrumental socio-economic pressures.

A general finding that is gained through this study is that, in Lithuania, there seems to be a gap between the existing cultural and disciplinary understandings of curriculum as expressed by university engineers and the new instrumental neoliberal logic as introduced through the standardized competence-based curriculum model. Academics demonstrate sceptical and cautious attitude towards the new curriculum trend. Their general response to the curriculum reform is one of silent opposition and the implementation in a 'copy-paste' manner. This response can be explained by cultural and discipline-related reasons.

First of all, in Lithuania, a shift towards the micromanaged outcome-based curriculum is not an unproblematic technical change but rather a cultural move, which involves the abolition of the traditional knowledge centrality in curriculum and the principle of an open pursuit of knowledge. Lithuanian academics seem to perceive the reform as bringing in an alien culture of curriculum and thus lacking meaning in the specific Lithuanian academic context, whereby curriculum has been traditionally knowledge or input, rather than competence or outcome, based. Also, what can be seen from the interviews is that Lithuanian academics' sensitivity and opposition to the externally prescribed outcome-based curriculum model have borne out of the shared negative historical experience of the authoritarian soviet regime and its top-down decision-making culture. For Lithuanian academics, the ambitious and optimistic yet bureaucratic language surrounding the competence-based reform, which places a strong emphasis on employability and instrumental competences, echoes the vain promises of the Communist government about the bright future. Hence, paradoxically, in the specific post-soviet context of Lithuania, the so-called 'progressive' competence-based approach and the rationale behind it are perceived by university academics not as progress but as a regression to the narrow utilitarian soviet-time mentality.

Moreover, a closer look at Lithuanian university engineers' narratives reveals that the new standardised curriculum model disregards broad academic and disciplinary traditions, in which the learning process is embedded. Interestingly, although the interviewed academic engineers acknowledge the applied and practical nature of engineering, they tend to think that the new standardised curriculum scheme imposes an overly instrumental logic, which is in dissonance with their discipline's purpose of developing scientifically and conceptually robust professional knowledge and skills. Rather than following standard criteria that are externally prescribed through the curriculum reform, engineers act upon the specific inner criteria of their discipline. What can be understood from the narratives is that, in the disciplinary context of engineering, the introduction of the competence-based curriculum framework has had negative rather than positive educational effects. The current heightened curriculum focus on generic competences tends to diminish the importance of the disciplinary engineering knowledge in the curriculum and, as a result, leads to fragmentized and overly instrumental students' knowledge. It should be noted that similar findings, as discussed in the case of engineering, were found in other three disciplines (physics, journalism, and history) that were at the focus of the original research on which this chapter is based. Given this, the argument could be made that academics' insistence that theoretical or conceptual knowledge needs to be at the centre of the university engineering curriculum reflects the broader traditional assumption that university education is primarily about developing knowledge and conceptual understanding, rather than the preparation for jobs.

What can be concluded from the present study is that competence-based reforms institute a de-contextualised and overly standardized approach to curriculum. They disregard the fact that different countries have different cultural and disciplinary traditions and thus require more nuanced approaches to curriculum. An important lesson that other countries, which have been restructuring their educational systems around the dominant outcome-based model, can learn from the Lithuanian case is that, in order to avoid curriculum policies that are culturally meaningless to the local academic community and implemented in a 'copy-paste' manner, it is important to build on, rather than shy away from, cultural traditions and meanings.

References

Adam, S. (2008). *Learning outcomes current developments in Europe: update on the issues and applications of learning outcomes associated with the Bologna Process.* Scottish Government.

Allais, S. (2012). Claims vs. practicalities: Lessons about using learning outcomes. *Journal of Education and Work, 25*(3), 331–354.

Allais, S. (2014). *Selling out education: National qualifications frameworks and the neglect of knowledge.* Sense Publishers.

Autio, T. (2016). Contested educational spaces—Some tentative considerations inspired by curriculum theory and history. *IJHE Bildungsgeschichte: International Journal for the Historiography of Education, Heft, 1–2016,* 111–117.

Autio, T. (2007). Towards European curriculum studies: Reconsidering some basic tenents of Curriculum and Didaktik. *Journal of the American Association for the Advancement of Curriculum Studies, 3.*

Bernstein, B. (2000). *Pedagogy, symbolic control, and identity: Theory, research, critique.* Rowman & Littlefield.

Braedley, S., & Luxton, M. (2010). *Neoliberalism and everyday life.* McGill-Queen's University Press.

Crosier, D., & Parveva, T. (2013). *The Bologna process: Its impact in Europe and beyond.* UNESCO.

European Commission. (2010). *Europe 2020: A strategy for smart, sustainable and inclusive growth.* Communication from the Commission.

European Commission. (2012). *Re-thinking Education: Investing in skills for better socio-economic outcomes.*

Gieda, A. (2013). *Istoriografija ir visuomenė: Istorika, istoriko profesijos ir istorinės kultūros aspektai Lietuvoje 1904–1940* [Doctoral thesis].

Goodson, I. F. (2013). *Developing narrative theory: Life histories and personal representation.* Routledge.

Lorenz, C. (2010, July 12). Higher education policies in the European Union, the 'knowledge economy' and neo-liberalism., EspacesTemps.net, Travaux.

Lorenz, C. (2006). Will the universities survive the European integration? Higher education policies in the EU and in the Netherlands before and after the Bologna Declaration. Retrieved https://research.vu.nl/ws/portalfiles/portal/2172135/Sociologia+Internationalis.pdf

Magalhaes, A. M. (2010). The creation of the EHEA, 'learning outcomes' and the transformation of educational categories in higher education. *Educaēćo, Sociedade & Culturas, 31,* 37–49.

Muller, J., & Young, M. (2014). Disciplines, skills and the university. *Higher Education, 67*(2), 127–140.

Scott, P. (2002). Reflections on the reform of higher education in central and Eastern Europe. *Higher Education in Europe, 27*(1–2), 137–152.

Sursock, A. (2015). *Trends 2015: Learning and teaching in European universities*. European University Association.

Tuning Educational Structures in Europe. (n.d.a). *Approaches to teaching, learning and assessment in competence based degree programmes*. Available from: http://tuning.unideusto.org/tuningeu/images/stories/archivos/TLA%20PARA%20LA%20PAGINA.pdf

Tuning Educational Structures in Europe. (n.d.b). Competences. Available from: http://www.tuning.unideusto.org/tuningeu/index.php?option=content&task=view&id=173&Itemid=209

Ward, S. C. (2012). *Neoliberalism and the global restructuring of knowledge and education*. Routledge.

Wheelahan, L. (2010). *Why knowledge matters in curriculum: A social realist argument*. Routledge.

Young, M. (2011). The future of education in a knowledge society: The radical case for a subject-based curriculum. *Journal of the Pacific Circle Consortium for Education, 22*(1), 21–32.

Rūta Petkutė is a former language teacher in higher education and is currently a PhD candidate in social sciences at Tallinn University's School of Educational Sciences (Estonia). The primary focus of her current research is on the sociology of higher education and knowledge, higher education policy, the transformation of the university, and curriculum studies. Her most recently published work draws on her PhD research project based in Lithuania and uses life history and narrative methods to explore political restructuring of higher education, academic knowledge and curriculum, as well as the professional lives of university academics.

The East Asian Picture: Confucian Ideals and Curriculum Reforms

Nationalism and Globalism as Epistemic Entanglements: China's *Suyang* Curriculum Reform as a Case Study

Weili Zhao

China's Modernization, Globalization & Western Modernity

Modernization, globalization, and nationalistic glocalization never occur simply as one against another along a power vs. resistance dynamic. Instead, they are contested and entangled in a multi-layered power relation wherein varying mechanisms, say, nationalism, globalism, culture, economy, state power, ideology, epistemology, and social control are interpellated in play with and against each other. For example, it is often claimed that China was forced onto its modernization trek through the 1840 Opium War, which ended China's three thousand years' isolation as a Confucian civilizational state (although it is debatable whether imperial China was in fact not as "modern" as the then West). China's modernization, as Ambrose King (2018) puts, is both a response to the intrusion of Western modernity (the "modern" Western civilization that has already undergone the modernization process) in the forms of imperialism and colonialism and the renewal and further development of traditional Chinese civilization. Globalization, King explains, is the global or universal diffusion of Western modernity conceptualized by Western scholars. Sociologists like Max Weber for example mainly conceptualize the Western "modern" in linkage with technological and bureaucratic organizations and ground the "modern" episteme on an economic, i.e., instrumental or means-ends, rationality. Modernity primarily expresses itself in capitalist or industrial economy, nation-state polity structure, and cultural values such as democracy, human rights, and freedom.

From the late Qing dynasty to the 1930s, China's modernization trek, reductively put, witnessed a radical change in the attitude of Chinese literati (officials) and government toward Western modernity. Namely, initial ethnocentric superiority and

---

W. Zhao (✉)
Department of Curriculum and Instruction, The Chinese University of Hong Kong, Hong Kong SAR, China
e-mail: weilizhao18@cuhk.edu.hk

© The Author(s), under exclusive license to Springer Nature Singapore Pte Ltd. 2021
W. Zhao and D. Tröhler (eds.), *Euro-Asian Encounters on 21st-Century Competency-Based Curriculum Reforms*,
https://doi.org/10.1007/978-981-16-3009-5_9

thus despise of Western modernity gave way to a self-subjection to and wholistic embracing of the latter (see, Wong, 2005). When some radical intelligentsia and political elites in late nineteenth century Qing dynasty advocated to study Western materials and technological advancements as a model and paradigm, conservatives argued to retain "Chinese studies as the fundamental base as against Western learning for practices use" (*zhongxue wei ti, xixue wei yong*). Nevertheless, the 1905 abolishment of the imperial civil service examination system, the 1911 Revolution led by Dr. Sun Yat-Sen and the 1919 New Cultural Movement transformed China from a civilizational state into a modern nation-state polity, advancing the "local-Chinese vs. global-Western" debate in a new direction. Specifically, Confucian traditions were to be eradicated and replaced by advanced Western modernity in the name of modernization and globalization up to the late twentieth century.

King (2018) maintains that a dominant, yet inadequate, sociological viewpoint prevails in the modernization and globalization literature, namely, "globalization is an inevitable result of modernization" (p. 121). That is, the Western modernization process by economic rationality has universal applications, and all modernized societies will ultimately take on similar or identical forms of modernity, including but not confined to market economy, nation-state polity, and individualism. Many Western and non-Western societies have indeed transformed into a convergent form of modernity, featuring the growth of scientific consciousness, secularization of religions, development of instrumental rationality, changes in social movements, and industrialization. However, such a Weberian understanding of modernity, albeit dominant for over two centuries, is critiqued as being "a-cultural" (Taylor, 1992) in that its focus on social change excludes culture as an indispensable factor of modernization and modernity. To Taylor, such an a-cultural theory of modernity wrongly interprets everything modern as derived from the "Enlightenment package" and fails, as King's (2018) paraphrases, "to see the full gamut of 'alternative modernities' that are in the making in different parts of the world" (p. 125).

As King rightly vociferates, modernity in East Asia serves as one such alternative "localized" modernity in the making. Though doomed to modernize, the modernization process in East Asia countries embody its own characteristics on top of adopting features of universal Western modernity. For example, we can take cultural tradition like Confucian wisdom into consideration as a rich resource for us to account for and construct China's modernization and modernity in the making. As Berger (1988) discerns, whilst capitalism and individualism are two inseparable expressions of Western modernity, East Asian countries embody a non-individualistic version of capitalist modernity.

China's Education at the Tensions of Globalism and Nationalism

In this chapter, I select education as a domain to further scrutinize China's "localized" modernity in its making at the intersection of modernization, globalization, and nationalistic localization. As a social practice, China's education has also been neoliberalized as a universal effect of globalizing Western modernity through market economy and economic rationalization. However, China's education remains primarily a Confucian cultural practice of "person-making" (Zhao and Deng, 2016), foregrounding a credo of "establishing a person with virtues" (*lideshuren*). Furthermore, China's education has been a political tool of nation-building and state governance, partly an imprint of Confucian tradition.

As I have argued elsewhere (see, Zhao, 2019a), Confucian education is termed "*jiaohua*" (literally *teaching-transforming*) and interlocks with state governance such that the sovereign-subject relationship is configured along a teaching-learning dynamic, with Confucian literati populating the state-governing structure. This education-governance link can be traced to Confucius' envisioning of teaching and learning in his Yijing commentary. Specifically, he interprets the *guan* hexagram image of "wind blowing over the earth" (the hexagram itself depicts a scenario whence a virtuous King is performing a highest-ranking ritual with his subjects observing from below) as an ideal teaching and learning movement/interaction between the Son of Heaven and his subjects. Specifically, Confucius mobilizes the hexagram image of "wind blowing over the earth" and an inherent sense of "transforming" within the Chinese character "wind", instantiating an education-governance bondage along a wind-like teaching-as-transforming dynamic (see, Zhao, 2019a, b).

Education, as Piattoeva and Tröhler (2019) argue, is becoming increasingly nationalistic in most nation-states, subject to an international comparative logic and striving to demonstrate excellence in international benchmark practices like PISA. Due to its historical-cultural bondage with state-governance and cultural value cultivations, China's education is especially so. China has been striving to catch up with the West since the 1840s; with its rapid economic development and growing international influence, China is turning to a rising nationalism and localism as against the Western hegemonic globalism. Expressions of such nationalism include the "China/ese dream", "cultural revival", and "building a shared community for the globe", all proposed by the Xi administration. Put differently, "the-local-Chinese-versus-the-modern/global-West" debate has taken a new trajectory since the early twenty-first century, engendering new tensions and entanglements between nationalism and globalism, tradition and modernity. In re-making China's localized modernity, education stakes more and more crucial in the nation's globalization and (inter)national development, striving to make its educational subjects into globally competitive and yet nationally patriotic "talent" (Zhao, 2019c). Put differently, China's education becomes the very site of epistemic contestation between nationalism and globalism in its nationalistic state-building against globalism (Zhao, 2019d).

Before I address the epistemic entanglements as expressed in China's on-going *suyang* curriculum, a brief revisit of China's curriculum reform history is helpful to provide broader context. In the early twentieth century, Confucian teaching and learning of classical texts as a canon of imperial China gave way to schooling systems and educational theories and practices imported from the West. Various educational models, from Japan (1900s–1920s), the Soviet Union (1950s–1960s), and the United States (since 1990s), were tested before China finally reformulated its nine-year compulsory education system and curriculum guides during the so-called Principal Stage (1990s–2001) (Law, 2014). These curriculum guides, distinct from previous ones, re-focus upon cultivating humanistic values in students and prioritized "moral-value education" or "socialist core values". Such values included both Confucian values and Western-modern values like democracy, freedom, and equality. The proposed student-centered curriculum guides were refined and implemented nationwide during "the 2001–2011 Fine-Tuning Stage" as a gesture to make them more compatible with China's economic development, educational commodification, and nationalistic cultural revival. In 2013, China launched a new round of competency-based reforms largely modelled upon the OECD's and USA's twenty-first-century competencies-skills frameworks. These new reforms, termed "*suyang* curriculum" are being implemented with full force at the programmatic and school levels.

Put reductively, China's curriculum or education reform since the early twentieth century up to the 1990s has been to learn from the Western countries in order to catch up with the latter, in the name of going modern. Beneath such a developmental mindset is an epistemic (dis)ordering that imperial China with its grounding Confucian cultural heritage is premodern or not modern as against the Western science and technology. Henceforth the entire twentieth-century China has been striving to learn from and catch up with the advanced Western epistemes, educational system, and curriculum reforms. However, since late 1990s, with its rapid economic development and growing international influence, China started to claim to recover its cultural soft power as an expression of a rising nationalism in going global. Henceforth, curriculum development in post-1990s China bespeaks an "increasing tension between globalization and nationalism" (Law, 2014, p. 332) as the Chinese state strives to make students into both globally competitive workers and patriotic citizens (see, Zhao, 2019c). Put differently, international models are often culturally and institutionally re-written or over-written by nationalism in the name of re-contextualization or glocalization to better encase national contexts. The next section explicates China's on-gong *suyang* curriculum as an example of epistemic contestations between localism and globalism.

Epistemic Entanglements with China's *Suyang* Curriculum Reform

To revisit King's (2018) argument, modernization originated in the West and globalization, as a universal diffusion of Western modernity, often bespeaks a disguised form of Western colonialism and imperialism. Beyond transforming non-Western countries along an economic development rationality and intonation-state polities, modernization and globalization further instil in the latter Western cultural values of democracy, human rights, and freedom. Along with these colonial effects, modernization and globalization, i.e., Western modernity, also lead to an epistemic killing, or what Boaventura de Sousa Santos (2016) terms an "epistemicide", in the colonized places. Namely, Western and modern epistemic rules replace and overwrite local-cultural forms of knowledge and styles of reasoning. For example, native languages are replaced by English, and local modes of reasoning and meaning making may be marginalized or overwritten by the now "planetary" Western conceptual mode of signification, representational thinking, and/or a binary style of reasoning (see, Foucault, 1973). Seen this way, "colonialism is constitutive of, rather than derivative from, modernity" (Andreotti, 2011, p. 383), and modernity is intricately entangled with a coloniality of knowledge, power, and being. Coloniality, according to Nelson Maldonado-Torres (2007), refers to the memory or legacy of colonialism, which defines culture, labor, intersubjective relation, and knowledge production well beyond the limits of and long after the end of a colonial administration.

Over the years, I have been problematizing China's modernization of its language and its popularization of global Western discourses as a form of modernity-coloniality at the juncture of globalization and localization (see, Zhao, 2019a, b, 2020a). Specifically, the modern Chinese language has been Westernized since the early twentieth century to the extent that its meaning making rationale is transformed-modernized into a conceptual mode of signification. That is, the cultural epistemes nurtured within the Chinese monograph words are eclipsed, transforming the Chinese language into a representational and enclosed system akin to English. As a coloniality expression, new terms and concepts continue to be coined in China today as glosses of English concepts, increasingly turning the modern Chinese language into a heteroglossia. However, China's rising nationalism, call for "cultural revival", and growing power on the global platform are shifting the country's take on modernization, globalization, and glocalization. Among these, the cultural re-invocation as competitive soft power on the international archipelago can be viewed as China's resistance and countering against "hegemonic" Western globalism. In so doing, China is claiming and foregrounding its own voice and identity, or re-making its own localized modernity, after its claimed "catching up with" the West economic development wise.

As one big expression of such modernity re-localization process, China finalized its *Core Suyang [Competency] Definitions for Chinese Student Development* in 2016 as a gesture of going global and keeping abreast of the West. Specifically, the OECD and the USA began in the 1990s defining core competencies and skills for the twenty-first century, initiating a globalization movement of competency-based curriculum reform thereafter in non-Western nation states. China's *suyang* curriculum reform is a best example of nationalistic recontextualization of international models in two aspects. On one hand, it is a clear imitation of the Western conceptual framework and a gesture of globalization alongside the West. On the other hand, China claims its *suyang* definitions are more than a replica of the Western frameworks in that they build upon Confucian traditions of *learning, body-cultivation (xiushen), and governing* (Lin, 2016; Ministry of Education, 2016). Combining Confucian tradition with Western modernity, China's *suyang* framework aims to train students into holistic human beings or "talents" (Zhao, 2019c) with both internationally competitive knowledge-skills and patriotic Confucian values.

Simply put, China's re-contextualization of the Western competency-based curriculum models is subjected to a disguised nationalism, and the OECD's and USA's models are culturally and institutionally re-written or over-written by nationalism in the name of better fitting into the national cultural-political-historical contexts. China's nationalistic re-contextualization is first expressed in the naming of its curriculum as "*suyang* curriculum", *suyang* being a re-invoked cultural notion constitutive of the two Chinese monographs *su* and *yang*. Due to its strong cultural and linguistic cohesiveness, *suyang* immediately became a household catchword in China (Cui, 2016). Furthermore, the semantic repertoire of *suyang* was expanded to include "character-traits" and "emotions-attitudes-values" on top of the "competencies-skills-literacies" defined in the OECD's and USA's documents. That is, compared to the OECD's and USA's framing of competencies primarily as "skills, knowledges, and abilities", China's *suyang* definitions encompass "desirable character-traits (*pinge*) and key competencies-skills-literacies" as well as (Confucian) "emotions-attitudes-values" (Ministry of Education, 2016). In this sense, *suyang* becomes both a gloss and a counter gloss (Zhao, 2021a) of the English "competencies-skills-literacies", bespeaking China's double gesture of going global and remaining local.

However, as I have discussed elsewhere (see, Zhao, 2020a, b, 2021a), a linguistic reinvocation doesn't promise a cultural-epistemic regeneration or reinvigoration, and China's nationalistic efforts in making *suyang* curriculum as more than a replica of the international models have failed as a rhetorical trap or trope. This is primarily because Chinese scholars and policy makers are still subjected to the grip of Western modernity as an effect of coloniality yet unconscious of their epistemic subjugation. There are several expressions of this epistemic entrapment of Western modernity. One is a naturalized conceptual mode of signification that encases Chinese scholars and policy makers to treat *suyang* as a modern concept, a semantic equivalent of the English words "competency-skill-literacy", i.e., *suyang* = competency (see, Cui, 2016; Zhong and Cui, 2018; Zhang, 2016). In so doing, the underlying epistemic rules regulating phonetic English and monographic Chinese are eclipsed, failing to take stock of the etymological senses nurtured within the two Chinese monographs, *su* and *yang*, constituting *suyang*.

Another expression is to treat the "character-traits" and "emotions-attitudes-values" register of *suyang* as psychological terms, or as cognitive "principles" that a learner (often conceptualized as autonomous and rational individual) can come to acquire through behavioural change (Zhao, 2021a). Such an epistemic ordering is in no way comparable to a Confucian understanding of learning as making a person into a virtuous and consummate person (*junzi*). As Ames (2011) maintains, Confucian notions of a "human being" or "person" doesn't signify a Western modern individual who is autonomous and rational. Rather, Confucian personhood is to be made through playing varied contextualized roles in daily life practices and Confucian learning is to learn how to play these varied roles in relation to others to its optimal effect and relation. Simply put, Confucian "emotions-attitudes-values" are no longer reducible to a modern conceptualization of ideas and categories but a mode of being to be lived and practiced (Hattam and Baker, 2015).

While these two expressions are not exhaustive of the Western modernity episteme, globalism and localism/nationalism are epistemically entangled in modern China and inseparable from each other. Chinese policy makers and scholars hope to re-invoke and re-generate *suyang* [and other Confucian discourses like "establishing persons with virtue" (*lideshuren*) and "making educational subjects into *talent*" (*rencai*)] in its nationalistic cultural revival through education as counter-discourses against the global Western ones. However, they are nevertheless reasoning with a modern-Western mindset unbeknown to them due to an imprint of Western modernity-coloniality. Put differently, the Chinese intellectuals and institutions have subscribed to the murder of their own cognitive matrix (Paraskeva, 2018). While it is true that China's re-contextualization of the Western competency-based curriculum models is subjected to a disguised nationalism, we can flip the statement to argue that such nationalization is simultaneously subjugated to an unrecognized coloniality effect of modernity. This embrace of the Western modernity-coloniality episteme has marginalized and erased China's traditional culture, producing an academic aphasia in post twentieth-century China.

Chinese Body-Thinking as a New Episteme for *Suyang* Curriculum Reform

King (2018) argues that China may also be "condemned to modernization" and "condemned to modernize" (p. 119) like other countries. By that, King means modernization has brought a future to China, but has also displaced Confucian and other cultural values. China's modernization and globalization, it can be argued, are simultaneously an intentional imitation and a forced coloniality of the Western modernity. Since modern Chinese people are already epistemologically governed by the Western modernity episteme, it is no longer justifiable to stick with a clear-cut East-West division nor a tradition-modernity division. As argued earlier on, globalism and localism, and tradition and modernity, are all entangled epistemologically. Given this, how is it possible for us to recognize the varied expressions of modernity-coloniality and to furthermore de-colonize the grip of modernity-coloniality episteme?

In my case, I have been using a Heideggerian-Foucauldian language-discourse perspective I recently rephrased as a de-colonial language gesture (see, Zhao, 2021a) in alignment with Paraskeva's (2016) de-colonial thinking. Foucault (1973) claims that critics of modernity need to "work [their] way back from opinions, philosophies, and perhaps even from sciences, to the words that made them possible, and, beyond that, to a thought whose essential life has not yet been caught in the network of grammar" (p. 298). One of his strategies is "to disturb the words we speak, denounce the grammatical habits of our thinking, and dissipate the myths that animate our words, to render once more noisy and audible the element of silence that all discourse carries with it as it is spoken" (ibid.). Inspired, I have suspended the Chinese term *suyang* into a form of *su + yang*, explicating a (w)holistic Chinese "body-thinking"

(Wu, 1997) episteme (see, Zhao, 2020a). "Body-thinking", Wu Kuang-Ming (1997) maintains, means the *body thinks, and thinking is enacted through bodily engagement*. It is not "bodily thinking" or "thinking has a bodily dimension", but the "body enacts thinking ontologically" such that the "body is thinking and thinking embodies itself in bodily engagements" (Zhang, 2010).

Specifically, I (see, Zhao, 2020a) have pinpointed an etymological and linguistic linkage between *suyang* and *jiaoyu* (education) as *yang* and *yu* both convey the semantic gesture of "bringing up or nurturing". This etymological linkage indicates a cultural convergence between parent-child interrelationships and teaching-learning in Confucian culture that resonates with the Confucian tradition of learning, body-cultivation (*xiushen*), and governing. That is, the (w)holistic Chinese body-thinking episteme retreats "emotions-attitudes-values" and "personality traits", the Confucian cultural register of *suyang*, as being intertwined with a (w)holistic psychosomatic way of living and being, rather than as psychological traits or "principles or even categorical imperatives above lived experience itself" (Zhang, 2012, p. 639). Intriguingly, the two complicated Chinese characters, "*tai*" (態 attitude) and "*neng*" (能 competency), graphically relate their morphological linkage and difference. Namely, the complicated Chinese character *tai* 態 (attitude) is comprised of the character of *neng* 能 (competency) on top of a radical for *xin* 心 (heart), succinctly dividing competencies-skills from emotion and attitude. However, this visual-etymological linkage does not appear in the simplified depiction of *neng* 能 and *tai* 态. Our common trans-lingual ordering of *taidu* = attitude further overwrites the crucial "heart" difference between "competency" and "attitude".

Seen this way, the Chinese body-thinking episteme nurtured within the cultural notion *suyang* can work as an alternative framework to recalibrate China's on-going *suyang* curriculum reform beyond the constraint of Western modernity-coloniality. In other words, the Chinese body-thinking episteme can play an alternative epistemic-cultural role in China's localized modernity in the making, not reducible to the mind-thinking episteme of Western modernity. My grammatical transfiguration of *suyang* into "su + yang" also significantly proves that the purpose of translation is not to produce "equivalents that successfully mediate between (cross-cultural) differences, but precisely the partly opaque relationship we call 'difference'" (Chakrabarty, 2000, p. 17).

Furthering the Globalization/Globalism and Localization/Localism Argument …

So far, I have argued that globalism and localism are entangled epistemologically. Chinese "body-thinking" is shared as an example of how to use language as a de-colonial tool in constraining the coloniality of Western modernity and constructing a

Chinese localized modernity episteme. My example also raises ethical and paradigmatic concerns in recalibrating the tensions and entanglements of globalism and localism/nationalism.

As King (2018) rightly observes, "modernity is an extremely complex sociocultural system, and its genesis and development cannot rely on any single factor, be it economic interest, ideology, geographic environment, or the particular character of an individual leader" (p. 124). In renewing and regenerating the Confucian body-thinking episteme in constructing the Chinese modernity, we need to take caution not to ossify it as the standard, nationalistic, and thus hegemonic, form of modernity. It is also not possible to completely discard the western "Enlightenment package" nor to nostalgically revive Confucian tradition without any adjustment and revision. As King (2018) vociferates, "building a new modern Chinese civilizational order involves not only a process of deconstructing the cultural tradition but also a process of reconstructing it. For the new Chinese civilization, after all, needs to be both 'modern' and 'Chinese'" (p. 128).

I unpack *suyang* not only as an "alternative thinking of curriculum" but also as "alternative thinking of alternatives" (see, Santos 2007b). That is, body-thinking is an alternative mode of mind-thinking in the epistemological and ideological terrain. As a form of decolonial thinking, it doesn't begin anew in the old West-Eurocentric cartography of knowledge but finds an entirely new ecological beginning in the distinct Chinese space of knowledge. It delinks itself from the rhetoric of modernity, democracy, post-modernity, or post-colonialism, all of which are grounded in the Occident, hoping instead to bring to the foreground "a silenced and different genealogy of thought" (Paraskeva, 2016, p. 80) by critiquing the validity of knowledge itself. This body-thinking, I believe, adds a nuanced dimension to the (re)making of Chinese modernity in the twenty-first century.

Furthermore, the Eastern and Western forms of modernity should not be opposed as one against the other, or as one being epistemically superior to the other. Instead, all forms of modernity and epistemes are ontologically equal and epistemologically different, needed and valued toward building a "cognitive justice" (Santos, 2007a, 2016) and "ecologies of knowledges" (Santos, 2007b, 2016). While the former recognizes the equal value of all forms of knowledge, the latter advocates a harmonious coexistence of varied forms of knowledge. For example, even within the Western scholarship, varied modes of thinking along the post-turns like post-humanist and new materialist scholarship related to the body/affect turn have critiqued the Enlightenment modernity, the foundational individualism, the representational episteme, the Anthropocene, the mind-body dualism, and the means-ends economic rationality. Scholars both within and without the West are enriching these post-turn scholarships with insights from non-Western epistemes and wisdom. For example, as Ames (2011) observes, the Confucian non-individualistic ordering of a person supplements the Enlightenment "individual" trap. I have also unpacked how the Chinese ancient onto-episteme of *qi* cosmology can inform the current post-humanist thinking, with rich implications for research methodology and pedagogy (see, Zhao, 2021b). Similarly, the Chinese holistic body-thinking resonates with the Western scholarship on "embodied curriculum" (Stephanie, 2008).

In other words, we need to de-colonize a binary mode of reasoning as a modern Western episteme toward an "itinerant" entanglement. Paraskeva's (2016) argumentation on a de-colonial theorization along an "itinerant" trajectory is helpful here. To Paraskeva, besides questioning whose knowledge gets taught as official knowledge in curriculum studies, we need to ask what other forms of knowledge exist in the first place. A de-colonial itinerant curriculum theorization, Paraskeva argues, is to expose and suspend the "darker side" of the Western modernity-coloniality of knowledge, power, and being toward global "cognitive justice". It is "sentient of the wor(l)ds behind and beyond the Western epistemological platform, wor(l)ds that are non-monolithic" (p. 86). Yet, it cautions against eulogizing any form of episteme as the ossified standard or center on the world civilization platform. Being itinerant, it means globalism and nationalism/localism undergo with, interact with, and inform each other, away from both a relativist nationalism and a hegemonic globalism.

References

Ames, R. T. (2011). *Confucian role ethics: A vocabulary*. Chinese University Press.
Andreotti, V. (2011). (Towards) decoloniality and diversity in global citizenship education. *Globalisation, Societies and Education, 9*(3–4), 381–397. https://doi.org/10.1080/14767724.2011.605323
Berger, P. (1988). An east Asian development model. In P. L. Berger and Michael Hsin-Huang Hsiao (Eds.), *In search of an east Asian development model*. Brunswick.
Chakrabarty, D. (2000). *Provincializing Europe: Postcolonial thought and historical difference*. Princeton University Press. https://doi.org/10.1086/ahr/106.4.1322
Cui, Y. H. (2016). Suyang: Yige rangren huanxi rangrenyou de gainian [Suyang as a concept that pleases and worries people]. *Huadong shifan daxue xuebao, 1*, 3–5.
Foucault, M. (1973). *The order of things: An archaeology of the human sciences*. Vintage Books.
Hattam, R., & Baker, B. (2015). Technologies of self and the cultivation of virtues. *Journal of Philosophy of Education, 49*(2), 255–273. https://doi.org/10.1111/1467-9752.12140
King, A. (2018). *China's great transformation: Selected essays on confucianism, modernization, and democracy*. Chinese University Press.
Law, W. W. (2014). Understanding China's curriculum reform for the 21st century. *Journal of Curriculum Studies, 46*(3), 332–360. https://doi.org/10.1080/00220272.2014.883431
Lin, C. D. (Ed.). (2016). *21 shiji xuesheng fazhan hexin suyang yanjiu* [Study on developing students' core suyang in 21st century 21]. Beijing Normal University Press.
Maldonado-Torres, N. (2007). On the coloniality of being. *Cultural Studies, 21*(2–3), 240–270. https://doi.org/10.1080/09502380601162548
Ministry of Education. (2016). *Zhongguo xuesheng fazhan suyang* [Core suyang definitions for Chinese student development]. http://www.jyb.cn/basc/sd/201609/t20160914_673105.html
Paraskeva, J. M. (2016). *Curriculum epistemicide: Towards an itinerant curriculum theory*. Routledge.
Paraskeva, J. M. (Ed.) (2018). *Toward a just curriculum theory: The epistemicide*. Routledge.
Piattoeva, N., & Tröhler, D. (2019). Nations and numbers: The banal nationalism of education performance data. *International Journal for the Historiography of Education, 9*(2), 245–249.
Santos, B. S. (2007a). Beyond abyssal thinking: From global lines to ecologies of knowledges. *Review (Fernand Braudel Center), 30*(1), 45–89.
Santos, B.S. (2007b). Introduction. In B. de Souza Santos (Ed.), *Cognitive justice in a global world: Prudent knowledges for a decent life* (pp. 1–12). Lexington Books.

Santos, B. S. (2016). *Epistemologies of the south: Justice against epistemicide*. Routledge.
Stephanie, S. (2008) *Body knowledge and curriculum: Pedagogies of touch in youth and visualculture*. Peter Lang.
Taylor, C. (1992). *Sources of the Self: The Making of Modern Identity*. Harvard University Press.
Wong, L. W. (2005). From 'controlling the Barbarians' to 'wholesale westernization': Translation and politics in late imperial and early Republican China, 1840–1919. In E. Hung & J. Wakabayashi (Eds.), *Asian translation traditions* (pp. 109–134). St. Jerome Publishing House.
Wu, K. M. (1997). *On Chinese body thinking: A cultural hermeneutic*. Brill Academic Publishing.
Zhang, H. (2016). Lun hexinsuyang de neihan [On the FFDFconnotations of core suyang]. *Quanqiujiaoyuzhanwang [Global Eduacation], 45*(4), 10–24.
Zhang, X. L. (2012). Time in familial reverence-deferance: A comment on Roger T. Ames' confucian role ethics. *Frontiers of Philosophy in China, 7*(4), 635–639.
Zhang, Z. L. (2010). Kuang-ming Wu "zhongguo shenti siwei" lunshuo [On Kuang-ming Wu's Chinese body thinking]. *Philosophy Trends, 3,* 43–49.
Zhao, W. (2019a). Re-invigorating the being of language in international education: Unpacking Confucius' 'wind-pedagogy' in Yijing as an exemplar. *Discourse: Studies in the Cultural Politics of Education*. https://doi.org/10.1080/01596306.2017.1354286
Zhao, W. (2019b). *China's education, curriculum knowledge and cultural inscriptions: Dancing with the wind*. Routledge.
Zhao, W. (2019c). China' s making and governing educational subjects as 'talent': A dialogue with Foucault' s biopower. *Educational Philosophy and Theory, 52*(3), 300–311. https://doi.org/10.1080/Q600131857.2019.1646640
Zhao, W. (2019d). Numbers, Nationalism, and the Governing of Education in China. *International Journal for the Historiography of Education, 2,* 260–263.
Zhao, W. (2020a). Problematizing "epistemicide" in transnational curriculum knowledge production: China's suyang curriculum reform as an example. *Curriculum Inquiry*. https://doi.org/10.1080/03626784.2020.1736521
Zhao, W. (2020b). Returning to the cultural foundations of China's curriculum reform: ICT and confucian "wind" education. In J. Paraskeva (Ed.), *Curriculum theory: A comprehensive reader*. Myers Educational Press.
Zhao, W. (2021a). Toward a de-colonial language gesture in transnational curriculum studies. In B. Green, P. Roberts, & M. Brennan (Eds.), *Curriculum challenges and opportunities in a changing world: Essays in transnational curriculum inquiry*. Palgrave Macmillan.
Zhao, W. (2021b). Eastern Ethico-Onto-Epistemologies as a Diffracting Return: Implications for Post-qualitative Pedagogy and Research. In K. Murris et al. (Eds.), *Navigating the Postqualitative, New Materialist and Critical Posthumanist Terrain Across Disciplines: An Introductory Guide*. Routledge.
Zhao, G. P. & Deng, Z. Y. (Eds.) (2016). *Re-envisioning Chinese education: The meaning of person-making in a new age*. Routledge.
Zhong, Q. Q., & Cui, Y. H. (Eds.). (2018). *Hexin suyang yanjiu* [Study on core suyang]. East China Normal University Press.

Weili Zhao is an assistant professor in the Department of Curriculum and Instruction at the Chinese University of Hong Kong, China. With interdisciplinary training in linguistics and sociolinguistics, critical discourse studies, language philosophy, and curriculum studies, she has been doing research on China's education and curriculum reforms at the nexus of tradition and modernity, East and West. Her dissertation-turned book, *China's Education, Curriculum Knowledge and Cultural Inscriptions: Dancing with The Wind*, was out in June 2018 with Routledge, and she was the recipient of 2019 AERA Early Career Outstanding Research Award, SIG 171 (Confucianism, Taoism, Buddhism and Education).

Unpacking the Global-Local Entanglements in Hong Kong's Curriculum Reform

Min Lin and Yundan Zheng

Introduction

In recent decades, educational and curriculum reforms worldwide have been shaped by globalized discourses, especially by the OECD (Organisation for Economic Co-operation and Development)-initiated concepts. Like many other countries and regions, Hong Kong has undergone rounds of curriculum reform to keep abreast of global changes and of the evolution of a knowledge-based economy. Since the 1980s, Hong Kong has been formulating and updating its curriculum reform(s) blueprint with reference to trends in education in international organizations and other countries (CDC, 2017; Chee, 2012). However, unlike previous reform documents, the recent renewal version of educational reform document 'Basic Education Curriculum Guide—To Sustain, Deepen and Focus on Learning to Learn (2014/2017)' (also known as 'Learning to Learn 2.0') foregrounds a value/attitude/moral cultivation component on the OECE's competency model.

This significant change in Hong Kong's curriculum documents (CDC, 2014, 2017) draws our attention to national/local reading of globalizing education reforms. For a long time, research highlighting East-West and global-local dialogues have taken globalization as a 'problem space' (Ong and Collier 2005). For example, according to the 'Ongoing Renewal of the School Curriculum—Secondary Education Curriculum Guide (2017)' mandated by the Curriculum Development Council, the ongoing curriculum renewal occurs/is occurring 'in response to changing context' so as to prepare students 'to meet the dynamic challenges in the twenty-first century world' and to be 'in alignment with the general directions of the major economies in the world' (p. 19). This official narrative treats globalization as a 'problem space': one

---

M. Lin (✉) · Y. Zheng
Department of Curriculum and Instruction, The Chinese University of Hong Kong, Hong Kong SAR, China
e-mail: lmlinmin@link.cuhk.edu.hk

© The Author(s), under exclusive license to Springer Nature Singapore Pte Ltd. 2021
W. Zhao and D. Tröhler (eds.), *Euro-Asian Encounters on 21st-Century Competency-Based Curriculum Reforms*,
https://doi.org/10.1007/978-981-16-3009-5_10

needs to get prepared to respond to and meet challenges as the 'solutions'. There are also a number of transnational policy studies revolving around how Asian countries borrow and translate Western educational policies or pedagogies into Eastern soil and how these policies and pedagogies are incompatible in Eastern context (for example, see Liu and Feng, 2015). Globalization indeed transmits issues and problems to indigenous cultures, but that is not the focus of this chapter. Rather, we are concerned with the dominant global-local, central-peripheral logic represented in the above narratives from the education policy mobility research field, and the multi-layered power relations and varying mechanisms entangled within.

In this chapter, we aim to develop a more nuanced understanding of globalization that extends beyond the global/local binary by unpacking Hong Kong's latest Learning to Learn curriculum reforms. A detailed discourse analysis on Hong Kong's curriculum reform case will offer new insights for discussion in globalization literature for the following reasons. First, as a small city prospering under UK's 155-year governance from the end of the First Opium War (1842) until its handover from British colonial rule back to China sovereignty (1997), Hong Kong has been a meeting place of Eastern and Western civilization, with a unique blending of globalization, Chinese localization, and Western modernity. Hence, Hong Kong's educational reforms represent a unique (dis)assemblage of heterogenous elements. Second, while there are sufficient researchers who investigate how national education agendas are indigenized in the local context despite the transnational pressure created by globalization (see, for example, Ozga and Lingard, 2007), most of them are situated in the Western context; little attention has been given to Asia, let alone to Hong Kong.

To move beyond dominant global/local and central/peripheral bilateral transnational policy borrowing pattern, we adopt Savage's (2020) theoretical framework of 'assemblage' as a conceptual tool to investigate how varying heterogeneous elements, such as the OECD's dominant core-competency model, Hong Kong's economic conditions, politic environment etc., are held together in a flux to create the conditions of possibilities for a/the specific curriculum reform framework to emerge in Hong Kong. Assemblage approach has been widely harnessed in recent education policy research, with a particular focus on the role of OECD in generating a new global space of educational governance (see, for example, Hartong, 2018; Savage and Lewis, 2018). However, much of the research has focused on the powerful influence of the OECD education framework (featured with standardized assessments, league table and evidence repositories, etc.) in shaping national education system into new topological assemblages. For example, by using an assemblage approach to trace the development of national teaching standards in Australia, Savage and Lewis (2018) argue that it is misleading to explain Australian national schooling reform policies as simply products of national schooling policies; they are also strongly informed by diverse components such as the transnational flows of policy actors, ideas, and practices. This chapter, however, sets aside the view that OECD has brought a globalizing phenomenon of education homogeneity and instead foregrounds the *culture* of education policy making in globalizing circumstances by situating a contextual analysis of Hong Kong's latest value-foregrounded education reform. By saying the *culture* of education, we mean there are place-based and culture-specific ways of national education policy making in globalizing circumstances. In other words, as

Olwig and Hastrup's (2005) anthropological work suggests, it is a kind of 'sitting culture' that involves new sites of cultural construction which embody the interrelationship between local frameworks of life and global transitory flows of relation. Therefore, cultures can be conceptualized as unique entities corresponding to particular localities, say, historical, linguistic, economic, and political situatedness. Here culture is more than what we commonly take as language, music, social relations, or other components, but is a 'deep structure' embedded in people's everyday life and social/political behavior (Sun, 2015, p. 9). Seen this way, education systems are the bearer of the nation-states, where different historical, economic, and political components are held together.

This chapter unfolds in three steps in order to make evident how the culture of Hong Kong's education underpins Hong Kong's curriculum reform against the backdrop of globalization. The first part of this chapter briefly introduces Hong Kong's emergent curriculum reforms since the 1990s in relation to the OECD education framework. We then shift our focus to the latest value-prioritized Learning to Learn curriculum reforms, which are rich in Confucian cultural connotations in comparison to the OECD's psychological based values and attitudes. The second part proposes the 'assemblage' approach as a helpful theoretical framework and conceptual tool in thinking about Hong Kong's curriculum reforms and key competencies in a globalization age. The third part illustrates how heterogenous components are forging and resisting in the making of Hong Kong's curriculum reforms, especially its value education.

Hong Kong's Curriculum Reform(s) in Relation to the OECD Reform Framework

In the transnational educational policy research field, a common view on the debate of 'globalizing education policy' is that local education systems are re-formulating and re-formatting their curricula according to a/the 'global format'. Supernational agencies such as the OECD, the World Bank, and the UNESCO, according to Lingard, Rawolle and Taylor (2005), are powerful players that influence regional education formation. The OECD, for instance, is a global agency that privileges neoliberal education agenda in education reform.

The beginning of the twenty-first century has seen the return of large-scale education reform worldwide. In 1996, the OECD launched 'The Knowledge-based Economy' guideline, fully recognizing the importance of knowledge and technology as the driver of productivity and economic growth in modern OECD economies. Skills and dispositions such as creative abilities, higher-order thinking, and cooperative and communication skills were identified as new human capital requirements for the new global economy. The OECD further initiated the Program for International Student Assessment, which has since been one of the most important instruments and impetus for global curriculum reforms. To better measure students' performance and the quality of education, the OECD-Definition and Selection of Competencies (DeSeCo) project brings a wide range of expert and stakeholder's opinions together and identifies key competencies necessary for the modern world. The *Recommendation* identifies eight key competences such as Literacy, Multilingualism, Numerical, etc., while values and attitudes are not prioritized, according to European Commission's 2006 *Recommendation on Key Competencies for Lifelong Learning*. Albeit some differences in expression, these key competencies soon became key words in worldwide curriculum reforms. Following this trend, a majority of countries and regions urgently jumped onto the wagon of knowledge-based reform in preparation for the emerging information society and globalized economy. Among this global educational reform tide, the Curriculum Development Council of Hong Kong released the consultation document 'Learning to Learn: The Way Forward in Curriculum Development' in 2000, and officially launched the 'Learning to Learn' reform in 2001 as a response to the world fashion.

According to the OECD document (1997), competency is more than just knowledge and skills; it also concerns the ability to meet complex demands by drawing on and mobilizing psychological resources like attitudes. 'To cope with the challenges of the twenty-first century' and to keep Hong Kong 'abreast of the global trends' (CDC, 2001), the 'Learning to Learn' reform? shares a lot in common with the OECD framework in both the form and discourses. For example, we see similar three-level patterns of framework, including knowledge (key learning areas in Hong Kong framework), skills, values, and attitudes, and common emphasis on life-long learning, generic skills, critical/creative thinking skills, etc. (see Table 1). Like many other countries and regions, the OECD key competencies and PISA have become the most significant instruments for assessing/measuring Hong Kong's curriculum reforms. In the ongoing renewal of curriculum reform guidelines? (CDC, 2017), the Hong Kong 2001 'Learning to Learn' reform is deemed as a success and on the 'right' direction over the ten-year curriculum reform because Hong Kong students have achieved outstanding results in PISA and many other international assessments like TIMSS and PIRLS. Thus, according to the report, schools have achieved greatly in the past decade in preparing students to succeed in a knowledge-based, technologically advanced, and increasingly globalized world (CDC, 2014, 2017).

Interestingly, while it is widely accepted that the 2001 Learning to Learn curriculum reform is in alignment with the general direction of the world's major economies, the role of values and attitudes is emphasized in the Hong Kong reform document for whole-person and balanced development, compared to the OECD framework. Both the Learning to Learn consultation document (2000) and the official guideline (2001) assert that values and attitudes should be one of the three pillars of curriculum framework and hence learning outcomes of the educated. Moral and civic education has been regarded as the first among four key tasks for reform and is included as Chapter 3A in the 2001 CDC new reform document.

Closer textual analysis and comparison on the value and attitude dimensions of the OECD guidelines and Hong Kong reform documents well reflect the difference. According to the DeSeCo project report (Rychen and Salganik, 2000), competence is broader than knowledge and skills and places complex demands facing individuals

Unpacking the Global-Local Entanglements in Hong Kong's … 179

Table 1 Mapping of competencies: Hong Kong and the OECD

Education Reform	Competencies Framework in HK			Education Reform	Competencies Framework from OECD		
Learning to Learn: the way forward in Curriculum Development (CDC, Nov 2000)	Key learning areas—the bases for **knowledge building** • Chinese language' • English language' • Mathematics • Personal, social and humanities • Science • Technology • Arts • Physical	**Gentric skills**-the foundation for helping students to learn how to learn • Collaboration skills • Communication skills • Creativity • Critical Thinking skills • Information Technology skills • Numeracy skills • Problem Solving skills • Self-management skills • Study skills	**Moral and value** e-nurturing of students' personal dispositions • Perseverance • Respect for others • Responsibility • National identity commitment	The knowledge based-Economy (1996)	**Codified knowledge** might be considered as the material to be transformed	**Tacit knowledge** in the form of skills needed to handle codified knowledge • Capabilities for selecting relevant and disregarding irrelevant information • Recognizing patterns in information • Interpreting and decoding information as well as learning new	**Scientific knowledge** **Technological knowledge** **Diffusion and use of information and knowledge** **Linear model of innovation**

(continued)

Table 1 (continued)

Education Reform	Competencies Framework in HK			Education Reform	Competencies Framework from OECD		
Learning to Learn 2.0 from 2014 to 2017 (CDC, 2014–2017)	**Knowledge** • Chinese language • English language • Mathematics • Personal, social and humanities • Science • Technology • Arts • Physical	**Skills** **Basic skills:** communication skills/mathematical skills/information technology skills **Thinking skills:** Critical thinking skills/creativity/Problem solving skills **Personal and social skills:** Self-management skills/self-learning skills/collaboration skills	**Moral and value** • Perseverance • Respect for others • Responsibility • National identity commitment • Integrity care for others	OECD Future of Education and Skills 2030 (2019)	**Knowledge** Disciplinary knowledge/interdisciplinary knowledge/epistemic knowledge/procedural knowledge	**Skills** • Cognitive and meta-cognitive skills • Social and emotional skill • Practical and physical skills	**Values and attitudes** • Personal values • Social values relate to those principles and beliefs that influence the quality of interpersonal relationships • Societal values define the priorities of cultures and societies • Human values defined as transcending nations and cultures

at the forefront of the concept of competence. According to this viewpoint, competencies are structured around demands and tasks. Fulfilling complex demands and tasks requires not only knowledge and skills but also involves strategies and routines needed to apply the knowledge and skills, as well as appropriate emotions and attitudes, and effective management of these components. Thus, the notion of competencies encompasses cognitive but also motivational, ethical, social, and behavioral components. It combines stable traits, learning outcomes (e.g., knowledge and skills), belief-value systems, habits, and other *psychological* features (italic added).

Much similar to this elaboration, other OECD policy texts also designate key competences as 'the ability to successfully meet complex demands in varied contexts through the mobilization of psychological resources, including knowledge and skills, motivation, attitudes, emotions and other social and behavioral components' (see OECD, 2005; Rychen, 2009). From these statements, we can recognize that the OECD deems particular values, motivations, attitudes and dispositions as forms of psychological resources or as means necessary for a specific goal, that is, reflective and autonomous learning. In this regard, the values and attitudes internal to students are linked to the notion of 'trainability', or the 'instrumentalities of the market' subjected to assessments (Bernstein, 2000, p. 55), ultimately for a nation's economic productivity and social harmony.

In comparison, values and attitudes are much more emphasized and have a strong cultural connotation in Hong Kong's policy texts. Specifically, in Hong Kong's 2014 Learning to Learn 2.0 guideline, the seven learning goals of the reform guidelines were revised to place more emphasis on value. The first learning goal was updated from 'recognise their roles and responsibilities as members in the family, the society, and the nation; and show concern for their well-being' to 'know how to distinguish right from wrong, fulfill their duties as members in the family, society and the nation, and show acceptance and tolerance towards pluralistic values'. Values and attitudes are still one of the three foundations and main components of the curriculum framework (see Figs. 1 and 2), and Moral and Civic Education one of the five essential learning experiences. But the five priority values and attitudes recommended by the *Basic Education Curriculum Guide—Building on Strengths (Primary 1 to Secondary 3)* (2002) was enlarged to seven values: 'perseverance, respected for others, responsibility, national identity, commitment', and newly-added 'integrity, care for others'. Along with these seven values, 'A Proposed Set of Values and Attitudes' (CDC, 2014) further identifies more than 70 personal and social values with cultural connotations, like honesty, courage, modesty, tolerance, etc. Schools are expected to nurture these seven prioritized values together with many other values through the adoption of a holistic curriculum.

Through the above reviews, the Hong Kong competencies clearly encompass features distinct from the OECD model. It is interesting to note that while Hong Kong is following a global format in its curriculum reform process, it is in a distinct cultural form. In the debate on globalizing education policy, thesis of homogenization of culture has been a common topic wherein globalization has become a popular phenomenon that caught the imagination of curriculum reforms. There are also a number of sociological and anthropological works that critique 'globalization' for

Fig. 1 Overview of the Hong Kong school curriculum (CDC, 2014, 2017)

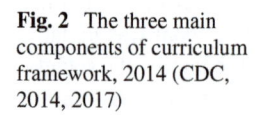

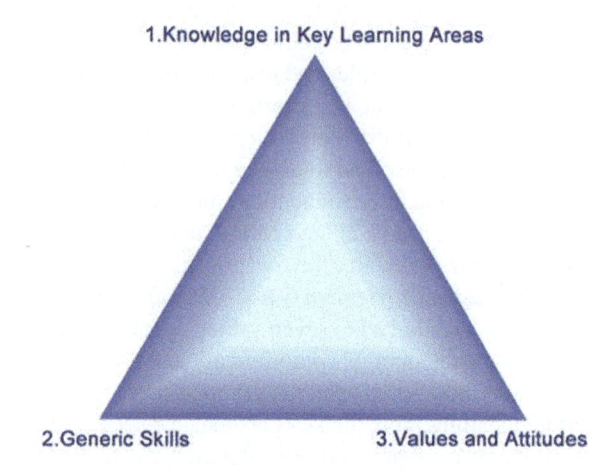

Fig. 2 The three main components of curriculum framework, 2014 (CDC, 2014, 2017)

limiting people from seeing the complex terrain of local culture form. However, the significant changes in the recent Learning to Learn 1.0 and 2.0 curriculum reforms suggest globalization is far from the only cause of educational change. In the following sections, we foreground cultural-specific ways in which Hong Kong mobilizes education policy, with the value-prioritized feature as a departure point of our analysis. We argue that assemblage thinking is a good conceptual tool to re-conceive the OECD model not as a totalizing external force in shaping Hong Kong's competency-based reform, but as something that can be formulated alongside local culture—a mix of local history, politics and global pressures. By saying local culture, we mean that the new assemblage of Hong Kong is the productive result of the intersection of China's national culture and British culture, but not part of, either one or the other system, due historical reasons.

Methodology, Theoretical Perspective, and Methods

Assemblage thinking has been widely applied in policy research. Commonly, assemblage thinking is adopted for a more nuanced understanding of policy *processes*: how policies move, mutate, and manifest in particular spaces and times, especially in a context of transnational flows of policy idea and practices (McCann and Ward, 2012; Peck and Theodore, 2015). With an intent to undermine structural ideas, assemblage generates enduring puzzles about 'process' and 'relationship' rather than falls into the tropes of classic social theory and the common discourse that it has shaped (Marcus and Saka, 2006). It has been a generative tool for addressing the limits of established debates and concepts, especially those relating to policy transfer, borrowing, and diffusion. For example, Clarke et al. (2015) has focused on bringing together assemblage with the related concept of 'translation' to capture the process of translation that policies undergo as they travel and are reassembled in new locations. The use of 'assemblage' as a conceptual tool helps us shift our attention to globalizing education policy beyond the global/local binary, which has dominated the discussion of global education policy studies.

The deployment of the term 'assemblage' can be traced to the work of Deleuze and Guattari (2003), who used this concept to understand the heterogeneous composition of complex and non-social formations (Savage, 2020). According to Deleuze and Guattari (2003), 'assemblage' is a topological concept that designates the actualizations of the virtual causes or causal processes that are immanent in an open system of intensities that is under the influence of a force that is external (or heterogeneous) in relation to it. Assemblages are causally productive (machinic) results of the intersection of two open systems but are not part of either system considered in isolation. In other words, it is an anti-structural (Marcus and Saka, 2006) concept that allows researchers to shift their attention away from global/local, central/peripheral binary to the emergence and heterogeneity of policies. Therefore, assemblage thinking is an appropriate conceptual resource to examine the heterogeneous components that are arranged within transnational education policies.

To understand the term 'assemblage' more systematically, Savage (2020) generates a conceptual framework for policy assemblage research built on three core foundations that are central to a policy assemblage approach: (1) relations of exteriority and emergence; (2) heterogeneity, relationality and flux; (3) attention to power, politics, and agency. First, Savage (2020) borrows De Landa's (2006) theories to demonstrate the 'relations of exteriority and emergence', or in other words, parts and wholes, when adopt an assemblage approach. Put differently, a policy is neither a coherent thing nor definable as the sum of its constitutive components; rather, it emphasizes the dynamics and interactions between components and how the components are arranged in specific ways but not others. Second, assemblages are heterogenous, comprised of a multiplicity of component parts that have been strategically arranged and held together 'without actually ceasing to be heterogeneous' (Allen, 2011, p. 145). These component parts serve strategic functions with contingently obligatory relations that are always evolving in form, rather than in ways that are logically necessary to make the whole what it is. As such, an assemblage approach requires relational thinking to understand relations between components as a core part of policy analysis work. Thirdly, with roots in Deleuzian theory, which is closely related to Foucauldian theory, assemblage thinking takes power as immanent and relational in nature—not fixed in a certain somewhere, but instead is everywhere and always/constantly flowing through things. That is, power is de-centered and polycentric in nature, extending across space in new ways without a singular ruling center from which it might extend its forces. Therefore, it is necessary to focus on the interactions of various actors, agents, politics, and contexts involved in creating the conditions of possibility for certain policies to emerge.

In sum, policy assemblage is to examine how multiple heterogeneous components are arranged to create governable forms. Through strategically harnessing the relational capacities of multiple component parts, assemblages represent a gathering together of political imaginations, rationalities, technologies, infrastructures, and agents towards steering individuals and groups in particular directions (Savage, 2020). Yet, given the heterogeneous and emergent form of assemblages, and the complexities of understanding and analyzing relations of exteriority, assemblage theory offers both highly complex yet potentially very productive ways of understanding power, politics, agency, and the context dependent ways these forces result from and contribute to the making of policy. In other words, policy ideas, practices, and forms of influence might be strongly informed by not only transnational flows but also the conditions of possibility for such policies depend largely on the local context.

The concept of assemblage has been adopted in recent education policy research with focus on the role of the OECD in generating a new global space of educational measurement and governance (Hartong, 2018; Savage and Lewis, 2018). Through a vast array of new metrics, standardized assessments, league tables, and evidence repositories that claim to offer evidence about 'what works' to improve education systems globally, the OECD has brought geographically distant and diverse political systems into a new transnational field of commensurability, thus creating a new closeness between education systems both near and far in ways that are having significant implications for how national and subnational education systems are governed and how core policy definitions are understood and debate. Assemblage thinking has also been adapted by Ong and Collier (2005) to investigate global-local interactions. By focusing on how global forms interact with other elements, they argue the product of unstable, uneasy interrelationships would be called the actual global, or the global in the space of assemblage. As a composite concept, the term 'global assemblage' suggests inherent tensions: global implies broadly encompassing, seamless, and mobile; assemblage implies heterogeneous, contingent, unstable, partial, and situated (2005, p. 12).

For the work of this chapter, the notion of assemblage will provide a frame of specific complexity around the vision of an/the unstable, heterogeneous structure. When the OECD policy components are assembled in the Hong Kong context, the components themselves will be contoured by numerous context-dependent factors. The specific historical, cultural, political, and economic conditions create possibilities that will render the components place-specific and result in new relations being established and maintained between these components and existing components in the new environment. We see, therefore, that the OECD key competencies undergo forms of mutation and re-assemblage as they travel to Hong Kong policy contexts.

With a discourse analysis method, we read into Hong Kong's curriculum reform guidelines since the 1980s, especially into how value and moral education is articulated in these documents. To investigate what the language is used for and how the discourse reflects the underlying way of reasoning (Foucault, 1973), we understand Hong Kong's value and moral education within in large web of interrelated entanglements of social context, cultural, historical, economic, and political background, and epistemes. Therefore, in order to unpack the principles of thoughts in organizing Hong Kong's Value/Moral Education in a cultural-specific way, we analyze how values and attitudes are articulated in the reform documents at different times and how they are interrelated with Western rationality and Confucian philosophy. We thus point out the new assemblage or conflation of epistemes as the very challenge of Hong Kong curriculum reform(s).

Unpacking Hong Kong's Value/Moral Education

In the previous section, we concluded that although Hong Kong's Learning to Learn reforms largely follow the OECD model, they more importantly stress values and attitudes. That is, the Hong Kong reforms' proposed set of values have Confucian cultural connotations with emphasis on whole-person moral traits like perseverance, honesty, respect for others, modesty, tolerance, etc., while the OECD values are deemed as 'psychological resources' for fulfilling demands and tasks. However, in this section, we argue the discourse of value/moral education in Hong Kong is sometimes self-contradictory. Mostly, moral education is narrowly educated for specific moral values, demanding adherence to static principles. This is different from Confucian education for morality, which seeks to develop a 'human being capable of sustaining and fulfilling his humanity and creating a social context of interhuman relationships of trust and respect' (Cheng, 2006). In the following section, we will unpack the discourse of Hong Kong's value/moral prioritized key competencies based on the conceptual notion of 'assemblage'.

Understood through assemblage thinking, the Hong Kong reform is neither a product nor a constitutive component of the global education policy; rather, it should be thought of in terms of the dynamics and interactions between heterogenous components, say, global and local forces. With this in mind, it is necessary to unpack various agents like history, politics, and economy in creating the conditions of possibility for certain value/moral educational policies to emerge. First, let us introduce the contextual background of Hong Kong's education. Situated near the south-eastern coast of China, Hong Kong evolved from a small fishing village into a densely-populated, industrialized, modernized, and multiethnic metropolis by the 1950s, and soon thereafter became one of the world's largest trading and financial centers. Following over 150 years of British colonial governance, Hong Kong is left as nothing more than a set of liberal frameworks within which capitalism flourished. As such, Hong Kong is depicted as a 'utopia of laissez-faire economics' and 'capitalist paradise' (Wing, 2009, p.1) influenced by British utilitarian tradition. Unlike other former British colonies, Hong Kong remained not a colonial entity, but a neutral arena where both Western and Eastern cultures compete with each other and intermingle. Specially, in order to strengthen the British superiority, colonists privileged Hong Kong Chinese elite and marginalized other Chinese residents by providing exclusive assess of English Education to a selected stratum of Hong Kong Chinese. As a result, while British culture was prevalent in Hong Kong as a symbol of privilege, traditional Chinese culture was also well reserved, especially among poor, immigrant Hong Kong people.

As Western and Eastern cultures intermingled, traditional Confucianism in Hong Kong was gradually distorted, not only due to influence from British capitalism, but also because of social and historical factors. A large proportion of Hong Kong's older generations, according to Lau (1984), are from pre-modern rural Southern parts of China, who arrived in Hong Kong as refugees, fleeing the political turmoil in China during the Chinese Civil War (1927–1949), WWII (1939–1945), and the Cultural Revolution (1966–1976). These people came to the Colony seeking stability and quick material gains; at the same time, they absorbed British culture voluntarily so as to move upward to elite social class. Therefore, the Hong Kong Chinese, as Lau (1984) termed, are characteristically utilitarian, materialistic, and family-oriented. King (2018) also holds the view that Hong Kong people have a long tradition of pursuing material wealth on their list of priorities. He argues, while literary education, becoming literati, and attaining government official positions were the yardstick for measuring social prestige in traditional China, the situation was different in Hong Kong. Literati never came into existence as a status group, because the most promising route to social eminence for Hong Kong people was not a career in politics, which was denied to Chinese in the Colony, but through gaining wealth in the business world. Industrial-business elites are status groups par excellence in Hong Kong. As a result, for a long time, education was viewed by most people as a prerequisite for material wealth, predominantly a highly utilitarian means to economic and vocational ends.

Hong Kong Chinese's pursuit for material wealth is accountable for their flexibility in moving in and out of Chinese and Western traditions, as long as it is effective in some circumstances. Such Hong Kong cultural assemblage is termed by King (2018) as 'rationalistic Confucianism'. What is distinctive about social and family life in Hong Kong is to seize the opportunity to live a better life by taking advantage of the uniqueness of Hong Kong as a unique assemblage of both Chinese traditions and modern civilizations in the world. Therefore, a pragmatic attitude is widespread. They have maintained Chinese culture, but have also absorbed cultural influences from Great Britain. The mixture of two heterogenous rationalities, the indigenous values and Western influences, has led to the existence of a transformed kind of Confucianism King (2018) terms 'rationalistic traditionalism'. This kind of new culture does not necessarily grant Hong Kong a distinct national identity of its own but leads to creation of a mixed cultural identity. King (2018) writes,

> The Chinese in Hong Kong no longer live uncritically under the traditional Confucian familistic persuasion, though they remain 'modern Chinese' in the sense that they still, ideologically and behaviorally, attach importance to some Confucian familistic values…Through a continuous process of cognition selection, the Hong Kong Chinese have, whether consciously or subconsciously, transformed Confucianism into a kind of rationalistic traditionalism. By this, I mean that traditions are not necessarily always treasured affectively for their intrinsic goodness but are selectively preserved mainly, though not exclusively, for their extrinsic usefulness in pursing economic goals. (p. 225)

Our point in stating Hong Kong's tradition is to claim that a constant reinterpretation of the needs of its economy is a part of Hong Kong's cultural characteristic in its education policy making. Due to its tradition of seeking material wealth, the heterogenous component parts of OECD's economic logic and Confucianism have been strategically arranged and held together to serve strategic functions. The OECD's neoliberal elements are soon absorbed and organically merged with Hong Kong's education policy. In other words, the economic side of Hong Kong's curriculum assemblage is neither a replica of the globalizing educational phenomenon nor the product of the OECD key competencies; rather, the 'culture' of Hong Kong is an assemblage compressed in Hong Kong's global assemblage. An assemblage is always the product of multiple determinations that are not reducible to single rationality (Ong and Collier, 2005). These heterogenous categories and elements are (re)assembled into new forms that are always evolving, dependent on the context. Thus, an assemblage should not be understood 'in terms of a priori coordinates—a fixed stage upon which events occur' (Savage and Lewis, 2018)—it is always in flux. Hence, it comes as no surprise that the economic-based Learning to Learn reforms underpinned by instrumental and neoliberal rationality have value and attitude prioritized characteristics with underlying tradition of Confucianism.

It is easy to notice the discursive legacy of Confucianism in the latest 'Moral and Civic Education' reform documents (CDC, 2014, 2017). Values and attitudes, as articulated by the Learning to Learn guidelines (2014, 2017), are not merely for tackling today's complex mental tasks and for autonomous learning within the OECD psychological framework but have broader Confucian cultural connotations. According to the seven priority values and attitudes recommended by the Learning to Learn curriculum guidelines, an individual is understood within the framework of what Ames (2011) terms 'Confucian relational personhood' and 'Confucian role ethics'. That is, a student who is whole person cultivated not only lies in his/her 'perseverance' to overcome challenges and failures towards personal goals, but also his/her 'responsibility' to develop a caring and helpful attitude to live harmoniously within the community, society, and even the nation. In other words, a person is understood within interlinked Confucian role ethics: morally self-cultivated (perseverance, integrity, commitment), capable to regulate his/her family and community (care for others, respected for others, responsibility), and finally to order well his/her states (national identity). These dimensions are linked together, reflecting a Confucian philosophy of cultivating learners. Nevertheless, moral self-cultivation as described in the curriculum guidelines does not extend to mind-body cultivation to rectify a person's heart and seek to be sincere in his/her thoughts. Sometimes the discourse is self-contradictory, as it is narrowly educated for specific moral values, demanding adherence to goal-oriented principles and trapped by neoliberal pragmaticism. That is why we claim that value-attitude-moral education in Hong Kong is strongly influenced by Confucianism but is different from Confucian education for morality.

As a distinct part of the Learning to Learn curriculum reforms, the cultivation of value and attitude is mainly expected to be fulfilled in moral and value education, which is often integrated with civic education in Hong Kong. However, Confucian values and attitudes cultivation were not necessarily integral parts of the Hong Kong colonial curriculum. In Morris and Chan's (1997) article, they tease out the contextualization of Hong Kong's moral and value education. In the period of 1945–1965, Hong Kong experienced a massive increase in population and economic growth, which consequently led to threats of public order and legitimacy to the colonial government. To counter the anti-government propaganda, the government created 'civics' as a school subject in 1953. In this period, the content of the civic curriculum focused on the responsibilities of good citizens and the constitutional relationship between Hong Kong and the UK. Then in the period of 1965–1984, 'civics' turned its focus on sensitive issues such as Hong Kong's continued close relations with mainland China, the tenuous legitimacy of the colonial government, and the substantial gulf between the government and the people. In order to avoid sensitive issues and social conflict, the rhetoric of terms such as 'citizenship', 'community', and 'belonging' were employed as key words in civic education to counter communist propaganda. Since 1982, the confirmation of Hong Kong's return to Chinese sovereignty has led to many changes in civic education. In view of the impending transfer of sovereignty, revised guidelines for civic education were produced to 'prepare students to become rational, active and responsible citizens' (Education Department, 1996). The nature of civic education during this period is still much western-oriented, with an aim to 'renew schools' commitment to the preservation of social order and the promotion of civic awareness and responsibility' (Education Department, 1985) and 'to prepare students to become rational, active, and responsible citizens in facing challenges arising from the above changes' (Education Department, 1996). At this period, the values emphasized mostly revolved around western notions like democratic, freedom, equality, and human rights, and other political elements. Additionally, critical/creative thinking, self-reflective abilities, and some other skills and abilities were foregrounded in understanding one's relation with the society, nation, and world.

When entering the post-1997 era, Confucian-evoking values began to be greatly emphasized in the curriculum guide. In society, the returning of Hong Kong to China in 1997 posed a great crisis to Hong Kong people, i.e., identity crisis of how to be Chinese (Fung, 2004). Turning to the global market economy, Hong Kong needed to retain its competitiveness as well as its uniqueness. Given increasing governmental demand for maintaining closer connection with mainland China and re-nationalizing Hong Kong under the value system of mainland China, Confucian values were drawn on as moral resource to address Hong Kong people's identities. The two abovementioned guidelines on civic education (Education Department, 1985, 1996) have been conjoined with moral education in the Learning to Learn curriculum reform. Out of this reason, moral education has no autonomous territory of its own, but is sub-merged into civic education, with a strong nationalistic flavor.

Actually, through the years, the government has paid great effort to the education reform advocating values; even government officials began taking new roles as moral teachers. Since September 2003, Mrs. Fanny Law, the Permanent Secretary of Education and Manpower, has written ten monthly public letters for young people on moral and civic education, each addressing a specific attitude or value. Furthermore, in 2013, the government planned to introduce Moral, Civic and National education in primary schools as a further gesture to implement moral education. However, even though Moral, Civic, and National Education is claimed by Hong Kong Education Bureau as 'an essential element of whole-person education which aims at fostering students' positive values and attitudes through the school curriculum and the provision of diversified learning experiences', we argue that these traditional values and other elements of Chinese traditions are utilized for achieving social and economic goals. Put differently, 'these Chinese traditions are not always cherished as something intrinsically sacred or good; instead, they are more often than not treated as cultural sources to be tapped and utilized according to instrumental considerations' (King, 2018, p. 232).

A close reading on 'Moral and Civic Education' in the Learning to Learn reform documents (CDC, 2014, 2017) well support this argument. While the moral education aims at whole-person development that fosters students' values and attitude, it at the same time targets enhancing 'students' commitments and contributions to analyzed the judge personal family, social, national and global issues', in response to 'rapid societal changes and the developmental needs of students' (CDC, 2014). When faced with difficulties and changes, students should 'be able to identify the values involved, analyse the issues objectively' (CDC, 2014) and 'make reasonable judgements and decisions about any negative influences that might impede the development of their fullest potential' (CDC, 2017). Here is an example of how 'perseverance' and 'respect for others' are reasoned along rationalistic rationality:

1. Perseverance: Perseverance enables students *to overcome challenges and failures* with courage and strive in the face of hardship *to achieve their goals*. Students' perseverance should be built on rational judgements and practical decision-making.

2. Respect for Others: In a diversified society like Hong Kong, it is easy for students to meet people of different backgrounds, abilities, races, religions, beliefs and lifestyles. When getting along with people having diverse or even conflicting views, students should accept the fact that everyone is unique and try to establish peaceful and friendly relationships with everyone *in order to live and work with others in harmony* (CDC, 2014, 2017; italic added).

In relation to the above discourses, at least two points of analysis can be made. First, while values with rich Confucian connotation are advocated in Hong Kong's recent curriculum reforms, the discourse of moral education has a strong neoliberal means-end instrumental flavor. Here, values and moral traits such as 'perseverance' and 'respect for other' are like any other knowledge and potential, waiting to be identified and analyzed to meet the requirements of a future workplace and of a sensible citizen in Hong Kong: perseverance is to overcome failures; respect is to stay peaceful with people with multiethnic background for a harmonious society; responsibility is for the betterment of the community and society. The ultimate purpose of the cultivation of internal moral traits is the prosperity and progress of Hong Kong society; in other words, to contribute to the future well-being of the nation and the world at large (CDC, 2001). Thus, moral education is narrowly educated for specific moral values, and it has an explicit moral objective to educate students accordingly. It is different from Confucian education for morality, which, according to Cheng (2006), is a much broader notion. Confucian education for morality goes beyond in identifying individual fulfillment and social development as guiding principles but focuses on the cultivation of the human person leading to his moral refinement. The Hong Kong value cultivation, as articulated by Learning to Learn curriculum guide, aims at 'maintaining our competitive edge and bring new opportunity for future development' and preparing students to 'demonstrate rational thinking and moral judgement competence, and to be courageous and with perseverance in putting positive values and attitudes into action' (CDC, 2014). Still with a strong western or OECD flavor, it once again falls into the trope of goal-oriented Tyler's curriculum design model (Zhong et al., 2018).

Second, as a unique assemblage of different cultures, traditional Confucian values have been transformed into 'rationalistic, instrumental' ones King terms as 'rationalistic Confucianism'. Therefore, although the intention of the Education Bureau to implement the Moral and National Education is to cultivate values of perseverance, respect for others, responsibility, etc., this intention is not easily accepted by Hong Kong public. Hong Kong people's reactions to the Moral and National Education Guideline suggest where their concerns lie. To Hong Kong people, the cultural-specific values and traditional Chinese spirits prioritized in the guideline are extrinsic elements useful for pursuing specific ends. Therefore, Hong Kong people tend to accept that Confucian values are used by the government with specific political objectives, say, to strengthen national identity. Therefore, the move of introducing Moral, Civic and National education in primary schools in 2013 quickly drew public backlash and concerns about political meddling. Finally, it resulted in the 'occupation movement' in August 2012, which aimed to compel the government to rescind its plans of Moral and National Education.

Under great social-political-educational tensions, the government ultimately postponed the commencement of the subject indefinitely. However, Hong Kong is still faced with various crises in its post-colonial sovereignty spanning across the economy, politics, culture, and identity. In the recently revised Learning to Learn 2.0 curriculum guide (2014/2017), a further gesture to re-evoke Chinese tradition and cultural identity, values and attitudes are emphasized more than ever.

Conclusion

There is no doubt the OECD and PISA have become globalizing agencies in turning national education policy into a 'global space of measurement' (Lewis and Lingard, 2015), but we should be careful not to fall into micro-reductionism and macro-reductionism. That is, we should avoid viewing global education policy as the sum of local education systems and Hong Kong education policy assemblage as a mere product of the global influences.

The central argument of this chapter is that we must take local culture into consideration when we analyze Hong Kong's emergent curriculum reforms. In summary, Hong Kong's Learning to Learn curriculum reform is an example of an assemblage launched by the government to rethink its education formula for staying competitive within the global economy, as well as for keeping close ties with mainland China. Global influence, specifically the OECD's neoliberal thinking, and traditional Confucianism are heterogenous components held together in making Hong Kong's education policy a unique assemblage that is constantly shifting and evolving. We argue Hong Kong's value prioritized curriculum reform assemblage is 'rationalistic Confucianism' motivated by its post-colonial crisis, which is unique to Hong Kong's culture of policy making. Confucian values and attitudes are harnessed to retain cultural heritage as a response to the rise of China. They are also moral resources to post-colonial identity issues.

Returning to OECD's ongoing framework, in the latest OECD Learning Compass 2030, attitudes and values are identified as key components towards well-being and future direction. In addition to former OECD value terminologies such as human dignity, equity, justice, and freedom, further humanistic terms like respect, integrity, and self-responsibility are (re)-cognized in the framework of key competencies. As the global policy in flux and relationality, the OECD key competencies are also interacting and merging with regional holistic competence frameworks, such as the German concept of *Bidung* and the Asian 'trinity' model (Moral-Knowledge-Body). Apparently, Hong Kong's value-attitude-moral education is re-assembled to a new form different from Confucian education for morality. Such new assemblage, however, brings great challenges and creates a dilemma in Hong Kong's value-attitude-moral education. On one hand, value-attitude-moral education is emphasized by the new reforms more than ever before. On the other hand, due to its mixture of Eastern and Western flavors, it seems that the value-attitude-moral does not touch the essence of humanity education, and is constantly challenged and refused by the Hong Kong public as a tool to get connected to mainland China's ideology. Thus, the key concern that lies ahead for Hong Kong is how to re-envision a holistic whole-person development competency framework while maintaining its cultural uniqueness and keeping abreast of global competitiveness.

References

Allen, J. (2011). Topological twists: Power's shifting geographies. *Dialogues in Human Geography, 1*(3), 283–298.
Ames, R. T. (2011). *Confucian role ethics: A vocabulary*. Chinese University Press.
Bernstein, B. (2000). *Pedagogy, symbolic control and identity*. Rowman & Littlefield.
Chee, W. C. (2012). Negotiating teacher professionalism: governmentality and education reform in Hong Kong. *Ethnography and Education, 7*(3), 327–344.
Cheng, C. (2006). Education for morality in global and cosmic contexts: the Confucian model. *Journal of Chinese Philosophy, 33*(4), 557–570.
Clarke, J., Bainton, D., Lendvai, N., & Stubbs, P. (2015). *Making policy move: Towards a politics of translation and assemblage*. Policy Press.
Curriculum Development Council. (1985). *Guidelines on civic education in schools*. Education Department.
Curriculum Development Council. (1996). *Guidelines on civic education in schools*. Education Department.
Curriculum Development Council. (2000). Education blueprint for the 21st century: learning for life, learning through life reform proposals for the education system in Hong Kong [Ershiyi shiji jiaoyu lantu: zhongshen xuexi, quanren fazhan Xianggang jiaoyu jizhi gaige jianyi] (Hong Kong, Government Printer) (Published in both English and Chinese).
Curriculum Development Council. (2001). Learning to learn: Life-long learning and whole-person development the way forward in curriculum development [Xuehui xuexi: zhongshen xuexi, quanren fazhan kecheng fazhan luxiang] (Hong Kong, CDC) (Published in both English and Chinese).
Curriculum Development Council. (2002). *Basic education curriculum guide—Building on strengths (Primary 1 to Secondary 3)*. www.edb.gov.hk. https://www.edb.gov.hk/en/curriculum-development/doc-reports/guide-basic-edu-curriculum/index.html
Curriculum Development Council. (2014). Learning to Learn: Basic Education Curriculum Guide (Primary 1–6). cd.edb.gov.hk. https://cd.edb.gov.hk/becg/english/index-2.html
Curriculum Development Council. (2017). Learning to Learn: Secondary Education Curriculum Guide. www. edb.gov.hk. https://www.edb.gov.hk/en/curriculum-development/renewal/guides_SECG.html
De Landa, M. (2006). *A new philosophy of society: Assemblage theory and social complexity*. New York Continuum.
Deleuze, G., & Guattari, F. (2003). *A Thousand Plateaus, 10th printing*. University of Minneapolis Press.
Foucault, M. (1973). *The order of things: An archaeology of the human sciences*. Vintage Books.
Fung, A. (2004). Postcolonial Hong Kong identity: Hybridising the local and the national. *Social Identities, 10*(3), 399–414.

Hartong, S. (2018). Towards a topological re-assemblage of education policy? Observing the implementation of performance data infrastructures and 'centers of calculation' in Germany. *Globalisation, Societies and Education, 16*(1), 134–150.

King, Y. C. (2018). *China's great transformation: selected essays on confucianism, modernization, and democracy.* The Chinese University Press.

Lau, S. K. (1984). Utilitarianistic familism: The basis of political stability. In King & Lee (Eds.), *Social Life and Development in Hong Kong.* Chinese University Press.

Lewis, S., & Lingard, B. (2015). The multiple effects of international large-scale assessment on education policy and research. *Discourse: Studies in the Cultural Politics of Education, 36*(5), 621–637.

Lingard, B., Rawolle, S., & Taylor, S. (2005). Globalizing policy sociology in education: Working with Bourdieu. *Journal of Education Policy, 20*(6), 759–777.

Liu, S. N., & Feng, D. M. (2015). How culture matters in educational borrowing? Chinese teachers' dilemmas in a global era. *Cogent Education, 2*(1).

McCann, E., & Ward, K. (2012). Policy assemblages, mobilities, and mutations: Toward a multidisciplinary conversation. *Political Studies Review, 10*(3), 325–332.

Marcus, G. E., & Saka, E. (2006). Assemblage. *Theory, Culture & Society, 23*(2–3), 101–106. https://doi.org/10.1177/0263276406062573

Morris, P., & Chan, K. K. (1997). The Hong Kong school curriculum and the political transition: politicisation, contextualisation and symbolic action. *Comparative Education, 33*(2), 247–264.

Ong, A., & Collier, S. J. (2005). *Global assemblages: Technology, politics and ethics as anthropological problems.* Blackwell.

Olwig, K. F., & Hastrup, K. (2005). *Siting culture : The shifting anthropological object.* Routledge.

OECD. (1997). Definition and Selection of Competencies. http://www.oecd.org/education/skills-beyondschool/definitionandselectionofcompetenciesdeseco.htm

OECD. (2005). *The definition and selection of competencies: executive summary.* www.oecd.org/dataoecd/47/61/35070367.pdf

Ozga, J., & Lingard, B. (2007). Globalisation, education policy and politics. In B. Lingard & J.Ozga (Eds.), *The Routledge Falmer reader in education policy and politics* (pp. 65–82). Routledge.

Peck, J., & Theodore, N. (2015). *Fast policy.* University of Minnesota Press.

Rychen, D. S. (2009). Key competencies: overall goals for competence development. In R. Maclean and D. Wilson (Eds.), *International handbook of education for the changing world of work.* Springer.

Rychen, D. S., & Salganik, L. (2000). A Contribution of the OECD Program Definition and Selection of Competencies: Theoretical and Conceptual Foundations Definition and Selection of Key Competencies.

Savage, G. C. (2020). What is policy assemblage? *Territory, Politics, Governance, 8*(3), 319–335. https://doi.org/10.1080/21622671.2018.1559760

Savage, G. C., & Lewis, S. (2018). The phantom national? Assembling national teaching standards in Australia's federal system. *Journal of Education Policy, 33*(1), 118–142.

Sun, L. G. (2015). *Zhongguo wenhua de 'shenceng jiegou'* [The 'deep structure' of Chinese culture]. China Citic Press.

Wing, S. (2009).*Collaborative colonial power.* Hong Kong University Press.

Zhong, M., Li, Z., Qin, W., & Jiang, H. (2018). Value education in curriculum reform of Hong Kong: Retrospect and prospect. *Hong Kong Teachers' Centre Journal, 17*, 19–35.

Min Lin is a Ph.D. candidate in the Department of Curriculum and Instruction at The Chinese University of Hong Kong. She is interested in doing comparative curriculum studies from a postmodern perspective. She is currently working on her doctoral research project *Rethinking China's Core-competency 'Suyang' Curriculum Reform: A Critical Discourse Analysis.*

Yundan Zheng is a doctoral student in the Department of Curriculum and Instruction at the Chinese University of Hong Kong. She is interested in unpacking curriculum reforms in mainland China and Hong Kong SAR at the crossroads and as the (dis)assemblages of the Confucian traditions and Western modernity and globalization. She is working on her doctoral research project *Moral Education and Its Historical Transformation: Back to Traditional Shuyuan for Its Modern Construction in China.*

Competency-Based Curriculum Reform and Its Making of Korean Global Citizens

Ji-Hye Kim

Intro: South Korean Curriculum Reform

In 2015, the South Korean government declared a new version of the national curriculum. The new curriculum was officially called the *2015 Curriculum*, and its other official name is the *Competency-Based Curriculum*. By referring to the new curriculum as "competency-based", the South Korean government affirmed that the society's focal concern for the education of future generations is students' competencies. Due to the centralized education system of South Korea, the new curriculum was gradually implemented right after the Ministry of Education issued it, and multiple teacher training courses on the concept of competency and ways to coordinate existing teaching materials with the competency-based curriculum were widely spread. In 2020, after five years of implementing the curriculum, the term "competency-based curriculum" became a part of everyday language among Korean teachers and educators.

Up until the *2015 Curriculum* was released, there had been a lot of research on the idea of competency. At the same time, the needs of the integration of competency into Korean education gained much interest from the late 2000s. At first, the Korean *Presidential Committee on Education Reform* reported the need for "competency-focused" education in 2007. According to the committee, future society requires new abilities such as creativity, problem-solving, artistic sensibility, and sociality. In the report, these abilities were described as being attainable through reforming Korean education from being knowledge-focused to core competency-focused (Presidential Committee on Education Reform, 2007: 22). In order to support its argument, this report stressed the growing global education competition which can be represented by the OECD's Programme for International Student Assessment (PISA) (16–17).

J.-H. Kim (✉)
Korean Educational Development Institute, Jincheon-gun, South Korea
e-mail: jihyekim@kedi.re.kr

Various studies on competencies were published in Korea's education field after the committee's report was released. Studies which recognized the need of competency-focused education commonly used the idea of "global tendency" to persuade educators and the public (Lee et al., 2018). In other words, applying competency into Korean education was justified mostly because it was the way other countries, especially OECD member countries, were taking. For this reason, ostensibly, the competency discourse seemed like it has traveled and been plugged into South Korean education from the "global" space. However, there are various historical and cultural aspects which have made a specific style of South Korean competency-based curriculum, which never can be simplified as an inter-/trans-national curriculum policy of borrowing and lending phenomenon.

This paper investigates how the educational discourse organized around the concept of competency has traveled to South Korea and how it is re-territorialized as cultural principles in the Korean national curriculum reform. However, this paper does not assume that there is a single notion of "global discourse on competency" or a single actor which propagates the discourse. Although the OECD and its various educational projects impact many countries' education policies, the OECD or an uncertain entity, "global actor", do not exist as a single influencer. Rather, this paper considers that competency discourse is one of multiple discourses which has performativity, and it de-/and re-territorializes as it travels around the world. In this sense, the paper tries to steer by the dualism of global and local, especially being drawn by the center-periphery theory.

Therefore, this paper will explore multiple layers of the South Korean competency-based curriculum released in 2015 by the theoretical lens of the global education policy and education philosophy. First, this paper will examine Korean Confucianism and the idea of the traditional ideally educated person. In order to explore the traveling of global competency discourse into South Korea, it is important to have an epistemological understanding of an educated person in Korean culture. Second, this paper will analyze the South Korean curriculum reform in 2015. By examining the documents such as the national curricula, education policy reports, and teachers' guide, this paper will discuss how the Korean curriculum reform embodies the effort to make the ideal Korean citizen by translating the global competency discourse together with Korean history and culture. Third, this paper will discuss the reaction of Korean teachers and national curriculum developers to the new competency-based curriculum. Referring to the case of South Korea, this study reveals the connectivity between global and local education reform as well as contextual differences which have emerged from the nation-state's own process of re-territorialization.

Traveling of Educational Policy

The idea of policy borrowing and lending is widely used in the field of education policy studies (Phillips, 2000; Steiner-Khamsi, 2004). According to this idea, a good education policy or educational practices can be borrowed and lent between countries. However, most borrowers are under-developed countries, and the lenders are comparably more developed or advanced countries. In other words, the developed countries in the center provide ways to modernize and advance to the underdeveloped periphery countries. For this characteristic of center-periphery, the policy borrowing and lending theory was actively used in international development studies. Due to this uni-directional idea of policy movement and its colonial characteristic, this idea of policy borrowing and lending has been criticized by many educational researchers. In the field of curriculum studies, João M. Paraskeva (2011, 2016) applied the notion of epistemicide on the phenomenon of borrowing Westernizing curriculum theories and practices by developing countries. By calling it "curriculum epistemicide", he argues that the Western-Eurocentric education discourses are prevailing in the world, which is causing the epistemic suicide of other forms of knowledge.

Different from the unidirectional transport of an educational policy, traveling theories and the notion of translation provides the possibility of epistemic conversation between the two sides (Kim, 2017a). For example, Said (1994) suggested a notion of "traveling theory", which claims that ideas and theories can travel from one place to another with intellectual changes. According to him, the traveling ideas and theories sometimes lose or gain power and rebelliousness while they travel. If Said's traveling theory suggests variation of the original ideas or theories, the idea of translation provides more possibility for change of the traveling by the receivers' sides.

Picking up from Michel Serres's metaphor of "translation", scholars used the idea to explain the movement of cultural phenomena (Czarniawska & Sevón, 2005; Löfgren, 2005). Translation engages transformation, and it changes both the translator and the translated (Czarniawska & Sevón, 2005). When educational policies travel, the trajectory encompasses the process of translation. For the country which brings new ideas from the outside, the policy is newly understood, re-defined, and translated in its own language. Through this process, the traveling policy takes on a new existence. Through the culture, history, and mode of thinking of the new place, the initial policy is newly territorialized and enacted (Kim, 2017a).

The policy borrowing and lending theory evokes the possibility of the policy's originality after it arrives in the new place. Its visual power of the center-periphery also makes epistemic imperialism possible by simply plugging in a policy. On the other hand, the idea of traveling unpacks the multi-layered process of translation. Specifically, in the field of education research, the term "traveling libraries" has been used to describe similar phenomenon. According to Popkewitz (2008), traveling libraries stands for sets of "assemblages, flows, and networks through which intelligibility is given to the changes" (p. 10). Education philosopher John Dewey is an example of a traveling library. He functioned as a metonym for modern pedagogy, a cosmopolitan child, and democracy as his ideas traveled the globe. However, the traveling ideas were translated and applied differently from country to country based on the history and culture of the country's society (Popkewitz, 2008).

In terms of the global education reform movement about competency-based education, its burgeoning impacts on multiple nation-states can be understood through the idea of traveling (Kim, 2017a, b). Curriculum reforms in South Korea, China, America, Australia, New Zealand, and many European countries have been done based on the idea of competencies. However, their actual curriculum documents redefine and articulate the idea of competency differently. As this edited book focuses, the variety makes interesting international dialogues happen, and allows for the new possibility of policies and practices on competency-based education.

Focusing on Confucianism and traveling theories, this chapter unravels the cultural characteristics of the South Korean understanding of competency. By exploring the case of South Korea, where the competency-based curriculum has been positioned as an important frame for both K-12 education and higher education, this paper will explore the religious-cultural dialogues for which the traveling discourse of competency gave rise. In here, "religious" does not only carry the meaning of cultural epistemology, but also includes the religious characteristics of the traveling discourse which propagates a certain sciento-social epistemology in the realm of education policy.

Korean Confucianism and Its Ideal Person

"Confucianism" can be interpreted in multiple ways depending on context. It can be understood as a type of religion, a type of culture prevailing in East Asia, and a mode of being including the Confucian worldview. In Korean society, Confucianism is a social value which is deeply rooted in every part of society. From family traditions to social structures, Confucianism is working as a value system. Nevertheless, some of the Confucian values are often criticized as South Korean society receives modern democratic values. For example, the traditional Confucian image of women, being quiet and less socially active, is contested by the modern values of gender equality. Or the importance of social class which framed Confucian Korean society once in history has mostly disappeared in modern Korean society. Likewise, the Confucian values remaining in the current Korean society can be different from how they were in pre-modern Korean society (Kim, 2006).

Due to its moral characteristics and its cultural impacts in Pan Asia, Confucianism is often compared to Christianity in Europe. However, Confucianism in South Korea needs to be interpreted more as a culture than a religion because it has lost most of its religious rituals in Korean society. Moreover, Confucianism is not something someone can choose to believe or refuse in Korean culture because it already exists in every part of society. In order to understand the unique characteristics of the competency-based curriculum in South Korea, Confucianism as a social value and culture needs to be considered.

The Joseon dynasty (A.D. 1392-1910), which was the last imperial society in Korea, officially accepted Confucianism as both a religion and governing ideology. Previous dynasties also had followers of Confucianism; however, it was not in the form of a national religion or a basic social values system. Scholars argue that it is uncertain when Chinese Confucianism was first introduced to Korea. However, historical artifacts prove that in 372 B.C., there was a royal educational institute, Taehak, which taught Confucianism as its main curricular content (Kim, 2009). In the Joseon dynasty, Confucianism was reframed in the name of Neo-Confucianism which included the theoretical frame of Taoism in existing traditional Confucianism (Park, 2011). Compared to traditional Confucianism, Neo-Confucianism reinforces the importance of the human mind and the principle of the universe. For example, the composition of the universe, the relationship between human and non-human beings, and the reason for humans to be moral were the main topics of Neo-Confucianism (Ahn, 2015). Neo-Confucianism in the Joseon era was a religion, political ideology, and mode of the people's lives at the same time. During the long history after Confucianism arrived in the fourth century B.C., Koreans developed their own interpretation and study of Neo-Confucian philosophy.

To educate people Confucian ideology, there were multiple educational institutes for students. From Seodang (today's elementary schools) to Sungkyunkwan (today's colleges), the institutes' curricula were organized with reading materials written by Confucian scholars. One of the central philosophies of the curricula was *Sugichiin*, meaning cultivating an individual's Confucian ethics to create influence in the broader society. The word is a combination of two words, *Sugi* and *Chiin*. The first word, *Sugi*, represents the importance of training of oneself. By reflection and self-training of the body, one develops his or her human morality. The second word, *Chiin*, means governing a society. In this context, the 'governing' (*Chi*) does not mean a way of control by one's political power, but it means developing a broader social community based on one's ability earned by self-development. As shown in the meaning of the key term, *Sugichiin*, Korean Confucian culture emphasizes one's contribution to society. Thinking of a person in multiple relationships between parents-child, king-subject, student-teacher, human-universe, individual, and regional- and political-community, one's personal and moral development was considered important due to its future contribution to the relationships and the society.

The philosophy of *Sugichiin* still remains strong in Korean culture (Lee, 2014). Furthermore, the philosophy is embedded in the education policy and curriculum. In the 2015 competency-based curriculum as well, South Korea's Confucian culture is interwoven together with today's traveling international competency discourse. Although the philosophy is not definitely written in the official document, it is, however, providing a strong bedrock of the reform.

What Is "Korean Core Competencies"?

In the late 1990s, the Organization for Economic Co-operation and Development (OECD) initiated the DeSeCo (Definition and Selection of Competencies) program. In the report, the researchers suggested three areas of competencies which are required for one to live a successive life and for a society to function well in the future. These competencies are "acting autonomously and reflectively", "using tools interactively", and "joining and functioning in socially heterogeneous groups" (Rychen and

Salganik, 2000). After this program, the OECD started the "Future of Education and Skills: The OECD Education 2030" project, which can be understood as an updated version of the DeSeCo from 2017. The goal of the project is to identify key competencies required for people who will successively live in 2030 and to provide an educational direction to educate future generations (OECD, 2018). After the OECD conducted these two projects, the idea of competencies emerged as a keyword in international education reforms in places such as Australia, Germany, New Zealand, and the USA (Yoon, 2007). South Korea as well, joined in the reform movement. In order to identify core competencies for future Koreans, national education research institutes conducted multiple forms of research on the core competencies required for future education. For example, the core competencies in the era of a life-long learning society and future vocations, inter/national research on future education, knowledge, and skills were conducted (Lee, 2008, 2013; Lim, 2008; Yoon, 2016).

In the 2015 competency-based national curriculum documents, the ideas of competency and "core competencies" of the new curriculum were officially introduced. According to the document, core competencies are the abilities of creative-interdisciplinary type human resources who will be needed by the future society (Ministry of Education, 2015). In order to grow the ideal person, core competencies were pursued through every subject of elementary and secondary education. The competencies were self-management competency, communication competency, community competency, creative thinking competency, knowledge-information processing competency, and aesthetic-emotional competency, whose descriptions are listed below (Ministry of Education, 2015).

- Self-management competency: The ability to live a self-directed life with a self-identity and self-confidence with basic skills and qualities necessary for one's life and career.
- Knowledge-information processing competency: The ability to process and utilize knowledge and information in various areas to solve problems reasonably.
- Creative thinking competency: The ability to create new things by fusing knowledge, skills, and experiences in various specialized fields based on extensive basic knowledge.
- Aesthetic-emotional competency: The ability to discover and enjoy the meaning and value of life based on the empathic understanding of humans and cultural sensitivity.
- Communication competency: The ability to effectively express one's thoughts and feelings, listen to, and respect others' opinions in various situations.
- Community competency: The ability to actively participate in community development together with appropriate values and attitudes required for members of local, national, and global communities.
(Ministry of Education, 2015)

Starting in 2017, the first and the second year elementary school students learned the 2015 Curriculum. In 2018, the third and the fourth year elementary school students and the first year middle and high school students started learning the 2015 Curriculum. In 2020, every student in K-12 is currently learning every subject based on the 2015 Curriculum. Together with the national curriculum document, the Korean Ministry of Education provides multiple teacher training courses, monitoring services, and teaching materials for teachers. With these efforts, it is hard to deny that the idea of 'core competencies' became a focus of K-12 education. However, South Korean teachers are experiencing difficulties in conducting the national curriculum with the new focus on competencies due to its vague characteristics and a shortage of resources for teachers (Lee et al., 2018).

When the idea of the six core competencies were introduced, they were explained in relation to the historical ideal person, *Hongikingan* (弘益人間). In the first chapter of the Korean national curriculum document, there is an explanation about *Hongikingan*, meaning a person who benefits the world. *Hongikingan* is a traditional educational philosophy, and an image of the ideal educated person. As a final goal of K-12 education, students are expected to grow like *Hongikingan* through the Korean education system. Thus, when the new core-competencies were introduced, they were listed as if they were closely related to the existing Korean educational philosophy. *Hongikingan* is more than a traditional education philosophy since it is also Korea's founding principle. Moreover, the idea shares much similarity with the education philosophy of Confucianism for several reasons (Sunwoo, 2012). First, the Confucian ideal society, *Datongsahoi* (大同社會), is closely related to the world which will be made by *Hongikingan*. According to *Liji*, the book of Confucius, *Datongsahoi* is the ideal world where all of humanity lives peacefully and humanely (Kwon & Bok, 2018). Similar to the *Hongikingan* philosophy, the social values of equality and peace are important in these two ideal worlds. Second, in Confucius's writing about education, the *Book of Learning*, Confucius stated that the path of great learning is to be close to goodness by lightening the world and loving others. In terms of the importance of social returns, the idea of *Hongikingan* and Confucianism's purpose of learning are tightly linked together (Sunwoo, 2012). Third, Confucius reinforces the importance of *Sushin* (修身), meaning training one's body and mind. Through *Sushin*, an individual's moral character and personality will mature, thus, he or she can benefit the family and the world. Gradual expansion of an individual's good will starting from the self to the world is also an important focus of these philosophies. These characteristics prove that the traditional idea of *Hongikingan* as an educational goal and philosophy is tightly linked to Confucianism. Yet, the origin of Confucius's learning came from China and the great philosopher's literature, and the idea of *Hongikingan* are based on the Korean traditional worldview which shares much similarity with the Confucian idea of learning.

When the Korean Ministry of Education introduced the new concept of the six core competencies to the public, they were visually dispositioned with the idea of *Hongikingan*. In other words, by explaining these competencies as skills and knowledge required for the ideal person, the new western traveling idea of competencies became an acknowledgeable being to the Korean traditional philosophy of education.

The Korean Ministry of Education's six core competencies and their relation to the bigger idea of the ideal Korean person are expressed in following Fig. 1.

On the top of the figure, *Hongikingan*, which functions as a philosophical direction to the whole Korean education system, is located as an over-arching goal of K-12 education. Under the umbrella of the traditional *Hongikingan* philosophy, there are the four characteristics of the ideal educated person which are self-directed, harmonious, creative, and cultivated. And the six core-competencies are listed in the circle as the components to grow a person with these characteristics. In the inner circle, there is a title for the newly-defined ideal person for the twenty-first century who is "a creatively-interdisciplinary type human resource who has desirable characters". In this figure, through the six core-competencies, not only the traditional ideal educated person but also the modern ideal human resource is possible. The tight relation between these elements strengthens the logic of the figure. For example, the "self-management competency" of the ideal human resource is linked to the "self-directed person", which is one of the characters of *Hongikingan*. In other words, the six core-competencies are suggested as specified scientific ways to grow the ideal educated person with the four characteristics.

Through this figurative explanation, the traditional Korean educational philosophy is demonstrated convincingly by the modern language of competencies (Kim, 2017a). The traditional philosophy about the ideal educated person looks vague and intangible. However, when the philosophy is dissected by sub-categories and detailed competencies, the ideal person seems reachable and reasonable. Moreover, the 'old' idea is reshaped by the new modern technology of competencies which are internationally accepted and scientifically proven. In the national curriculum, the core competencies are introduced as being "required for a human resource who is

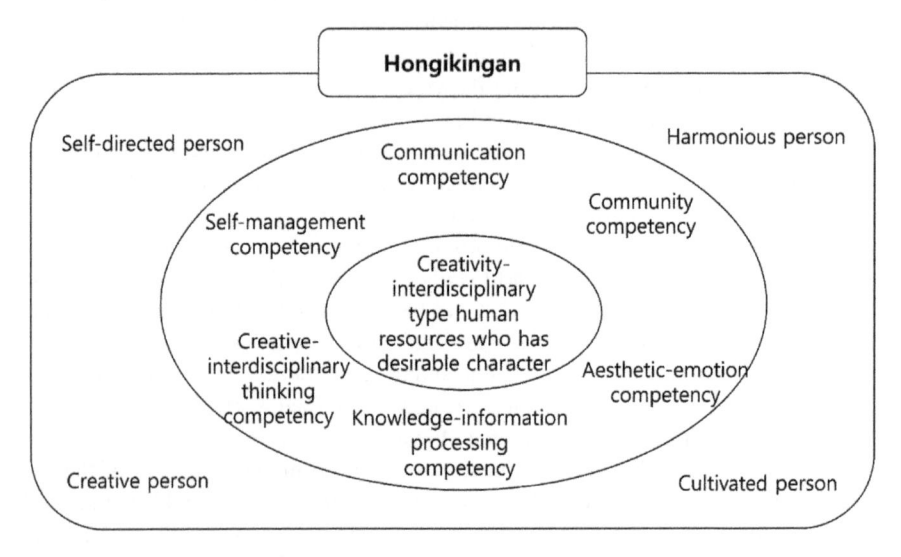

Fig. 1 Core-competencies of 2015 curriculum (Ministry of Education, 2015)

requested by the future society" (Ministry of Education, 2015). As a way to prepare for the uncertain future of the society, competencies are welcomed and reassembled with the traditional education philosophy. In this sense, the traditional ideal person is transformed into a "human resource", with a fancy explanation, "creatively-interdisciplinary type human resources who have a desirable character" (from the inner circle of Fig. 1). Thus, the traditional idea of *Hongikingan* does not need to be rejected, but welcomed again in twenty-first century Korea as a renewed educational goal.

Traveling of Competency Discourse and Making of an Ideal Korean Citizen

Then, how were these Korean core-competencies discovered? In order to understand the advent of the new core-competencies in the Korean national curriculum, it is important to look at the journey of the traveling of competency discourse into South Korea.

Process of Developing the 2015 National Curriculum

In the *Research on the Final Version of the General Curriculum Draft of the 2015 National Curriculum Revision* published by the Ministry of Education and National Curriculum Revision Research Committee (Kim et al., 2015), core competency is introduced as an "international reform movement" (58). As the document explains, the competency discourse received attention by Korean educational researchers after the OECD released a report on the DeSeCo (Definition and Selection of Competencies). After the release, the Presidential Committee on Education Reform (2007) pointed out that the competencies will be a new focus of the curriculum compared to the past curriculum which put more importance on knowledge. Since then, the Ministry of Education, Korean Institute for Curriculum and Evaluation, Korean Educational Development Institute, and individual curriculum researchers paid much more attention to the core competencies.

Most of the basic research for the development of the new national curriculum had chapters of foreign examples of core-competency movement. To describe core-competencies as an international trend, cases from the USA (California), Canada (Quebec, British Columbia, Alberta), New Zealand, Australia, Thailand, England, Germany (Hesse), and Finland were analyzed (Kim et al., 2015; Lee, 2013, 2019; Park, 2017). By referring to the foreign cases, researchers found similarities between these countries' core-competencies, compared each nation to Korea's educational environment, or drew insights to develop the Korean version of the core-competencies. In addition, all researchers referred to the OECD's report on core-competencies as an anchor of the argument that the core-competency movement is an international trend for preparing for the future.

After looking at the cases of other countries, Korean researchers used various research methods to devise the Korean version of the core-competencies. First, they studied previous literature on competencies in the fields of psychology and education, the characteristics of future society (knowledge-economy society), and the paradigm shift from previous education to competency-focused education. Based on the literature analysis, a draft of the competencies was produced. Second, the researchers surveyed 40 curriculum experts using the Delphi method and conducted multiple interviews. In addition, about 700 people were invited to do a survey on the draft. The participants were teachers, educational administrators, professors, and general people from every part of Korean society. They were asked to provide feedback on the Korean draft of the core-competencies. By the reviewing process by multiple people, the draft was revised. Third, the final version of the core-competencies was finalized. In order to include the core-competencies in the national curriculum document, the description part about the ideal educated person was changed as well. The four characteristics of the *Hongikingan* were explained in relation to the new competencies, and the twenty-first century version of an ideal educated person was introduced in the form of a "human resource" (Choi et al., 2017; Yoon, 2007).

The Process of Making Competent Future Korean Citizens

The process of discovering the core-competencies of the Korean curriculum was continuous acts of looking abroad, looking ahead, and comparison. In other words, the Korean researchers studied international trends on competency-focused education reform, found characteristics of the future society and its education, and compared a Korean version of the core-competencies with other countries' preparations for the future. In this process, most importantly, fear about an uncertain future and about being left behind in the global competition were located deep within the research. As found in the Presidential Committee's report on education reform published in 2007, there was serious reflection on the quality of South Korean education compared to other countries. For South Korea, the competency-focused national curriculum was a way to prepare society for the fast-changing global economy. Not to be left behind, researchers looked for cases from mostly western and developed countries. Curriculum reform focusing on competencies was required for Korean society to become a leading country in the uncertain future.

At the same time, the curriculum reform was a process of translation. The object of translation was not only the global competency discourse or curricula of other countries, but also Korea's previous education, including its philosophy, ideal educated person, and curriculum documents. As pointed out earlier, the idea of *Hongikingan* was revisited and re-framed as a human resource. In order for Korean education to make the future generation competent human resources, the ideal Korean educated person, *Hongikingan*, needed a new form of existence. Thus, in the new curriculum, the four characters of the ideal educated person functioned like bridges between the core competencies and the traditional education philosophy. By detailing the ideal person's characteristics, the *Hongikingan* could be linked to the competencies. With the competencies, *Hongikingan* can be successfully perceived as "human resources", which is a new version of the ideal Korean educated person. In this sense, the Korean traditional education philosophy can be maintained in the twenty-first century.

The case of "community competency" shows well about how the idea of competency is linked to Korean culture and history (see Fig. 2). One of the unique characteristics of the Korean version of core competency is the "community competency". According to the new curriculum, a person with community competency actively participates in developing his or her community with proper values and attitudes required for citizens of the local area, nation, and world. In addition, its higher category, "a harmonious person", is an ideal person who is also a democratic citizen, has a sense of community, lives together with others, cares and helps others, and communicates with the world. Most especially, the 'sense of community' is emphasized to make students learn a responsive attitude for the local area, nation, and the world.

Both in the idea of *Hongikingan* and in the Confucian ideal person, a person's relationship and responsibility for family, the local community, nation, and world (including nature and the universe) is very important. According to Confucian scholars, one's public contribution to the community is considered more important than one's individual success (Lee, 2007). One's learning is not limited to one's individual growth, but strongly related to his or her social return to the community. For this reason, education is not a choice or parents' responsibility, but a responsibility of the whole society. In the research report for the new curriculum development "a warm community with love, care, and sharing" is described as important as "a democratic

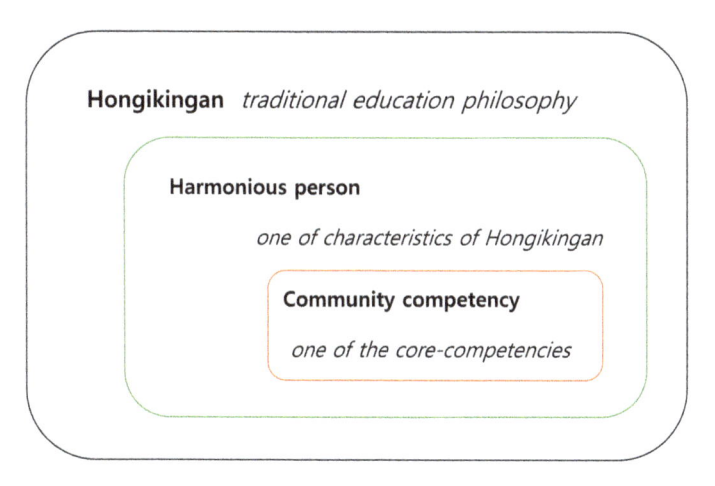

Fig. 2 Connection between community competency and Hongikingan

society where various values and resources are equitably protected and shared" for a human to grow properly (Kim et al., 2015: 57). In other words, education is considered as an important public responsibility to grow future generations; at the same time, an individual has a comparably heavy responsibility to their family, local community, and the nation. Due to this characteristic, in Korea, the success of a student is considered as the success of a family, a school, a local community, and a nation. In this tight relation between a person and his or her community, *Hongikingan's* idea of social contribution is emphasized again in the name of "community competency". Although it is written in a modern scientific language of competencies, the signified has the characteristics of Confucian culture and the spirit of *Hongikingan.*

In this sense, Korean education scholars' effort to make their own version of the core-competencies is a way of translating a global education reform trend into Korean culture and history. In this traveling of "competencies" and continuous process of reading (the global trend) and re-writing (Korean national curriculum), re-territorialization happens. According to Deleuze and Guattari (1987), a nomad's traveling creates new relations to the earth constituted by re- and de-territorialization. Since the de-territorialization always has the potential of a new assemblage of the de-territorialized elements entering into a new relation, re-territorialization can happen along with the movement of the traveler. In the traveling of competency reform movement, similarly, it created a new assemblage when it entered into the South Korean educational environment. With the existing culture, philosophy, and history, a Korean version of the competency reform becomes possible with its unique cultural characteristics. Furthermore, in the process of making a new competency-focused national curriculum, the South Korean idea of an ideal educated person is also re-created as a new assemblage. In this sense, the traveling of competency is a process of re-territorialization of South Korean education.

The Reaction of Korean Society and Teachers to the New Competency-Based Curriculum

After the new competency-based curriculum was released, there were various reactions to the changes. Starting in 2017, the new curriculum has gradually expanded to reach all grade levels by 2020. During the past five years between 2015 and 2020, many teachers and education researchers expressed worry and perplexity about the idea of competencies.

First of all, teachers expressed perplexity about the new entering of competencies into the national curriculum. According to the survey and interview of teachers on the new competency-based curriculum, teachers answered that they do not have a consensus about the need of core-competencies in general (Lee et al., 2018). Interestingly, the teachers who participated in the survey knew that "competency" is becoming a very important keyword in the global field of education. For this reason, their responses show that they agreed with the new direction of the national curriculum being competency-focused. Nevertheless, to the teachers, competency seemed an abstract notion which was irrelevant to their everyday teaching. Moreover, some teachers felt that their previous lesson planning had also been targeting the growth of student competencies even before the curriculum reform. In other words, the new curriculum does not add much more than the previous curriculum but rhetorical explanations on competencies (Choi et al., 2017; Hong, 2017; Lee et al., 2018). In addition, teachers' awareness and reactions to the competency-based curriculum were different from school to school. For example, teachers in "innovative schools",[1] which are a few selected schools funded by provincial offices of education to make school reforms, accepted the new curriculum more than other teachers in general schools (Lee et al., 2018: 144).

There were contradictory arguments among the developers of the new national curriculum as well. For example, developers who were responsible for the general guidelines of the new curriculum argued that the idea of competency is more of a philosophy than a fixed definition which can be practically applied to content knowledge (Lee et al., 2018: 116). As a new philosophical pillar, the general guideline developers of the national curriculum wanted the subject-content developers to organize each curriculum based on the newly devised Korean core-competencies. On the other hand, subject curriculum developers tended to think that the notion of competencies in the new curriculum did not add much to the previous subject-specific curriculum. Moreover, depending on the curriculum developers' level of understanding, the role of core-competencies in the final version of the new curriculum was understood differently. Some people considered core-competencies as a purpose of Korean education, and some people considered it as a result of teachings or student activity. Due to the disagreement of curriculum developers, the process of developing a national curriculum was very controversial (Lee et al., 2018). As explained, applying core-competencies into the Korean national curriculum was a long process of theoretical persuasion and negotiation between different understandings.

The new entering of competencies into the South Korean national curriculum brought confusion not only for curriculum developers and researchers but also for teachers. After the new curriculum was released, the Korean Ministry of Education offered multiple teacher training programs to provide resources and a better understanding of the competency-based curriculum. As a result, teachers who participated in the training understood the changes of the national curriculum better and experienced fewer difficulties in conducting the new curriculum (Lee, 2019). However, still, the *event* of curriculum revision brought huge burdens to teachers. With the new focus on competencies, teachers had to fight against their anxiety made from a lack of confidence about the new idea of competencies. At the same time, teachers had a new obligation to make their students into competitive future human resources with the six core-competencies.

---

[1] Funded by provincial offices of education, innovative schools are public schools which have much autonomy in terms of school administration, curriculum reconstruction, and teachers' professional development.

Conclusion: The Transnational Traveling of Competency Discourse

The process of finding South Korea's core-competencies is still ongoing. Right after the release of the competency-focused national curriculum in 2015, South Korea participated in "The Future of Education and Skills: The OECD Education 2030 Project". The purpose of the project is to refine a notion of core-competency and to suggest a new future learning frame which can be applied to schools in every country. By participating in the Education 2030 project, South Korean education researchers are continuously comparing the OECD's core competencies and Korean competencies, as well as reframing the future competencies of South Korea (Lee et al., 2018).

The conversation between global and local entities is continuously happening in various forms. Participation in the OECD project is a kind of conversation, and this chapter's analysis on the South Korean curriculum reform is another kind of conversation between global and local entities. This case of the South Korean curriculum reform shows that the conversation is not one-way communication or the delivery of a fixed message. Rather, during the traveling of competency discourse, it dismantled the previous South Korean idea of the ideal educated person. At the same time, the global competency discourse is also destructed and re-assembled with Korean culture, history, and epistemology. The sciento-social epistemology of competency discourse territorializes Korean education as a mission of Protestants; however, the discourse becomes a new assemblage during the process of translating it into Confucian epistemology.

The new Korean K-12 curriculum's core-competencies could be interpreted as a case of education policy borrowing from the OECD and many different (mostly western) countries which are preparing well for the future with the idea of competencies. However, when it was examined with the microscopic lens of culture and philosophy, it was revealed that the Korean traditional understanding of an ideal educated person and its Confucian characteristics are embedded in the new discourse of Korean competencies. Moreover, a new idea of an educated Korean citizen as a human resource was formulated and proposed in the 2015 curriculum using the language of competencies. If the idea of policy borrowing and lending only spotlighted a one-way direction from the center to the periphery, with this perspective of traveling, multiple conversations between global education discourse and each nation-state's epistemology can be heard. This chapter on the case of South Korea contributed to make the noisy conversations become un-muted.

References

Ahn, Y. (2015). *What is the neo-confucianism.* Saemoonsa.

Choi, S., Lee, J., Kim, E. Y., Kim, H., Paik, N., Kim, J., et al. (2017). *A study on OECD Education2030 project: Analyzing validity of OECD competencies framework and exploring practices of competency-based education in South Korea*. Korean Educational Development Institute.

Czarniawska, B., & Sevón, G. (2005). Translating is a vehicle, imitation its motor, and fashion sets at the wheel. In B. Czarniawska & G. Sevón (Eds.), *Global ideas. How ideas, objects and practices travel in the global economy* (pp. 7–14). Liber & Copenhagen Business School Press.

Deleuze, G., & Guattari, F. (1987). *A thousand plateaus: Capitalism and schizophrenia*. University of Minnesota Press.

Hong, W. (2017). Revisiting competency-based curriculum in Korea: Focused on theoretical and practical challenges. *The Journal of Curriculum Studies, 35*(1), 239–254.

Kim, U. (2006). Confucianism, democracy, and the individual in Korean modernization. In Y-S. Chang & S. H. Lee (Eds.), *Transformations in twentieth century Korea* (pp. 221–244). Taylor & Francis.

Kim, K.-N. (2009). The introduction and development of Confucian thought in Korea. *Korean Association of National Thought, 3*(2), 125–165.

Kim, J-H. (2017a). Fabricating the future: Making up the Korean global citizen in the era of PISA. (Unpublished doctoral dissertation). University of Wisconsin, Madison, WI, USA.

Kim, J.-H. (2017b). The traveling of PISA: Fabricating the Korean global citizen and the reason of reforms. In: *A Political Sociology of Educational Knowledge* (pp. 53–68). Routledge.

Kim, K., Guak, S., Back, N., Song, H., On, J., Lee, S., Han, H., Hur, B., & Hong, E. (2015). *Research on final version of general curriculum draft of 2015 national curriculum revision*. Ministry of Education & National curriculum Revision Research Committee.

Kwon, J., & Bok, D. (2018). A study on Da-tong society in Liji. *Journal of Korean Classical Chinese Literature, 36*, 357–385.

Lee, C. S. (2007). Significance and problems of "confucian communitism" in the "globalization" era. *Epoch and Philosophy, 18*(3), 137–178.

Lee, D. (2014). An educational interpretation of Chong Yak-yong's theory of 'Co-perfection of Self-cultivating and People-governing'. *The Journal of Moral Education, 26*(2), 187–213.

Lee, G. (2008). *Research on the vison of elementary and secondary curriculum to enhance future Korean's core competencies: Focusing on the sub-element by the core competencies*. Korea Institute of Curriculum and Evaluation.

Lee, G. (2013). *Improvement plan of the subject curriculum based on the key competencies-focusing on the alignment of curriculum, teaching-learning methods and educational assessment*. Korea Institute of Curriculum and Evaluation.

Lee, J. (2019). An analysis of the effect of teacher training on understanding and implementation of the 2015 revised curriculum. *The Journal of Curriculum Studies, 37*(1), 191–216.

Lee, S., Kim, E., Kim, S., Yoo, Y., Choi, S., So, K., et al. (2018). *A study on OECD Education 2030 project: Exploring the application of competencies to educational policy in South Korea*. Korean Educational Development Institute.

Lim, E. (2008). *Research on the core competencies required for the vocation world of future society*. Korea Research Institute for Vocational Education & Training.

Löfgren, O. (2005). Cultural alchemy: Translating the experience economy into Scandinavian. In B. Czarniawska & G. Sevón (Eds.), *Global ideas. How ideas, objects and practices travel in the global economy.* (pp. 15–29). Liber & Copenhagen Business School Press.

Ministry of Education. (2015). *2015 National curricula revision*. Retrieved from: http://ncic.kice.re.kr/nation.revise.board.list.do

Organisation for Economic Co-operation and Development (OECD). (2018). *The future of education and skills: Education 2030*. OECD.

Paraskeva, J. M. (2011). *Conflicts in curriculum theory: Challenging hegemonic epistemologies*. Palgrave

Paraskeva, J. M. (2016). *Curriculum epistemicide: Towards an itinerant curriculum theory*. Routledge.

Park, J. (2011). The changes and characteristics of Joseon's Confucianism curriculum. *The Korean Journal of History of Education, 33*(3), 1–24.

Park, I. (2017). Core value and virtue of Character Education Promotion Act, competency, and law education. *Proceeding of the 21st annual conference of Korean Law and Human Right Education,* 117–147.

Phillips, D. (2000). Learning from elsewhere in education: Some perennial problems revisited with reference to British interest in Germany. *Comparative Education, 36*(3), 297–307.

Popkewitz, T. S. (2008). *Inventing the modern self and John Dewey: Modernities and the traveling of pragmatism in education.* Macmillan.

Presidential Committee on Education Reform. (2007). *Education vision 2030: Vision and strategies of future education for realization of learning society.* Seoul, South Korea: Presidential Committee on Education Reform.

Rychen, D. S., & Salganik, L. H. (2000). *Definition and selection of key competencies.* The Ines Compendium (Fourth General Assembly of the OCDE Education Indicators programmme) (pp. 61–73). OECD.

Said, E. W. (1994). Traveling theory reconsidered. *Reflections on exile and Other essays* (pp. 436–452). Harvard University Press.

Steiner-Khamsi, G. (2004). *The global politics of educational borrowing and lending.* Teachers College Press.

Sunwoo, M. (2012). Confucianism philosophical consideration of the educational idea, 'Hongikingan'. *The Journal of Eastern Philosophy, 70,* 181–220.

Yoon, H. (2007). *Research on elementary and middle school's curriculum vision to enhance future Korean's core competency: Focusing on core competency standards and area setting.* Korea Institute of Curriculum and Evaluation.

Yoon, J. (2016). *Current situation and future tasks for 'OECD education 2030: future education and competencies'.* Korea Educational Development Institute.

Ji-Hye Kim is an associate researcher at Korean Educational Development Institute in South Korea. After obtaining B.A. and M.A. in Education at Ewha Womans University, she earned her Ph.D. in the Department of Curriculum and Instruction at the University of Wisconsin-Madison. She studies the styles of reasoning behind the traveling of global curriculum reforms and how the reforms construct subjects which embody double gestures of discerning who they are and who they cannot be. Her recent research includes curriculum reform of DPRK and education experience of immigrants including North Korean defector students.

A Holistic Model of Competence: Curriculum Reforms for Pre-school Education in Singapore

Sandra Wu and Charlene Tan

Introduction

Curriculum reforms are taking place across all levels of schooling in education jurisdictions around the globe. Despite divergence in the contents of educational changes, a converging trend is an attention to the promotion of competencies based on global frameworks such as the core competency definitions by the Organisation for Economic Co-operation and Development (OECD). This chapter discusses the competency-based curriculum reforms for pre-school education in Singapore by highlighting the key changes, potential and challenges. It examines how and the extent to which recent changes for pre-school curriculum in Singapore transcend the definition of competencies as discrete skills to promote a set of complex and integrated attributes (knowledge, attitudes, values and skills) in children so that they could thrive as confident individuals and active members of the community. The chapter also explores how the interactions of top-down and ground-up forces and social actors contribute to the quality of pre-school education in Singapore. The aim of our chapter is to illustrate how concepts and theories on competence that originate from Anglo-American settings ('the West') can be synthesized with Confucian/Eastern values and practices using the example of Singapore. The first part of the chapter introduces the concept of competence with a focus on a holistic model of competence. The next section examines the curriculum reforms for pre-school education in Singapore by drawing upon the holistic model of competence. The last section explores the key implications for pre-school education and reforms from the experience of Singapore.

S. Wu (✉) · C. Tan
National Institute of Education, Nanyang Technological University, Singapore
e-mail: sandra.wu@nie.edu.sg

The Concept of Competence and a Holistic Model of Competence

At the outset, it is important to clarify that 'competence' is not identical to 'skill'. Scholars and agents of reform have highlighted significant differences between them. A skill refers to the capacity to perform a task proficiently by overcoming the technical difficulties efficiently (Wallace, 1978). There are different types of skills such as the skills of production (e.g. creating crafts), skills of performance (e.g. dancing), and processual skills (e.g. editing prose) (Stalnaker, 2010). Competencies, unlike skills, denote capacities but go beyond them to include also other "internal mental structures" such as "motivation and value orientation" (PIAAC Numeracy Expert Group 2009, p. 10). The OECD elaborates:

> A competency is more than just knowledge and skills. It involves the ability to meet complex demands, by drawing on and mobilising psychosocial resources (including skills and attitudes) in a particular context. For example, the ability to communicate effectively is a competency that may draw on an individual's knowledge of language, practical IT skills and attitudes towards those with whom he or she is communicating. (Ananiadou and Claro, 2009, p. 8)

In the context of schooling, competence reveals "what an individual knows and can do in a subject area however that knowledge and skill is acquired, whether through instruction or experience or whatever" (Messick, 1984, p. 217). A review of literature points to a variety of notions, forms and practices of competence (Tan, 2019a). For example, Glaesser (2019) identifies two types of competence models: models of competence structures and models of competence levels. The former "assume the existence of several aspects of a particular competence and they examine the relationship between these aspects and how they relate to the overarching competence under study, whereas the latter describe various levels of competence which differ qualitatively in terms of the task a person is able to perform given a particular level of competence" (Glaesser, 2019, p. 74). Xiao and Chen (2009), on the other hand, expound on two main types of competence that adhere to different rules: "the ability to follow the regulative rules to meet the demands of certain human relationships and situations involving interactions"; and "the ability to exploit the constitutive rules so as to construct a status and situation that favour one's position in an interaction" (p. 68). Jones and Moore (1995) further differentiate between a behaviouristic model and a structuralist model. The former focuses on empirically defined performance standards whereas the latter attends to the foundational and generative capacity of competence.

A helpful way to summarise the diverse conceptions of competence is to refer to the behaviourist, generic and integrated formulations of competence (Gonczi, 1994). The behaviourist conception is similar to Jones and Moore's behaviouristic model where the focus is on task completion and direct observation of performance (Gonczi, 1994). This conception also emphasises the need to follow regulative rules as highlighted by Xiao and Chen (2009). The generic conception goes beyond discrete behaviours to foreground the general qualities of the practitioner such as personal attributes and thinking dispositions. Transferable and context-independent, the generic conception is consistent with Jones and Moore's (1995) structuralist model and Xiao and Chen's (2009) point on one's ability to utilise constitutive rules.

It is noteworthy that the competency-based curriculum reform movement across education jurisdictions is largely focused on the behaviourist and generic approaches to competence. A survey of twenty-first century skills or competencies frameworks such as the *twenty-first Century Skills and Competences for New Millennium Learners in OECD Countries* and the *Framework for twenty-first Century Learning* reveals a tendency to underline practical and workplace capabilities. Despite their differences, all the frameworks place a premium on the following core skills/competencies: creativity, critical thinking, innovation, communication, collaboration, Information and Communication Technology-related competencies, social and/or cultural awareness (Voogt and Roblin, 2012; Tan et al., 2015). These frameworks reflect OECD's call for countries to strengthen their human capital through technological and scientific know-how for routines and specifications (Avgerou and McGrath, 2007; Barnett, 1994; Grant, 1999; Jordon and Powell, 1995; Roberts, 1996; Schön, 1983, 1987; Schultze and Leidner, 2002; Tan, 2019b).

Distinguished from the behaviourist and generic approaches to competence is the integrated or holistic conception. This conception seeks to marry the general attributes approach to the context in which these attributes will be employed. This approach looks at the complex combinations of attributes (knowledge, attitudes, values and skills) that are used to understand and function within the particular situation in which professionals find themselves. To put it simply, the notion of competence here is relational. It brings together disparate things—abilities of individuals (deriving from combinations of attributes) and the tasks that need to be performed in particular situations. Thus, competence is conceived of as the complex structuring of attributes needed for optimal performance in particular contexts (Gonczi, 1994). Gonczi's (1994) integrated conception underscores the contextual dimensions of competence. Jones and Moore (1995) concurs with Gonczi that "cultures are the essential, historical repositories of competencies" (p. 90).

Putting together the works of Gonczi (1994) and Jones and Moore (1995), a *holistic model of competence* is characterised by three main features. First, it presents a strong *communal dimension* by emphasising the relationship between the inner (the person) and the outer (the social). The accent is on "how the person both acquires and demonstrates the capacity to be publicly acknowledged as an accepted ('competent') individual—as a member of a group or community" (Jones and Moore, 1995, p. 87). Accordingly, a competent person is one who manifests one's cultural awareness in terms of social norms and processes specific to a locality or community. Closely accompanying the communal dimension is the *social practice* for the acquisition and transfer of competence. A holistic model of competence occurs in everyday settings which are informal, routinised and contextually located. A competent person thrives in social practice by reflecting "intrinsic standards of excellence that are systematically extended over time through practice and reflection" (Stalnaker, 2010, p. 410). The last attribute of a holistic model of competence is *personal mastery* that is witnessed by confident, spontaneous and non-reflexive conduct. Such a person exhibits tacit achievement by not limiting oneself to external regulation and discrete skills. Instead, he or she displays the internal regulation and skilful harmonisation of knowledge, values, dispositions and actions. Jones and Moore (1995) aver that "the processes whereby the outer becomes inner and the social constitutes the individual as a social being are realised in the routine exercise of tacit skills in the everyday world (competence)" (p. 88).

It is important to point out that the holistic model of competence described above is largely derived from Western histories and experiences. What remains underexplored in the existing literature and reform movement on competencies are theories and practices from non-Western traditions. To fill this research gap, we would like to propose a holistic model of competence from a Confucian perspective. Our model anchors Jones and Moore's model of competence on the Confucian notion of *person-making*. A Confucian classic, *Zhongyong* (*Doctrine of the Mean*) states in Chapter 20 that "a person of humanity is what it means to be human" 仁者,人也 (translated by the second author). It is a salient point that the Confucian virtue of humanity *ren* 仁 is etymologically equivalent to "person" 人 (also pronounced as *ren*). Although 仁 and 人 are homophones, a crucial difference between them is that 仁 is not just about being a human. Person-making, from a Confucian viewpoint, is about being a *certain* type of human—one who is authentic, fully human and perfectly realized (Tan, 2020). That is why a holistic model of competence is necessary—everyone needs to cultivate humanity (*ren*) through personal mastery and social practice within communal settings. In short, a holistic model of competence is pivoted on a lifelong process of person-making where the self is formed and evolved alongside fellow human beings in a community (Li, 1999).

Having outlined a holistic model for competencies, the next section details the chronology of curriculum reforms for pre-school education in Singapore and discusses the nation's policies and curriculum frameworks in relation to the holistic model of competence.

Curriculum Reforms for Pre-school Education in Singapore

Before discussing the competency-based curriculum reform in Singapore, it is necessary to give some background information on pre-school education in the country. In Singapore, pre-school education begins at eighteen months and ends at six years as children enter primary school at the age of seven. While pre-school education is encouraged, it is not mandatory as compulsory education begins at primary school. Historically, pre-school education operates under a split and parallel system as child care centres and kindergartens are also set up for different policy objectives—child care for custodial care and kindergartens for educational purposes (Khoo, 2010; Tan, 2017). The two main types of pre-school education are child care centres and kindergartens, differentiated by child care centres operating under the auspices of Ministry of Community development, Youth and Sports (MCYS) (now known as the Ministry of Social and Family development (MSF)), and kindergartens under the purview of the Ministry of Education (MOE) and included in the 1958 Education Act (Khoo, 2010). This split system creates a view that care and education perform separate functions in early childhood when they should serve complementary roles in pre-school education (Tan, 2017). Concurrently, child care centres and kindergartens also operate in a parallel system as they cater to children between four and six years of age (Khoo, 2010). Consequently, this leads to fragmentation and inefficiencies in pre-school education as it goes against a global trend of countries moving towards an integrated system of care and educational services in early childhood (Tan, 2017). Today, pre-school education is regulated by the Early Childhood Development Agency (ECDA) that was set up in 2013 as the government recognises the need for harmonisation in the sector (Bull and Bautista, 2018). Despite so, pre-school education in Singapore occupies an interesting position in the nation's education policies as it is located in the market driven private sector while regulated by the government for quality standards and assurance (Lim, 2017).

The curriculum in a diverse pre-school landscape is fundamentally different from the curriculum in schools for formal education that is mandated under the centralised system of MOE as centres draw upon different curriculum models and offer different programmes, depending on the centre and operator type (Wu, 2017). Despite calls for the centralisation of pre-school education, the government had consistently indicated that it would not take over pre-school education so as to preserve the diversity of the landscape (Sum et al., 2018). Instead, MOE has announced that it will raise the quality of pr-eschool education through four key leverage areas: (1) Determining the desired outcomes of pre-school education, (2) Setting out curriculum recommendations and research, (3) Examining teacher training and professional development and (4) Regulating kindergarten education. Therefore, curriculum reforms in pre-school education indicate the government's efforts towards supporting pre-school education as a precursor to formal education in children's learning trajectory. When MOE first articulated the desired outcomes of pre-school education in 2000 (Ang, 2012), it was a significant milestone that marks the first of many curriculum reforms in pre-school education.

The chronology of curriculum reforms thus began with the desired outcomes envisioned for pre-school education in 2000, followed by a Framework for Kindergarten Curriculum that was rolled out in 2003 (Ang, 2012; Sum et al., 2018). This framework was designed for children from four to six years, enrolled in kindergarten programmes. In 2008, the Kindergarten Curriculum Guide was introduced as a resource to help teachers and leaders unpack the framework and apply it to the teaching and learning practices in their centres (Ang, 2012). The framework and guide are to be used in tandem to direct kindergarten education in Singapore. This signals MOE's role in helping the sector raise the quality of pre-school education through its focus on kindergarten education as children generally prepare for formal schooling in these two years prior to primary education. In fact, although pre-school education is not mandatory, almost all Singaporean children have attended at least one year of pre-school education prior to entering primary school (Tan, 2017).

In a country where English is the first language and the language of instruction in formal schooling, possessing English language proficiency becomes critical to children's learning (Wu, 2018). Recognising the importance of early literacy, MOE introduced the Focused Language Assistance in Reading (FLAiR) programme in 2006 to help Kindergarten 1 and 2 children level up so as to enter primary school with a level of English proficiency that would enable them to learn in schools (Ang, 2012). This programme is aimed at helping children from disadvantaged backgrounds and serves as a bridging programme for those with little to no exposure to pre-school education to help them transit to primary 1 (Sum et al., 2018). It was first rolled out to 10 kindergartens and then increased to 90 in 2007 (Ang, 2012). By 2017, the programme had supported over 21,000 children and continue to provide language support for children in need (MOE, 2017b).

Between 2011 and 2012, MOE also reviewed the framework and guide, resulting in the launch of a refreshed framework, the Nurturing Early Learners (NEL) framework, along with the NEL Educators' Guide. Concurrently, MSF rolled out the Early Years Development Framework (EYDF) for Child Care Centres in 2011, as a complementary curriculum framework to the NEL framework to support the continuum of pre-school education from eighteen months to six years (Ang, 2012). In 2013, the NEL Framework for Mother Tongue Languages (MTL) and the NEL Educators' Guide for MTL were enacted to cater to the MTL teachers teaching pre-school education in the three MTL, Chinese, Malay and Tamil (MOE, 2012a, 2013a, b, 2015a). In 2017, ECDA also introduced the EYDF Educarers' Guide for the early years (ECDA, 2017).

With globalisation, the advent of digital literacy became prominent in the early childhood education. In response to the increasing use of technologies in the pre-school classroom, MOE introduced the Teaching and Learning Guidelines on the Use of Information and Communication Technology (ICT) in Pre-school Centres (MOE, 2017a). It serves to support educators to help them plan, implement and review ICT learning activities, and provide broad directions for ICT use in pre-school teaching and learning (MOE, 2017a). Table 1 chronicles the curriculum reforms that have taken place since 2000 under MOE, MSF and ECDA.

Curriculum reforms from 2000 to 2017 in Singapore's pre-school education demonstrate the government's efforts in uplifting pre-school education. The government's role in raising the quality of pre-school curriculum is evident in the national curriculum frameworks and the teaching and learning resources developed for the sector. The government continually updates these frameworks and resources so as to keep up with new developments in early childhood education and the changes brought about by globalisation. However, how these reforms translate into centre and classroom practice, given the diversity in pre-school education, can be problematic. This is because centres may interpret these resources differently in their settings and adopt them according to their centre philosophy and curriculum model, which also explains why the government does not enforce these reforms as mandatory but instead, introduce these reforms as a form of support for educators and centres, so that the social actors on the ground can have the autonomy to interpret and adopt the top-down policies in their centres.

As seen from the Table 1, MOE has played a major role in shaping the curriculum reforms in pre-school education as it is the ministry that charts the nation's direction

Table 1 Curriculum Reforms for Pre-school Education

Year	Curriculum reform	Government body
2000	Desired outcomes for pre-school education	Ministry of Education (MOE)
2003	Introduction of a framework for a kindergarten curriculum	
2006	Focused Language Assistance in Reading (FLAiR) programme	
2008	A kindergarten curriculum guide	
2011	Early years development framework (EYDF) for child care centres	Ministry of Social and Family development (MSF)
2012	Nurturing Early Learners (NEL)—A curriculum framework for kindergartens in Singapore NEL framework: A guide for parents	Ministry of Education (MOE)
2013	NEL educators' guide NEL framework for mother tongue languages	
2015	NEL educators' guide for mother tongue languages	
2017	Teaching and learning guidelines on the use of information and communication technology (ICT) in Pre-school centres	
	Early years development framework (EYDF) educarers' guide	Early Childhood Development Agenc (ECDA)

in education policies (Bull and Bautista, 2018). Policies will continue to evolve as the nation progresses and changes according to national priorities and the nation's needs. Education has long been used as a tool for human capital development since Singapore gained independence as its people are the nation's only resource and best asset (MOE, 2015b). Through effective educational policies, Singapore has produced knowledge workers for the local and global economy. But beyond the pragmatic lens of viewing people as human capital for economic growth and progress, the government has also recognised that individuals must not only possess knowledge and skills but also sound values, which in turn build character and shape the beliefs, attitudes and actions of individuals (MOE, 2010). This reflects the holistic model of competence where developing the people comprises knowledge, attitudes, values and skills, evidenced by MOE's twenty-first Century Competencies (21CC) framework. The third column of Table 2 shows the core values, social and emotional competences, and emerging twenty-first century competences in the twenty-first Century Competencies (21CC) framework.

The Singapore education system is grounded in the 21CC framework. Although curriculum in pre-school education is not centralised under MOE, the inclusion of the key stage outcomes of pre-school education in the trajectory of education journey marks the first step towards achieving the desired outcomes of education. A close

Table 2 Mapping of outcomes and competencies

Key stage outcomes of preschool education	Desired outcomes of education	Twenty-first century competencies framework
At the end of pre-school education, children should	**By the completion of formal education, every Singaporean is**	**Core Values** Respect Responsibility
Be comfortable and happy with themselves Know what is right and what is wrong Be able to listen and Speak with understanding Be able to relate to others	A confident person who has a strong sense of right and wrong Adaptable and resilient, knows himself Discerning in judgment, thinks independently and critically Able to communicate effectively	Integrity Care Resilience Harmony **Social and Emotional Competencies** Self-Awareness Self-Management Social Awareness Relationship Management Responsible Decision-Making **Emerging twenty-first century competencies** Civic Literacy, Global Awareness and Cross-cultural Skills Critical and inventive thinking Communication, collaboration and information skills
Be curious and able to explore Have developed physical co-ordination, healthy habits, participate in and enjoy a variety of arts experiences	A self-directed learner who takes responsibility for his own learning Able to question, reflect and persevere in the pursuit of learning	
Be willing to share and take turns with others	An active contributor who is able to work effectively in teams able to exercise initiative, take calculated risks is innovative and strives for excellence	
Love their families, friends, teachers and school	A concerned citizen who is rooted to Singapore Able to demonstrate a strong civic consciousness Informed, and takes an active role in bettering the lives of others around him	

Adapted from MOE (2012b, 2018a, b)

examination of the desired outcomes of pre-school and formal education, and the twenty-first century competencies reveals the government's political aspirations that focus on the holistic development of its people. In Table 2, the key stage outcomes that children should achieve at the end of pre-school education (first column) are mapped against the desired outcomes of education that every Singaporean should achieve by the completion of their formal education (second column). The table maps out the alignment between the two first columns, complemented by the third column that identifies core values, social and emotional competencies and the emerging twenty-first century competencies in the 21CC framework (MOE, 2012b, 2018a, b).

It is a pertinent point that the six core values, namely, respect, responsibility, integrity, care, resilience and harmony, are aligned with the Confucian notion of person-making (Tan and Tan, 2014). As explained earlier, Confucian thinkers exhort all to attain humanity (*ren*) because this is what it means to be more fully human. Humanity is a supreme virtue that encompasses other qualities such as respect, harmony and care. For example, Confucius teaches that respect is the root of humanity (*Analects* 1.2) and that harmony is critical if one wishes to follow the way of the sage-kings (*Analects* 1.12) (for details, see Tan, 2013). Although MOE's twenty-first Century Competencies (21CC) framework is not officially based on Confucian traditions, scholars such as Tu (1984) and Chua (1995) have maintained that Confucian values such as frugality, industriousness, self-discipline, loyalty and considerateness have contributed to Singapore's economic, political and social success.

This section elaborates on the key stage outcomes of pre-school education and how they lead towards the desired outcomes of education. At the end of pre-school education, the six year old child should "be comfortable and happy with themselves, know what is right and what is wrong, be able to listen and speak with understanding, be able to relate to others" and by the end of their formal education, it is hoped that they will become "a confident person who has a strong sense of right and wrong, adaptable and resilient, knows themselves, discerning in judgment, thinks independently and critically, able to communicate effectively" (MOE, 2012b, 2018a). These are important aspects of personhood that one should cultivate from early childhood. In this process of person-making, children's sense of curiosity should be supported so that they would eventually become self-directed learners (MOE, 2012b, 2018a). When child is "willing to share and take turns with others", they have the potential to become "an active contributor who is able to work effectively in teams, able to exercise initiative, take calculated risks, is innovative and strives for excellence" (MOE, 2012b, 2018a). Finally, when the child is able to "love their families, friends, teachers and school", they will become "a concerned citizen who is rooted to Singapore, able to demonstrate a strong civic consciousness, informed, and takes an active role in bettering the lives of others around them" (MOE, 2012b; 2018a). To achieve these outcomes, children cultivate and develop the core values of the 21CC in the early years that will eventually come to shape and define their character. In turn, these values will underpin the knowledge and skills acquired through the course of education (MOE, 2018b). The stress on values-inculcation as part of the competence-based curriculum reform in pre-school education demonstrates MOE's promotion of a holistic notion of competence. Every child in Singapore should acquire the knowledge, attitudes, values and skills that they can apply according to the situation that calls for it (Gonczi, 1994). Values shape a person's beliefs, attitudes and actions and the six core values that form the core of the 21CC framework (MOE, 2018b).

These core values are followed by the social and emotional competencies and the emerging twenty-first century competencies that all Singaporeans are aspired to develop, acquire and continue to hone through lifelong learning. The reference to 'social and emotional competencies' testifies to an all-embracing notion of competence adopted by MOE that transcends technical rationality. The focal point on social and emotional development is also in concert with Confucian person-making where individuals develop the virtue of humanity through interpersonal relationships. Confucius gives examples of humanity-based conduct in everyday life:

出門如見大賓,使民如承大祭。己所不欲,勿施於人。在邦無怨,在家無怨。

When in public, behave as though you are receiving important guests; when employing the services of the common people, behave as though you are overseeing a great sacrifice. Do not impose upon others what you yourself do not desire. In this way, you will have no ill will in public or private life (*Analects* 12.2, translated by the second author).

There are five social and emotional competencies and three emerging twenty-first century competencies in the 21CC framework and they are (1) Self-awareness, (2) Self-management, (3) Social awareness, (4) Relationship management and 5. Responsible decision-making; and (1) Civic literacy, global awareness and cross-cultural skills, (2) Critical and inventive thinking and (3) Communication, collaboration and information skills (MOE, 2018b). Overlaying the holistic model of competence delineated in the previous section to the 21CC framework, Fig. 1 demonstrates how developing the inner self in the early cultivation of the six core values can translate into the outer, social self, where the person partakes in social practices and demonstrates personal mastery of the desired competencies which are the social-emotional and emerging twenty-first century competencies. In so doing, individuals

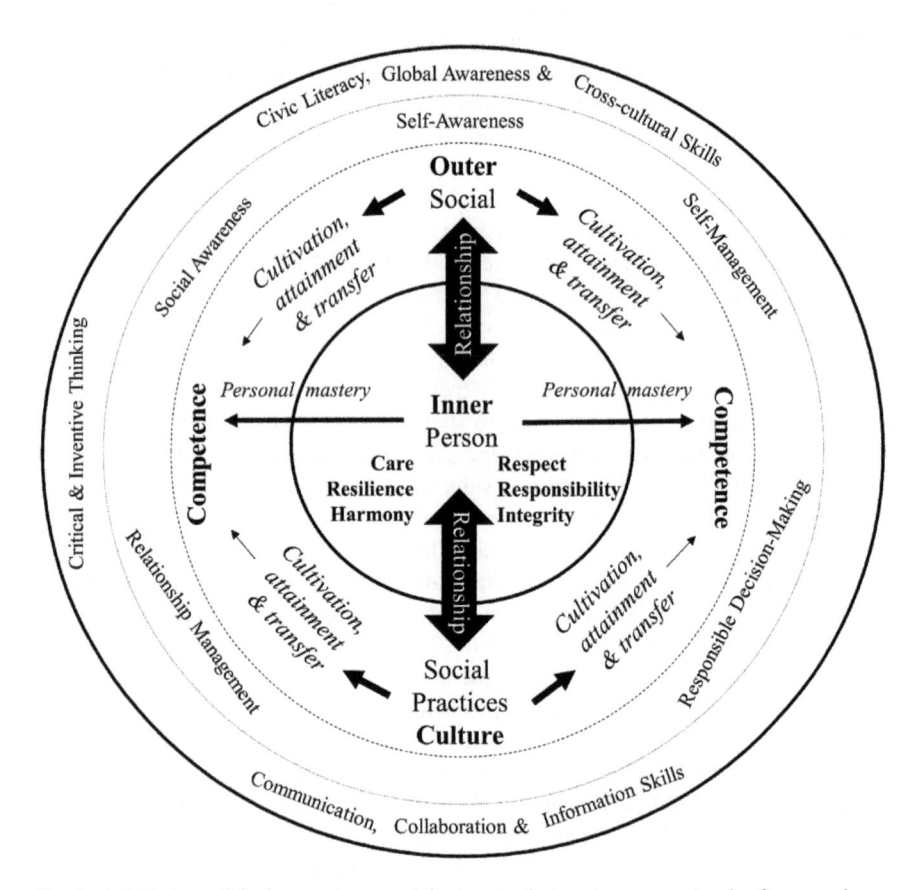

Fig. 1 A holistic model of competence and the twenty-first century competencies framework

engage in person-making through cultivating the virtues of humanity and other values in a moral community.

In the holistic model of competence discussed earlier, there is a strong communal dimension which correlates to the social context that the child is born into. The child is situated at the centre of the social ecological systems surrounding such a one; from infancy, the child's growth, learning and development are supported and facilitated by the nurturance, caregiving, sustenance received from the adults in one's life, which would be one's parents, caregivers and family (Bronfenbrenner, 1994; Bronfenbrenner and Morris, 1998). Through these relationships and interactions with the adults in the child's life in the outer social dimension, the child develops one's inner self, acquiring and demonstrating the capacity and competencies as a member of the group and community one's belongs to and over time, learns the norms and conventions of the culture they live in through this social conditioning process. The child participates in and engages with the social practices, learning the knowledge, skills, abilities and acquiring desirable attributes and dispositions expected of them. The contexts for child development and pre-school education are therefore dynamic as each person influences and is influenced by all other persons in the system (Shaffer and Kipp, 2010). These early relationships also align with Confucian's hierarchy of cardinal relationships that delineates the roles the child takes on as they grow as a daughter/son, sibling, spouse, friend and a citizen of Singapore (Cline, 2015).

As the child cultivates the core values in one's inner self, the child is able to demonstrate them through social practices and relationships. For example, when the child develops one's inner person, such as "knowing what is right and what is wrong", they develop the moral compass to become someone "who has a strong sense of right and wrong" (MOE, 2012b, 2018a). This translates into integrity in adulthood. Henceforth, the individual attains social and emotional competencies, where they have self and social awareness, self management skills and are able to engage in responsible decision making and manage the relationships in their life. The key characteristics of the communal dimension and social practice in a holistic model of competence are brought to the fore here as the learner cultivates one's values, dispositions and behaviours within informal, routinised and contextually located contexts. Rather than being asocial or individualistic, the child learns to become "an accepted ('competent') individual—as a member of a group or community" (Jones and Moore, 1995, p. 87). The targeted outcome is a competent person who is not only equipped with practical skills but also, and more importantly, exemplifies intrinsic standards of excellence through practice and reflection (Stalnaker, 2010). Such a person has realised one's humanity through person-making as envisaged by Confucius.

From the core values and social and emotional competencies, the child develops the twenty-first century competencies of civic literacy, global awareness and cross-cultural skills, critical and inventive thinking, and communication, collaboration and information skills. The process of mastering these competencies begins in early childhood, starting from pre-school education. Hence, pre-school education enables children to cultivate desirable values in their inner selves from young which are manifested through their outer self and social practices, demonstrating the personal mastery and acquisition of competencies over time. Tan (2017) observes that the government targeted its efforts at high leverage areas on raising the quality of preschool education instead of making it mandatory and part of the formal education system. Such a stance reflects pragmatic policymaking in influencing a privatised sector through reforms and policies (Sum et al., 2018).

The developments between 2000 and 2017 reflect a well calibrated, top down approach that social actors on the ground—namely the centres, teachers and leaders, children and parents, actively interpret and adopt. In these reforms, the government ensured that the key stage outcomes of pre-school education are developmentally appropriate and relate to the developmental milestones of six-year-old children (Sum et al., 2018). The desired outcomes at pre-school level align with the outcomes at the end of education, which focus on developing children with a positive outlook in life and to possess the knowledge, skills and dispositions for lifelong learning (Bull and Bautista, 2018). Hence, pre-school education sets the important foundation for children to grow to become hardworking citizens who value and abide by law and order and are respectful and considerate to others, which is why qualities such as perseverance, reflectiveness, appreciation, inventiveness, sense of wonder, curiosity and engagement are encouraged in the national framework (Bull and Bautista, 2018).

The NEL framework for pre-school education in Singapore espouses six pedagogical principles, known as the iTeach principles for educators to develop the desired competencies in pre-school children (MOE, 2012a). They are as follows: (1) Integrated approach to learning, (2) Teachers as facilitators of learning, (3) Engaging children in learning through purposeful play, (4) Authentic learning through quality interactions, (5) Children as constructors of knowledge and (6) Holistic development (MOE, 2012a). There are six learning areas spelt out in the framework: (1) Aesthetics and creative expression, (2) Discovery of the world, (3) Language and literacy, (4) Motor skills development, (5) Numeracy and (6) Social and emotional development (MOE, 2012a). These principles and learning areas serve to guide the design and delivery of pre-school curriculum and programmes in child care centres and kindergartens. The NEL framework promotes the desired outcomes of pre-school education, although the extent of centres adopting the framework in their curriculum and how teachers are enacting the teaching and learning guidelines in the classrooms is not known (Sum et al., 2018). Thus, while the curriculum reforms are well intended, the subscription to policy is still not known, and this indicates a gap between policy and practice. While the reforms points towards a holistic model of competence, there is still room for improvement in implementing a competency-based curriculum reform for pre-school education.

The foregoing shows that the overall approach to pre-school education in Singapore pivots on a holistic model of competence. As noted earlier, the communal dimension and social practice of competence are given prominence in the pre-school curriculum. Furthermore, personal mastery which is the third characteristic of a holistic model of competence is also apparent, where the children are nurtured to act confidently, spontaneously and reflectively. Finally, the Confucian value of humanity and principles such as moral cultivation and human interdependence are embedded in the pre-school educational philosophy in Singapore. In sum, the children are guided to evince the internal regulation and skilful harmonisation of knowledge, values, dispositions and actions through "the routine exercise of tacit skills in the everyday world (competence)" (Jones and Moore, 1995, p. 88).

A Key Implication for Competency-Based Curriculum Reform for Pre-school Education

A major implication from the example of the orientation of competence based preschool education in Singapore is a need to go beyond a behaviouristic approach to competence for students in general and preschoolers in particular. It is evident that the conception of competence privileged by MOE in Singapore for pre-school education is not limited to workplace skills, discrete tasks or meeting performance targets. Rather, it is congruous with the broader understanding of competence as "the ability to meet complex demands, by drawing on and mobilising psychosocial resources (including skills and attitudes) in a particular context" (Ananiadou and Claro, 2009, p. 8). Against a backdrop of a trend towards competence-based reforms across all educational sectors and levels, researchers have underscored the importance of embracing the appropriate conception of competence (Glaesser, 2019).

A holistic model of competence is needed to address a current trend of overemphasising the behaviourist conception of competence. This conception draws attention to 'trainability' that refers to "the shaping of particular forms of dispositional and cognitive capabilities of social actors—in particular 'the ability to profit from continuous pedagogic reformations', complying as and when required" (Tsatsaroni and Evans, 2014, p. 170). The focus on the behaviourist conception of competence is to be expected in light of the skills and competencies agenda in a globalised and digital age. This agenda centres on disaggregated skills and quantifiable standards of performance and portrays a competent worker as one who is skilful at monitoring "the skill requirements of changing skill niches and 'skill[s] up' accordingly" (Muller, 1998, p. 190; also see Jones and Moore, 1995; Tan, 2019a). In a nutshell, what is valued is the instrumental value of learning or upskilling for economic development and success rather than the development of holistic competencies and ethical values.

Eschewing an over-emphasis on the behaviourist conception of competence, the MOE in Singapore has implemented competence-based curriculum reform for preschool education that is geared towards holism. As noted earlier, the key driver for change for Singapore stems from the need to raise the quality of pre-school education, and to ensure continuity in children's education journey. Therefore, the key stage outcomes of pre-school education in Singapore chart the direction towards the desired outcomes of education, underpinned by the values and competencies spelt out in the 21CC framework. It is recommended that policymakers and educators, in introducing competence-based curriculum reforms for pre-school education, consciously adopt an all-encompassing model of competence. We have proposed in this article one such model that shows up the communal dimension, social practice and personal mastery with regards to competence. Furthermore, the framework advanced by the MOE is in tandem with a Confucian approach to competence that promotes person-making. Maintaining that decision-makers and curriculum designers should not reduce competence to measurable standards, Glaesser (2019) calls for educators to be given "enough freedom in their choice of teaching content and methods so that the danger of teaching to the test may be contained" (p. 84).

Conclusion

This chapter has discussed the competency-based curriculum reform for pre-school education in Singapore. The educational changes are generally oriented towards a behaviourist conception of competence that is task-based and focuses on direct observation of performance. Our analysis is drawn upon Gonczi's (1994) and Jones and Moore's (1995) holistic model of competence. We have explained that this model is marked by three distinctive characteristics. First, it contains a strong communal dimension by emphasising the relationship between the inner (the person) and the outer (the social). Secondly, the model emphasises social practices where competence takes place within informal, routinised and contextually located activities. Finally, the model underlines personal mastery by interpreting competent performance as spontaneous, natural and non-reflexive. We further extend this model by offering a Confucian interpretation where holism revolves around person-making. We have also investigated how and the extent to which recent changes for pre-school curriculum in Singapore transcend the definition of competencies as discrete skills to promote a set of complex and integrated attributes (knowledge, attitudes, values and skills) in the children so that they could thrive as confident individuals and active members of the community. We argued that the interaction of top-down and ground-up forces and social actors intersect to improve pre-school education in Singapore.

The experience in Singapore highlights the key changes that have taken place over the years, demonstrating how the government had balanced public governance with the affordance of freedom expected in a private market (Bull and Bautista, 2018). In this intricate balance, the government was able to roll out reforms for the pre-school sector to keep up with the changes and developments of time. The NEL framework focuses on promoting a set of complex and integrated attributes (knowledge, attitudes, values and skills) which are spelt out in the key stage outcomes of pre-school education. The framework is also in line with the desired outcomes of education and the 21CC framework to provide guidelines for pre-school curriculum so that children can grow to become confident individuals and active contributors to the country. Further research needs to be done to understand how top-down and ground-up forces and social actors interact with one another, thereby contributing to the quality of pre-school education and the success in these curriculum reforms.

References

Ananiadou, K., & Claro, M. (2009). *21st century skills and competences for new millennium learners in OECD countries* (Education Working Paper No. 41). Paris, France: Organisation for Economic Co-operation and Development. Retrieved from http://www.oecd.org/officialdocuments/public displaydocumentpdf/?cote=EDU/WKP%282009%2920&doclanguage=en

Ang, L. (2012). *Vital Voices for Vital Years: A study of leaders' perspectives on improving the early childhood sector in Singapore*. Singapore: Lien Foundation. Retrieved from: http://www.lienfo undation.org/pdf/publications/vitalvoices.pdf

Avgerou, C., & McGrath, K. (2007). Power, rationality, and the art of living through socio-technical change. *MIS Quarterly, 31*(2), 295–315.

Barnett, R. (1994). *The limits of competence: Knowledge, higher education and society*. Open University Press.

Bronfenbrenner, U. (1994). Ecological models of human development. In M. Gauvain & M. Cole (Eds.), *International encyclopaedia of education* (pp. 37–43). Freeman.

Bronfenbrenner, U., & Morris, P. A. (1998). The ecology of developmental processes. In W. Damon (Ed.), *Handbook of child psychology: Vol 1. theoretical issues* (Vol. 1, pp. 993–1028). Wiley.

Bull, R., & Bautista, A. (2018). A careful balancing act: Evolving and harmonizing a hybrid system of ECEC in Singapore. In Kagan, S., L. (Ed.). *The early advantage: Early childhood systems that lead by example* (pp. 155–181). Teachers College Press, Columbia University.

Chua, B. H. (1995). *Communitarian ideology and democracy in singapore*. Routledge.

Cline, E. M. (2015). Moral cultivation, filial piety, and the good society in classical confucian philosophy. In Cline, E., M. (Ed.), *Families of virtue: Confucian and Western views on childhood development* (pp. 1–27). University of Minnesota. https://doi.org/10.7312/columbia/9780231171557.003.001

Early Childhood Development Agency (ECDA). (2017). *Early Years Development Framework (EYDF) Educarers' guide*. Retrieved from https://www.ecda.gov.sg/Educators/Pages/Early-Years-Development-Framework-(EYDF)-Educarers-Guide.aspx

Glaesser, J. (2019). Competence in educational theory and practice: a critical discussion. *Oxford Review of Education, 45*(1), 70–85.

Gonczi, A. (1994). Competency based assessment in the professions in Australia. *Assessment in Education, 1*(1), 27–44.

Grant, J. (1999). The incapacitating effects of competence: A critique. *Advances in Health Sciences Education, 4*(3), 271–277. https://doi.org/10.1023/A:1009845202352

Jones, L., & Moore, R. (1995). Appropriating competence: The competency movement, the new right and the 'culture change' project. *British Journal of Education & Work, 8*(2), 78–92.

Jordon, R., & Powell, S. (1995). Skills without understanding: A critique of a competency-based model of teacher education in relation to special needs. *British Journal of Special Education, 22*(3), 120–124. https://doi.org/10.1111/j.1467-8578.1995.tb00918.x

Khoo, K. C. (2010). The shaping of childcare and preschool education in Singapore: From separatism to collaboration. *International Journal of Child Care and Education Policy, 4*, 23–34. Retrieved from https://link.springer.com/article/10.1007/2288–6729-4-1-23#citeas

Li, C. (1999). *The tao encounters the West: Explorations in comparative philosophy*. State University of New York Press.

Lim, S. (2017). Marketization and corporatization of early childhood care and education in Singapore. In M, Li, J. L. Fox, & S. Grieshaber (Eds.), *Contemporary issues and challenges in early childhood education in the Asia-Pacific region* (pp. 17–32). New Frontiers of Education Research, Springer Nature.

Messick, S. (1984). The psychology of educational measurement. *Journal of Educational Measurement, 21*(3), 215–237.

Ministry of Education (MOE). (2010). *Nurturing our young for the future, competencies for the 21st century*. Retrieved from: http://www.moe.gov.sg/education/21cc/

MOE. (2012a). *Nurturing early learners—A curriculum framework for kindergartens in Singapore*. Retrieved from https://www.moe.gov.sg/docs/default-source/document/education/preschool/files/kindergarten-curriculum-framework-guide-for-parents.pdf

MOE. (2012b). *Nurturing early learners—A curriculum framework for kindergartens in Singapore: A guide for parents*. Retrieved from https://www.moe.gov.sg/docs/default-source/document/education/preschool/files/kindergarten-curriculum-framework-guide-for-parents.pdf

MOE. (2013a). *NEL educators' guide*. Retrieved from https://www.nel.sg/qql/slot/u143/Resources/Downloadable/pdf/nel-guide/nel-edu-guide-overview.pdf

MOE. (2013b). *NEL framework for mother tongue languages*. Retrieved from https://www.nel.sg/qql/slot/u143/Resources/Downloadable/pdf/nel-framework/nel-framework-for-mtls.pdf

MOE. (2015a). *NEL educators' guide for mother tongue languages*. Retrieved from https://www.nel.sg/qql/slot/u143/Resources/Downloadable/pdf/nel-guide/nel-edu-guide-chinese.pdf

MOE. (2015b, March 24). *Speech by minister for education's message to students on Mr Lee Kuan Yew (1923–2015)*. Retrieved from: http://www.moe.gov.sg/media/speeches/2015/03/24/minister-for-educations-message-to-students-on-mr-lee-kuan-yew.php

MOE. (2017a). *Teaching and learning guidelines on the use of information and communication technology (ICT) in pre-school centres*. Retrieved from https://www.nel.sg/qql/slot/u143/Resources/Downloadable/pdf/(MOE)ICT%20Guidelines_Final.pdf

MOE. (2017b). *MOE FY 2017 committee of supply debate speech by Minister of State Dr Janil Puthucheary*. Retrieved from https://www.moe.gov.sg/news/speeches/moe-fy-2017-committee-of-supply-debate-speech-by-minister-of-state-dr-janil-puthucheary

MOE. (2018a). *Desired outcomes of education*. Retrieved from https://www.moe.gov.sg/education/education-system/desired-outcomes-of-education

MOE. (2018b). *21st century competencies*. Retrieved from https://www.moe.gov.sg/education/education-system/21st-century-competencies

Muller, J. (1998). The well-tempered learner: Self-regulation, pedagogical models and teacher education policy. *Comparative Education, 34*(2), 177–193.

PIAAC Numeracy Expert Group. (2009, November 24). [Gal, I. (Chair), Alatorre, S., Close, S., Evans, J., Johansen, L., Maguire, T., Manly, M., Tout, D.], *PIAAC numeracy framework, OECD Education* (Working Paper No. 35). OECD Publishing. http://www.oecd.org/officialdocuments/displaydocumentpdf?cote=edu/wkp(2009)14&doclanguage=

Roberts, J. (1996). Management education and the limits of technical rationality: The conditions and consequences of management practice. In R. French & C. Grey (Eds.), *Rethinking management education* (pp. 54–75). Sage.

Schön, D. A. (1983). *The reflective practitioner: How professionals think in action*. Basic Books.

Schön, D. A. (1987). *Educating the reflective practitioner*. Jossey-Bass.

Schultze, U., & Leidner, D. E. (2002). Studying knowledge management in information systems research: Discourses and theoretical assumptions. *MIS Quarterly, 26*(3), 213–242.

Stalnaker, A. (2010). Virtue as mastery in early Confucianism. *Journal of Religious Ethics, 3*, 404–428.

Shaffer, D., & Kipp, K. (2010). *Developmental psychology: Childhood and adolescence*. Wadsworth.

Sum, C. W., Lim, S. M., & Tan, C. T. (2018). Pragmatism in policy making: Influencing a largely privatized early childhood education and care sector in Singapore. In C. Pascal, T. Bertram, & M. Veisson (Eds.), *Early childhood education and change in diverse cultural contexts* (pp. 51–76). Routledge.

Tan, C. (2013). *Confucius*. Bloomsbury.

Tan, C. T. (2017). Enhancing the quality of kindergarten education in Singapore: policies and strategies in the 21st century. *International Journal of Child Care and Education Policy, 11*(7). Retrieved from https://ijccep.springeropen.com/articles/10.1186/s40723-017-0033-y#citeas

Tan, C. (2019a). Beyond the competencies agenda in large-scale international assessment: A Confucian alternative. *Philosophical Inquiry in Education, 26*(1), 20–32.

Tan, C. (2019b). *Comparing high-performing education systems: Singapore, Shanghai, and Hong Kong.* Routledge.
Tan, C. (2020). *Confucian philosophy for contemporary education.* Routledge.
Tan, C., & Tan, C. S. (2014). Fostering social cohesion and cultural sustainability through Character and Citizenship Education in Singapore. *Diaspora, Indigenous, and Minority Education, 8*(4), 191–206.
Tan, C., Chua, C. S. K., & Goh, O. (2015). Rethinking the framework for 21st-century education: Toward a communitarian conception. *The Educational Forum, 79*(3), 307–320.
Tsatsaroni, A., & Evans, J. (2014). Adult numeracy and the totally pedagogised society: PIAAC and other international surveys in the context of global educational policy on lifelong learning. *Educational Studies in Mathematics, 87*(2), 167–186.
Tu, W.-M. (1984). *Confucian ethics today: The Singapore challenge.* Curriculum Development Institute of Singapore and Federal Publications.
Voogt, J., & Roblin, N. P. (2012). A comparative analysis of international frameworks for 21st century competences: Implications for national curriculum policies. *Journal of Curriculum Studies, 44*(3), 299–321. https://doi.org/10.1080/00220272.2012.668938
Wallace, J. D. (1978). *Virtues and vices.* Ithaca, NY: Cornell University Press.
Wu, P.-H. S. (2017). *Exploring pedagogical leadership in the early childhood context of Singapore* (Unpublished doctoral dissertation). Nanyang Technological University, Singapore.
Wu, P.-H. S. (2018). Translation of language policy from pre-school to primary school. In Chua, C., S. K., Chew, P. G. L., Taylor-Leech, K. & Williams, C. (Eds), *Un(intended) language planning in a globalising world: Multiple levels of players at work* (pp. 267–289). De Gruyter Open.
Xiao, X., & Chen, G.-M. (2009). Communication competence and moral competence: A confucian perspective. *Journal of Multicultural Discourses, 4*(1), 61–74.

Sandra Wu is a lecturer at the National Institute of Education, an institute of the Nanyang Technological University in Singapore. She obtained her Doctor in Education from the university she now serves, and her Master of Teaching from the University of Melbourne. Prior to joining academia, she had worked in government ministries serving early childhood education. She has conducted research in the pre-school and primary school contexts in Singapore and early childhood arts education in Melbourne. Her research interests are policies and leadership in early childhood and primary education and the sociology of education.

Charlene Tan Ph.D., is an associate professor at the National Institute of Education, Nanyang Technological University. A former schoolteacher, she has over two decades of teaching experience in a variety of educational settings. She has been a visiting professor at East China Normal University, Sungkyunkwan University and Brock University. Her research centres on Confucian Heritage Cultures, with a particular focus on Chinese philosophy and East Asian educational systems. Her recent books are *Comparing High-performing Education Systems: Understanding Singapore, Shanghai, and Hong Kong; and Confucian Philosophy for Contemporary Education.*

The Global Inside the National and the National Inside the Global: 'Zest for Living,' the *Chi, Toku and Tai* Triad, and the 'Model' of Japanese Education

Keita Takayama

Education and Competencies

Throughout the different stages of historical development since the second half of the nineteenth century, Japanese political leaders have always viewed and used public education as one of the central state mechanisms to address urgent political and economic challenges they faced. What the Meiji political leaders did in the late nineteenth century was a case in point, when the newly established education system was deliberately geared towards instilling in the mass a strong sense of national consciousness and values and dispositions required by the profound cultural and political shifts towards mo2009dernity. Mass enlightenment/Westernization through education was pursued to protect Japan's political independence against the encroaching Western powers (Duke,). The postwar education reform led by the US Occupation was another case in point, where pacifist and democratic values were infused through the radically transformed education system (Beauchamp, 1987). Likewise, the postwar education reforms in the 1960s and 1970s have been credited for the country's unprecedented economic growth; they were driven by and aligned closely with the changing human resource needs of the country (Aso and Amano, 1972). These historical examples of educational transformation were guided by an imagery of desired citizens with a set of particular dispositions and skills—or 'competencies' in today's education policy lingo—to be nurtured through the education system.

The 1980s was the crucial turning point in the postwar reform of Japanese education. Often coined as the 'third' great education reform, the series of reform ideas, originally developed in the late 1970s and the 1980s, were pursued much more

---

The earlier version of this chapter was published elsewhere (see Takayama, 2009). I have substantially updated and reframed it for this chapter.

K. Takayama (✉)
Graduate School of Education, Kyoto University, Kyoto, Japan
e-mail: takayama.keita.7w@kyoto-u.ac.jp

© The Author(s), under exclusive license to Springer Nature Singapore Pte Ltd. 2021
W. Zhao and D. Tröhler (eds.), *Euro-Asian Encounters on 21st-Century Competency-Based Curriculum Reforms*,
https://doi.org/10.1007/978-981-16-3009-5_13

incrementally than the previous two 'great' reforms in the Meiji Restoration and the Occupation era. From the late 1970s, by which time Japan's economic 'miracles' were widely acknowledged by Western observers (e.g., Vogel, 1979), Japanese leaders declared the end of 'catch-up' with the advanced Western economies (Kariya, 2020). A major shift in educational reform discourse was registered, where educational changes for quality over quantity, flexibility over bureaucratic rigidity, individuality and freedom over conformity, and spirituality over materiality were called for. Shared among the reformers at the time was the view that the excessive drive to modernize the country since the Meiji era and the postwar pursuit of rapid economic growth achieved remarkable success, and yet the whole society now suffered from social and psychological consequences of 'compressed modernity.' These undesirable effects were claimed to appear in the most condensed form in children's education. A consensus was reached that the education system, developed around efficiency and productivity, now must be reoriented towards well-balanced emotional, social and cognitive development of children in the post-catch-up epoch.

This chapter focuses on the subsequent development of Japan's education reform from the 1990s onward. It does so by looking closely at the genealogy of one of the most used policy keywords over the last three decades, 'zest for living' (*ikiru chikara*), the latest articulation of competencies to be developed through education reform. As will be detailed shortly, 'zest for living' epitomizes particular dispositions and skills deemed essential for children to survive the new social and economic conditions characterized by knowledge economy, advanced information and communication technology and various social and cultural manifestations of globalization. Just like any keywords designated to represent a set of desired skills and dispositions, however, a close look at 'zest for living' suggests that it has served as a sliding signifier, assuming different meanings in different times in response to different policy necessities and circumstances.

Of particular note in understanding the trajectory of this policy keyword is that the period under investigation was characterized by the increasing influence of transnational policy actors, including UNESCO and OECD and by the simultaneous processes of renationalization of education policy discourses. The former's universalist language frames education within "the ideology of a culturally indifferent world of education" (Tröhler, 2013, p. 158), most typically characterized by the notion of 'best practices.' It de-territorializes the national education policy, and 'best practices' are supposed to work as 'a silver bullet,' irrespective of the particular historical, cultural and institutional contexts (Kamens, 2013). Such a de-territorializing policy discourse, however, provokes the re-territorializing language of education policy that domesticates the globally circulated ideas and foregrounds the nationally specific characters of education. These two contradictory ways of framing education policy are mutually dependent; the articulation of the national requires the notion of the global against which the former registers its distinctiveness, and vice versa. Hence, deterritorialization (denationalization) and reterritorialization (renationalization) occur simultaneously, blurring any meaningful distinctions between the global and the national (see Alasuutari, 2013; Popkewitz, 2000; Takayama, 2014).

Informed by this conceptualization, this chapter demonstrates how the transnational discourse of lifelong learning and the domestic reform discourse shaped the initial articulation of 'zest for living' in the late 1990s, when the proposed reform focused on rectifying the psychological, emotional and social ills of Japanese children, the consequences of 'compressed modernity.' And then, it shows how the same keyword was rearticulated to OECD's notion of 'key competencies,' when PISA results were accepted as the confirmation of 'crisis' of Japanese education and when PISA itself gained tremendous policy tractions in the early 2000s. Finally, the chapter demonstrates how 'zest for living' came to be reterritorialized as it was framed more prominently within the putatively 'traditional' framing of education in Japan, the triad of *chi, toku and tai* (knowledge, moral and physical). This was when the 'recovery' of Japanese education was confirmed through PISA 2009, 2012 and 2015 results and subsequently when the Ministry began actively using the triad to define the 'model' of Japanese education for overseas exportation. At this point, I take the discussion back to the particular historical moment of Japan's early modernization in the late nineteenth century, when the triad framing of education as *chi, toku and tai* emerged. In so doing, I illuminate the strong intellectual influences of British sociologist/social evolutionist Herbert Spencer and Prussian education in the original constitution of the Japanese 'tradition' now redefined as the 'essence' of the Japanese education 'model.'

Hence, through tracing the shifting articulations of 'zest for living' over the last thirty years, this chapters demonstrates the complex intersections between national and transnational and their increasingly blurred distinctions in the notion of 'competencies' to be developed through Japanese education. It uses the Japanese case to problematize the uncomplicated demarcation between these two spatial categories and proposes a view that the national constitution of 'competencies,' or national education policy in general, has always been both transnational and national simultaneously. In so doing, it rejects the view of the nation-state as a 'container' and the conception of the national and the global in a zero-sum competition. The global has always been constitutive part of the national, inside the national, from the early foundational history of nation state. What is deemed 'national,' 'indigenous' and 'traditional' are products of intense interactions between the national and global forces, and they are constantly invented and reinvented through a localization or domestication of the global (see Alasuutari, 2013; Popkewitz, 2000; Sassen, 2010). Vice versa, the reverse is also the case; the national is a constitutive part of the global (see Tröhler, 2013). The Japanese case servers to illuminate this mutually-constitutive relationship between the global and the national in education policy.

'Zest for Living' as a Contested Policy Keyword

The policy keyword, 'zest for living' emerged out of the 'humanizing' policy discourse actively promoted by MEXT (Japan's Ministry of Education) since the mid 1980s. By this time, the end of 'catch-up' economy was widely accepted, and a radical shift in social systems, economic structures and cultural orientations was called for. Education in particular was perceived as central to this reconstruction of Japanese society beyond the postwar catch-up phase. Then Prime Minister Yasuhiro Nakasone's Ad hoc Council for Education Reform demanded that Japan shift from materialistic (quantitative) expansion to spiritual (qualitative) enrichment in life. It identified children, in particular, as the primary victim of the postwar pursuit of materialistic prosperity; 'today's children' were deemed morally, emotionally, physically, and socially 'deficient.' The series of education reform proposals made by the Ad Hoc Council therefore called for individualizing and humanizing the bureaucratic and competitive education system, which was organized around efficiency and productivity.

Reflecting this humanizing policy discourse, the MEXT's main deliberative committee, the Central Council of Education's (CCE) reports and MEXT policy documents in the 1990s extensively used two policy keywords, *yutori* (relaxing) and *kosei* (individuality). They were utilized to justify a set of reform measures aimed supposedly at nurturing children's emotional and social well-being (Takayama, 2009). More concretely, the humanizing effort was translated into reducing the curricular content and number of schooling days and introducing moral teaching, integrated learning opportunities, and the child-centric, constructive pedagogic approach.

It is out of this policy discourse that 'zest for living' first appeared in the 1996 CCE report. The report closely articulated the term with *yutori*, as indicated in the subtitle of the report: "we shall give our children *ikiru chikara* and *yutori*" (CCE, 1996, Section I). In the same report, CCE provides a definition of 'zest for living,' which can be summarized as: (1) "an ability to identify problems, learn and think independently, make an autonomous judgement and act accordingly, and solve problems;" (2) "self-discipline, cooperation with others, empathy for others, emotion, and rich humanity;" and (3) "health and stamina for robust living" (CCE, 1996). The report calls for reconsideration of the nature of education thus far which it claims has focused disproportionately on transmission of knowledge. It hence proposes the harmonization of *chi, toku and tai* (knowledge, moral and physical) to facilitate children's sound development of rich humanity and robust body. Though not explicitly stated, the definition of 'zest for living' presented in the CCE report is clearly framed through the triad focuses. The use of the three Chinese characters evokes the impression of 'tradition,' though, as will be discussed later, the triad concepts have a complicated transnational genealogy deeply entangled with Japan's early history of modernization.

Underpinning this humanizing policy discourse was the dismal representation of the social and educational conditions under which children allegedly lived. According to the same CCE (1996) report, children today spend a large portion of the day studying at school or *juku* (afterschool preparatory schools), leaving little time for sleep. In addition, extended exposure to the electronic media (such as TV and computer games) leaves little time for their authentic experience in nature or rich socializing experiences. Growing up in nuclear families of few children, the report further argues, today's children are deprived of opportunities to learn social skills and moral values, and they suffer from superficial social relations. These descriptions resonated with the rising number of media reports on children's 'pathological' problems, including *ijime* (bullying), *tōkōkyohi* (school refusal), *hikikomori* (social withdrawal), and *gakkyuhōkai* (out of control classrooms). Hence, by the 1990s, the 'salvation' of children's soul through humanizing and moralizing interventions was firmly established as MEXT's master policy narrative (Takayama, 2009).

Driving the deficit construction of 'today's children' was the desocializing discourse of moral conservatism, which became prominent in the second half of the 1990s, when conservative political forces gained popular support against the backdrop of the prolonged economic recession (Takayama, 2009). The desocialized discussion of 'youth problems' became abundant, with considerable media attention given to the aforementioned educational pathologies. It bracketed out the sociocultural and economic transformations of the time that had contributed to the rise of such school-related problems. The MEXT policy documents in the late 1990s subscribed to this deficit construction of children, calling for *kokoro no kyōiku* (education for a rich heart/spirituality, often translated into moral and patriotic education) and tougher disciplinary measures. Moralizing language about sympathy with others, self-discipline, cooperation with others, and respect for adults and the nation were now fully integrated into the humanizing policy discourse.

The rise of the humanizing policy discourse also mirrored the particular shift in the nation's capital accumulation strategies in the 1990s. This was the period when the Japanese political economy underwent a 'regime shift' (Pempel, 1998); the postwar economic, social, and political settlements, central to the nation's stability since the end of the Second World War, were recognized as 'out of sync' with the fast-changing reality of advanced globalized capitalism. Corporate sectors demanded the radical restructuring of the nation's economic, political, and social institutions to revitalize its global economic competitiveness. In so doing, they drew on the humanizing discourse in their proposals for education reform with humanization redefined as the 'liberation' of children from government regulations, thus rearticulating it into their preferred neoliberal discourse of deregulation, market and choice. By the late 1990s, therefore, humanization came to be articulated into three competing languages: (1) the competition-free, child-centered liberal education, (2) the conservative language of morality, ethnics, self-discipline, and patriotism; and (3) the neoliberal language of choice, deregulation, and market. As will be demonstrated shortly, these somehow contradictory and yet overlapping policy discourses shaped the way international policy ideas around 'lifelong learning,' 'knowledge economy,' and 'key competencies' were subsequently translated into 'zest for living.'

Domesticating the Global

Actively promoted by such intergovernmental organizations as UNESCO, the European Commission, and OECD, the notion of lifelong learning achieved a global policy consensus by the 1990s and was enthusiastically endorsed by advanced industrial nations thereafter, though the extent to which the idea was actually implemented varied from country to country (Field, 2006). Echoing this international trend, Japanese MEXT began drawing on the same de-territorialized, transnational policy discourse. Unlike some of the nations where lifelong learning remained merely political rhetoric, Japan implemented a series of relevant policy measures to promote this new concept of learning (Field, 2006). According to Kaori Okumoto (2008), this was partly due to the appeal that the notion of lifelong learning presented to MEXT, which was searching at the time for a 'humanizing' solution to the institutional and operational rigidity and uniformity of its educational system.

It was right at this moment that 'zest for living' emerged as part of MEXT's policy discourse. Though the term sounds like a uniquely Japanese concept (see Sato, 2000, p. 33), its underlying concept clearly parallels the international policy discourse of learning society and lifelong learning. Ikuo Arai (2001) locates the origin of part of the keyword, *ikiru* (to live) in UNESCO's so-called Fall Report, *Learning to be* (UNESCO, 1972). Drawing on Robert Hutchins' (1968) *The Learning Society* and the 1972 UNESCO Fall Report, Arai (1993, 2001) maintains that in a lifelong learning society, schooling must encourage children to 'learn to be' (one must learn to be self-motivated to achieve one's goal and lead a fulfilling life); and that education systems need to be flexible enough to encourage such individual volitions 'to be.' In Arai's mind, many of the reforms undertaken by MEXT throughout the 1990s under the name of 'zest for living' and *yutori* represent the shift towards the twenty-first century model of *gakushū shakai* ('learning society') (see UNESCO, 1996). In this model, public education shifts its focus from *chiiku* (teaching facts based on subject disciplines) to teaching 'skills and knowledge for life' with teachers acting as the 'facilitator' for their self-motivated learning.

From the late 1990s, OECD has become the key advocate of 'lifelong learning' and 'learning society,' initially promoted by UNESCO (see Rychen, 2004). Unlike UNESCO, however, OECD situated lifelong learning more explicitly within the sphere of formal schooling and in terms of its contribution to nation's human capital development strategies (Field, 2006; Takayama, 2013). In the late 1990s, OECD proposed school curricular reform that promotes new forms of knowledge: "know-why, know-how, and know-who" kinds of knowledge rather than "know-what" or factual knowledge/recall" (OECD, 2000, p. 3). Reflecting this conceptualization of new schooling, OECD designated PISA to assess "young people's capacity to use their knowledge and skills in order to meet real-life challenges," hence "knowledge and skills for life" (OECD, 2001, p. 1). Later, OECD published the notion of 'key competencies,' which refers to the ability to meet complex demands using "cognitive and practical skills, creative abilities and other psychosocial resources such as attitudes, motivation and values" (OECD, 2005, p. 8, emphasis added).

The Japanese term 'zest for living' partly reflects this international discourse of lifelong learning, whereby the focus of pedagogic intervention and assessment is placed on individual learners' "psychosocial resources,"—their desire, interest, attitude, and motivation—what is internal to them, or what is often summed up as "non-cognitive" (Honda, 2005; Yamada, 2011). As discussed earlier, the 1996 CCE report defines 'zest for living' as composed of the following three domains: (1) "an ability to identify problems, learn and think independently, make an autonomous judgement and act accordingly, and solve problems;" (2) "self-discipline, cooperation with others, empathy for others, emotion, and rich humanity;" and (3) "health and stamina for robust living" (CCE, 1996). The report argues that these are the key attributes and capabilities that children must acquire in the emerging lifelong learning society. Clearly, the first domain resembles UNESCO and OECD's international policy discourse of twenty-first century schooling. Despite this clear resemblance, the MEXT and CCE documents published at that time make no reference to any transnational influence on 'zest for living.'

However, 'zest for living' was not simply the Japanese 'silent borrowing' of the transnational policy discourse, either. The last two domains in the definition not only resonate with the increasing international recognition of learners' 'non-cognitive,' or 'psychosocial resources' as central to the development of key competencies. They also draw explicitly on the domestic discourse of moral conservatism, discussed earlier. It is also important to note that the triad-domain framework in the definition of 'zest for living' derives from *chi, tolu, and tai*, a popular pedagogic expression that has been used in Japan to signify a well-rounded learning experience. As will be discussed shortly, this triad framework becomes more pronounced in recent years, when MEXT explicitly recognizes the holistic approach to education, represented by the triad framing, as the key features of Japanese 'model' of schooling that the Ministry attempts to export overseas. What we see in the 1996 CCE report, however, is that it embeds the transnational policy discourse of learning society and key competencies within the domestic policy discourse of 'humanization' as well as the 'traditional' triad conceptualization of quality learning. This domestication of the global allows for a particular representation of the policies under 'zest for living': They are 'our' solutions to 'our' unique problems. This was the time when MEXT enjoyed relatively strong policy legitimacy, hence not needing to resort to an external source of legitimacy, including OECD and UNESCO.

"Crisis" of Humanizing Reform and the Rise of PISA

Soon after the 1997 release of the CCE report, MEXT publicized the new National Course of Study to be implemented in 2002. It featured *yutori* as the overarching keyword of the reform. The reform involved a 30 percent reduction in curricular content, the introduction of complete five-day schooling (as opposed to six-day schooling), a new definition of teachers as learning 'facilitators,' and a new cross-curricular subject (*sōgō gakushū no jikan*). Soon after, the so-called debate over declining academic standards took place wherein the *yutori* reform became the focus of intense public criticism (see Takayama, 2007). Cultural conservatives and other social critics perceived the 'relaxing' reform as undermining the nation's moral, economic, and cultural foundations. With the release of the PISA 2003 results, which registered a drop in Japanese students' international ranking in many tested areas, a public consensus was formed that the scholastic 'crisis' was real and that the *yutori* reform was to blame (see Takayama, 2007, 2008a). In the course of the debate, the term *yutori* and the humanizing policy discourse that encompassed it quickly lost political legitimacy. Many critics interchanged *yutori* with a similar-sounding and yet derogatory term *yurumi* (slack, or lazy), making it impossible for the Ministry to salvage the term as its policy keyword.

The backlash against the humanizing policy caused a subtle and yet notable shift in the articulation of 'zest for living.' After the PISA 2003 shock, MEXT and CCE dropped *yutori* and instead featured 'zest for living' much more explicitly in their presentation of reform measures (e.g. CCE, 2002, 2003). However, given the widespread public concern about declining academic standards and the view that the humanizing (now seen as slacking) policy measures were the culprit, the Ministry could not continue with the same articulation of 'zest for living.' A closer look at the CCE reports in 2002 and 2003 reveals an expansion of the definition of the term; now it includes as its key domains *tashikana gakuryoku* (solid academic abilities), which signifies the idea of academic basics and rigors. It was announced in 2002 by then Education Minister Atsuko Tōyama in response to the mounting criticism of *yutori* reform (MEXT, 2002).

This slight expansion of the definition was quickly mirrored in the 2005 CCE report on structural education reform. The report defines one of the missions of compulsory education as fostering children's 'zest for living' and explains that the concept encompasses the following three domains: *tashikana gakuryoku* (solid academic abilities), *yutakana kokoro* (rich spirituality), and *sukoyakana karada* (healthy body). Under 'solid academic abilities,' the report stresses the compatibility of teaching basics on the one hand and fostering creativity, problem-solving skills, and autonomous thinking on the other, which are now all subsumed within the first domain of 'zest for living' (CCE, 2005a, Section II, Chapter 1). Likewise, the report's executive summary (CCE, 2005b) stresses in its definition of 'zest for living' a "thorough teaching of basic knowledge and skills" along with an "ability to learn and think on their own" (p. 4). This was an explicit discursive move to disarticulate 'zest for living' from the now unpopular humanizing/slacking policy discourse.

Globalizing the National and Renationalizing the Global

The MEXT and CCE documents, published after the PISA 2003 'shock,' register a clear shift in the articulation of 'zest for living.' By this point, the OECD and PISA had gained powerful referential status in the Japanese education policy discourse with the triennial publications of the PISA results and the ranking rise and fall of

Japanese students becoming a major media event. Accordingly, Education Ministers and bureaucrats started explicitly referring to the PISA reports and other OECD publications in characterizing and legitimizing policies (see MEXT, 2007, 2010), while continuing with 'zest for living' as the key feature of the policy direction. For instance, the two CCE reports published in 2008 (CCE, 2008a, b) prominently feature the term and OECD's terminologies, including 'knowledge-based society' and 'key competencies,' throughout the documents. It is noteworthy that these reports provide a description of 'key competencies' immediately after discussing 'zest for living' (CCE, 2008a, p. 10, b, p. 6), though at the time these reports were published, 'key competencies' and 'zest for living' were not explicitly articulated to each other. Of particular note here is that 'zest for living,' originally introduced in 1996, was revamped in 2008 (see OECD, 2012, p. 52), when OECD's notion of 'key competencies' was gaining more policy tractions in Japan.

The subsequent CCE and MEXT documents related to the new National Course of Study (*gakushūshidōyōryō*), scheduled to be implemented in 2011, reveal a more explicit re-embedding of 'zest for living' within the transnational policy discourse. For instance, the 2009 CCE report (CCE, 2009) regarding the new Course of Study, along with the associated promotional brochure also titled *Zest for Living* (MEXT, 2008), explicitly includes OECD's 'knowledge-based society' and 'key competencies' as part of the definitional discussion of 'zest for living.' Furthermore, these documents go as far as to assert that 'zest for living' actually precedes OECD's development of these terminologies (see also CCE, 2008b, p. 6; MEXT, 2008, p. 2). All these MEXT and CCE documents continue with the same definition of 'zest for living' emphasizing its triad components: 'solid academic ability' (*chi*), 'rich heart/spirituality' (*toku*), and 'healthy body' (*tai*), while failing to acknowledge that 'solid academic ability' was not part of the definition in the 1990s.

Interestingly, the increasing embedding of 'zest for living' within the transnational, de-territorializing discourse proceeded simultaneously with the contradictory shift towards re-nationalization of the same keyword. While the 'traditional' triad framing of education—*chi* (knowledge), *toku* (moral) and *tai* (body)—had been consistently used in the shifting articulations of 'zest for living,' it become much more foregrounded after the controversial revision to the fundamental law of Education in 2006. The revision included as its educational goals specific references to acquisition of broad knowledge and culture (*chi*), enriched emotions and morality (*toku*) and sound body (*tai*) (MEXT, 2006, Article 2 (1)). The highly contested revision of the Fundamental Law of Education was driven by cultural nationalists who were in power at the time, and the inclusion of the triad as the educational goals was viewed largely as part of their political agenda (Takayama, 2008b).

Soon after the legal revision, the balance among *chi, toku* and *tai* was repeatedly stressed as one of the central educational goals (see CCE, 2008a). Reflecting this explicit focus on *chi, toku and tai*, MEXT began to articulate the notion of 'zest for living' more explicitly within the triad concepts. Entitled *Zest for Living*, MEXT's (2008) promotional brochure for the new national course of study slated for 2009, states that 'zest for living' refers to the harmonization of *chi, toku* and *tai*, which respectively refer to sound academic competencies (both basics and application), enriched humanity (self-discipline, willingness to work with others and sympathy for others) and healthy and strong body for life. The CCE report, on the basis of which the new national course of study was developed, clearly situates 'zest for living' as the central concept for the new course of study. As discussed earlier, the same report suggested that 'zest of living' preceded OECD's notion of key competencies (CCE, 2008b; see also MEXT, 2008).

It was around this time that Japan was featured by many OECD publications. OECD's (2010) *Strong performers and successful reformers in education: Lessons from PISA for Japan* described Japan as a case of 'sustained excellence" where "one of the world's best-educated and most productive workforces" is produced (p. 137). The expanded edition of the same OECD report published subsequently (OECD, 2012), continues with a glowing review of Japanese education and features 'zest for living' reform (see p. 52). The report states "the reform (under 'zest for living') not only set clear objectives, but it also highlighted the conditions that would enable students to achieve such objectives (solid academic abilities, rich humanity and health and stamina) and as a result develop both cognitive and non-cognitive competencies" (p. 52). Of note here is the articulation of 'zest for living' as closely aligned with the transnational policy discourse around non-cognitive competencies. OECD's affirmative appraisal of MEXT's reform direction was timed with the improving trajectories of Japanese 15 years old students in PISA 2009, 2012 and 2015.

Renationalizing the Global: The Rise of Triad and 'Model'

PISA 2009, 2012 and 2015 results are believed to have 'confirmed' Japan's upward trajectories since the worst performance in PISA 2003 (see Takayama, 2008a for details). In PISA 2015, Japan ranked the second out of 72 participating countries in scientific literacy, the 5th in mathematical literacy and the 8th in reading literacy. The confidence is clearly registered in 2016 CCE report (CCE, 2016), which stresses the G7 Education Ministers' meeting in Kurashiki in May 2016, the OECD policy dialogue where Japan's curricular reform was praised, and Japan's proactiveness in response to OECD's 2030 agenda. The report mentions these examples of international engagements to assert Japan's leading role in education reform: the international community expects "Japan to lead the world, rather than catching up with the world, in the area of curricular reform" (CCE, 2016, p. 12). As confidence in the national education system permeated MEXT and CCE reports, references to OECD's key competencies in their discussion of 'zest for living' was pushed in the background. The 2016 CCE report for the next revision to the National Course of Studies continues to resort to 'zest for living' as the central keyword, and yet it entirely drops any references to OECD's key competencies, except for a brief reference to it in a footnote (see Footnote #43). Now that it is established that 'zest for living' not only encompasses key competencies but actually preceded it, the former no longer needs to rely on the external legitimacy that the latter might confer.

What lies behind the rising confidence was a new policy initiative pursued by MEXT from the 2016 onward. In August 2016, MEXT established the so-called EDU-Port Nippon, the private, public and NGO consortium designed to export the 'model' of Japanese education overseas. This unusual partnership between Ministry and private interests was made possible due both to the rising international interest in Japanese schooling, as expressed by developing countries in Asia and Africa and to the increasing interest of Japanese edu-businesses in exploring overseas markets due to the shrinking domestic market. This policy shift was clearly registered in the Education Minister's call for the forthcoming CCE deliberation, issued in 2019. After proclaiming that Japan maintains "the world top level standard of education in PISA 2015" (CCE, 2019), the report quickly relates this success to what it calls the Japanese 'model' of schooling characterized by its integrated approach to *chi, toku and tai*. It argues that this triad focus, along with 150 years of professional experience with subject-based teaching since Meiji, has materialized in the success as demonstrated in PISA and national assessments (p. 1). In the supplementary document for the CCE deliberation, MEXT visually presents *chi, toku and tai* as the distinctive features of Japanese schooling compared to education systems abroad. It shows distinctive differences between *gakkō* (the Japanese term for schools) and schools overseas, highlighting the expansive roles of Japanese *gakkō*, whose roles encompass those performed by churches, sport clubs and families in other countries. It is this holistic approach to schooling, maintains the CCE (2019) report, that resulted in what OECD (2010) calls Japan's 'sustained excellence' (p. 137).

The sudden foregrounding of *chi, toku and tai* reflects the growing policy emphasis on what was earlier referred to as 'other psychosocial resources' in OECD's notion of key competencies. The notion of key competencies is now developed and popularized as 'non-cognitive' or 'socio-emotional skills' by OECD (2015), referring to students' perseverance, sociability and self-esteem. The Japanese focus on *chi, toku and tai* demonstrates a striking resemblance to "a balanced set of cognitive, social and emotional skills," which OECD (2015) proposes as the central focus of education (p. 13). While it is unclear whether the policy correspondence was carefully coordinated or a product of mere coincidence, there is no doubt that the resemblance has given MEXT external legitimation for its resuscitation of the 'traditional' triad focus.

Tokkatsu (special activities) was one curriculum activity of Japanese schooling that became featured in the ongoing effort to export the 'model' of Japanese schooling overseas. It is a formally designated curricular activity that includes a wide range of non-academic activities, including student-led class deliberation and decision-making, cleaning duties, afterschool club activities and excursions. As Ryoko Tsuneyoshi (2019), one of the most active proponents of *tokkatsu*, argues, "a major characteristic of the Japanese model of schooling is that the school is seen as a place for an education for life, including subject matter and experiences which aim to strengthen noncognitive areas from an educational view point" (p. 29). Once again, the use of the term 'noncognitive' is significant here, as it speaks directly to OECD's discourse of key competencies and socio-emotional competencies. The rise of non-cognitive as part of the transnational, de-territorializing discourse of learning resulted in the re-assessment of *chi, toku and tai,* the triad that has long been articulated within the discourse of cultural nationalists; it is now squarely placed as the central component of 'zest for living' and the Japanese 'model' of education. In the rising sense of national pride in its education system and MEXT's policy push towards exporting its 'model' overseas, the most recent articulation of 'zest for living' has been renationalized, with its deep, complicated transnational entanglements erased from any of the recent MEXT documents.

'Tradition,' Spencer and Modernity

Little acknowledged in any of MEXT references to the triad of *chi, toku and tai* is its complicated genealogies. Tracing that history leads us to question the assumed 'traditional' status of the triad and the roles of 'indigenous foreigners' in the very constitution (Popkewitz, 2000). It was first articulated by the diplomat and the first Minister of Education, Arinori Mori, who established the modern education system in Japan in the late nineteenth century. Faced with the encroaching threat of Western imperial powers, Japan was under increasing pressure to establish its modern state system as well as to modernize industries and economies to defend its sovereignty. The task for the early modern Japanese leaders, such as Mori, was to achieve the profound cultural, social and political shifts, achieved by Western advanced economies over the previous few hundred years, in an 'compressed' fashion. They considered this as the only way to rectify the series of unequal bilateral agreements that Japan was forced into vis-à-vis Western powers soon after its opening to the outside world. Rapid modernization was believed essential for Japan to be accepted as part of the 'civilized' world and hence to equalize the uneven trade and diplomatic relationships (Duke, 2009; Majima, 2014). To this aim, Mori considered as the model for Japan the Prussian education system of the early 1880s, where the schools was "designed to strengthen the power and prosperity of the state" and "to produce a citizenry to meet that goal" (Duke, 2009, p. 315). Following the Prussian model, Mori introduced a comprehensive education system, where "the needs of interests of the individual are superseded by the needs of the state" (Duke, 2009, p. 320).[1]

Mori resorted to the direct, intrusive state intervention in achieving mass enlightenment and conceived education as the central state mechanism towards this goal. The focus of the newly established national education system under Mori's leadership was to transform the mass population into modern national citizens from inside, and this enlightening project required a comprehensive involvement of state in "reforming" people's habitualized mode of living and being. It turned the comprehensive range of everyday life of children into the focus of state disciplinary controls (Okita, 1987, p. 41). In the case of early modern Japan, hence, the enlightenment as a cultural and political project did not emerge from the "maturation" of civil society and individuality as in the European context, but rather it was a thoroughly state-centric, top-down initiative from the onset (Okita, 1987).

As many scholars suggest, Mori's political and educational thoughts were strongly influenced by Hebert Spencer with whom he was acquainted during his stay in London (Swale, 2000). To being with, Mori's focus on the three faculties, *chi, toku and tai*, derived directly from Spencer's notion of education; Spencer published a book on education titled *Education: Intellectual, moral, and physical*, wherein he stressed the harmonization of the three aspects of education (Godart, 2016). Among the three faculties of educational goals, Mori was particularly concerned about *tai*, physical (Okita, 1987), and this emphasis on physical is also the key feature of Spencer's discussion of education (Swale, 2000). Having lived extensively in USA and England, Mori was acutely aware of the physical inferiority of the Japanese vis-à-vis Europeans. This was the racialized view widely shared among the Japanese political leaders at the time. Informed by various versions of Social Darwinism, they construed physical difference as a visible manifestation of the 'civilizational gap,' or the temporal distance between different 'evolutionary' stages (Majima, 2014). In Mori's view, the overall improvement of physical robustness of the mass was central to Japan's rapid modernization project. Mori first introduced military style physical education as part of teacher education curriculum and then subsequently through the entire public education system. For Mori, the military style physical education had little to do with militarism. Rather, it was a way to instill in the Japanese people "the behavioral patterns reflecting the institutional structure of modern order" (Sonoda, 1993, p. 285; see also Duke, 2009; Okita, 1987).

Hence, from the onset Japanese schools encompassed a whole range of everyday activities above and beyond the focus of cognitive development of children. Unlike in UK or US, where schools were much more focused on children's cognitive development, schooling in Japan was arranged from its inception as "a place of everyday life" (*seikatsu no ba*), where schools take charge of children's comprehensive range of human development (*sōgōtekina ningen keisei*), including moral and physical development. The all-encompassing nature of schooling did not remain dominated by state interests, however. As Hajime Kimura (2015) maintains, educators disarticulated schools from the totalizing state interests to achieve relative autonomy. Before the rise of ultra-nationalism in the late 1930s, for instance, Japanese educators were able to turn schools into a quasi-autonomous space where unique pedagogic practices and cultures grounded in the lives of children were developed (see e.g., Hiraoka, 2011). The same holistic approach to schooling, or the so called 'whole-person education' (*zenjin kyōiku*), was kept in place during the US-led Occupation's democratization and demilitarization of Japanese education.

It is this legacy of Japanese education that many Western observers highlighted in the rise of Japan as the economic power house in the 1980s and the subsequent international scholarly interest in Japanese education (see White, 1988; Lewis, 1995; Sato, 2004). These international researchers identified the strength of Japanese education in its notion of whole-person education, where "cognitive, social, and affective spheres are not isolated into sperate categories" (Sato, 2004, p. 52). And then, in more recently years, those same aspects of Japanese schools attracted considerable international attention from developing countries in Africa and Asia (Tsuneyoshi, 2019). Reflecting this broader policy context, CCE's recent report (CCE, 2018) stresses that the holistic approach to schooling in Japan, including students serving school lunch to each other (*kyūshoku*) and extracurricular activities, accounts for Japanese students and adults' success in various OECD assessments (p. 13). The same report lists the exportation of Japanese 'model' of education as one of the 21 goals set out for MEXT (p. 91). In the description of the goal, the report identifies the central feature of Japanese primary and early secondary as a sound balance among *chi, toku and tai* (knowledge, moral and physical) and recognizes it as central to the 'model' of Japanese education (p. 91). Little acknowledged here is the particular historical circumstances under which the holistic conception of schooling was developed. It was early modernizing reformers' desperate attempt to "progress from a third-rate country to a second-rate country, and then to a first-rate power" (Duke, 2009, p. 329). The comprehensive state intervention in every aspect of children's lives were deemed necessary for the country to leap through the ladder of 'social evolution' in a fast-tracked fashion. It is now thoroughly de-historicized and rearticulated as the central characteristics of Japanese 'model' of schooling, reframed as preceding the rising international attention to 'non-cognitive' and 'phyco-social competencies.' The irony is that this tradition was reinvented in a time when Japanese political leaders has long declared the end of century old tradition of 'catch-up' with the West.

The Global Within the National and the National Within the Global

The genealogical tracing of 'zest for living' has shown how the Japanese articulation of 'competencies' in the last three decades has resulted from continuous mixings of transnational and national policy discourses. It was so consistently made and remade in response to the emerging political situations and expediencies that the demarcation between the national and the transnational was increasingly difficult to establish. What the Japanese case suggests, though, is that the global and the national do not operate in a zero-sum manner but are constitutive part of each other. The recent re-invention of *chi, toku* and *tai* as a constitutive part of the 'model' of Japanese education would not have taken place, for instance, had there not been a strong presence of the transnational, de-territorializing discourse of 'non-cognitive' and 'psycho-social competencies.' It was only through the international attention to 'non-cognitive' that *chi, toku* and *tai* gained political tractions both inside and outside Japan, and subsequently redefined as the 'essence' of the Japanese 'model.' Vice versa, the same 'traditional' Japanese triad has now 'gone global,' as it is fully integrated into the exportable 'model' of Japanese education. In the process, the particular historical circumstances of early modern Japan out of which the triad was originally defined and developed, was erased. Instead, it is now repackaged as a concrete set of pedagogical practices (e.g., *tokkatsu*) that can be exported to different cultural and political contexts. They are 'Japanese' pedagogic practices grown out of the distinctive historical experience of compressed modernity, and yet they are increasingly framed within the OECD's de-territorialized language of 'non-cognitive' and 'psycho-social competencies' to achieve the global 'transferability.'

The global spread of "the ideology of a culturally indifferent world of education" has led many education scholars to lament over the disappearance of the national in education policy discourse. Kamens (2013), for instance, argues that education is "no longer a cultural project of the nation, aimed at reproducing cultural cohesion and community" (p. 122; see also Meyer and Benavot, 2013). The old assumptions about the uniqueness of national traditions and the value of national sovereignty are no longer upheld by national and transnational policy actors, he maintains. Kamens (2013) further points out that "(t)he uniqueness of national educational systems is now a possible source of new models, not an artifact of national sovereignty to be celebrated and reified" (p. 123). Indeed, the 'model' of Japanese education is underpinned by Japanese uniqueness, and yet its national uniqueness is assumed to be compatible with the universalist notion of 'transferability,' the assumption that "a practice that works in, say, Finland will work as well in the United States or Germany" (Kamens, 2013, p. 130).

While the disappearance of the national in the current education discourse is worrisome, it is important to stress that education has never been a purely national initiative from the start. The Japanese case is illustrative in this sense, as it has shown that even some of the concepts that are largely accepted as 'foundational' to Japanese education are a product of eclectic amalgamations of various international and transnational influences (e.g., the Prussian 'model' of the early 1880s and Herbert Spencer). Hence, the global was also deeply imbedded in the construction of the national in the first instance. And then, it is this product of domesticating the global that is currently globalized in the MEXT's policy push to export the 'model' of Japanese education. Unfortunately, such evolving and dynamic interactions between the global and the national are erased by those who actively advocate the 'model' of Japanese education. For instance, Tsuneyoshi (2019), in explaining the distinctiveness of the 'model' of Japanese education, stresses the fact that "Japanese education developed relatively independent of the west" (p. 18). Tsuneyoshi's effort to promote a non-Western model of education reform is laudable, and yet her articulation of Japanese 'model' does not adequately acknowledge the essentially hybrid nature of the model itself. Nor can the same complexity be adequately captured by the current scholarship of education policy that stresses the overpowering presence of transnational actors and their policy discourses (Kamens, 2013; Meyer and Benavot, 2013). Their romanticized and essentialized notion of 'the national' is predicated upon the usual national-global binary and the view of this relationship as in a zero-sum competition. The distinct contribution of this chapter, then, is to caution us against any totalizing, static and zero-sum view of the relationship between the global and the national. It has shown that national education has always been thoroughly transnational and that the global and the national operate in a mutually dependent and constituting way that fundamentally undercuts any easy demarcations.

Note

1. It is interesting to note that Horace Mann, the Secretary of the Massachusetts Board of Education, also used Prussia as the model for education in Massachusetts 30–40 years earlier. But unlike Mori, Mann deemed the Prussian 'model' incompatible with the democratic and republican spirits that American common schools were to nurture. Mann was particularly attracted to the strict organization and teacher education in the Prussian system, but not its tendency to breed passive obedience to the government (see Rust et al., 2009, p. 125). I thank the editors (Weili and Daniel) for bringing this comparative point to my awareness.

References

Alasuutari, P. (2013). Spreading global models and enhancing banal localism: The case of local government cultural policy development. *International Journal of Cultural Policy*, *19*(1), 103–119.

Arai, I. (1993). *"Ikikata" wo kaeru gakkōjidai no taiken: raifukōsu no shakaigaku* [School experience that changes "one's life": sociology of life course]. Gyōsei.

Arai, I. (2001). *Yutori no manabi yutori no bunka: 21 seiki no gakushū shakai* [Low pressure learning and low pressure culture: 21st century learning society]. Kyōiku shuppan.

Aso, M., & Amano, I. (1972). *Education and Japan's modernization*. Ministry of Foreign Affairs.

Beauchamp, E. (1987). The development of Japanese educational policy, 1945–85. *History of Education Quarterly 27*(3), 299–324.

CCE. (1996). *Nijūisseiki wo tenbōshita wagakuni no kyōiku no arikata ni tsuite (Daiichiji tōshin)* [The new vision of our education towards the 21st century (First report)]. MEXT.

CCE. (2002). *Atarashii jidai ni okeru kyōyōkyōiku no arikata ni tsuite* [On the foundation education in the new era]. MEXT.

CCE. (2003). *Shotō chūtō kyōiku ni okeru tōmen no kyōiku kadai oyobi shidō no jujitsu kaizen hōsaku ni tsuite* [On the educational agenda and strategies for improvement in primary and secondary education]. MEXT.

CCE. (2005a). *Atarashii jidai no gimu kyōiku o sōzō suru* [Imagining compulsory education for the new era]. MEXT.

CCE. (2005b). *Gimu Kyōiku no kōzō kaikaku chuūō kyōiku shingikai tōshin no gaiyō* [Summary of the CCE report on structural reform of compulsory education]. MEXT.

CCE. (2008a). *Kyōiku shinkō keikaku ni tsuite: kyōiku rikkoku no jitsugen ni mukete* [On the educational promotion plan: Towards the realization of education nation]. MEXT.

CCE. (2008b). *Atarashii jidai wo kirihiraku shōgai gakushū no shinkōhōsaku ni tsuite* [Policy promotion for lifelong learning in the new era]. MEXT.

CCE. (2009). *Yōchien, shōgakkō, chūgakkō, kōtōgakkō oyobi tokubetsu shien gakkō no gakushū shidōyōryō tou no kaizen ni tsuite* [On the revision to the national course of study for kindergarten, primary, secondary and special schools]. MEXT.

CCE. (2016). *Yōchien, shōgakkō, chūgakkō, kōtōgakkō oyobi tokubetsu shien gakkō no gakushū shidōyōryō tou no kaizen oyobi hitsuyōna hōsku ni tsuite (Tōshin)*. MEXT. https://www.mext.go.jp/b_menu/shingi/chukyo/chukyo0/toushin/__icsFiles/afieldfile/2017/01/10/1380902_0.pdf

CCE. (2018). *Daisanki kyōiku shinkō kihon keikaku ni tsuite (Tōshin)* [Regarding the third education promotion basic plan (Report)]. MEXT.
CCE. (2019). *"Atarashii jidai no shotō chūtō kyōiku no arikata ni tsuite" kankei shiryō* [Regarding primary and secondary education in the new era, a reference material]. MEXT. https://www.mext. go.jp/component/b_menu/shingi/toushin/__icsFiles/afieldfile/2019/04/18/1415875_3_1.pdf
Duke, B. (2009). *The history of modern Japanese education: Constructing the national school system, 1872–1890*. Rutgers University Press.
Field, J. (2006). *Lifelong learning and the new educational order*. Trentham Books.
Godart, C. G. (2016). Spencerism in Japan: Boom and bust of a theory. In B. Lightman (Ed.), *Global Spencerism: The communication and appropriation of a British evolutionist* (pp. 56–77). Brill.
Hiraoka, S. (2011). The ideology and practices of "Seikatsu-Tsuzurikata": Education by teaching of expressive writing. *Educational Studies in Japan: International Yearbook 6*, 21–31.
Honda, Y. (2005). *Tagenka suru 'nōryoku' to nihonshakai* [Multifaceted 'capability' and Japanese society]. NTT shuppan.
Hutchins, R. M. (1968). *The learning society*. Praeger.
Kamens, D. (2013). Globalization and the emergence of an audit culture: PISA and the search for 'best practices' and magic bullets. In H. Meyer & A. Benavot (Eds.), *PISA, power, and policy: The emergence of global educational governance* (pp. 117–139). Symposium Books.
Kariya, T. (2020). *Oitsuita kindai kieta kindai: Sengo nihon no jikozō to kyōiku* [Who killed Japan's modernity? What comes after 'catch-up'?]. Iwanami shoten.
Kimura, H. (2015). *Gakkō no sengoshi* [Postwar history of schools]. Iwanami shoten.
Lewis, C. (1995). *Educating hearts and minds: Reflections on Japanese preschool and elementary education*. Cambridge: Cambridge University Press.
Majima, A. (2014). *"Hadairo" no yūutsu: Kindai nihon no jinshu taiken* [Melancholy of "skin color": Racial experience of modern Japan]. Chuōkōron Shinsha.
Meyer, H., & Benavot, A. (2013). PISA and globalization of education governance: Some puzzles and problems. In H. Meyer & A. Benavot (Eds.), *PISA, power, and policy: The emergence of global educational governance* (pp. 9–26). Symposium Books.
MEXT. (2002). *Tashikana gakuryoku no kōjō no tameno 2002 api-ru* [2002 appeal for improvement of solid academic abilities]. MEXT.
MEXT. (2006). *Kaisei zengo no kyōiku kihonhō no hikaku* [Comparison of the fundamental law of education before and after the revision]. https://www.mext.go.jp/b_menu/kihon/about/06121913/002.pdf
MEXT. (2007). *PISA 2006 no kekka o uketa kongo no torikumi* [The cabinet responses to PISA 2006 results]. MEXT.
MEXT. (2008). *Ikiru chikara* [Zest for living]. MEXT. https://www.mext.go.jp/a_menu/shotou/new-cs/pamphlet/20080328/01-16.pdf
MEXT. (2010). *Gakuryoku kōjō ni kansuru koremade no seisaku to PISA 2009 no kekka* [Existing strategies for improving academic standards and the results of PISA 2009]. MEXT.
OECD. (2000). *Schooling for tomorrow*. OECD Scenarios, OECD.
OECD. (2001). *Knowledge and skills for llfe: First results from PISA 2000: Executive summary*. OECD.
OECD. (2005). *The ssefinition and sselection of key competencies: Executive summary*. OECD.
OECD. (2010). *Lessons from PISA for Japan. Strong performers and successful reformers in education.*. OECD.
OECD. (2012). *Lessons from PISA for Japan*. Paris: OECD Publishing. https://doi.org/10.1787/9789264118539-9-en
OECD. (2015). *Skills for social progress: The power of social and emotional skills: OECD skills studies*. OECD Publishing.
Okita, Y. (1987). Mori Arinori no keimō to kyōiku (Ge) [Arinori Mori's enlightenment and education (Volume II)]. *Jinbungaku [Doshisha University Studies in Humanities], 144*, 23–48.
Okumoto, K. (2008). Lifelong learning in England and Japan: Three translations. *Compare, 38*(2), 173–188.

Pempel, T. J. (1998). *Regime shift: Comparative dynamics of the Japanese political economy.* Cornell University Press.

Popkewitz, T. (2000). Globalization/regionalization, knowledge, and educational practices: Some notes on comparative strategies for educational research. In T. Popkewitz (Ed.), *Changing relationship between the state, civil society and educational community* (pp. 3–27). SUNY Press.

Rust, V., Johnstone, B., & Allaf, C. (2009). Reflections on the development of comparative education. In R. Cowen & A. Kazamias (Eds.), *International Handbook of Comparative Education* (pp. 121–138). Springer.

Rychen, D. (2004). Key competencies for all: An overarching conceptual frame of reference. In D. S. Rychen & A. Tiana (Eds.), *Developing key competencies in education: Some lessons from International and national experience* (pp. 5–34). UNESCO International Bureau of Education.

Sassen, S. (2010). The global inside the national: A research agenda for sociology. *Sociopedia.isa.* http://www.columbia.edu/~sjs2/PDFs/National.pdf

Sato, M. (2000). *"Manabi" kara tōsōsuru kodomotachi* [Children running away from learning]. Iwanami shoten.

Sato, N. (2004). *Inside Japanese classrooms: The heart of education.* RoutledgeFalmer.

Sonoda, H. (1993). *Seiyōka no kōzō: Kurofune, bushi and kokka* [Structure of Westernization: Black ships, worriers and state]. Shibunkaku Shuppan.

Swale, A. (2000). *The political thought of Mori Arinori: A study in Meiji conservatism.* Japan Library.

Takayama, K. (2007). A nation at risk crosses the Pacific: Transnational borrowing of the U.S. crisis discourse in the debate on education reform in Japan. *Comparative Education Review, 51*(4), 423–446.

Takayama, K. (2008a). The politics of international league tables: PISA in Japan's achievement crisis debate. *Comparative Education 44*(4), 387–407.

Takayama, K. (2008b). Japan's Ministry of Education 'becoming the right': Neoliberal restructuring and the Ministry's struggles for political legitimacy. *Globalisation, Societies, and Education 6*(2), 131–146.

Takayama, K. (2009). Is Japanese education the "exception"?: Examining the situated articulation of neoliberalism through the analysis of policy keywords. *Asia Pacific Journal of Education 29*(2), 125–142.

Takayama, K. (2013). OECD, 'key competencies' and the new challenges of educational inequality. *Journal of Curriculum Studies 45*(1), 67–80.

Takayama, K. (2014). Global 'diffusion', banal nationalism, and the politics of policy legitimation: A genealogical study of "zest for living" in Japanese education policy discourse. In P. Alassutari & A. Qadir (Eds.), *National policy-making domestication of global trends* (pp. 129–146). Routledge.

Tröhler, D. (2013). The OECD and cold war culture: Thinking historically about PISA. In H. Meyer & A. Benavot (Eds.), *PISA, power, and policy: The emergence of global educational governance* (pp. 141–161). Symposium Books.

Tsuneyoshi, R. (2019). The Tokkatsu framework: The Japanese model of holistic education. In R. Tsuneyoshi, H. Sugita, K. Kusanagi, & F. Takahashi (Eds.), *Tokkatsu: The Japanese educational model of holistic education.* World Scientific Publishing.

UNESCO. (1972). *Learning to be.* UNESCO.

UNESCO. (1996). *Learning: The treasure within.* UNESCO.

Vogel, E. (1979). *Japan as number one: Lessons for America.* Harvard University Press.

White, M. (1988). *The Japanese educational challenge: A commitment to children.* he Freee Press.

Yamada, T. (2011). Hyōka/senbatsu [Assessment/selection]. In N. Ishido & S. Imai (Eds.), *Shinsutemu toshite no kyōiku o saguru* [Exploring education as a system] (pp. 97–117). Keisōshobō.

Keita Takayama is a professor of the Graduate School of Education, Kyoto University, Japan. He spent nearly 12 years teaching at University of New England, Australia before taking up professorship in Kyoto. His research focuses on globalization of education policy and educational research. He was the 2010 recipient of CIES's George Bereday Award.

Lightning Source UK Ltd.
Milton Keynes UK
UKHW020608190722
406062UK00002B/11